Challenging Behaviour and Intellectual Disability: A Psychological Perspective

Robert S.P. Jones
Caroline B. Eayrs

Editors

British Library Cataloguing in Publication Data
A CIP record for this book is available from the British Library
ISBN 1 873791 63 1

First Published 1993. Second impression 1997
© **Copyright 1993 BILD Publications**

BILD Publications is the publishing office of the
British Institute of Learning Disabilities
Wolverhampton Road
Kidderminster
Worcestershire
United Kingdom
DY10 3PP
Telephone: 01562 850251
Fax: 01562 851970
e-mail bild@bild.demon.co.uk.

BILD Publications are distributed worldwide by
Plymbridge Distributors Limited
Estover House
Plymouth
United Kingdom
PL6 7PZ
Telephone: 01752 202300
Fax: 01752 202333

Printed by The Cookley Printers Limited, 56 Bridge Road, Cookley, Kidderminster, Worcs. DY10 3SB

Cover design by HotHouse Image, 26 Lower Wood, The Rock, Telford TF3 5DN

Authors

Dr Robert Jones is a Senior Lecturer in Clinical Psychology at the University of North Wales in Bangor. He trained as a clinical psychologist in his home town of Dublin and was awarded the B.P.S. diploma in clinical psychology in 1984. As a clinical psychologist he has worked in services for people with intellectual disabilities in Ireland, England and Wales. He obtained a research PhD from Trinity College Dublin in 1986 for his work on reducing stereotyped and self-injurious behaviour using differential reinforcement techniques and has continued to research and publish in the area of challenging behaviour. He is married with three children and has lived in North Wales since 1987.

Dr. Caroline Eayrs currently holds a joint appointment with Clwyd Health Authority and the University College of North Wales in Bangor as a clinical psychologist and lecturer. She completed her training as a clinical psychologist in Birmingham, where she obtained a PhD in clinical psychology in 1981 for work on group treatment for anxiety management. She subsequently moved into the field of intellectual disabilities and has recently been researching and publishing in the area of charity advertising. She is married with one son and has lived in North Wales since 1987.

Contributors

Edward Blewitt
Department of Psychology,
Ysbyty Bryn-y-Neuadd,
Llanfairfechan,
Gwynedd, LL33 OHH
NORTH WALES

Caroline B. Eayrs
Department of Psychology,
University College of
North Wales,
Bangor, Gwynedd, LL57 2DG
NORTH WALES

David Felce
Mental Handicap in Wales,
Applied Research Unit,
55 Park Place, Cardiff, CF1 3AT
SOUTH WALES

Amanda Goza
Department of Psychology,
Southwest Institute for
Developmental Disabilities,
Abilene, Texas, TX 79604,
U.S.A.

Donna Head
Westcotes House,
Westcotes Drive,
Leicester, LE3 OQU

Tony Holland
Academic Department of
Psychiatry,
P.O. Box 189,
Addenbrook's Hospital,
Cambridge, CB2 2QQ

Robert S. P. Jones
Department of Psychology,
University College of
North Wales,
Bangor, Gwynedd, LL57 2DG
NORTH WALES

Chris Kiernan
Hester Adrian Research Centre,
The University of Manchester,
Manchester, M13 9PL

Renee E. McCaughey
Nant-y-Glynn Resource Centre,
Nant-y-Glyn Road,
Colwyn Bay, LL29 7RB
NORTH WALES

Andy McDonnell
Department of Psychology
University of Birmingham,
Egbaston, Birmingham, B15 2TT

Shelagh MacKinnon
The Elms, 50 Cowley Hill Lane
St. Helens, WA 10 2AP
Merseyside

Glynis Murphy
Department of Psychology,
Institute of Psychiatry,
De Crespigny Park
Denmark Hill, London, SE5 8AF

Chris Oliver
Department of Psychology,
Institute of Psychiatry,
De Crespigny Park
Denmark Hill, London, SE5 8AF

R. Glynn Owens
Faculty of Health Studies,
Health Studies Research Division,
University College of
North Wales,
Upper School.
St David's Hospital,
Bangor, LL57 4SL
NORTH WALES

Alan C. Repp
Department of Educational
Psychology,
Counselling and Special
Education,
Northern Illinois University
DeKalb, IL 60115, U.S.A.

Robert Ricketts
Department of Psychology,
Southwest Institute for
Developmental Disabilities,
Abilene, Texas, TX 79604,
U.S.A.

Peter Sturmey
Department of Psychology,
Abilene State School,
Abilene, Texas TX 79604-0451
U.S.A.

Sandy Toogood
Intensive Support Team,
Broughton Hospital,
Broughton Nr.Chester
Clwyd, CH4 ODT
NORTH WALES

Peter A. Woods,
Department of Psychology,
Ysbyty Bryn-y-Neuadd,
Llanfairfechan,
Gwynedd, LL33 OHH
NORTH WALES

Contents

Foreword

Challenging behaviour is a term that has become popular in recent years, probably for two reasons: (a) it is a relatively neutral term and is, therefore, more appealing than terms such as maladaptive or inappropriate behaviour which are more value laden and contradict the general movement away from such labels; and (b) it directs the attention of the responsible person (e.g., therapist, teacher) to the behaviour as one we are supposed to solve instead of one that belongs to the individual in some invariant way. The challenge then belongs to us to determine the manner by which we can change behaviour.

This is not a new idea, and is indeed one that Skinner offered at least 55 years ago in the *Behaviour of Organisms*. For some reason, however, it is an idea now readily adopted by non-behaviourists as well. Ironically, both the behaviourists and the non-behaviourists now agree on a very fundamental point; some behaviour is often controlled by the environment, and the challenge is for us to learn which consistuents of the environment control behaviour and how we can manipulate them to produce better lives for people we are trying to help.

For many years, we met this challenge by using an Antecedent-Behaviour-Consequence model, at least superficially. For the most part, while we first considered the conditions under which responding occurred, we then ignored them during intervention and manipulated only the contingencies between behaviour and consequences. We developed a function analysis with behaviour as the dependent variable and the consequence as the independent variable. The question for years was, Is the rate of challenging behaviour a function of the new (or old) consequences? This approach has been criticised; however, it has been a very reasonable one as we too respond under behavioural principles, i.e., we were successful sometimes and unsuccessful other times, in no particular order – the very definitions of a variable ratio schedule that should maintain our behaviour at a fair ratio.

Recently, and primarily in the field of challenging behaviour, we have begun to concentrate on the relationship between antecedent conditions and behaviour. We have returned to the A-B-C analysis but are truly examining a three-term (A-B-C) rather than a two-term (B-C) contingency. The schema from my perspective is as follows:

where (a) R– is the challenging behaviour; (b) its consequence serves the function of

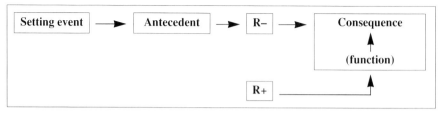

the behaviour; (c) the antecedent is a condition or event, the presence of which alters the probability of R–; (d) the setting event is a condition or event, the presence of which alters the probability that an antecedent will in turn alter the probability of R–; and (e) R+ is an appropriate response we would like to substitute for R–.

Today, the term functional analysis is used to describe the relationship of the challenging behaviour and events that precede it. We in applied behaviour analysis should not, however, repeat our prior mistake and concentrate only on events preceding the target behaviour. Instead, a full functional analysis should consider antecedents, setting events, consequences, the target behaviour, and competing behaviours. Additionally, we should consider these elements as they affect acquisition (of R+), maintenance, and generalisation.

Functional analysis is really a series of contingency tables representing if-then statements of the following order:

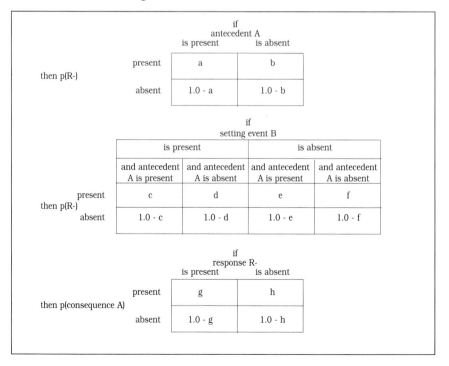

The question in addressing behaviour becomes, Does event A influence the probability of event B? This book has addressed that question in several interesting ways. For example, the chapter on housing addresses residence and elements of residency as setting events for challenging behaviour. Similarly, chapters on the aversives debate, the law, and normalisation address setting events that may affect our behaviour when we are confronted by a client's challenging behaviour. Certainly these areas have changed the way we as a field act in the presence of the antecedent of challenging behaviour compared with the way we acted 20 or 30 years ago. Similarly, the chapters on functional analysis may act on the behaviour of us, the readers, as we adopt new procedures for addressing these behaviours. Hopefully, those ways will involve a more efficient, sensitive, and far -reaching manner for addressing these problems.

This book has presented many fine ideas for achieving this objective. The challenge is now for us: Can we adopt new ways of analysing challenging behaviours? With this book as a framework, I think we can.

Alan Repp

CHAPTER 1

Challenging Behaviour, and Intellectual Disabilities: An Overview

Robert S. P. Jones
University College of North Wales, Bangor
and
Caroline B. Eayrs
University College of North Wales, Bangor, and Clwyd Health Authority

The presence of disturbed behaviour is undoubtedly one of the major stressors in the lives of parents, educators, and direct-care staff who live and work with people with intellectual disabilities. Although prevalence figures show wide variation, it is clear that a significant minority of people with intellectual disability engage in some form of behaviour which can be regarded as inappropriate (Cipani, 1989; Emerson *et al.*, 1987; Gorman-Smith and Matson, 1985; Harris & Russell, 1990; LaGrow and Repp, 1984; Lennox *et al.*, 1988; Matson and Taras, 1989; Quereshi & Alborz, 1992). An analysis of the relevant literature reveals that the inappropriate behaviours which have aroused most concern are: physical attacks on others, self injury, destructive behaviour, and other socially or sexually unacceptable behaviour (Qureshi & Alborz, 1992).

Writing from an American perspective, Cipani (1989) has stated the problem as follows:

'Behavior problems, in one form or another, concern almost all personnel in the developmental disabilities field. Discipline/behavior problems have commonly been cited as a major factor in staff turnover and "burnout," as well as in the failure to maintain clients in less restrictive educational and residential environments. Concerns regarding the management of severe behavioral problems can cause problems for even the best trained personnel' (Cipani, 1989).

In the last decade, research has shown that not only are maladaptive behaviours stigmatising and devaluing (Jones, Wint & Ellis, 1990), but that the presence of these behaviours can result in the reduced attainment of independent living skills, the breakdown of family placements (Rousey, Blacher & Hanneman, 1990), admission to institutionalised placements (Borthwick-Duffy, Eyman & White, 1987), the breakdown of community placements and subsequent readmission (Lakin, Hill, Hauber, Bruininks & Heal, 1983) and a reduced probability of discharge (James, 1986). Community-based research also suggests that once returned to institutional environments, individuals displaying behavioural difficulties remain unpopular with staff, are often segregated in special wards, and may continue to exhibit behavioural difficulties over an extended timescale. (Emerson, 1990; Mansell & Beasley, 1990).

This volume presents a psychological perspective on challenging behaviour and examines the phenomenon from a wide conceptual standpoint. All the authors in this volume have taken their subject matter beyond the simple analysis of observable behaviour and their need to do this shows how complex the field of intellectual disabilities has become in recent years. The subject matter is so complex that the issues involved in understanding challenging behaviour inevitably necessitate an overlap with other perspectives. Thus, a broad-based psychological approach will interface with systemic, sociological and even philosophical issues in the quest for an in-depth understanding of challenging behaviour in people with intellectual disabilities. One of the first obstacles in understanding the relationship between intellectual disabilities and difficult behaviour is posed by the term 'challenging behaviour' itself. The next section outlines some of the issues involved in the use of this term.

Definition

Originally adopted by the Association for Persons with Severe Handicaps (TASH) in the U.S.A., the term 'challenging behaviour' first gained popularity in the U.K. following a King's Fund publication by Blunden and Allen (1987) entitled *Facing the Challenge*. The use of this term was designed to emphasise a move towards regarding inappropriate behaviour as being a challenge to the system rather than being seen as isolated within the individual. Thus, it suggested a move away from viewing inappropriate behaviour as a characteristic inherent in individuals, and towards a focus on services and the ways in which they might respond to the challenges presented by particular behaviours in the context of a commitment towards social role valorisation (normalisation) and deinstitutionalisation. Whether or not this change is a mere euphemistic word play is a debatable point. Broderick (1988) has commented that to dismiss the term challenging behaviour as euphemistic is to miss an important change of attitude.

'This substitution of terms reframes the situation from one of 'how to eliminate the disturbed behaviour?' to 'how do we seek to meet the needs of the person

2

despite the difficulties his (sic) behaviour represents?' - a framing which permits of a wider range of solutions than that of eliminating the behaviour. Of course it does not rule out the possibility of concentrating on eliminating the behaviour, if on consideration this is deemed appropriate. But should the attempts at eliminating the behaviour prove unsuccessful, one still has a range of alternatives remaining that one can explore.'

Although the ideological basis of this change in terminology seems laudable, the utility of using a global term such as challenging behaviour can be questioned. Any attempt at a definition of challenging behaviour must recognise that the term is over-inclusive and covers a wide range of behaviours. In addition, the concept of challenging behaviour is essentially socially defined. Whether or not a particular behaviour is regarded as challenging depends upon a number of factors. In particular, the resources, skill and experience of service providers as well as the quality of local facilities will determine the nature, or indeed the existence, of any 'challenge'. Thus, apparently identical behaviour may be seen as challenging by staff in one setting but not in another. For example, Qureshi (in press) gives the example of passive, withdrawn behaviour which

'may not be seen as challenging by over-worked staff in an environment where it is a struggle to achieve containment and the meeting of physical needs. However, where staff are attempting to increase the level of a person's community participation, such behaviour may pose considerable challenges. Thus, if, in an attempt to assess the prevalence of challenging behaviour, staff across different settings were asked to identify people whose behaviour was challenging, it is likely that this would give rise to a group of people selected by a number of quite different sets of criteria related to existing norms and expectations, the characteristics of the setting and the variety of goals pursued.'

Thus, it appears that the social consequences a particular behaviour will vary along a number of dimensions. Consequently, unless any definition of challenging behaviour contains some reference to the form or topography of particular behaviours, then those behaviours must be defined solely in relation to these variable social consequences. Emerson *et al.*, (1987), for example, have formulated the following definition of the term:

'Severely challenging behaviour refers to behaviour of such an intensity, frequency or duration that the physical safety of the person or others is likely to be placed in serious jeopardy, or behaviour which is likely to seriously limit or deny access to and use of ordinary community facilities.'

3

This definition makes no reference to the form of the behaviour but rather emphasises the consequences to the individual of displaying the behaviour. The nature and severity of the 'challenge' is therefore determined chiefly by the severity of the behaviour's social consequences. In an effort to overcome this rather arbitrary way of defining challenging behaviour, some researchers have suggested more specific definitions. Dockrell, Gaskell, Rehman and Normand (1992), for example, suggested that the concept of challenging behaviour covers two quite distinct sets of behaviours. They proposed a distinction between 'dangerous' and 'problem' behaviours. *Dangerous behaviour,* included 'physical violence, use of weapons, suicide attempts and SIB, child abuse and fire setting' whereas *problem behaviour* consisted of 'temper tantrums, verbal abuse, pestering, and throwing things'. Similarily, as part of a survey of the epidemiology of challenging behaviour in adults, Qureshi and Alborz (1992) constructed a series of detailed questions concerning various dimensions of 'serious' challenging behaviours. On the basis of the range of information available from their survey, Qureshi (in press) formulated a working definition of challenging behaviour. In this study, people were defined as showing challenging behaviour if they:

'Had at some time caused more than minor injuries to themselves or others, or destroyed their immediate living or working environment;
OR
Showed behaviour at least weekly which required intervention by more than one member of staff for control, or placed them in physical danger, or caused damage which could not be rectified by immediate care staff, or caused at least an hour's disruption;
OR
Caused more than a few minutes disruption at least daily.'

Other studies which have investigated specific behaviours have used definitions which are less dependent on the social consequences of the behaviour. For example, Oliver, Murphy and Corbett (1987) used a clear and precise definition of self-injurious behaviour whereas in other definitions, topographical and social aspects are mixed within the same definition. For example, in their community survey of aggressive behaviour, Russell and Harris (1992) constructed the following working definition:

'While we are primarily interested in identifying people who present serious problems such as biting, kicking, scratching, etc. which result in injury to others, for example bruising, bleeding, or other tissue damage, we would also like to include all individuals whose actions such as shouting/screaming at others, or violence towards objects may not necessarily result in injury but do present serious management difficulties because of the threat or risk of injury to others.'

4

From this small sample of studies it can be seen that challenging behaviour has been defined in various ways and using a variety of criteria. While this situation is unsatisfactory from a number of perspectives, it is particularly difficult to ask even the most basic questions concerning the prevalence of challenging behaviour while there is such variation between definitions.

Prevalence

In assessing the occurrence of any disorder, it is usual to estimate both incidence and prevalence. Incidence refers to the number of cases arising in a population whereas prevalence relates to the number of cases within an age group or total population (Fryers, 1990). It is clear that the estimate of both of these statistics will ultimately depend on the quality and consistency of the definition of the disorder. As seen previously, different researchers use different definitions and even where the same definition is used across studies, differences in service response can affect estimates of prevalence. It is not surprising, therefore, to find considerable variation in estimates of the prevalence of challenging behaviour across a number of different studies. For example, Beange & Bauman (1990) reviewed the prevalence rates for 'behavioural problems' across 9 separate studies which were carried out between 1968 and 1986. They found a range of between 17% and 56% across studies. This variation is almost certainly due to the different definitions employed. Similarly, Eyman & Call's (1977) study of maladaptive behaviour found rates of physical aggression to be as high as 28% whereas Jacobsen (1982) found a much lower prevalence rate of 10%.

Some studies, however, have undertaken more careful analyses of prevalence. For example, the Oliver *et al.*, (1987) study mentioned earlier, used a very precise definition of self-injurious behaviour. Not only was this study able to demonstrate a high level of inter-rater reliability, but the reported prevalence rate of 12% was very similar to the rate of 13.8% found by Griffin *et al.*, (1986) in a similar study carried out in the U.S.A.

In summary it would seem that while a global term such as challenging behaviour may have utility as a generic term, it is of limited use in forming the basis of research studies unless more detailed operational definitions are incorporated. Despite the difficulties in assigning specific numerical data, a number of general trends emerge from the host of prevalence studies which have been undertaken in the last decade:

Challenging behaviour is more common in institutions than in the community and is more common in residential services than in day services. It is more usual for individuals to display more than one challenging behaviour (e.g., both self-injury and physical attacks on others) than to engage in a single discrete problem behaviour (e.g., physical aggression alone). The majority of challenging behaviours are seen in people with profound or severe disabilities although specific (usually low rate) challenging behaviours such as arson and sexual offences are more

5

commonly found amongst people with mild intellectual disabilities. Finally, challenging behaviour is most frequently seen in individuals between the ages of 15 and 30 years of age although in some cases rates can remain high into late middle age.

Summary of the book

The present volume presents a perspective on challenging behaviour which pays particular attention to current issues and emerging trends in analysis and treatment. Two issues reoccur as central themes throughout this volume. These involve a) the recent emphasis on the interface between ideological and empirical issues in service provision and b) the continuing emphasis on ecological analysis in understanding the functions of challenging behaviour. In addition, two chapters are presented which address neglected issues in the literature on intellectual disability. These are the relationship between challenging behaviour, psychiatric disorder and the law (Murphy & Holland) and the effectiveness of staff guidelines on the management of violent and aggressive behaviours (McDonnell & Sturmey).

Ideology and Empiricism

In terms of service provision, the relationship between ideology and empiricism has come into sharp focus in the last decade and in the past five years in particular. This volume has attempted to present a coverage of these issues by presenting a chapter on the aversives debate from an American perspective (Sturmey, Ricketts & Goza) and a chapter outlining the issues involved in the normalisation debate from a British perspective (Toogood). In addition, the relationship between ideology and empiricism is central to the contributions concerning gentle teaching (Jones & McCaughey) and the provision of ordinary housing for people with challenging behaviour (Felce).

This debate has developed a rather different emphasis on each side of the Atlantic. In the U.S. the 'aversives issue' has dominated the scene in recent years and has received much greater emphasis than the U.K. As shown by Sturmey *et al.*, the protagonists of each point of view have, on occasions, expressed their opinions with great intensity, even to the extent of making interpersonal attacks. As a consequence the debate has reached a highly emotional pitch at times and led to an unhelpful polarisation of positions. Characteristic of the U.S., there has also been a far greater use of litigation and involvement of the law courts. This has, in turn, stimulated the development of detailed codes of conduct and treatment procedures by organisations and establishments concerned with the care and treatment of people with intellectual disabilities While there are obvious advantages to the development of greater accountability and explicitness of treatment programmes, including the reduction of the use of psychotropic medication, there is also the danger of treatments being delayed because of excessive bureaucracy and dependence on court approval.

The situation on this side of the Atlantic, as outlined in the chapters by Toogood and by Jones & McCaughey, differs in a number of respects. The focus of the debate appears to be a much broader one encompassing the interface between applied behaviour analysis and social role valorisation (normalisation) in general.

Toogood gives a comprehensive, historical overview of the development of normalisation and Wolfensberger's more recent extension and refinements of the original concepts and examines the implications of normalisation for people who exhibit challenging behaviour in relation to O'Brien's five service accomplishments. In the light of this appraisal Toogood's chapter concludes on a much more optimistic note than perhaps other accounts of the aversives debate have done. Toogood suggests that there is a "false dichotomy" between applied behaviour analysis and normalisation theory and that "there is some evidence of a middle ground beginning to emerge . . . seek(ing) to marry values with technology". This sentiment is echoed in the chapter on gentle teaching by Jones & McCaughey. Whereas, again in the U.S., gentle teaching is the subject of much acrimonious and personal debate, Jones & McCaughey adopt a more constructive appraisal. They suggest that, at the present time, gentle teaching is better seen as "an ideology rather than a method of proven effectiveness". Nevertheless, like normalisation, it draws attention to a number of important implications for service delivery, such, as the need to focus on the whole environment.

A number of themes come to the surface in the three chapters which focus on service delivery in the context of normalisation (Toogood, Jones & McCaughey, Felce). Felce looks at the concept of "needs" and reminds us that some individuals may have "special needs" but that they also share the same ordinary needs as all human beings. He maintains that community services have to be designed to "deliver individually designed remedial programmes" while not overlooking more general needs. Toogood suggests that there has been a problem of 'throwing the baby out with the bath water' as normalisation confronts applied behaviour analysis. He highlights the issue of developing competencies and engagement and maintains that normalisation has been used by ill informed staff as a justification for non-intervention (Jones & McCaughey make the same point with respect to gentle teaching) and laments that the aspect of Normalisation and service provision which has the best empirically validated technology for its implementation should turn out to be the one which is given the least credence in services. Both Felce and Jones & McCaughey emphasise the importance of enabling people with behavioural challenges to increase independence skills as alternatives to challenging behaviour, as a means of reducing deviant imagery and as a vehicle for developing mutual positive regard between teacher and learner.

Related to the development of individual competencies is another recurring theme, that of staff training. Jones & McCaughey point out that "gentle teaching requires fundamental changes in staff as well as learners" and it is crucially important that staff receive appropriate management and supervision to help them to develop their own competencies and to avoid burnout. In his chapter Toogood makes the important point that if the gap between theory and practise is to be narrowed then we need to make the technology that does exist more available, credible, acceptable and 'user friendly' to the direct care staff.

Ecological Analysis
For many years behavioural psychology has been subject to harsh criticism both from within its own ranks and from critics from more ideologically-based perspectives. Oliver & Head (this volume) have phrased the situation as follows: 'Behavioural psychologists are fiddling while Rome burns and there are plenty prepared to chuck another log on'. The reasons for this criticism are complex but most focus on the fact that until the recent past, the behavioural literature resembled a battery of techniques more than an analysis of the determinants of behaviour. This was true on both sides of the Atlantic. For example, despite the heroic calls for analysis made in the first edition of the *Journal of Applied Behavior Analysis* (Baer, Wolf & Risley, 1968), one could be forgiven for assuming that the function of the majority of the papers published in the first 20 years in this journal was to prove that the Law of Effect (Thorndike, 1913) actually worked in applied settings. Not surprisingly, the critics claimed that applied behaviourism was cold, sterile, simplistic, authoritarian and dehumanising (see Oliver & Head, this volume). Unfortunately, it is still common to see behavioural principles taught as a battery of techniques in an oversimplistic and even naive manner and this undoubtedly enhances the appeal of less data-driven approaches (see Jones & McCaughey, this volume). There is however, a new and exciting emphasis in behaviourism and in the past decade the concept of analysis has reemerged slowly into the forefront of the field. Both functional and ecological analyses, are set to make major contributions to the understanding and treatment of challenging behaviour in the near future and the present volume presents a 'state-of-the-art' analysis of these new approaches. Woods & Blewitt present an outline of the major issues involved in these forms of analyses from a historical perspective and show how these complementary approaches can be applied in a variety of ways. Oliver & Head show how functional analysis can be applied to the understanding and treatment of self-injurious behaviour. They also point to some of the other advantages of this approach such as in the analysis of behaviour which may be motivated by neurotransmitter and neuro modulator disturbance and the new developments in the use of hand-held computers for real-time naturalistic observation and sequential lag analysis. Throughout the chapter, Oliver & Head point out that the apparent simplicity of functional analysis may mask a number of theoretical complexities which, while not insurmountable, point to the need to regard functional analysis as a process which is still evolving and contributing towards our understanding of human behaviour, rather than a series of specific techniques and procedures.

This latter point is echoed in the chapter by Owens & MacKinnon where they provide a theoretical perspective on functional analysis from the viewpoint of radical behaviourism. Owens & MacKinnon outline a number of examples where functional analysis needs to be sensitive to the complexity of human behaviour. They point to the relativity of such terms as 'antecedent', and 'consequence' and emphasise the need to see concepts such as 'functional equivalence' as contextually bound. In addition, when a person has a variety of sources of reinforcement and a large repertoire of behaviours (such as when the behaviour is under the control of a concurrent or conjoint schedule), then any functional analysis needs to reflect his complexity and avoid assuming that a particular challenging behaviour only serves a single function.

In their chapter on the relationship between challenging behaviour, psychiatric disorder and the law, Murphy & Holland present a historical perspective on the special legal provisions for people with intellectual disabilities since the middle ages. They discuss the difficulties with the identification and diagnosis of psychiatric disorders in people with intellectual disabilities, but suggest that in some cases, the failure to recognise the presence of a psychiatric disorder in an individual displaying challenging behaviour could result in the failure to treat a treatable disorder. They outline the procedures involved when an individual with intellectual disability commits a crime and the subsequent court procedures including the concepts of 'culpability' and 'fitness to plead' as well as the implications for assessment and treatment. Psychological assessment and treatment are discussed in relationship to violent and aggressive behaviour; sexual offences and arson. It appears that approaches to the assessment and treatment of high-rate challenging behaviour (e.g., self-injury) are considerably in advance of those routinely employed in the analysis of a low rate behaviour such as arson.

Similarly, considerable lack of clarity and analysis is evident in the available guidelines to staff for dealing with violent and aggressive behaviour. McDonnell & Sturmey have collected a number of 'guidelines' and report on their attempts to evaluate a number of procedures by task analysing them using trained martial artists. Although the majority of procedures were either impractical or too vague to be of use, some were found to pose a high risk of injury to both staff and clients. They suggest that the available evidence concerning the quality of information and training given to care staff at the present time is so poor as to be a major cause of concern.

Finally, Kiernan in his concluding chapter, deals in depth with several issues raised in the body of the book. These include the ethics of intervention, future theoretical developments and the shape of services in the era of community care and structural reorganisations such as advent of the internal market in the NHS.

Borrowing notions from the social work and medical ethics literature, he discusses the relative weight which should be afforded to the autonomy of the individual to behave freely and, in particular, when this is in conflict with parents'

9

or staff needs or more generally with social mores and laws. The influence of normalisation in services has often left staff lacking direction in dealing with situations where the apparent choice of behaviour by the client is inappropriate for a number of reasons. It is perhaps true that naive slavish application of normalisation principles have lead to the toleration of behaviour beyond appropriate limits and often with the ultimate cost of staff burnout. Kiernan also reminds us that it is all too easy to forget that people by virtue of the fact they may have intellectual disabilities do not necessarily relinquish all moral responsibility for their own behaviour. He suggests that the reframing of 'behavoural excesses' in terms of 'challenges to the system' has tended to shift us away from perceiving people with intellectual disability as having any control or choice over their own behaviour, a position which is, in itself, devaluing.

Challenging behaviour also poses a challenge to the theoreticians. Many of the authors in this volume point to the theoretical shortcomings at the present time. These are compounded by the broadranging nature of the subject matter in view of its socially determined definition and the heterogeneous nature of the client group. Kiernan highlights the need to develop analytic models which deal with aspects of different challenging behaviours; which can accomodate differences in dimensions such as language; which maintain the laws of parsimony; which present an "overall internally consistent approach"; and which furthermore have practical application in the real world. He ends with a plea for service providers to 'get their act together' in using effectively the expertise that already exists but which often is lost through ineffective management. Echoing Toogood he highlights the enormous need for the development of effective and, most importantly, sophisticated specialist behavioural analytic training for staff. We hope that this collection will go some way to focus the attention of both theoreticians and practitioners alike to forge ahead in all these endeavours.

References

Baer, D. M., Wolf, M. M. and Risley, T. R. (1968). Some current dimensions of applied behavior analysis. *Journal of Applied Behavior Analysis* 1, 91-97.

Beange, H. and Bauman, A. (1990) Health Care for the Developmentally Disabled. Is it necessary? In W. I. Fraser (ed.) *Key Issues in Mental Retardation Research*. London: Routledge

Blunden, R. and Allen, D. (1987). *Facing the challenge: an ordinary life for people with learning difficulties and challenging behaviour*. London: King's Fund.

Borthwick-Duffy, S. A., Eyman, R. K. and White, J. F. (1987). Client characteristics and residential placement patterns. *American Journal of Mental Deficiency*, 92, 24-30.

Broderick, B. (1988) Comments on Contemporary Issues in Addressing the Needs of People who have mental Handicap and Disturbed Behaviour. In R. McConkey and P. McGinley (eds.) *Concepts and Controversies in Services for People with Mental Handicap*. Galway: Woodlands Centre and Dublin: St. Michael's House.

Cipani, E. (ed.) (1989). *The Treatment of Severe Behavior Disorders*. Washington: American Association on Mental Retardation.

Dockrell, J., Gaskell, G., Rehman, H. and Normand, C. (1992) *The MIETS evaluation: Implications for service provision*. Paper presented at Challenging Behaviour in People with Learning Disabilities conference, Charterhouse Hotel, Manchester, 7-8th May, 1992.

Emerson, E. (1990) Designing individualised community based placements as alternatives to institutions for people with a severe mental handicap and severe problem behaviour. In W. I. Fraser (ed.) *Key Issues in Mental Retardation Research.* London: Routledge

Emerson, E., Barrett, S., Bell, C., Cummings, R., McCool, C., Toogood, A., and Mansell, J. (1987). *Developing Services for People With Severe Learning Difficulties and Challenging Behaviours.* University of Kent at Cantebury, Institute of Social and Applied Psychology.

Eyman, R. and Call, T. (1977). Maladaptive behavior and community placement of mentally retarded persons. *American Journal of Mental Deficiency,* 82, 137-144.

Fryers, T. (1990) Epidemiology of Severe Mental Retardation. In P. L. C. Evans, and A. D. B. Clarke, (Eds.) *Combatting Mental Handicap.* Oxon: A B Academic Publishers.

Gorman-Smith, D., and Matson, J. L. (1985). A review of treatment research for self-injurious and stereotyped responding. *Journal of Mental Deficiency Research,* 29, 295-308.

Griffin, J. C., Williams, D. E., Stark, M. T., Altmeyer, B. K. and Mason, M. (1986) Self-injurious behavior: A state-wide prevalence survey of the extent and circumstances. *Applied Research in Mental Retardation,* 7, 105-116.

Harris, P.and Russell, O. (1990). Aggressive behaviour among people with learning difficulties - the nature of the problem. In A. Dosen, A. van Gennep, and G. J. Zwanikken (Eds). *Treatment of Mental Illness and Behavioural Disorder in the Mentally Retarded.* Proceedings of the International Congress. Leiden, The Netherlands: Logon Publications.

Jacobsen, J. W. (1982) Problem Behavior and Psychiatric Impairment within a Developmentally Disabled Population 1: Behavior Frequency. *Applied Research in Mental Retardation* 3, 121-139.

James, D.H. (1986). Psychiatric and Behavioural disorders among older severely mentally handicapped patients. *Journal of Mental Deficiency Research,* 30, 341-345.

Jones, R. S. P., Wint, D. and Ellis, N. C. (1990). The social effects of stereotyped behaviour, *Journal of Mental Deficiency Research,* 34, 261-268.

LaGrow, S. J., and Repp, A. C. (1984). Stereotypic responding: A review of intervention research. *American Journal of Mental Deficiency,* 88, 595-609.

Lakin, K. C., Hill, B. K., Hauber, F. A. Bruininks, R. H. and Heal, L. W. (1983) New admissions and readmissions to a national sample of public residential facilities. *American Journal of Mental Deficiency* 88, 13-20.

Lennox, D. B., Miltenberger, R. G., Spengler, P., and Erfanian, N. (1988). Decelerative treatment practices with persons who have mental retardation: A review of five years of the literature. *American Journal of Mental Retardation,* 92, 492-501.

Mansell, J. and Beasley, F. (1990) Evaluating the transfer to community care. In W. I. Fraser (ed.) *Key Issues in Mental Retardation Research.* London: Routledge

Matson, J. L., and Taras, M. E. (1989). A 20-year review of punishment and alternative methods to treat problem behaviors in developmentally delayed persons. *Research in Developmental Disabilities,* 10, 85-104.

Oliver, C., Murphy, G. H. and Corbett, J. A. (1987). Self-injurious behaviour in people with mental handicap: a total population study. *Journal of Mental Deficiency Research,* 31, 147-162.

Qureshi, H., and Alborz, A. (1992). Epidemiology of challenging Behaviour. *Mental Handicap Research,* 5, 130-145.

Qureshi, H. (in press). Prevalence of challenging behaviour. In I. Fleming and B.Stenfert Kroese (Eds). *People with learning difficulties and challenging behaviour: Advances in research, service delivery and interventions.* Manchester: Manchester University Press.

Rousey, A.B., Blacher, J.B. and Hauneman, R.A. (1990). Predictors of out of home placement of children with severe handicaps: A cross-sectional analysis. *American Journal on Mental Retardation,* 94, 522-531.

Russell, O. and Harris, P. (1992) *Aggressive behaviour - findings from a community survey.* Paper presented at the Challenging Behaviour in People with Learning Disabilities conference, Charterhouse Hotel, Manchester, 7-8th May 1992.

Thorndike, E. L. (1913). Educational Psychology. Vol.2: The Psychology of Learning. New York: Teacher's College Columbia University.

CHAPTER 2

Self-Injurious Behaviour: Functional Analysis and Interventions

Chris Oliver
Institute of Psychiatry, London
and
Donna Head
Leicestershire Health Authority

Introduction

The acrimonious debate about the use of aversive stimuli to reduce self-injurious behaviour (SIB) in people with intellectual disabilities looks set to run and run and continue to dominate the behavioural literature. In the meantime there are two points worth noting. Firstly, out of nearly 600 people who showed SIB in a regional health authority in the U.K. only 12 were receiving any psychological therapy at all (Oliver, Murphy & Corbett, 1987). Secondly there has been an increase in the use of unproven and superficially seductive therapies which are not derived from mainstream psychology and consequently further marginalise people with intellectual disabilities (Clements, 1992). Behavioural psychologists are fiddling while Rome burns and there are plenty prepared to chuck another log on.

The factors contributing to this current state are inevitably numerous. The culture of behavioural psychology failed to root in the U.K., compared to the U.S.A., and against this backdrop technique-oriented behaviour modification has been disseminated. The hallmark of this approach is the empirical evaluation of the outcome of intervention methods, primarily the manipulation or introduction of contingencies, within controlled single-case designs. There is therefore, little attention paid to the necessity for a theoretical understanding of the methods or their derivation. The result of this endeavour has been the development and evaluation of techniques which can succeed in reducing a life-threatening behaviour and its attendant distress. In this respect this type of intervention research based in behavioural psychology is unparalleled in its contribution to ameliorating SIB by any other discipline or branch of psychology.

This brand of behaviour modification however, seems to have fallen from favour. Interestingly, not because of any new empirical evidence regarding its efficacy but for other reasons. The approach has been labelled cold, controlling, clinical and simplistic by opponents. These judgements have been uncritically accepted by some philosophies of service delivery which have then deemed that behavioural psychology itself is unacceptable. These dogmatic criticisms have simply gone unanswered, mainly because behavioural psychology in the field of intellectual disability failed to be widely disseminated as more than a battery of techniques. Criticism has also come from within. The development of intervention strategies, it is argued, should be based on the determinants of the target behaviour and not on the criterion of the overall efficacy of any given method (Carr, Robinson, & Palumbo, 1990). Ironically, it is this criticism of technique-oriented behaviour modification which is currently reviving the behavioural approach and relocating the study and treatment of SIB back within mainstream psychology.

This chapter is concerned with understanding the determinants of SIB. More specifically, its subject is the methodology of functional analysis. Whilst a functional analysis is most commonly conducted as an aid to developing effective interventions, this should not be the only reason why practitioners in behavioural psychology should develop expertise in this area. A brief scan of the most frequently cited references in papers on SIB, will show the influence of functional analysis on contemporary research and practice (see for example, Lovaas, Freitag, Gold *et al.*, 1965; Carr, 1977; Rincover & Devany, 1982; Iwata, Dorsey, Slifer, *et al.*, 1982; Carr & Durand, 1985a). It appears that improvements in interventions do not simply come from evaluating interventions but also from examining determinants. Functional analysis therefore, has helped to avoid the technological stagnation that afflicted behaviour modification and has significantly contributed to the changing face of behavioural psychology. Behavioural psychology stands apart from many other approaches because of its commitment to a scientific approach. Functional analysis is a basic tool of this approach which ensures that such a commitment continues. Its common use is critical to further developments in the application of behavioural psychology to the study of SIB.

Functional analysis and self-injurious behaviour
Reviews and studies of the functions of SIB describe two classes of reinforcement, negative and positive, which may maintain SIB. Escape from demands or instructional settings is the commonly cited mode of negative reinforcement (Carr, Newsom & Binkoff, 1976; Gaylord-Ross, Weeks & Lipner, 1980; Iwata, Pace, Kalsher *et al.*, 1990; and see Iwata, 1987) whilst social attention is the most frequently considered form of positive reinforcement (Carr, 1977; Iwata, Dorsey, Slifer *et al.*, 1982; Carr & Durand 1985a). (SIB maintained by avoidance is, interestingly, infrequently considered or described, Oliver, 1991a.) Sensory

13

stimulation accruing from SIB may be either a negative or positive reinforcer, it is often unclear which, and the term 'automatic reinforcement' has been suggested (Iwata, Pace, Kalsher *et al.*, 1990). More recently other positive and negative reinforcers have been described. Tangible stimuli can reinforce SIB (Edelson, Taubman & Lovaas, 1983; Durand & Crimmins, 1988) and so may the donning of physical devices, such as splints (Favell, McGimsey & Jones, 1978; Foxx & Defrense, 1984). Additionally social interactions void of instructional demands can comprise aversive stimuli which may be an establishing operation for SIB (Oliver, Murphy, Crayton *et al.* 1993; and see Michael, 1982, for a discussion of establishing operations).

It is important to note that SIB may not necessarily only be maintained by one class of reinforcer or one type of reinforcer within a class. Additionally the reinforcer(s) may change over time. In fact, for SIB there may be different functions:

- for the same type of self-injury between individuals (Iwata, Dorsey, Slifer *et al.*, 1982)
- for the same type of self-injury within an individual (Oliver, 1991a)
- for different types of self-injury within and between individuals (Durand, 1982; Carr & Durand, 1985b).
- for the same type of self-injury within an individual at different times (Murphy & Oliver, 1987)

The role of functional analysis is to identify which environmental events influence the probability that SIB will occur and thus attribute a function to the behaviour.

Functional analysis has been usefully described and defined by Kiernan (1973) and Blackman (1985). From both authors' accounts three important points arise which may be seen as the conditions which a functional analysis should fulfil. These are:

i) That behaviour (B) is considered in terms of the influence of events preceding the behaviour, or its antecedents (A), and the events consequent (C) upon it.
ii) That the influences of antecedents and consequences should be empirically demonstrated.
iii) That all necessary and sufficient conditions for a behaviour to occur should be considered.

From examining the commonly used methods of functional analysis, and considering these conditions, a number of problems are evident. Frequently it is one aspect of the first point which has become synonymous with the term functional analysis and this is examination of the temporal sequence of events, or, which A precedes B in time, and, which C follows B in time. Little attention appears to be paid to the functional relationship between A and B and B and C and even less to empirical demonstrations of such a relationship. Similarly, whilst it is clearly important that a functional analysis considers all of the possible sources of reinforcement documented above by published studies, it is equally important that it is not limited to these. If it is, then the second defining feature of a functional analysis (all necessary and sufficient conditions) will have been ignored. Finally, there is an emphasis on identifying reinforcers for SIB and little attention is paid to antecedents which may exert an equal influence on the probability of SIB occurring.

The methods of functional analysis of self-injurious behaviour
A potted history of empirical research into SIB would show that the first study of any influence (Lovaas, Freitag, Gold et al., 1965) employed a functional analysis and thus opened the door to behavioural psychology. Interest in functional analysis then lapsed, partly because of the leap into technological behaviour modification, and was only revived in the early 80's. Consequently there is a paucity of literature from which to draw conclusions about the utility and quality of a given method of functional analysis. It is necessary therefore to examine practice as well as evidence. As there is an increasing number of reviews which more than adequately document the various methods of functional analysis (see Durand & Crimmins, 1991, for a useful summary), this section will concentrate on describing and evaluating the main methods and consider their strengths and limitations.

The most common method of conducting a functional analysis for SIB is probably by interview with someone who knows the client. An interview will consider antecedents to SIB and the consequences which follow. Other information can be gained on broader setting events and relevant individual and environmental characteristics. Whilst this is a popular technique for conducting a functional analysis, its properties of validity and reliability are undetermined. Such a method relies almost exclusively on the observational abilities of the informant, with the attendant problems of selective recall and subjective interpretation. Its popularity therefore, probably lies in its ease of application and its ability to sample large periods of time and numbers of events. It should not be used in isolation prior to intervening and is most useful as a general guide to which antecedents and consequences, particularly uncommon ones, are related to SIB.

Carrying out direct natural observations of SIB and related events is a more objective method of collecting information on potential antecedent - behaviour - consequence chains. A similar method, commonly employed in practice, is the use of A-B-C charts to record the sequence of events (see Murphy, 1987). As with the method of clinical interview however, there is little appraisal of these approaches either in terms of the agreement with any other method or their ability to 'predict' the efficacy of a given intervention. Studies of the functional analysis of SIB using direct natural observations have yielded data on the observed, temporal relationship between SIB and other events. Maurice & Trudel (1982) for example, report that

15

from observing SIB in 36 people for a mean of 3.5 hours for each person, each 10 second interval in which SIB occurred was preceded by an observable event on only 6% of occasions. Similarly in the interval subsequent to SIB being observed, an observable event only occurred on 6.25% of occasions. A comparable method was employed by Edelson, Taubman & Lovaas (1983) who concluded that for 20 people who showed frequent SIB, there was no temporal relationship between observed staff presence and SIB and thus no 'positive' reinforcement of SIB by attention. They did, however, find clearer relationships between the observed events of demands and denials and subsequent SIB.

These studies demonstrate two problems associated with direct natural observations and A-B-C charts. The first is that such observations may prove inconclusive because there is no apparent relationship between SIB and surrounding events. The second is that the relationship between SIB and surrounding events, when it exists, may be weak. This method of functional analysis therefore gives rise to a difficulty in interpretation; on the one hand an absent or weak relationship between SIB and other events may simply mean that no functional relationship exists, conversely such a relationship may exist but the assumptions partly inherent in the method of direct natural observations obscure the relationship. This problem of interpretation is further discussed below together with other errors which may arise from this method of functional analysis.

The use of analogue conditions as a method of functional analysis has been pioneered by Iwata, Dorsey, Slifer *et al.*, (1982), Durand (1982) and Carr & Durand (1985a) (see Oliver, 1991b, for a review). This method systematically manipulates environmental events and observes their effect on SIB to determine which reinforcers are operative in the natural environment. The three analogue conditions employed by Carr & Durand (1985a) for example, involve: a high level of attention when an easy task is presented, a low level of attention when an easy task is presented and a high level of attention when a difficult task is presented. A higher rate of SIB in the second condition than the first would indicate that SIB is reinforced by attention, whilst a higher rate of SIB in the third condition than the first would indicate that SIB is reinforced by escape from demands. Similar reasoning is applied to the analogue conditions employed by Iwata, Dorsey, Slifer *et al.*, (1982), Durand & Crimmins (1988) and Oliver, Murphy, Crayton *et al.*, (1993).

Analogue methodology has become a popular method of functional analysis in the research literature by virtue of its inherent empiricism, its basis in the behavioural approach and its contribution to the understanding of SIB. Recent research has begun to address the issue of its ability to predict the efficacy of given interventions (Carr & Durand, 1985a; Mace, Page, Ivancic *et al.*, 1986; Durand & Crimmins, 1987; Durand & Carr, 1987; Steege, Wacker, Berg *et al.*, 1989; Iwata, Pace, Kalsher *et al.*, 1990) and how variants of early methods may provide a more detailed assessment (Murphy & Oliver, 1987; Day, Rea, Schussler *et al.*, 1988; Slifer, Ivancic, Parrish *et al.*, 1986)

Analogue methodology however, may not necessarily overcome all the problems associated with the functional analysis of SIB. Oliver, Crayton, Murphy *et al.*, (1988) compared the functional analysis of SIB using analogue conditions, direct natural observations and clinical interview and found poor agreement between these methods. Additionally, it was clear that errors could arise from the use of analogue methodology as well as other methods. These problems are discussed below together with recommendations as to the most productive use of analogue methodology and an appraisal of the contribution to decision making this method yields.

The most recent specific contribution to the functional analysis of SIB has been the development of the Motivation Assessment Scale (MAS) by Durand & Crimmins (1988). Whilst this instrument was preceded by some checklists and questionnaires (see for example Carr 1977; Wieseler, Hanson, Chamberlain *et al.*, 1985; Donnellan, Mirenda, Mesaros *et al.*, 1984 and Hauck, 1985) it is unique in that its reliability and validity have been assessed. The validity was assessed by correlating the results of a functional analysis by the MAS with comparable analogue conditions. Despite this the MAS has been criticised as it is not empirical (i.e., does not demonstrate a cause and effect relationship; see Iwata, Pace, Kalsher *et al.*, 1990). It is likely however to prove useful for screening purposes (see Bird, Dores, Moniz *et al.*, 1989; Durand & Kishi, 1987).

This brief review of the methods used in the functional analysis of SIB has only alluded to some of the difficulties inherent in different methods. From considering these methods against the three properties for a functional analysis described above the following points arise:

i) The method of clinical interview is useful because it samples large amounts of time and numbers of events but relies on anecdotal information. It therefore fulfils the first and third conditions but not the second.

ii) Direct natural observations and A-B-C charts are a more objective method of collecting data on A-B-C chains but the interpretation of the data rests on an assumption about the relationships within this chain. They may therefore only fulfil the first and third conditions but not the second.

iii) Analogue conditions proffer an empirical test of hypotheses regarding the function of SIB but frequently sample a restricted set of events. They may therefore only fulfil the first two conditions but not the third.

iv) The Motivation Assessment Schedule is an easily administered, validated instrument which provides valuable information but may be limited in its appraisal of all environmental determinants. It therefore fulfils the first condition, to some extent the second but not the third.

There are therefore strengths and limitations associated with the various methods of functional analysis. It is important to understand the implications of a method not fulfilling all three conditions so that the potential for errors is recognized. The following section demonstrates,via some brief case studies, how errors arise by examining the qualities of different methods.

The strengths and limitations of methods of functional analysis

There are two errors which may arise from not fulfilling all three conditions for a functional analysis when attempting to determine the functions of SIB. A reinforcer may not be identified as operative when it is in fact influential (an error of omission) and a reinforcer may be identified as operative when it is not in fact influential (an error of commission). These two errors may arise for a number of reasons which are discussed below. A different problem is that a functional analysis may not yield a conclusive result in terms of which functions are operative (e.g., Iwata, Dorsey, Slifer *et al.*, 1982). Similarly a functional analysis may not be possible when SIB is so intense or frequent that the potential for injury rules out free responding. These problems are addressed in a later section.

Errors of Omission
Errors of omission may arise for reasons which are associated with the methodology employed.

1. An error of omission may arise because a given methodology does not consider a particular type of reinforcement (as a possible consequence) or aversive stimulus (as a possible antecedent) (i.e., from not fulfilling condition 3).

The potential for this error is predominantly evident in studies employing analogue methodology. The possibility of tangible reinforcement, for example, is not considered by the analogue conditions used by Iwata, Dorsey, Slifer *et al.* (1982), Carr & Durand (1985a) and Oliver, Murphy, Crayton *et al.* (1993). This is perhaps overly critical of these studies which did not seek to assess this function, however as this function may exist for individuals it is important to note that these methods may be incomplete. This is particularly important as the study of Durand & Crimmins (1988) found that tangible reinforcement was the primary function for 48% of people showing SIB.

Similarly, most analogue studies do not empirically assess the possibility that SIB may be maintained by escape from social interactions which are void of demands (see Oliver, Murphy, Crayton *et al.*, 1993). One implication of this omission is that when employing analogue conditions a high rate of SIB in demand conditions does not necessarily indicate a function of escape from demands. It may simply be interaction with the other person which comprises the aversive stimulus. This problem is equally evident in the MAS (Durand & Crimmins, 1988) which omits social escape as a potential function.

This discussion points to the fact that functions may be omitted because a particular method does not consider that function, even though generally the class of

18

reinforcement (i.e., positive or negative) is considered. A good example is to be found in the results of Iwata, Pace, Kalsher et al. (1990). In this study one subject showed high rates of SIB only in a condition which involved a medical examination but not when more general demands were presented. Clearly the establishing operation is very specific and would not have been identified if the Iwata, Dorsey Slifer et al. (1982) 'standard set' of analogues had been employed.

A further example of this type of error of omission was seen in the study of Oliver, Crayton, Murphy et al. (1988). One subject, a 32-year-old man with profound intellectual disability, was exposed to a number of analogue conditions to conduct a functional analysis of his SIB (head punching and banging). Direct matural observations and clinical interview were also employed in parallel. The analogue conditions employed, which are relevant here, show SIB to be high when instructional demands were made (demands), but low when there was a social interaction with no demands (continuous attention) or attention was contingent on SIB (contingent attention) or when others were present but did not attend to the SIB (ignore). Figure 1 shows the rate of SIB under these four conditions for one set of the conditions.

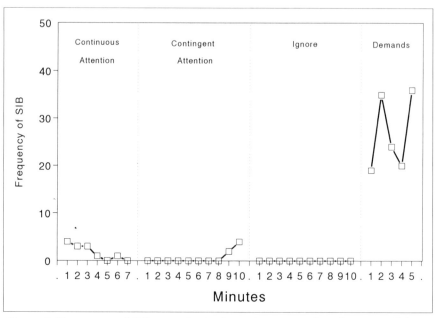

Figure 1. Frequency of SIB per minute shown in one set of analogue conditions.

Whilst it is clear from the data in Figure 1 that one of the primary reinforcers for SIB was escape from task demands, the results of other methods of functional analysis produces contradictory results. Most significantly direct natural observations lasting

19

3.5 hours failed to identify this function. The reason for this was that no demands were made during this period and this could have been due either to the low levels of engagement which occurred in the environment or because people were reluctant to present demands because they would evoke SIB (see Carr, Taylor, Robinson, 1991). In either case the method of direct natural observation led to an error of omission, The clinical interview did identify this function, presumably because it was able to sample a greater period of time and/or elicit the fact that demands were not presented because of the SIB. Interestingly, both direct natural observations and clinical interview also identified the function of escape from social interactions, whilst this was not identified by the analogue conditions employed. This may have been because interactions in the natural environment, which were at a very low level, were always associated with demands and the methods were unable to disentangle which establishing operation was operative (i.e., social interaction alone or paired with demands). In this case analogue conditions which controlled relevant aspects of interactions were perhaps more accurate (see Figure 1).

2. An error of omission may arise even if the function is considered by the methodology employed when invalid assumptions are made about the analysis (i.e., by not fulfilling condition 2).

An error of omission may arise in direct natural observations or A-B-C charts when SIB is maintained on a lean, intermittent schedule of, for example, social or tangible reinforcement. In this case SIB may be followed by a reinforcing consequence very infrequently. Observation or charting may therefore show only weak temporal contiguity between SIB and consequences and the relationship may be judged to have no functional significance. A potential example of this is given above in the Maurice and Trudel (1982) direct observation study. Consequences to SIB were observed on only 6.25% of occasions. Such a low frequency however does not necessarily indicate that the consequence is not an operative reinforcer, it may be operative but it is simply presented on a lean, intermittent schedule (see also Hall & Oliver, 1992).

A related error of omission arises when the antecedent is not necessarily a discrete and observable event. The study by Hall & Oliver (1992) demonstrated that an influential antecedent to SIB was the establishing operation of reinforcer deprivation (in fact the absence of social contact for a period of time). Such an antecedent, although operative and amenable to manipulation in an intervention, may simply not be recognized. It may be this problem which has led to such an increase in the examination of the negative reinforcement hypothesis. The establishing operation in the case of negative reinforcement (the presence of an aversive stimulus) is more easily observed and manipulated e.g., the presentation of a 'task demand'. In the case of positive reinforcement by attention however, the establishing operation may commonly be the absence of an observable stimulus.

20

There are then various ways in which errors of omission may arise. These are however, not insurmountable as they arise predominantly from the limited sampling of salient events and their definition. The methods employed can clearly be adapted to overcome this problem and this is further discussed in the concluding section.

Errors of Commission

Errors of commission predominantly arise because the functional significance of events related to SIB is assumed invalidly (i.e., condition 2 is not fulfilled). An example of this is given above where the methods of clinical interview and direct natural observations ascribed the function of escape from social interactions to SIB determined only by escape from demands. This error may have arisen because there was also an avoidance component to the SIB as opposed to simply an escape component. (There was evidence from further analogue conditions that this was the case; Oliver, 1991a.) Consequently any approach to the subject was likely to evoke SIB as it was reinforced by avoidance of a demands. However it was clear from analogues that it was not just the social interaction that determined SIB but the demands. In this case then, an error arises because the nature of the antecedent establishing operation is poorly evaluated by clinical interview and direct natural observations.

A different type of error of commission may arise because of an assumption inherent in the method of direct natural observations and, to some extent, clinical interview. The assumption in an A-B-C analysis, seems to be that if SIB is reliably followed by a given stimulus then that stimulus is a reinforcer. The definition of a reinforcer however, is that it increases the probability of a behaviour occurring. A good example of this problem arises when assessing eye poking. For the majority of people this behaviour is probably maintained by the resultant stimulation. This is presumably why it occurs when there is retinal damage but not when there is damage to the optic tract (Jan, Freeman, McCormick *et al.*, 1983). If it is observed however, that each instance of eye poking is followed by a reprimand and physical restraint, it may be incorrectly assumed that this consequence is a reinforcer for the behaviour. In this case a function which does not exist is ascribed to the behaviour and a function (self stimulation) which does exist is not ascribed.

When employing analogue conditions it is possible to make an error of commission when artificially reinforcing a self-injurious response. For example, if the test of attention maintained SIB is the presentation of such reinforcement contingent on each response, it is plausible that responding can be more frequent in this condition than in control conditions, simply because the person has learned to self-injure in the test situation (c.f. Lovaas, Freitag, Gold *et al.*, 1965). This higher frequency therefore, does not necessarily mean that in the natural environment SIB is reinforced in this way. Iwata, Dorsey, Slifer *et al.*, (1982) who used this method reported that this did not occur for the 9 subjects. It is however, possible. For this reason, and for the obvious reason that it is undesirable to 'create' a function, it is

21

perhaps better to use a test involving the establishing operation of reinforcer deprivation (see Carr & Durand, 1985a; Murphy & Oliver, 1987).

Errors of commission may also arise when different topographies of SIB are inappropriately combined. This point can be demonstrated from the functional analysis by analogue conditions of the hard and soft head hits shown by V, a 15 year old girl with severe intellectual disabilities. The conditions employed were sitting alone on a mat (a preferred activity), 1:1 continuous attention at a table, being ignored at the table and being required to engage in a task. (The last 3 conditions are similar to those employed by Carr and Durand, 1985a). The effect of these conditions on soft and hard hits is shown in Figure 2.

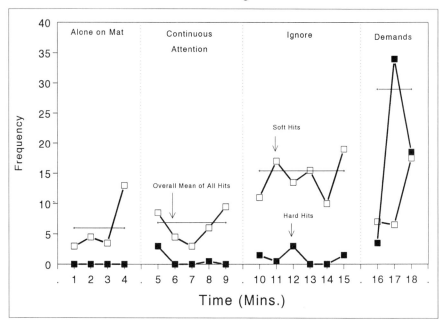

Figure 2. Mean frequency per minute of hard and soft head hits shown by V from two trials of a set of four analogue conditions.

The data in Figure 2 show the highest rates of soft hits to occur when being ignored and the highest rates of hard hits to occur in demand conditions. The implication here is that two intensities of the same topography appear to be reinforced in different ways and consequently the manipulation of contingencies in an intervention should also differ (see Oliver, Murphy, Crayton *et al.*, 1993, for another example and Durand, 1982, for a related example). If the two forms of SIB had been combined it would have been assumed that they both had the functions of gaining attention and escaping demands thus errors of commission would have occurred for both intensities of SIB. This is not just an academic point. Extinction of soft hits as part of an overall intervention strategy is a viable option, extinction of hard hits is not, simply because of the potential for injury in an extinction burst.

Overcoming errors in functional analysis

The errors which may occur when conducting a functional analysis of SIB arise as a result of not fulfilling all 3 conditions for a functional analysis. Analogue conditions proffer control over relevant variables and ensure the presentation of salient aversive and reinforcing stimuli. They do however, potentially increase the possibility of errors of omission as they may sample a restricted variety of influential variables in 'unnatural' settings. Conversely, direct natural observations sample natural settings but cannot necessarily ensure that all relevant variables are considered. Finally both direct natural observations and clinical interviews to some extent run a greater risk of making errors of commission and omission by considering temporal and not functional relationships.

These problems are not insurmountable and can be overcome by combining the various methods. Clinical interview is useful for identifying potential functionally related events and thus acting as a screening device, as are A-B-C charts and direct observations of 'high risk' settings. It is important however, that hypotheses are tested systematically and analogue methodology is useful in this respect. For example, if in interview the teaching of self care skills is identified as a high risk period, it should be possible to compare the rate of SIB when such teaching occurs with a setting in which the person teaching is present but not making demands for a similar period of time on a number of occasions. If the latter setting does not occur it can be arranged (see Iwata, Pace, Kalsher *et al.*, 1990 for a good example of this). This type of functional analysis has the benefit of being controlled and of using natural settings and thus may avoid some of the errors described above.

This sort of process was employed with V, who participated in the analogue conditions shown in Figure 2. Initially two broad brush methods of functional analysis were employed. The first employed a variant of momentary time sampling of both SIB and, simultaneously, the type of engagement she was involved in. The teacher was asked to observe V every 30 minutes for 1 minute and record whether SIB occurred and whether she was involved in a 1:1 teaching session, a group activity, or alone and unoccupied. The results are shown in Table 1.

Table 1 shows that V is significantly more likely to engage in SIB if she is involved in a 1:1 teaching activity or a group situation. Conversely she is significantly less likely to show SIB if she is alone and unoccupied. The second method involved direct natural observations using lap held microcomputers (see Repp & Felce, 1990). Similar behaviours were recorded and the analysis consisted of determining the probability of SIB occurring given that a type of interaction was occurring. The results are given in Table 2.

The results shown in Table 2 are broadly similar to those from the momentary time sampling procedure employed by the class teacher. The conclusion drawn at

23

Unconditional probability of SIB	Type of Engagement	Conditional probability of SIB given engagement	Z Index*
0.38	1 : 1 or group activity	0.56	2.12
0.38	solitary activity or unoccupied	0.25	2.14

(* see Bakeman, 1978)

Table 1. Unconditional and conditional probabilities of SIB occurring, given types of engagement, calculated from teaching staff's 'momentary' time sampling records.

Unconditional probability of SIB	Type of Engagement	Conditional probability of SIB given engagement	Z Index
0.31	1 : 1 – engagement 4.	0.40	3.90
0.31	no engagement	0.25	2.98

Table 2. Unconditional and conditional probabilities of SIB, given types of engagement, calculated from direct natural observations.

this point was that a primary determinant of the hitting was social interactions, although it was unclear as to exactly how they were related to the SIB. Consequently the analogue methodology described above and in Figure 2 was employed to empirically determine the relationship. It is worth noting that before the analogue methodology was employed and detailed, controlled observation conducted, it was unclear as to whether being in a group activity increased SIB because it was associated with demands or whether there was an establishing operation of deprivation of reinforcing attention with a discriminitive stimulus present. Similarly the intensity of the hitting and the difference in function that appeared to exist had not been explored as the observational categories were combined for the direct natural observation.

In this section the strengths and limitations of various methods of functional analysis have been described and, hopefully, illustrated. The main point is that

24

functional analysis is essentially a hypothesis testing exercise and thus is subject to the usual rules governing the control of variables and conclusive demonstration. As has been discussed above the critical test of a functional analysis is whether manipulation of identified contingencies (A's or C's) changes the probability of the behaviour. Whilst this is a defining feature of functional analysis, it is also the point at which intervention may be said to begin (see Repp, Felce and Barton, 1988 for an example of this).

Functional analysis and interventions
The development of functional analysis has given rise to much optimism for enhanced efficacy of interventions. This is perhaps the most recent and important landmark in the application of behavioural approaches to SIB. The study of Carr and Durand (1985a) originally indicated the importance of determining function for intervention efficacy. More recently Iwata, Dorsey, Slifer et al.'s (1982) methodology has been applied by Mace, Page, Ivancic et al., (1986) and Steege, Wacker, Berg et al., (1989) to demonstrate the selection of interventions based on analogue conditions. Successful interventions have been also demonstrated in a similar way by Iwata, Pace, Kalsher et al. (1990). This growth area will undoubtedly continue to expand with further demonstrations. (Useful, recent reviews of the relationship between functional analysis and interventions are: Mace, Lalli & Shea, 1992; Durand & Crimmins, 1991; Carr, Robinson, Taylor et al., 1990). These studies however, naturally rely on the functional analysis being conclusive and this cannot always be achieved. Iwata, Dorsey, Slifer et al., (1982) could not determine function for 2 subjects (out of 9) and the SIB in all subjects in the Linscheid, Iwata, Ricketts et al., (1990) study did not show a clear function in analogue conditions.

There are therefore, clearly a number of people for whom functional analysis, in the forms discussed above, may be unhelpful in determining the nature of an intervention. It is likely that these people show severe and/or frequent SIB and that protective or restrictive orthoses are a common method of management (Oliver, Murphy & Corbett, 1987). Under these circumstances then, intervention is clearly essential and there is still a role to be played by functional analysis.

Two brief case examples may serve to illustrate this point. In the first a 10 year old boy, S, who was blind and had a profound intellectual disability, showed high rate and damaging eye poking, requiring both arms to be permanently restrained in splints. Functional analysis involving free responding was untenable because of the immediacy of damage to his eyes. The most likely hypothesis in this case was that the eye poking was automatically reinforced (by stimulation). To begin any intervention it was essential that there was a sufficient period between responding to allow an alternative response to occur so that it could acquire functional similarity (by applying positive reinforcement procedures). Consequently, a trial of response prevention was employed i.e. an adult simply physically stopped each response.

25

Under these circumstances an increase in the rate would indicate that attention of this kind could maintain the behaviour, and thus be a detrimental 'management' procedure, whilst a decrease in rate would indicate either that the behaviour was automatically reinforced (as the procedure under these conditions essentially approximates to sensory extinction, see Rincover and Devany, 1982) or that the prevention was aversive. The data from the first two trials of this procedure are shown in Figure 3.

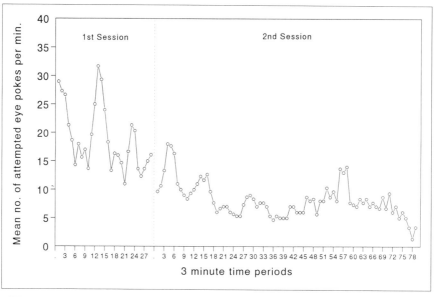

Figure 3. Mean frequency of attempted eye pokes per minute, shown by S, in the first two trials of response intervention. (A 3 point moving mean has been applied to the data to examine the general trend.

The data in Figure 3 show a clear decrease in responding over the first 2 sessions. Consequently it may be assumed either that the reinforcement for responding has been removed or that the physical prevention is aversive. In either case a management strategy, response prevention, had been identified which would not be detrimental in the long term i.e. it would not positively reinforce the behaviour. With this finding established, methods of teaching alternative ways of gaining stimulation combined with response prevention may be sought.

For a second person, D, a 23 year old woman with a visual impairment and profound intellectual disability, head punching occurred at a high rate when her chosen form of restraint was not employed. The restraint sought by D was in the form of 'filters' i.e. large plastic light covers with hand holes at both ends. She would push her hands through the holes and thus wear the filters on her arms. Interestingly, the presence of the filters did not physically prevent SIB, they did however reduce its probability considerably. Direct natural observations revealed that she wore these filters for 86.4% of the time (range 74 to 100%). Head punching predominantly occurred when the filters were removed, and then at a high rate and of dangerous intensity. Figure 4 shows the effect of removing these filters in a controlled fashion.

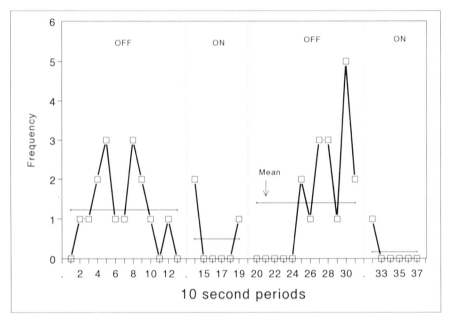

Figure 4. Frequency of head punching shown by D in a brief trial of removal of her preferred form of 'restraint'.

From the data in Figure 4 and the natural observations, the presence of the filters is obviously a major determinant of SIB. They are therefore, functionally related. Any further functional analysis was untenable because of the potential damage from head punching and it was unlikely that the rate would be further determined by other features of the environment.

From this necessarily restricted analysis two important findings arose. Firstly from the Premack principle the filters were almost certainly reinforcing. Additionally, D would often resist their removal and would actively put them on. Secondly they exerted almost total control over the SIB. The intervention in this case consisted of two strategies. On the basis of the finding that such restraints may be faded without SIB necessarily increasing (see Luiselli, 1992, for a brief review) the size of the filters was gradually reduced so that the control established to be present from the trial (Figure 4) was retained and the social acceptability of the restraints was enhanced. The second strategy based on the findings of Favell,

27

McGimsey & Jones (1978) and Foxx & Defrense (1984) was to only present the filters (positive reinforcers from the Premack principle), if they had been removed, following a period of no SIB. The results of this procedure are shown in Figure 5.

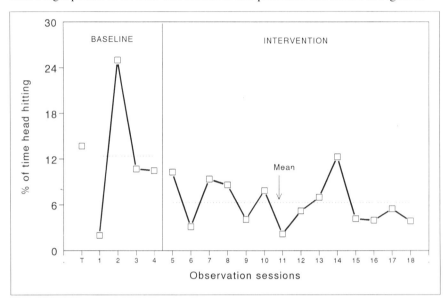

Figure 5. Mean percentage of time spent head-hitting by D, during a trial session (see Fig. 4) and during baseline and intervention phases. Behaviour was observed in the 'natural' environment.

The results of this intervention demonstrate that the amount of SIB occurring when the filters were off was reduced by about 50%, presumably because of differential reinforcement. Although the SIB continued to be a problem, a management procedure had been effected which was a necessary, but not sufficient, condition for a significant reduction in SIB.

These examples serve to demonstrate two general points. The first is that functional analysis should not just be used at the assessment phase to identify the reinforcer for self-injury. It should be used constantly during intervention to evaluate potential changes in function. What reinforces a behaviour during assessment may change during the intervention, precisely because there has been an intervention. In any event there may be more than one reinforcer for SIB and those of lesser potency may be more evident during intervention. Secondly it should be used to examine and predict the effects of management procedures. The laws of operant conditioning are not held in abeyance for reactive strategies and it is useful to rule out responses to SIB which reasonable predictions would show to be detrimental in the longer term.

Conclusions

Most reasons for conducting a functional analysis are obvious. It makes practitioners more effective, interventions logical and obvious. The literature on the contribution to intervention efficacy looks set to grow substantially in the 90's. There is also a good case to be made for constantly describing more stimuli which can evoke or reinforce SIB. Such lists are not really the stuff of applied behaviour analysis but they may contribute to an extensive initial screening procedure in checklist or questionnaire format. A more important reason for advocating the use of functional analysis is that it enables practitioners to understand why people self-injure and, with empirical demonstrations, can help others to understand. It is this feature of behavioural psychology which distinguishes it from dogma driven fashionable therapies. If the data do the talking you can put the flares in mothballs.

There is an additional and more fundamental role for functional analysis outside the applied field. Currently, neuromodulator and neurotransmitter disturbance are being proposed as potential determinants of severe SIB, and the main testing ground of these theories is pharmacological intervention (Oliver and Head, 1990). There are, however, other predictions that may be made about SIB if it was *only* determined by such mechanisms in a given individual. The level of SIB should be unaffected by analogue conditions for example, and in natural observations, all antecedents should appear at their unconditional probability prior to SIB. (Consequences may not as they may be temporally and not functionally related.) An examination of the theories from both perspectives (pharmacological and analytical) offers a more robust appraisal of the relative contributions of conditioning and neurochemistry. As ever, the smart money is on an interaction.

Looking ahead, functional analysis is about to take a significant leap forward. The major obstacles to conducting a sophisticated analysis of contingencies in the natural environment have been the onerous tasks of recording with pen and paper and raw data analysis. Consequently time sampling methods have dominated, with the attendant problems of estimation and non-sequential recording. Lap-held microcomputers can overcome these problems and others (see Repp & Felce, 1990; Repp Felce & Karsh, 1991). Behaviours can be recorded as they occur and in the order that they occur, without sampling. It is now possible to conduct lag analysis and thus examine contingencies in more detail than has previously been possible. Similarly, it is possible to examine the effect of SIB on the behaviour of others and thus expand the traditional remit of functional analysis (see Hall & Oliver, 1992). This area holds out much promise both to researchers and practitioners and deserves development.

The case made for functional analysis so far has been concerned with intervention efficacy, science and behavioural psychology. There is however, a much more compelling reason why it should commonly be employed and this is the empowerment of people with severe intellectual disabilities. It has been argued that SIB (and other challenging behaviours) are communicative in function and this is a useful metaphor for the behavioural position. The intervention question then becomes how may someone be taught to communicate in a more acceptable and less harmful way? Before this can be answered however, it is necessary to know what the person is communicating and why. This can be achieved by conducting a functional analysis which identifies the conditions that evoke the communication (the antecedents to the SIB) and how successful the communication is (the consequences or reinforcer for the SIB). Once this process is understood, a new form of communication with functional similarity may be taught and the individual retains control over their environment (Carr and Durand, 1985b). People cannot be empowered unless it is known what they want to control.

In the opening paragraphs of this chapter it was suggested that the early dissemination of technique orientated behaviour modification in the U.K. contributed to the decline of behavioural psychology in the 80's. (This is not a criticism, it is an observation). A necessary condition for this decline was the absence of a culture of behavioural psychology and an emphasis on techniques not analysis. The same error must not occur with the methods of functional analysis. The practitioner should not just be aware of how to use a method and its strengths and limitations. Conversely, it is important to understand that functional analysis is a scientific method of examining the determinants of behaviour and methodology is simply there to serve, not be served. Greater understanding of the determinants of behaviour will foster improvements in testing and tighter predictions. There is a need therefore, for practitioners to be more than just familiar with basic theory and it is against this background that the methodology of functional analysis should be set and developed. This will ensure that theory and practice remain closely linked and prevent another case of premature dissemination spoiling a relationship.

References

Bakeman, R. (1978). Untangling streams of behavior. In G. P. Sackett, (Ed.) *Observing behavior: data collection and analysis methods.* Vol. 2. Baltimore: University Park Press.

Blackman, D. E. (1985) Contemporary behaviourism: a brief overview. *In Behaviour Analysis and Contemporary Psychology,* C. F. Lowe, M. Richelle and D. E. Blackman, (Eds.), London: Lawrence Erlbaum Associates Ltd.

Bird, F., Dores, P. A., Moniz, D. and Robinson, J. (1989) Reducing severe aggressive and self-injurious behaviors with functional communication training. *American Journal on Mental Retardation,* 94, 37-48.

Carr, E. G. (1977) The motivation of self-injurious behavior: A review of some hypotheses. *Psychological Bulletin,* 84, 800-816.

Carr, E. G. and Newsom, C. D. and Binkoff, J. A. (1976) Stimulus control of self-destructive behavior in a psychotic child. *Journal of Abnormal Child Psychology,* 4, 139-153.

Carr, E. G. and Durand, V. M. (1985a) Reducing behavior problems through functional communication training. *Journal of Applied Behavior Analysis,* 18, 111-126.

Carr, E. G. and Durand, V. M. (1985b) The social-communicative basis of severe behavior problems in children. In S.Reiss and R.Bootzin (Eds.), *Theoretical Issues in Behavior Therapy* (pp. 219-254), Academic Press, New York.

Carr, E. G., Robinson, S. and Palumbo, L. W. (1990) The wrong issue: Aversive versus non-aversive treatment. The right issue: Functional versus non-functional treatment. In A. Repp and N. Singh

(Eds.), *Perspectives on the use of non-aversive and aversive interventions for persons with developmental disabilities* (pp. 361-379). Sycamore, IL: Sycamore Press.

Carr, E. G., Robinson, S., Taylor, J. C., and Carlson, J. I. (1990). Positive approaches to the treatment of severe behavior problems in persons with developmental disabilities: A review and analysis of reinforcement and stimulus-based procedures. *Monograph of the Association for Persons with Severe Handicaps*, 4.

Carr, E. G., Taylor, J. C. and Robinson, S. (1991). The effects of severe behavior problems in children on the teaching behavior of adults. *Journal of Applied Behavior Analysis*, 24, 523-535.

Clements, J.(1992) I can't explain. . . 'Challenging Behaviour': towards a shared conceptual framework. *Clinical Psychology Forum*, 39, 29-37.

Day, R. M., Rea, J. A., Schussler, N. G., Larsen, S. E. and Johnson, W. L. (1988) A functionally based approach to the treatment of self-injurious behavior. *Behavior Modification*, 12, 565-589.

Donnellan, A. M., Mirenda, P. L., Mesaros, R. A. and Fassbender, L. L. (1984) Analyzing the communicative functions of aberrant behavior. *Journal of the Association for Persons with Severe Handicaps*, 9, 201-212.

Durand, V. M. (1982) Analysis and intervention of self-injurious behavior, *Journal of the Association of the Severely Handicapped*, 7, 44-53.

Durand, V. M. and Carr, E. G. (1987) Social influences on 'self stimulatory' behavior: Analysis and treatment application. *Journal of Applied Behavior Analysis*, 20, 119–132.

Durnd, V. M. and Crimmins, D. B. (1987) Assessment and treatment of psychotic speech in an autistic child. *Journal of Autism and Developmental Disorders*, 17, 17-28.

Durand, V. M. and Kishi, G. (1987) Reducing severe behavior problems among people with dual sensory impairments: An evaluation of a technical assistance model. *Journal of the Association of Persons with Severe Handicaps*, 12, 2-10.

Durand, V. M. and Crimmins, D. B. (1988) Identifying the variables maintaining self-injurious behavior. *Journal of Autism and Developmental Disorders*, 18, 99-117.

Durand, V. M.and Crimmins, D. (1991) Teaching functionally equivalent responses as an intervention for challenging behavior. In: B. Remington, (Ed.) *The Challenge of Severe Mental Handicap: A behaviour analytic approach*, pp. (71-95). Chichester: Wiley and Sons.

Edelson, S. M., Taubman, M.T. and Lovaas, O.I. (1983) Some social contexts of self-destructive behavior. *Journal of Abnormal Child Psychology*, 11, 299-312.

Favell, J. E., McGimsey, J. F. and Jones, M. L. (1978) The use of physical restraint in the treatment of self-injury and as positive reinforcement. *Journal of Applied Behavior Analysis*, 11, 225-242.

Foxx, R. M. and Defrense, D. (1984) 'Harry': the use of physical restraint as a reinforcer, timeout from restraint and giving restraint in treating a self-injurious man. *Analysis and Intervention in Developmental Disabilities*, 4, 1-13.

Gaylord-Ross, R., Weeks, M., and Lipner, C. (1980). An analysis of antecedent, response, and consequence events in the treatment of self-injurious behaviour. *Education and Training of the Mentally Retarded*, 15, 35-42.

Hauck, F. (1985) Development of a behavior-analytic questionnaire precising four functions of self-injurious behavior in the mentally retarded. *International Journal of Rehabilitation Research*, 8, 350-352.

Hall, S. and Oliver, C. (1992) Differential effects of severe self-injurious behaviour on the behaviour of others. *Behavioural Psychotherapy*, 20, 355-365.

Iwata, B. A. (1987) Negative reinforcement in applied behavior analysis: An emerging technology. *Journal of Applied Behavior Analysis*, 20, 361-378.

Iwata, B. A., Dorsey, M. F., Slifer, K. J., Bauman, K. E. and Richman, G. S. (1982) Toward a functional analysis of self-injury. *Analysis and Intervention in Developmental Disabilities*, 2, 3-20.

Iwata, B. A., Pace, G. M., Kalsher, M. J., Cowdery, G. E. and Cataldo, M. F. (1990) Experimental analysis and extinction of self-injurious escape behavior. *Journal of Applied Behavior Analysis*, 23, 11-27.

Jan, J. E., Freeman, R. D., McCormick, A. O., Scott, E. P., Robertson, W. D. and Newman, D. E. (1983) Eye-pressing by visually impaired children. *Developmental Medicine and Child Neurology*, 25, 755-762.

Kiernan, C. C. (1973) Functional analysis. In *Assessment for Learning in the Mentally Handicapped*, Mittler, P. (Ed.), London: Churchill Livingstone.

31

Linscheid, T. R., Iwata, B. A., Ricketts, R. W., Williams, D. E., and Griffin, J. C. (1990) Clinical evaluation of the self-injurious behavior inhibiting system (SIBIS). *Journal of Applied Behavior Analysis,* 23, 53-78.

Lovaas, O. I., Freitag, G., Gold, V. J. and Kassorla, I. C. (1965) Experimental studies in childhood schizophrenia: Analysis of self-destructive behavior. *Journal of Experimental Child Psychology,* 2, 67-84

Luiselli, J. K. (1992) Protective Equipment. In: J. K. Luiselli, J. L. Matson, and N. N. Singh, (Eds.) *Self-injurious behavior: Analysis assessment, and treatments.* pp. 235-268. New York: Springer-Verlag.

Mace, F. C., Page, T. J., Ivancic, M. T. and O'Brien, S. (1986) Effectiveness of brief time-out with and without contingent delay: A comparative analysis. *Journal of Applied Behaviour Analysis,* 19, 79-86.

Mace, F. C., Lalli, J. S. and Shea, M. C. (1992) Functional analysis and treatment of self-injury. In: J. K. Luiselli, J. L. Matson, and N. N. Singh, (Eds.) *Self-injurious behavior: Analysis, assessment, and treatment.* pp. 122-152. New:York: Springer-Verlag.

Maurice, P. and Trudel, G. (1982) Self-injurious behavior: Prevalence and relationship to environmental events. In J. Hollis and C. E. Meyers (Eds.) *Life Threatening Behaviour: Analysis and Intervention* (pp. 81-104). Washington, DC: American Association of Mental Deficiency.

Michael, J. (1982) Distinguishing between discriminative and motivational functions of stimuli. *Journal of the Experimental Analysis of Behavior,* 37, 149-155.

Murphy, G. (1987) Direct observation as an assessment tool in functional analysis and treatment. In J. Hogg and N. V.Raynes (Eds.) *Assessment in Mental Handicap: A Guide to Assessment Practices, Tests and Checklists* (pp. 190-238), London: Croom Helm.

Murphy, G. H. and Oliver, C. (1987) Decreasing undesirable behaviours. In W. Yule and J. Carr (Eds.) *Behaviour Modification for People with Mental Handicaps* (2nd Ed., pp. 102-142), London: Croom Helm.

Oliver, C., Murphy, G. H. and Corbett, J. A. (1987) Self-injurious behaviour in people with mental handicap: a total population study. *Journal of Mental Deficiency Research,* 31, 147-162.

Oliver, C., Crayton, L., Murphy, G., Burgess, A., Clements, J. and Corbett, J. A. (1988) The Functional Analysis of Self-injurious Behaviour: A Comparison of Methods. Paper Presented at the Behaviour Therapy World Congress, Edinburgh.

Oliver, C. and Head, D. (1990) Self-injurious behaviour in people with learning disabilities: Determinants and interventions. *International Review of Psychiatry,* 2, 99-114.

Oliver, C. (1991a) Self-injurious behaviour in people with mental handicap: prevalence, individual characteristics and functional analysis. Unpublished Ph.D. thesis, University of London.

Oliver, C. (1991b) The application of analogue methodology to the functional analysis of challenging behaviour. In B. Remington (Ed.) *The Challenge of Severe Mental Handicap: A Behavioural Analytic Approach,* Chichester: Wiley and Sons.

Oliver, C., Murphy, G., Crayton, L. and Corbett, J. A. (1993). Self-injurious behaviour in Rett's syndrome: interactions between features of Rett's syndrome and operant conditioning. *Journal of Autism and Developmental Disorders,* 23, 91–109.

Repp, A. C., Felce, D. and Barton, L. E. (1988) Basing the treatment of stereotypic and self-injurious behaviors on hypotheses of their causes. *Journal of Applied Behavior Analysis,* 2l, 281-289.

Repp, A. C. and Felce, D. (1990) A microcomputer system used for evaluative and experimental behavioural research in mental handicap. *Mental Handicap Research,* 3, 21-32.

Repp, A. C., Felce, D. and Karsh, K. G. (1991) The use of a portable microcomputer in the functional analysis of maladaptive behaviour. In Remington, B. (Ed.) *The Challenge of Severe Mental Handicap: A behaviour analytic approach.* pp. 119-137. Chichester: Wiley and Sons.

Rincover, A. and Devany, J. (1982) The application of sensory extinction procedures to self-injury. *Analysis and Intervention in Developmental Disabilities,* 2, 67-81.`

Slifer, K. J., Ivancic, M. T., Parrish, J. M., Page, T. J. and Burgio, L. D. (1986) Assessment and treatment of multiple behavior problems exhibited by a profoundly retarded adolescent, *Journal of Behavior Therapy and Experimental Psychiatry,* 17, 203-213.

Steege, M. W., Wacker, D. P., Berg, W. K., Cigrand, K. K. and Cooper, L. J. (1989) The use of behavioral assessment to prescribe and evaluate treatments for severely handicapped children. *Journal of Applied Behavior Analysis,* 22, 23-33.

Wieseler, N. A., Hanson, R. H., Chamberlain, T. P. and Thompson, T. (1985) Functional taxonomy of stereotypic and self-injurious behavior. *Mental Retardation,* 23, 230-234.

Acknowledgements

Much of the research described in this chapter was funded by the Department of Health. The data analysis and the preparation of the manuscript were carried out on a PC generously donated by Viglen Ltd.

CHAPTER 3

Functional and Ecological Analysis: A Precursor to Constructional Intervention

Peter A. Woods
and
Edward Blewitt
Gwynedd Health Authority, North Wales

Introduction

It is now over 25 years since the methods developed by the *experimental analysis of behaviour* began to be applied to issues of human behaviour outside the laboratory. In 1968 this approach gained some institutional independence with the launch of the *Journal of Applied Behavior Analysis,* and over the intervening period it has achieved tremendous growth and influence. Whilst the focus has been on the interrelationship of responses with antecedent and consequent events (often referred to as the A-B-C model), the level of sophistication with which this model has been employed has varied considerably.

Recent years have seen the emergence and development of an approach which has attempted to move beyond the purely technological interests of mainstream applied psychology. This new wave of research and practice still has its roots in applied behaviour analysis, and seeks to develop within this tradition. However, it recognises that to increase the conceptual and pragmatic effectiveness of behaviour analysis there is a need to both expand the range of issues dealt with and the concepts required to deal with this expanded field of interest. It has attempted to do this in two main directions:

(a) Developing trends that already exist within behaviour analysis but which have not been incorporated as the main feature of most work within the discipline. Three such trends are discussed here:

1) the importance of identifying natural rather than arbitrary antecedents and consequences.

2) the desirability of constructing new adaptive repertoires of behaviour for individuals.
3) the importance of pre-intervention functional analysis.

(b) The incorporation of perspectives and concepts from allied approaches to applied behaviour analysis. Two such alliances have been attempted, but they have not been whole heartedly adopted by the discipline. Hence, the new wave tends to be a minority viewpoint. The two approaches are the *ecobehavioural* perspective of Edwin Williams, and *interbehaviourism* developed by J. R. Kantor

In this chapter we briefly review this development and examine it in relation to the study of 'challenging behaviour': Firstly the basic dimensions of applied behaviour analysis are described and some crucial, but often overlooked conceptual issues are considered. This is followed by an examination of the contrasting 'pathological' and 'constructional' applications of the A-B-C model. Next comes a brief discussion of the 'ecological analysis' of the mid-1970's. Finally, the adoption of the 'setting event' concept from the inter-behavioural psychology of J. R. Kantor is examined, and its potential contribution to further refinement of the process of analysis and intervention is considered.

Applied behaviour analysis
In their classic paper, 'Some current dimensions of applied behaviour analysis', Baer, Wolf & Risley (1968) outlined what they considered to be the defining characteristics of Applied Behaviour Analysis. They listed seven criteria which, briefly, were that it should be:-

Applied: That it should be concerned with concepts and problems that are of social interest and importance.
Behavioural: It should be pragmatic, explicit, and concentrate on the precise and reliable measurement of physical events.
Analytic: It should make use of a convincing experimental design capable of a believable demonstration of the events and conditions that may be responsible for the occurrence or non-occurrence of the behaviour under study.
Technological: That the techniques making up a particular behavioural application are completely identified and described.
Conceptual: That its behaviour-change methods make systematic, conceptual sense in terms of a comprehensive theory about behaviour.
Generalisable: This was seen as being crucial to the survival of the discipline. Generalisation across settings, across time, across people, etc., was something hoped and strived for in designing intervention procedures. However, in the following twenty years, the emphasis shifted to exploring the conditions that control appropriate generalisation (e.g., Stokes & Baer, 1977; Baer, 1982) rather than relying on good luck.

Effective: That measured change of target behaviour in desirable ways should result from implementation of the applied techniques.

Twenty years later, the same authors took stock of their discipline (Baer, Wolf & Risley, 1987) and concluded that, amongst other things:-

'A similar anthropological note today finds the same dimensions still prescriptive, and to an increasing extent, descriptive. Several new tactics have become evident, however, some in the realm of conceptual analysis, some in the sociological status of the discipline, and some in its understanding of the necessary systematic nature of any applied discipline that is to operate in the domain of important human behaviors.'

'. . . effectiveness for the future will probably be built primarily on system-wide interventions and high-quality failures, as we continue to bring theory to the point of designs that solve problems. But it should be current theory that is built on, not some replacement of it — current theory has worked far too well to be abandoned in the face of what are more parsimoniously seen as technological rather than theoretical failures.'

Although the dimensions of Baer *et al.,* (1968) simply required that applied behaviour analysis be conceptually systematic, and no particular model was explicitly called for, undoubtedly the implied model of preference was an operant one as espoused by proponents of the *experimental analysis of behaviour* (Skinner, 1953). Indeed, much of the early published work in this field consisted of reports in which 'principles' or 'techniques' derived from laboratory studies of the experimental analysis of behaviour could be 'applied' to social and clinical problems. In Britain, Cliffe, Gathercole & Epling (1974) exhorted applied researches and practitioners to search for '. . . a principle looking for applications', and informed them that 'There are a number of phenomena known to researchers acquainted with basic research that have not, so far, had practical application'.

Early studies which were concerned with challenging behaviours in people with intellectual disabilities generally focused on the effects of manipulating the environmental consequences of those behaviours. Amongst the 'principles' or 'techniques' that were investigated were *extinction* (e.g., Williams, 1959), *punishment* (e.g., Risley, 1968; Lovaas, Schaeffer & Simmons, 1965), and *differential reinforcement of other (or incompatible) behaviour* (e.g., Repp & Deitz, 1974).

Initially, applied behaviour analysis concentrated upon demonstrating that behavioural techniques were effective but, as the discipline matured, arguments for the subjective measurement and evaluation of behaviour change (e.g., Wolf, 1978) led to *social validation* (Kazdin, 1977) becoming a topic of importance for its exponents. As ethical considerations came more into central focus, the *public acceptability* of intervention procedures, the moral issues and social repercussions with their use, and their potential for abuse became of equal importance to their *effectiveness* (c.f. Florida Guidelines, 1974). To a large extent this echoed a caution that had been emphasised a decade previously by Michael & Meyerson (1962):

'A behaviour approach to human control does not consist of a bag of tricks to be applied mechanically for the purpose of coercing unwilling people.'

The role of aversive methods of controlling behaviour has always been a point of contention within applied behaviour analysis. Skinner himself has always been implacably opposed to the use of punishment (e.g., 1948, 1953) but others have proposed that the selective use of aversive procedures combined with 'reinforcement techniques' is justifiable and indeed necessary to solve some problems (Axelrod, 1987; Matson & Taras, 1989). In the last few years, this issue has again arisen with the growth of a 'non-punitive' lobby and the consequent debate over the use of aversive procedures with people with disabilities (e.g., LaVigna & Donnellan, 1986; Axelrod, 1987; Horner *et al.*, 1990; Helmstetter & Durand, 1990; Sturmey, Ricketts & Goza, this volume).

Some conceptual issues

The Three-Term Contingency
The operant model adopted in applied behaviour analysis was described by Skinner (1953, 1969) as the *three-term contingency:*

'An adequate formulation of the interaction between an organism and its environment must always specify three things: (1) the occasion upon which a response occurs, (2) the response itself, and (3) the reinforcing consequences. The inter-relationships among them are the contingencies of reinforcement'. (Skinner, 1969).

In many texts that offer guidance to 'front-line' staff such as teachers, nurses and residential care workers, the three term contingency is often referred to as the *ABC analysis.* An example of an explanation of these elements, taken from a recent guide by Presland (1990), is as follows:

'Antecedent: an event, object, or situation which has an influence on whether or not a particular behaviour occurs immediately or shortly afterwards. In the example, if George's colliding with Graham is an event which makes it more likely that Graham will kick him, the collision is an antecedent for the kicking. *Behaviour:* this is the action or actions for which an explanation is being sought. In the example, the behaviour is Graham's kicking.

37

Consequence: an event, object, or situation which occurs immediately or shortly after a particular behaviour and has an influence on whether or not that behaviour occurs again on a similar occasion in the future. In the example, if staff attention makes it more likely that Graham's kicking will be repeated, it is a reinforcer for that behaviour.'

This sequence can be represented by the following diagram:

Antecedent	Behaviour	Consequence
(For example, George bumps into Graham)	(For example, Graham kicks George)	(For examble, staff member lectures George)

Functional and Operational Definitions

Catania (1969, 1973, 1984) has noted that the term reinforcement is used in the literature to describe both an *operation* (i.e., the delivery of a consequence when a response occurs) and a *process* (i.e., particular responding increases because it produces a reinforcer). It is important to note that in strictly correct terms, a stimulus can only be described as a *reinforcer,* and reinforcement said to have occurred, when a functional relationship between the response and its consequence can be demonstrated. A parallel vocabulary is appropriate to *punishment* and *punisher,* with the difference being that a punishing consequence makes responding occur less rather than more often.

'If an organism responds more often because its response changes its environment, we say that the response was rewarded or reinforced; if an organism responds less often for the same reason, we say that the response was suppressed or punished' (Catania, 1984).

The qualifiers, *positive* and *negative,* of course, simply indicate whether the consequence of a behaviour involves the *presentation* or *removal* of a reinforcer or punisher, respectively. Thus negative punishment is the process by which a response is reduced or suppressed as a result of the contingent removal of a stimulus.

In discussing the vocabulary of *learning,* Catania (1986) examined the concept of *stimulus control* and Skinner's (1938) term *discriminative stimulus,* distinguishing it from Pavlov's (1927) *eliciting stimulus*:-

'When a stimulus is the primary cause of a response, we say that the stimulus produces the response is elicited. But when a response occurs in the presence of

38

a stimulus because the stimulus signals some consequence of responding, we say that the stimulus occasions or evokes the response and that the response is emitted' (Catania, 1984).

In many 'guide to practice' texts that use the ABC framework of analysis, the term *antecedent* has become virtually synonymous with the technical term *discriminative stimulus*, and instead of being described as an event which *'occasions'* a response, the term *'triggers a behaviour'* (e.g., Zarkowska & Clements, 1988) is often coined.

Arbitrary and Natural Reinforcement

Introductory texts on learning and behaviour modification often refer to the distinction between *primary* and *secondary* (or *conditional*) *reinforcers* (e.g., Nevin, 1973). However, a conceptual dichotomy that is of more relevance to the field of applied behaviour analysis and intervention is that between *arbitrary* and *natural reinforcers* (and *punishers*). The distinction was introduced by Ferster (1967) as a consequence of his work with 'autistic' children (e.g., Ferster, 1961; Ferster & DeMeyer, 1962), and is similar to what Skinner (1982) has termed contrived reinforcement (see also Vaughan & Michael, 1982; Dickinson, 1989; Deitz, 1989 and Horcones, 1987).

Perhaps the easiest way to explain the distinction between natural and arbitrary reinforcement is to contrast the following: (a) A child walks towards the door, turns the knob and walks through into the toilet and urinates. (b) A teacher instructs the child, "If you open the door, I'll give you a biscuit", the child walks towards to door and turns the knob to open the door. He then walks back to the teacher who gives him a biscuit and says "Good boy, David".

The first example illustrates a case of natural reinforcement. The child's walking to the door and opening it is reinforced by the opportunity to urinate and reduce the physical discomfort of a full bladder. The reinforcing consequence is closely tied to the behaviours it follows; it meets the current repertoire of the individual and meets his needs. Natural reinforcement begins with a performance already in the individual's repertoire which is reinforced by an event that occurs reliably in a particular setting. With many natural reinforcers there are often a number of behaviours that can reliably lead to their occurrence. In the example given, if the door did not open, the child might have gone outside and urinated behind a tree in the garden, or run upstairs to use the toilet there. Such behaviours are said to be members of the same *naturally occurring functional operant class*.

The second example illustrates a case of arbitrary reinforcement. The child's walking to the door is under the external control of another person. The controller (or contingency manager) not only narrowly specified the behaviour required to obtain the reinforcer, but also determines the consequence for carrying out this performance. The whole event is primarily in the interest of the controller rather than the performer; the controller can coerce a particular performance whatever the child's current repertoire. The defining characteristic of arbitrary reinforcement (and punishment) is that the consequence of behaviour is not one that would usually occur, given the social and physical ecology in which the person lives, but is an unusual or unnatural consequence for that behaviour that is *externally imposed* by another person. That is not to say that all other-person-mediated or social consequences of behaviour are arbitrary. Indeed, such consequences occur quite naturally for all of us, as illustrated in the example given from Presland (1990) previously in which a naturally occurring social consequence reliably followed the target behaviour.

Pathological and constructional approaches to intervention: Apposite paradigms

In examining the conceptual basis adopted by various clinical and theoretical orientations to analysis and intervention with problematic and distressful behaviour, Goldiamond (1974) and Schwartz & Goldiamond (1975) contrasted two apposite approaches; the pathological approach and the constructional approach. Goldiamond did not propose that either approach was 'correct', nor did he propose that they were incompatible or exhaustive of all possible approaches. However, in comparing the two approaches attention was given to the relative durability of their effectiveness, and to the extent to which their outcomes are genuinely 'therapeutic' (c.f. Cullen, Hattersley & Tennant, 1977) and produce sustained behaviour change. The main characteristics of these two approaches are outlined in the sections which follow.

The Pathological Approach

Essentially, a pathological approach views challenging behaviour as a *problem* that has to be suppressed or removed. Hence, the kinds of questions that would be posed with a view to selecting and implementing programmes of intervention would be of the nature, 'How can we get the client to stop . . . .' Intervention procedures that have resulted from this approach typically attempt to achieve their desired ends by *imposing* new contingent consequences for the challenging behaviour.

Intervention procedures that involve contingent denial of access to the naturally occurring reinforcing consequences of a challenging behaviour (i.e., an extinction paradigm), for example, can be described as adopting a pathological approach. A classic early example of an extinction procedure was described by Williams (1959) which focused on a child's tantrums as a *problem* behaviour that was targeted for *suppression.* In that example the *extinction operation* consistent of withholding an adults natural attentional consequences. Schematically, the removal or denial of a naturally occurring consequence of a challenging behaviour can be shown as in Figure 1.

Intervention procedures that make use of contingent administration of an arbitrary punishing consequence can also be described as adopting a pathological

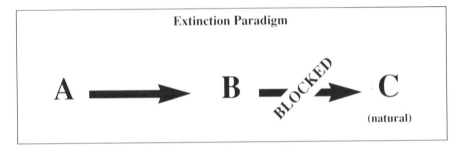

Figure 1

approach. An early study by Risley (1968) adopted a pathological approach by targeting the autistic behaviours of a deviant child for *suppression* by *superimposing* an arbitrary punishing consequence (electric shock) onto any naturally occurring consequence. Such an intervention paradigm can be shown as in Figure 2.

Many published studies which have adopted a pathological approach to intervention have reported effective suppression of targeted challenging behaviours (Axelrod & Apsche, 1983; Matson & DiLorenzo, 1984). However, it is generally the case that only intervention studies with *successful* outcomes are submitted for publication such that reviews of the literature alone could give a distorted picture of the efficacy of those which have adopted a pathological approach (or indeed any approach). In our own clinical experience, however, and indeed from that related to us by numerous colleagues, difficult, undesirable, and often most unpredictable outcomes can frequently result from adopting a pathological approach to challenging behaviour.

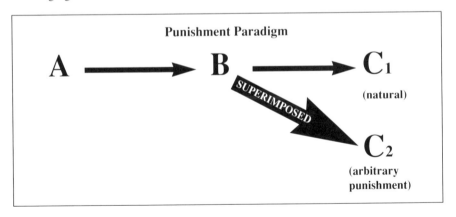

Figure 2

41

It should perhaps be noted at this point that most studies that have adopted a pathological approach have probably done so unwittingly. Virtually all interventions must surely be of good intent, and it is most unlikely that any intervention attempts purposely decide to adopt a pathological approach in preference to, say, a constructional approach. It is more likely that many researchers and practitioners have simply not undertaken the sort of conceptual analysis that would lead to labelling a particular intervention procedure as adopting a pathological approach or that they are immediately concerned with providing a reactive response to disturbing instances of a challenging behaviour.

Amongst the undesirable outcomes observed through adoption of a pathological approach to intervention with challenging behaviours that have been published, or reported informally, are the following examples:

a) A target challenging behaviour is not always totally suppressed when an arbitrary punishment contingency is introduced. Furthermore, the punishing effectiveness of such an *externally imposed contingency management procedure* can diminish over time, and the frequency or intensity of the behaviour gradually returns to near baseline levels.

For example, several years ago one of the present authors helped nursing staff at the hospital where he is based to design, implement and evaluate an externally imposed contingency management procedure with a resident who presented aggressive behaviours that resulted in physical injury to others. The procedure, which consisted of 'requiring' the resident to sit in a particular chair for five minutes immediately following every incident of aggressive behaviour, was carried out consistently every day by nursing staff for a period of three months. The outcome results for this clinical intervention are shown in Figure 3. The data were total number of defined aggressive acts (scratching, pinching and biting others) observed in eight random quarter hour periods per day, averaged over a week.

Clearly the graph in Figure 3 reveals that, although initially contingent implementation of this procedure led to suppression of the target challenging behaviours relative to *baseline* measures, over time the functional relationship changed with the *punishing* effectiveness diminishing. Needless to say this pathological approach was abandoned.

b) A major practical problem with any arbitrary, externally-imposed contingency management procedures, whether they use a reinforcement or a punishment paradigm, is that once they are removed, any desirable outcome effect they have on a target behaviour is lost, more often than not. As such they are often described as *prosthetic* (e.g., Cullen *et al.*, 1977; Lindsley, 1964; Woods *et al.*, 1984) and are said not to be genuinely *therapeutic* if lasting desirable changes in the frequency or conditional probability of a target behaviour is not maintained once the arbitrary intervention procedure has been withdrawn (e.g., Woods *et al.*, 1984).

Reliance on arbitrary, prosthetic contingencies being implemented consistently in all targeted circumstances and over time cannot always be guaranteed of course,

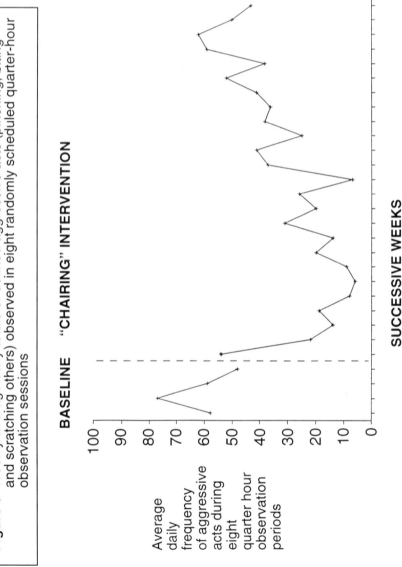

Figure 3 Weekly average daily totals of defined aggressive acts (pinching, biting and scratching others) observed in eight randomly scheduled quarter-hour observation sessions

Figure 3

43

and sometimes *procedural decay* can occur in which the precision and diligence with which the procedures are carried out gradually drifts and becomes more 'sloppily' carried out (if at all). As a consequence, over time a gradual return to pre-intervention levels of behaviour often results (e.g., Woods & Cullen, 1983).

c) Generalisation to non-intervention settings/people/times rarely occurs, unless it is actively programmed for (c.f. Stokes & Baer, 1977; Baer, 1982). Indeed *behavioural contrast* has sometimes been reported in which the occurrence of a behaviour targeted for decrease in one setting actually increases in non-intervention settings.

d) *'Symptom substitution'* often occurs in which although the targeted challenging behaviour is suppressed, another behaviour which is perhaps equally challenging will increase and occur in similar circumstances to the target behaviour. The present authors have had considerable experience in their early 'fix-me-a-programme' days when, for example, a contingency management procedure such as 'exclusion time-out' would successfully reduce the frequency of 'attacks on staff', only to find that the frequency of 'breaking windows' would increase. When the procedure was then introduced for 'breaking windows', the frequency of 'smearing faeces' would increase. And so on. This phenomenon has been reported in the literature on interventions with severely handicapped learners (e.g., Evans & Meyer, 1985) and has been explained as a case where the different challenging behaviours are members of the same functional operant class (Helmstetter & Durand, 1990).

The Constructional Approach

The constructional approach views challenging behaviour as a successful *means of serving a function*. Given the learning histories and restricted behavioural repertoires of many people with an intellectual disability, a challenging behaviour can be seen as a legitimate and logical path to a desired natural consequence, albeit costly and distressful to the person or others. The goal of the constructional approach, therefore, is to establish new, less distressful behaviours that will serve the *same* function and lead to the *same* natural consequences.

Schematically, the teaching of a new adaptive behaviour to hopefully *replace* the challenging behaviour can be shown as in Figure 4.

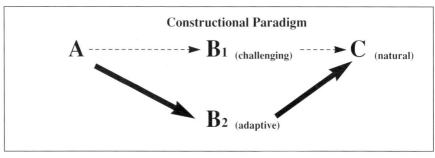

Figure 4

In a constructional approach to intervention the focus is upon *replacing* rather than simply *removing* the challenging behaviour. To be classified as a constructional intervention, it is not sufficient to teach an alternative adaptive behaviour. Constructional interventions are characterised by the establishment of alternative behaviours that are 'occasioned' *naturally* by the same naturally occurring antecedents that would trigger the challenging behaviour, and that *naturally* lead to the same natural consequences as the challenging behaviour. Only then can it be said that the alternative behaviours are *functionally equivalent* to the challenging behaviour. Apart from the alternative behaviour producing the same consequence produced by the challenging behaviour, it must also do so with less or similar *response effort*. Consider this example:

John used to be able to produce social attention by slapping his face and shouting, but now he has to run up the stairs twice, do twenty press-ups and sing 'Yankee Doodle' to get the same attention! The two behaviours require vastly different degrees of response effort. It is unlikely that John's behaviour will shift from 'face slapping and shouting' to 'run-up-stairs-twenty-press-ups-Yankee Doodle' - it's not worth the effort.

Important considerations to take into account, therefore, when identifying acceptable alternatives to the challenging behaviour, are (1) that the alternative should be as, if not more effective, in producing the consequence(s) that maintained the challenging behaviour, and (2) should involve less response effort than the challenging behaviour.

It is important to note that DRO, DRI and DRA procedures are not constructional interventions if they do not result in the alternative behaviour being triggered by the natural antecedent that previously would trigger the challenging behaviour, and/or they do not lead to the natural consequences. Such 'schedules of reinforcement' usually make use of arbitrary consequences (as defined previously), and even if they do try to use consequential events that are similar to the naturally occurring ones, they are 'delivered' arbitrarily, and the alternative behaviours are not always triggered by the natural antecedents.

An example of an approach to challenging behaviour that is truly constructional is that which makes use of the *functional communication hypothesis* (e.g., Donnellan *et al.*, 1984; Carr & Durand, 1985), which can be stated as follows:

Challenging behaviours may function like verbal communicative acts to *request* specific reinforcers (positive and negative) that are socially mediated. Therefore if a challenging behaviour is construed as a non-verbal request for attention, the suggested intervention strategy might involve teaching a verbal means of obtaining attention. Similarly, if a challenging behaviour is construed as a *non-verbal request* to escape from an '*aversive demand situation*', the suggested intervention strategy might involve teaching a verbal means for obtaining assistance which, once provided, should help to reduce the aversive nature of the task.

,s clearly a constructional approach involving specifically verbal, functionally
,ivalent, replacement behaviours. A recent example study by Carr & Durand
,985) used controlled analogue assessments (e.g., Iwata *et al.*, 1982) to identify
possible functional determinants of the aggressive behaviour of handicapped
children who were required to work on a matching task in a classroom situation.
Successful interventions were demonstrated involving the teaching of a) verbal
requests for attention, and/or b) verbal requests for obtaining assistance with a
difficult task, that were based on the analogue assessments.

Functional analysis
In a constructional approach, it is essential to determine *'why'* the challenging
behaviour occurs *before* intervention strategies are introduced. However, until
recently the focus of initial data gathering and analysis has often been limited to
temporally and spatially contiguous behaviours and environmental events. For
example:

> 'Essentially, the term "functional analysis" refers to the determination of the
> function of the various stimuli impinging upon the 'target' individual . . . the aim
> being to discover whether there are discriminative stimuli which 'trigger' the
> occurrence of the undesirable behaviour and whether there are identifiable stimuli
> which act as reinforcers, and maintain the undesirable behaviour . . . Typically,
> this would require the recording of antecedents (what happened before the target
> behaviour), the target behaviour itself and consequences (what happened after-
> wards) for every occurrence of the target behaviour . . . Once sufficient records
> have been collected (i.e., at least 20 occurrences of the target behaviour), then the
> analysis of the functions of the various stimuli may begin' (Murphy, 1987).

Collection of ABC observation data, where A is the immediately preceding
(more noticeable) array of environmental events and conditions, often reveals
findings such as:

(i) Challenging behaviours are sometimes low-rate but high intensity. For example,
arson behaviours might only occur once every two years with a particular person.
(ii) Variations can occur over time in the occurrence of challenging behaviours
which may be more episodic or cyclical than regular and consistent.
(iii) Considerable variation in the likelihood that an identified discriminative event
would serve to instigate challenging behaviour in a particular person over time, e.g.,
teasing may do so on some occasions, but not on others. Difficulty in predicting which
occurrences of a stimulus event will be followed by the behaviour is often the case.
(iv) Some challenging behaviours seem to be triggered by any of a very broad range
of immediate antecedent events, and sometimes 'nothing in particular' seems to
precede its occurrence.

Theoretically, if controlling antecedent stimulus conditions can be identified and modified, a means of influencing the occurrence of the challenging behaviour should exist. However, it is often the case that one specific topographically defined behaviour may serve more than one function for an individual (i.e., be a member of more than one operant class) at different times. For example, Carr (1977) identified three possible maintaining factors for self-injurious behaviour in the same subject; positive reinforcement by attention, negative reinforcement by escape from an aversive demand situation and self-stimulation/sensory reinforcement. It is also the case that the same topographically defined behaviour may serve different functions for different people (e.g., Carr & Durand, 1985).

That is, the following alternatives might be possible with the same person, for example: In a work situation, a person may be observed to be verbally aggressive when teased by other people. However, he may not always be verbally aggressive when teased; on some occasions teasing may lead to him acting coy and giving a 'shy' look, and on other occasions of teasing he may simply give the teaser an angry annoyed look without saying anything. Also, it may be the case that events other than teasing may lead to verbal aggression. It might be that on some occasions when his work is corrected by a supervisor such behaviour occurs, and indeed that on some occasions such verbal aggression follows praise from the supervisor. Using an ABC framework of analysis, these various possibilities could be represented as in the schematic diagram shown in Figure 5. Careful observation and recording could be undertaken in order to determine the conditional probability of each A-B sequence (c.f. Gardner *et al.*, 1986).

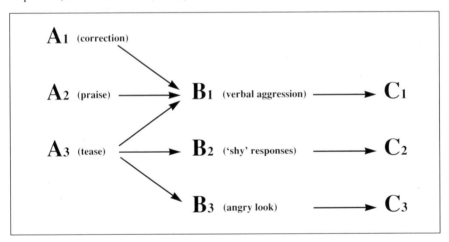

Figure 5

Assuming that all behaviour is not capricious, but is lawfully determined, it becomes necessary to unravel the complexity of factors which, for example, will determine which of the above A-B combinations is most likely to occur at any one instance. An expanded framework of analysis is clearly required. A more comprehensive functional analysis methodology that moves beyond a temporal and spacial 'narrow band' ABC model is clearly called for.(see Owens & MacKinnon, this volume)

Ecobehavioural analysis

Willems (1974), in a classic paper entitled 'Behavioural technology and behavioural ecology', introduced the notion of an ecological perspective in applied behaviour analysis. He drew attention to the possibility of interventions with particular behaviours inadvertently producing unanticipated side effects on an entire ecology of behaviours. He presented examples from the literature in which the introduction of intervention procedures for specific target behaviours (including challenging behaviours) had resulted in various side effects. Indeed, he pointed out that a wide range of side effects are possible embracing:

'(a) desirable, neutral, or undesirable behaviours may be affected; (b) the behaviours may increase or decrease; (c) the target subjects, other persons, or both may be affected; (d) effects may occur in the setting where the manipulation occurred, other settings, or both; and (e) effects may occur immediately, somewhat later, or much later' (Willems, 1974).

Willems was also concerned with the inconsistent outcomes of specific procedures, and proposed that these could be accounted for in terms of the *pre-treatment behaviour ecology*. A further issue he highlighted for consideration was that of the difficulties often experienced in ensuring across-setting generalisation and long-term maintenance of behaviour change. There was ample evidence to show that behaviour change was possible within the confines of the 'experiment', but a relative paucity of data to show that once a study came to an end the change continued.

In order to overcome these deficiencies and blind-spots of applied behaviour analysis, Willems suggested a shift of focus away from the *outcomes* of behavioural interventions and towards the *broad antecedent conditions*. He contended that only by acquiring firm knowledge about the environmental conditions that maintained behaviour could effective and long-term change be achieved.

Although Willems (1974) cautioned against indiscriminate use of behavioural interventions, his paper presented an impetus for examining relationships between behaviour and its broader ecology for the purpose of improving behavioural intervention strategies (see also Willemsn, 1977). His lead was taken up by Rogers-Warren & Warren (1977) and by Rogers-Warren (1984) who have attempted to incorporate the theory and methodology of ecological psychology with that of applied behaviour analysis in what has been called *ecobehavioural analysis*.

In appraising the two 'parent disciplines' of ecobehavioural analysis, Rogers-Warren (1984) notes that applied behaviour analysis is characterised by its emphasis on the *identification of functional relationships* between environmental events and behaviour, but argues that the units of analysis it uses are defined relatively narrowly. In particular, its focus on the environment is typically limited to the temporally and spatially contiguous interface between environmental events and the individual's particular behaviour under study. This is contrasted with the major purpose of empirical inquiry for ecological psychology which is to *describe* naturally-occurring environmental influences on behaviour. Much of ecological psychology centres on studying broader environmental settings for behaviour and molar patterns of behaviour; the latter being defined in terms of related actions or episodes occurring within the *natural stream of behaviour* (Kantor, 1959) rather than in discrete, arbitrarily defined units. She points out that the hybrid ecobehavioural analysis combines the broader definitions of behaviour and environment found in ecological psychology with the functional analysis of behaviour for therapeutic purposes. In doing so it investigates a larger set of environment-behaviour relationships at a variety of levels, and thus it expands the continuum of strategies for intervention by identifying a larger set of environmental variables which influence behaviour.

Ecobehavioural analysis may include the range of behaviour and environmental units used in the parent disciplines, and Rogers-Warren (1984) cites examples (e.g., Patterson, 1982) where multiple units of measurement (discrete events and behaviours, episodes or patters of behaviour) have been used in the same study. Indeed, studies in this area have attempted to identify 'natural' units of analysis from within the stream of behaviour as opposed to those imposed by investigators. Interestingly Skinner (1938) had also stressed the importance of searching for the 'natural lines of fracture' in the quest for units of analysis. Rogers-Warren & Warren (1977) and Rogers-Warren (1984), for example, in studies concerned with naturally-occurring incidental teaching in classrooms for young handicapped children focused on such broader variables as lesson scheduling, the nature of classroom activities, child-teacher ratios and the pattern of exchange between child and teacher. Their findings indicated that such *molar* categories could be incorporated and manipulated in a functional analysis.

The expanded set of behaviour and environment relationship to be explored through functional analysis, that ecobehavioural analysis introduces, includes *behaviour/behaviour* relationships in which behavioural covariation related to the effects of intervention are studied. In a classic study, Wahler (1975) employed a coded observational system to investigate interrelationships between behaviours within settings, across settings and over time with two predelinquent boys over a period of three years. Through correlational analysis his data revealed molar covariation patterns of 'clusters' of behaviours over time and, in some cases, across settings and suggested that behaviours within the covarying clusters were related to one another rather than controlled by the same set of environmental events.

Baseline measures showed that each child emitted a group of behaviours that covaried and that the groupings were specific to home and school settings. When contingency management procedures were introduced into one setting, across-setting effects were recorded. However, these intended effects were accompanied by unintended effects in the second setting. For one boy increases in classroom school-work were associated with increases in self-stimulation at home and a reduction in social interactions. For a second child, reduction in oppositional behaviour at home was associated with increased peer intervention and reduced opposition at school.

His study has been said to illustrate the use of response covariation as an intervention procedure with challenging behaviours;

'If a child's behavior repertoire is indeed organised into functional 'clusters', it is conceivable that his or her deviant actions might be modified indirectly. Thus behaviors difficult to deal with directly, such as stealing, might be modified by the contingent management of behaviors more easily dealt with' (Wahler, 1975).

Interbehavioural Psychology
In a recent collection of writings, edited by Schroeder (1990), *ecobehaviourism* has been portrayed as a 'menage a trois' which links radical behaviourism, ecological psychology (e.g., Barker, 1968) and the *interbehavioural psychology* of J. R. Kantor (1924, 1926, 1959, 1970). A full exposition of the latter is beyond the scope of this chapter, but aspects of the conceptual framework it adopts that have strongly influenced the developing methodologies of ecobehavioural analysis include;

a) A thoroughly *naturalistic* standpoint that is strongly anti-mentalistic and anti-reductionist. Way back in 1924, Kantor stated that:

'We deem it the essence of valid scientific method . . . to study any fact as it actually transpires and not to reduce it to something else, not even to a simple part of itself'.

b) For Kantor, the subject matter of psychology is the history of interactions of biological organisms with their environments. These reciprocal stimulus-response interactions always occur within a specific context of setting factors which condition the event. These interactions are part of a continuous *stream of behaviour* and not a series of discrete ones. As Kantor and Smith (1975) put it:

'The behavioral life of an organism is absolutely continuous as long as the individual is active. There is never a moment that it is not interacting with things.

50

Psychological phenomena must be likened to a flowing stream, rather than to barbs set side by side on a wire.'

It has been acknowledged that Kantor's writing style is not the easiest to follow and in an attempt to explain the essential features of interbehavioural psychology, Blewitt (1978) commented that:

'What he is saying is that single behavioural events cannot be studied in isolation from the preceding and succeeding behavioural events. One may be able to fix a definite spatio-temporal unit, but it is essential that the *context* in which it occurs be considered. Kantor is also pointing to the notion that the divisions of the behaviour stream cannot be *imposed* by the psychologist; rather that the properties of the stream indicate to the investigator where the important divisions are.'

c) From emphasis placed upon the context of interbehavioural events (reciprocal stimulus and response interactions), a concept of *setting factors* emerged and was at the heart of Kantor's explanations. For example:

'. . . it is an indubitable fact that the person is stimulated not only by things but also by their setting or background. From a behavior standpoint the setting of the stimulus object is of extreme importance in influencing the behavior of the individual and in conditioning in a large way what the person will do and how it is done.' (Kantor, 1924).

'Such setting factors as the hungry or satiated condition of the organism its age, hygiene or toxic condition, as well as the presence or absence of certain environing objects clearly influence the occurrence or non-occurrence of interbehavior . . . setting factors as general surrounding circumstances operate an inhibiting or facilitating conditions of behavior segments . . .' (Kantor, 1959).

In the next section we examine how in recent years investigation of *'setting factors'* has been used to investigate challenging behaviours in both descriptive and experimental analyses. However, before leaving the conceptual bases of inter-behavioural psychology, it is interesting to consider how the current vogue for con-trived *analogue assessments* (e.g., Iwata *et al.*, 1982; Durand, 1990) can be reconciled with Kantor's emphasis on the importance of studying the *naturally occurring stream of behaviour*. For example, Mace, Lalli, & Lalli (1991) have noted that:

'. . . it may be risky to assume that a contingency that controls a response under experimental conditions is the same contingency that maintains the behavior in the natural environment . . .

51

'. . . interventions based on a functional analysis are likely to be effective to the extent that the contingencies/stimuli in the analogue conditions parallel those in the subjects natural environment. For example, a functional analysis of analogue conditions may identify social disapproval as a positive reinforcer for self-injury and suggest that attention be withheld to extinguish the response (e.g., Carr, 1977). However, if social disapproval does not occur contingent on self-injury in the natural environment and the behavior is controlled by other unidentified contingencies, withholding attention is not likely to reduce the aberrant behavior'.

This recognition that the functional relationship established in the analogue setting can be different to that which exists in the natural setting of the behaviour, does not necessarily imply that analogue procedures are invalid. Rather, it suggests caution in deciding what to introduce into the analogue setting. Instead of arbitrarily establishing relationships between response and antecedent and consequent events based on broad theoretical principles, it is necessary to establish relationships based on an observation of what occurs in the natural setting, on how, for example, social attention is typically distributed. Having abstracted one aspect of the natural setting and investigated it in the analogue setting, it is important to also carry out the manipulations in the natural setting to confirm its validity and to determine the power of the relationship in the context of other relationships.

Thus, there is a three stage process:
(a) Formal/informal observation of natural setting
(b) Abstraction of part of the total field to the analogue setting
(c) Return of the part into the natural setting to determine through manipulation
    (i) validity of the finding from the analogue
    (ii) the power of the relationship in context.

Analogue procedure, therefore, should not substitute for the investigation of behaviour in its natural setting but should be seen as a stage in a three phase process.

Setting events: A definition
It is only in recent years that the term 'setting event' has been adopted in the applied behaviour analysis literature. The main influence for this has been the work of Sidney Bijou (e.g., Bijou, 1976; Bijou & Baer, 1961, 1965; Krasner, 1977), who suggested that 'setting events' should be added to form a four-term contingency. However, this suggestion did not have much impact at the time. It was with the work of Wahler (Wahler & Fox, 1981; Wahler & Graves, 1983) that the concept was taken up in the applied behaviour analysis literature which led to a number of discussions of the compatibility and value of the concept to behaviour analysis (e.g., Leigland, 1984; Michael, 1982; Morris, 1982, 1984; Morris & Midgley, 1990).
    Since the concept of setting events is a major feature of Kantor's approach, it is

useful to examine his definition of the term. In *Interbehavioral Psychology* (1959, p59) Kantor defined setting factors as . . . 'the general surrounding circumstances [that] operate as inhibiting or facilitating conditions in behaviour segments'. To put it more fully, as a result of its interbehavioural history the individual develops a repertoire of *response functions* to corresponding *stimulus functions*. Having acquired this complex repertoire, the issue is one of identifying which specific factors increase or decrease the probability of a specific response function occurring at a specific time to a specific stimulus object. It is this wide range of factors that are referred to as setting events. The specification of such events is begun by locating them in one of the following categories:

(a) *in the organism;* Events include the hygiene of the organism, the state of deprivation or satiation (food, sex, sleep and other needs), the presence of drugs, and the state of physical fitness.
(b) *in the environment;* The presence or absence of certain objects or people, the general setting (e.g., school, bank, home), the noise level, availability of activities, instructions, demands of the setting, humidity, the weather and other ecological features.
(c) *stimulus response interactions;* Not simply a durational condition or event but of both an environmental event and the person's response to that event which simply because it has occurred will affect other stimulus-response relationships which follow it.

Whether such factors are functional for any individual or for any specific stimulus-response interaction is an empirical question, dependent on the interbehavioural history the person has passed through. Furthermore, the temporal relationship between setting events and the specific stimulus-response functions is an open one. Whilst Kantor (1959) refers to setting events as the 'immediate circumstances', others such as Wahler & Fox *et al.,* (1981) and Gardner, Cole, Davidson & Karan (1986) also include events which occur well before the present action in both space and time. An example of the influence of an event that occurs well before the 'target' behaviour is Wahler's (1980) finding that mothers who engage in aversive interactions with relatives and helping agency personnel are less likely to maintain positive reinforcement procedures with their children, and more likely to engage in aversive exchanges. However, it is not clear if this result is due to the influence of distant or immediate setting factors. An alternative possible explanation is that mothers who have had an aversive interaction with a relative or agency member are still engaging in negative feeling behaviour (i.e., are angry or upset) immediately prior to a specific occurrence of their child's behaviour. Those readers who are more comfortable with a different descriptive system might call this an "emotional atmosphere". However, whatever the appropriate explanation, Wahler's general point is still valid, events that occur more than a few seconds before an interaction *could* exert an influence. But in each case this needs to be demonstrated and not merely assumed.

According to the interpretation made by Bijou (e.g., Bijou & Baer, 1961) a distinction is made between 'setting events' and 'stimulus functions'. The latter refer to specific environmental stimuli which function to (a) elicit (b) set the occasion for, or (c) strengthen a response. That is, discriminative stimuli and reinforcing stimuli are conceptualised as distinct from setting events. In contrast, setting events are general and more complex stimuli than the presence, absence, or change of simple, discrete stimuli. The role they play as background events is to determine whether specific stimuli are functional or not. Thus, the relationship of setting events to the three-term contingency can be represented by the schematic shown in Figure 6.

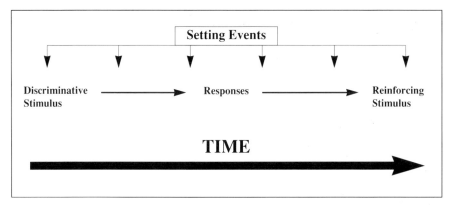

Figure 6

This meta-functional role of setting events is very closely allied to concepts developed by Michael (1982) who proposed the adoption of the term *'establishing operation'* (and the related *'establishing stimulus'*) to refer to operations that have two effects: (a) to increase the effectiveness of some object or event as reinforcement, and (b) to evoke the behaviour, via the establishing stimulus, that has in the past been followed by that object or event. That these concepts share some of the same conceptual territory as 'setting events' is acknowledge by Michael (1982):

'Students of J. R. Kantor may see some similarity to his term 'setting factor', but I believe that his term includes operations that have a broader or less specific effect on behaviour than the establishing operations . . .' (emphasis added).

Thus, establishing operations are related to their effect on specific antecedent stimuli and consequences, and would not include the wider range of events researchers have investigated (see end of this section). However, the concept of establishing operation has not been taken up by those interested in human behaviour

54

in its natural setting. Some other concepts sharing the same explanatory function as setting events are: *potentiating variables* (Goldiamond, 1983); *initial and boundary conditions* (Marr, 1984); *contingency-specifying stimuli* (Blakely & Schlinger, 1987; Schlinger & Blakely, 1987); *pinpointed interaction events, temporary ongoing activity events and enduring setting events* (Moxley, 1982). While this flurry of concepts is confusing, it does point to an important development: the recognition that the concept of 'discriminative stimulus' cannot do all the explanatory work demanded of it, as the solitary antecedent event in the three-term contingency.

From this discussion it can be seen that setting events refer to a very broad range of factors. It is this breadth which is both its advantage and disadvantage. It is an advantage in that it does not close off particular events from investigation of their function in increasing or decreasing the possibility of responding. However, it is a disadvantage in that the concept does not specify the event or the type of controlling function it exerts, unlike the concept of 'discriminative stimulus' (Leigland, 1984). It is necessary, therefore, that whenever setting events are referred to that a specific event is pointed to and that the way it produces its influence is indicated. If the term is used in a vague and general way it will be of no theoretical or practical value, degenerating into a behavioural pseudo-explanation (whose only merit is that it is not 'cognitive'). To avoid this fate, the concept must move from the abstract and imprecise to the concrete and specific. A sampling of the literature referring to setting events produces the following list of events:

* material activity
* physical location of mother
* persons present
* socio-economic status
* social isolation
* material conflict
* surveillance
* spatial density
* progressive relaxation
* diet
* eating schedule
* sleeping pattern
* rapport
* noise level
* density of housing
* predictability of events
* aversive social interactions
* outset of puberty
* clothing

Setting events and challenging behaviour

Even though the concept of setting events is not new to theoretical discussions, it is new to behaviour analysis research. Consequently, there is not a great deal of empirical research to draw upon in order to build up practical procedures to change and maintain behaviour. Of this already small data base, an even smaller part is related to 'challenging behaviour'. Before going on to look at some of this research, a few words on the difference between analytical and technical (or technological) approaches (or emphases) to behaviour change. Both these tendencies are features of applied behaviour analysis as defined by Baer *et al.*, (1968).

In the analytical emphasis there is a concern with *identifying* the factors that maintain the behaviour being studied, and it is on this basis that an attempt is made to change behaviour. Over the years, the analytical approach has lost ground in applied behaviour analysis (Hayes, Rincover & Solnick, 1979). The inter-behavioural approach is supportive of the analytical trend, in that the focus for both is on describing behaviour in its natural setting (Blewitt, 1985).

The technical emphasis, which has come to dominate applied behaviour analysis (Hayes *et al.*, 1979), has as its primary aim the development of a technology of behaviour change. It is not sympathetic to developments which have no immediate pragmatic implications (e.g., Baer, 1974; Baer *et al.*, 1987). Since the setting event concept is a difficult one to use, the technological approach does not see much value in pursuing its implications for both a revision of the theory and practice of applied behaviour analysis. In the rest of this section brief reference is made to research from both tendencies to illustrate how differently they use the concept of setting events.

The Analytic Emphasis

In terms of work relating to 'challenging behaviour' the work of Gardner (e.g., Cole, Gardner & Karan, 1985; Gardner, Cole, Berry & Nowinski, 1983; Gardner, Cole, Davidson & Karan, 1986) provides the most appropriate example. He reports that the use of the three procedural approaches developed by the operant model (i.e., stimulus control, reinforcement control and alternative responses) have been effective in work with adolescents and adults with chronic conduct disorders. However, in a number of cases these procedures have not been effective. In particular, a number of difficulties have arisen: (a) variability in responding; (b) across subject differences in types of antecedent events controlling challenging behaviours: (c) unpredictability and variability in degree of control exerted by antecedent events. This led Gardner to look at the potential contribution of setting events. In the attempt to specify a range of possible events, he devised a Setting Event Checklist (see Table 1). This checklist was devised in order to study the aggressive behaviour of people with moderate and severe intellectual disabilities. The events included were identified through discussion with residential staff who had been asked to describe situations or events that resulted in (a) a more than

56

momentary state of emotional agitation, such as anger, prolonged disappointment, bad mood, and/or (b) verbal ruminations about events. Staff completed the checklist prior to each day the subjects attended a community work training setting.

Table 1
Setting Event Checklist

Client: *Date:*
Completed by:

Check any of the following events that occurred last evening (pm) or this morning prior to work (am).

	AM	PM
Was informed of something unusually disappointing		
Was refused some requested object/activity		
Fought, argued, or had other negative interaction(s)		
Was disciplined/reprimanded (behavior or disciplinary action was atypical)		
Was hurried or rushed more than usual		
Sleep pattern (including duration) was unusual		
Was under the care of someone new/favourite caretaker was absent		
Experienced other major changes in living environment		
Learned about visit/vacation with family/friends (will or will not occur)		
Visitors arrived/failed to arrive		
Medication was changed/missed		
Has menstrual period		
Appeared excessively tired/lethargic		
Appeared excessively agitated		
Appeared to be in a bad mood		
Appeared/complained of being ill		
Other		

(From Gardner *et al.*, 1986)

Since a number of the events on the checklist were global rather than discrete, and difficult to manipulate experimentally, Gardner used a *correlational analysis* to identify possible relationships between setting events and aggressive behaviour. In one study (Gardner *et al.*, 1986) it was found that the following setting events increased the probability of verbal aggression: (a) home visit with brother present;

(b) difficulty in getting up in the morning, (c) arguments with peers at home or on the bus to work, and (d) the presence of a specific staff member at home.

The Technological Emphasis
Illustrative of the technological approach to setting events is the use of exercise to reduce inappropriate behaviour (e.g., Bachman & Fugua, 1983; Bachman & Sluyter, 1988; Baumeister & Maclean, 1984; Jansma & Combs, 1987; Kem *et al.*, 1982; McGimsey & Farell, 1988; Walters & Walters, 1980). In none of these studies is it argued that lack of exercise is what maintains the inappropriate behaviour under study; the issue of maintenance is simply not addressed. The aim of these researches is to evaluate whether exercise can be added to the environment of people with disabilities in order to reduce levels of inappropriate behaviour. From the data then present, it can be concluded that in the first two hours following periods of physical exercise the frequency of a wide range of inappropriate behaviours (hyperactivity, self-stimulation, aggression, and self-injury) can be reduced. The level of effect varies across individuals, but it is not clear what level or duration of exercise is needed and further research is proposed to more closely specify the parameters of these factors.

Other "techniques" for altering setting events that have been proposed include "room management therapy" (Porterfield, Blunden and Belwitt, 1980) in which it is hypothesized that implementation of procedures designed to increase levels of "adaptive engagement" should result in decreases in challenging behaviours (although some research findings do not entirely support this; e.g., Horner, 1980). A recent review of the technological approach to setting events was provided by Helmstetter and Durand (1991).

Data Collection
Apart from Gardner's *Setting Event Checklist*, two other data collection instruments which acknowledge the range of events that could function as setting events have been developed by Groden (1989) and Van Houten & Rolinder (1989).

Groden (1989) has designed three forms to collect and organize behavioural information:
Detailed Behaviour Report (see Figure 7)
Detailed Behaviour Report Checklist
Detailed Behaviour Report Analysis
In describing his guide to conducting a comprehensive functional analysis, Groden refers to the need to identify immediate and distant antecedents. Immediate antecedents consist of four main types (1) the activity engaged in; (2) social/interpersonal events - what others were doing or saying to the client; (3) covert events - what the client was thinking about, and (4) organismic/affective events - emotional behaviour, medication, bodily state. Distant antecedents refer to

58

Figure 7: DETAILED BEHAVIOR REPORT (DBR)

Client:	J K	Staff:	B R
Unit: Adolescent Residence		Date:	3/16/88
Behavior: Aggression		Recording Frequency:	Every Occurrence

Day, Date and Time		Wednesday, 16 March 1988, 9.00 pm
Target Behavior (describe in detail)		Hit Bob Roberts (staff) fairly strongly on the chest with both fists and was about to hit him again.
Location of Incident		Residence living room, in front of TV.
Immediate Antecedents	Activity	Going over contract.
	Social/Interpersonal (who doing/saying what to whom, etc)	"J" had not earned a reinforcer which would have been due at this time and I told her, without raising my voice, "J, you didn't earn your ice cream because you didn't put your clothes away", as we were going over contract item by item.
	Covert	None apparent
	Organismic/Affective (drugs, bodily state, anger, nervousness)	"J" was very tense (body stiffened and tight lipped) when she was told that she wasn't going to get her ice cream
	Other	None
	Distant Antecedents	Disruption earlier in the day (threw a book).
Consequences	Program	Response prevention by staff until calm. Was required to put her clothes away after this and did not earn her reinforcer for the next interval (the interval in which the aggression occurred).
	Environmental	None

events that occurred from several minutes to 24 hours or more before the behaviour occurred, and includes such things as an earlier disruption or the cancelling of a planned event. As Groden states, these distant antecedents are `more tentative than an immediate antecedent in that the connection is more speculative' (1989).

Van Houten & Rolinder (1989) devised the *Stimulus Control Checklist* to try to identify relevant antecedent events. This is too long to present here, but some of the questions are:

59

- *Does the behaviour occur more when the environment is noisy?*
- *Does the behaviour occur more when the room is warm?*
- *Does the behaviour occur when the individual has to wait for an item or activity?*
- *Does the person show signs of being upset, angry or otherwise agitated immediately prior to as well as while engaging in antisocial behaviour?*
- *Does the behaviour occur following a transition, regardless of the direction of change?*

From this discussion it would appear that reference to setting events improves both the understanding of why specific responses occur as well as potential ways of changing them. However, it is recognised that the concept is broad and difficult to specify. This does not mean that it is not a useful term (Leigland, 1984); only that it is a difficult one to use. Unlike the terms *'discriminative stimulus'* and *'reinforcer'*, which point to specific events in the immediate setting of behaviour, *'setting events'* refers to a wide range of events. Since it is far less specific in pointing to events, it makes it difficult to decide which events to focus on out of the large complex of potential setting events. Indeed, because the particular setting events functional for each stimulus-response function can vary within and between individuals, there is no simple way of identifying them. The only way of successfully identifying setting events is to get to know the individual and the settings they occupy, arrive at some 'hunches' and follow them up. Thus instead of applying a particular technique one has to carry out a functional analysis before devising an individually tailored intervention. Whilst such a strategy is time-consuming there is the counter-balancing advantage of a greater likelihood of achieving a more effective constructional intervention that can be maintained for longer, and be generalisable to a wider range of settings.

The complexity of behavior determination could well include that of several setting events exerting their effect on a specific stimulus-response interaction, some of which may be facilitative and some inhibiting. Clearly a more sophisticated *technology* of data collection and analysis is required, but this should not be confused with the *technological tendency* as described in this chapter.

Once again, the apparent conflict between the analytic and technological tendencies is operative. Those advocating a technical approach are concerned with immediate pragmatic implications, whereas the analyst is concerned with the descriptive and explanatory value of the setting event concept *as well as* the technological implications. The issue is one of how to best deal with a problem; the short-term technological fix concerned with *'symptoms'*, or the long-term analysis of *'causes'* which then forms the foundation for remedial action. Put another way, the technological tendency may be adopting a *pathological* approach, with all its shortcomings, whilst the analytic tendency clearly adopts a *constructional* approach.

Conclusion

In this chapter we have argued for the need to carry out a functional analysis of responses that are challenging to the social environments inhabited by individuals with intellectual disabilities. This has been done by showing that such a strategy is firmly grounded in certain approaches that have been developed within the wider applied behaviour analysis movement which is concerned with the broader ecological context of behaviour. However, the currently most prominent approach within the field, and the model most widely disseminated to non-psychologists is that based on applying certain 'techniques'.

The position we have taken is that this concern for a broader ecological analysis needs to be developed by the introduction of concepts and research models borrowed from two allied perspectives; the ecological approach of Willems and the interbehavioural psychology of Kantor. Over the past 15 years such an alliance has been developing and has now become identified with the term *ecobehaviourism* (Schroeder, 1990). As with all alliances the interests and viewpoints of all the parties are not wholly identical, but there is sufficient shared ground that the differences and contradictions are minimised. Ecobehaviourism is grounded on tradition, it is not a traditional set of practices. It is not concerned with merely repeating old and well-worn procedures, but with opening-up and developing new territory and practices. It looks to the future rather than the past, and it is primarily concerned with the development of constructional approaches to intervention.

References

Axelrod, S. (1987). Doing it without arrows: a review of LaVigna and Donnellan's Alternative to Punishment: Solving Behavior Problems with Non-Aversive Strategies. *The Behavior Analyst* 10, 243-257.

Axelrod, S. and Apsche, J. (Eds). (1983). *The Effects of Punishment on Human Behavior* New York: Plenum.

Bachman, J. E. and Sluyter, D. (1988). Reducing inappropriate behaviors of developmentally disabled adults using antecedent aerobic exercise. *Research in Developmental Disabilities* 9, 73-83.

Bachman, J. E. and Fugua, R. W. (1983). Management of inappropriate behaviors of trainable mentally impaired students using antecedent exercise. *Journal of Applied Behavior Analysis* 16, 477-484.

Baer, D. M. (1982). The role of current pragmatics in the future analysis of generalisation technology. In R. B. Stuart (Ed). Adherence, *Compliance and Generalisation in Behavioral Medicine*. New York: Brunner/Mazeb, pp 192-212.

Baer, D. M. (1974). A note on the absence of a Santa Claus in any known ecosystem: a rejoinder to Willems. *Journal of Applied Behavior Analysis* 7, 167-170.

Baer, D. M., Wolf, M. M. and Risley, T. R. (1968). Some current dimensions of applied behavior analysis. *Journal of Applied Behavior Analysis* 1, 91-97.

Baer, D. M., Wolf, M. M. and Risley, T. R. (1987). Some still current dimensions of applied behavior analysis. *Journal of Applied Behavior Analysis* 20, 313-327.

Barker, R. G. (1968). Ecological Psychology. Stanford: Stanford University Press.

Baumeister, A. A. and Maclean, W. E. (1984). Deceleration of Self-injurious and stereotypic responding by exercise. *Applied Research in Mental Retardation* 5, 385-393.

Bijou, S. W. and Baer, D. M. (1961). *Child Development I: Systematic and Empirical Theory.* Englewood Cliffs: Prentice-Hall.

Bijou, S. W. and Baer, D. M. (1965). *Child Development II: Universal Stage of Infancy.* Englewood Cliffs: Prentice-Hall.

Bijou, S. W. (1976). *Child Development III: Basic State of Early Childhood.* Englewood Cliffs: Prentice Hall.

Blakely, E. and Schlinger, H. (1987). Rules: function-altering contingency-specifying stimuli. *The Behavior Analyst* 10, 183-187.

Blewitt, E. (1978). Introductory notes on J. R. Kantor's interbehavioral psychology. *Behavior Analysis* 1, 8-13.

Blewitt, E. (1985). *An Analysis of Environmental Influences on Developmentally Retarded Behavior.* Unpublished M Sc Thesis, University of Wales.

Carr, E. G. (1977). The motivation of self-injurious behavior: a review of some hypotheses. *Psychological Bulletin* 84, 800-816.

Carr, E. G. and Durand, M. (1985). Reducing behavior problems through functional communication training. *Journal of Applied Behavior Analysis* 18, 111-126.

Catania, A. C. (1969). On the vocabulary and the grammar of behavior. *Journal of the Experimental Analysis of Behavior* 12, 845-846.

Catania, A. C. (1973). The nature of learning. In J. A. Nevin and G. Reynolds (Eds). *The Study of Behavior: Learning, Motivation, Emotion and Instinct.* Glenview, Ill: Scott, Foreman, pp 31-68.

Catania, A. C. (1984). *Learning* (2nd ed). Englewood Cliffs N J: Prentice-Hall.

Cliffe, M. J., Gathercole, C. and Epling, W. F. (1974). Some implications of the experimental analysis of behavior for behavior modification. *Bulletin of the British Psychological Society* 27, 390-397.

Cole, C. L., Gardner, W. I. and Karan, O. C. (1985). Self management training of mentally retarded adults presenting severe conduct difficulties. *Applied Research in Mental Retardation* 6, 337-347.

Cullen, C., Hattersley, J. and Tennant, L. (1977). Behaviour modification - some implications of a radical behaviourist's view. *Bulletin of the British Psychological Society* 30, 65-69.

Dickinson, A. M. (1989). The detrimental effects of extrinsic reinforcement on 'intrinsic motivation'. *The Behavior Analyst* 12, 1-15.

Deitz, S. M. (1989). What is unnatural about 'extrinsic reinforcement'?. The Behavior Analyst 12, 255.

Donnellan, A. M., Mirenda, P. L., Mesaros, R. A. and Fassbender, L. L. (1984). Analysing the communicative function of aberrant behavior. *Journal of the Association for the Severely Handicapped* 9, 201-212.

Durand, V. M. (1990). *Severe Behavior Problems: A Functional Communication Training Approach.* New York: Guilford Press.

Evans, I. and Mayer, L. (1985). *An Educative Approach to Behavior Problems: A Practical Decision Model for Interventions with Severely Handicapped Learners.* Baltimore: Paul H Brookes.

Ferster, C. B. (1961). Positive reinforcement and behavioral deficits of autistic children. *Journal of Child Development* 32, 437-456.

Ferster, C. B. (1967). Arbitrary and natural reinforcement. *Psychological Record* 17, 341-347.

Ferster, C. B. and DeMeyer, M. (1962). A method for the experimental analysis of the behavior of autistic children. *American Journal of Orthopsychiatry* 32, 89-98.

Florida Division of Retardation and Florida State University. (1974). *Guidelines for the Use of Behavioral Procedures in State Hospitals for the Retarded.* Unpublished Report.

Gardner, W. I., Cole, C. L., Berry, D. L. and Nowinski, J. M. (1983). Reduction of disruptive behaviors in mentally retarded adults: a self management approach. *Behavior Modification* 7, 76-96.

Gardner, W. I., Cole, C. L., Davidson, D. P. and Karan, O. C. (1986). Reducing aggression in individuals with developmental disabilities. *Education and Training of the Mentally Retarded* 21, 3-12.

Goldiamond, I. (1974). Toward a constructional approach to social problems. *Behaviorism* 1, 1-84.

Goldiamond, I. (1983). Discussion. In I. Goldiamond. *The Interdependence of Formal, Basic and Applied Behavior Analysis.* Symposium of ABA, Milwaukee.

Groden, G. (1989). A guide for conducting a comprehensive behavioral analysis of a target behavior. *Journal of Behavior Therapy and Experimental Psychiatry* 20, 163-169.

Hayes, S C., Rincover, A. and Solnick, J. V. (1979). The technical drift of applied behavior analysis. *Journal of Applied Behavior Analysis* 13, 275-285.

Helmstetter, E. and Durand, V. M. (1991). Nonaversive interventions for severe behavior problems. In L. H. Meyer, C. A. Peck, and L. Brown (Eds). *Issues in the Lives of People with Severe Disabilities.* Baltimore: Paul H Brookes, pp 559-600.

Horcones, L. (1987). The concept of consequences in the analysis of behavior. *The Behavior Analyst* 10, 291-294.

Horner, R. D. (1980) The effects of an environmental "enrichment" program on the behavior of institutionalizsed profoundly retarded children. *Journal of Applied Behavior Analysis*, 13, 473_492.

Horner, R. H., Dunlap, G., Koegal, R. L., Carr, E. G., Sailor, W., Anderson, J., Albin, R. W. and O'Neill, R. E. (1990). Toward a technology of 'nonaversive' behavioral support. *Journal of the Association for Persons with Severe Handicaps* 15, 125-132.

Iwata, B., Dorsey, M., Slifer, K., Bauman, K. and Richman, G. (1982). Toward a functional analysis of self-injury. *Analysis and Intervention in Developmental Disabilities* 2, 3-20.

Jansma, P. and Combs, C. S. (1987). The effects of fitness training and reinforcement on maladaptive behaviors of institutionalised adults classified as mentally retarded/emotionally disturbed. *Education and Training in Mental Retardation* 22, 268-279.

Kantor, J. R. (1924,1926). *The Principles of Psychology*. Chicago: Principia Press.

Kantor, J. R. (1959). *Interbehavioral Psychology*. Granville: Principia Press.

Kantor, J. R. (1970). An analysis of the experimental analysis of behavior (TEAB). *Journal of the Experimental Analysis of Behavior* 13, 101-108.

Kantor, J. R. and Smith, N. W. (1975). *The Science of Psychology: An Interbehavioral Survey*. Chicago: Principia Press.

Kazdin, A. E. (1977). Assessing the clinical or applied importance of behavior change through social validation. *Behavior Modification* 1, 427-451.

Kem, L., Koegal, R. L., Dyer, K., Blew, P. A. and Fenton, L. R. (1982). The effects of physical exercise on self-stimulation and appropriate responding in autistic children. *Journal of Autism and Developmental Disorders* 12, 399-419.

Krasner, L. (1977). An interview with Sidney W. Bijou. In B. C. Etzel, J. M. LeBlanc and D. M. Baer (Eds). *New Developments in Behavioral Research*. New York: Lawrence Erlbaum Associates, pp 587-599.

LaVigna, G. W. and Donnellan, A. M. (1986). *Alternatives To Punishment: Solving Behavior Problems With Non-Aversive Strategies*. New York: Irvington.

Leigland, S. (1984). On 'setting' events and related events. *The Behavior Analyst* 7, 41-45.

Lindsley, O. R. (1964). Direct measurement and prosthesis of retarded behavior. *Journal of Education* 147, 62-81.

Lovaas, I., Schaeffer, B. and Simons, J. (1965). Building social behavior in autistic children by use of electric shock. *Journal of Experimental Research in Personality* 1, 99-109.

Mace, F. C., Lalli, J. S. and Lalli, E. P. (1991). Functional analysis and treatment of aberrant behavior. *Research in Developmental Disabilities* 12, 155-180.

Marr, M. J. (1984). Some reflections on Kantor's (1970) 'An Analysis of the Experimental Analysis of Behavior (TEAB)'. *The Behavior Analyst* 7, 189-196.

Matson, J. L. and DiLorenzo, T. M. (1984). *Punishment and Its Alternatives*. New York Springer.

Matson, J. L. and Taras, M. E. (1989). A 20 year review of punishment and alternative methods to treat problem behaviors in developmentally delayed persons. *Research in Developmental Disabilities* 10, 85-104.

McGimsey, J. F. and Farrell, J. E. (1988). The effects of increased physical exercise on disruptive behavior in retarded persons. *Journal of Autism and Developmental Disabilities* 18, 167-179.

Michael, J. L. (1982). Distinguishing between discriminative and motivational functions of stimuli. *Journal of the Experimental Analysis of Behavior* 37, 149-155.

Michael, J. L. and Meyerson, L. (1962). A behavioural approach to councelling and guidance. Harvard Educational Review 5, 382-402.

Morris, E. K. (1982). Some relationships between interbehavioral psychology and radical behaviorisms. *Behaviorism* 10, 187-216.

Morris, E. K. (1984). Interbehavioral psychology and radical behaviorism: some similarities and differences. *The Behavior Analyst* 7, 197-204.

Morris, E. K. and Midgley, B. D. (1990). Some historical and conceptual foundations of ecobehavioral analysis. In S. R. Schroeder (Ed). *Ecobehavioral Analysis and Developmental Disabilities*. New York: Springer-Verlag, pp 1-32.

Moxley, R. (1982). Graphics for three-term contingencies. *The Behavior Analyst* 5, 45-51.

63

Murphy, G. (1987). Direct observation as an assessment tool in functional analysis and treatment. In J. Hogg and N. V. Raynes (Eds). *Assessment in Mental Handicap: A Guide to Assessment Practices, Tests and Checklists*. London: Croom Helm, pp 190-238.

Nevin, J. A. (1973). Conditioned Reinforcement. In J. A. Nevin and G. S. Reynolds (Eds). *The Study of Behavior*. Glenview, Ill; Scott, Foresman.

Patterson, G. R. (1982). *Coercive Family Precesses: A Social Learning Approach*. Champagne: Research Press.

Pavlov, I. P. (1927). *Conditioned Reflexes*. London: Oxford University Press.

Porterfield, J., Blunden, R. and Blewitt, E. (1980) Improving environments for profoundly handicapped adults; Using prompts and social attention to maintain high group engagement. *Behavior Modification*, 4, 225–241.

Presland, J. L. (1990). *Overcoming Difficult Behavior: A Guide and Sourcebook for Helping People with Severe Mental Handicaps*. Kidderminster: BIMH.

Repp, A. C. and Deitz, S. M. (1974). Reducing aggressive and self-injurious behavior of institutionalised retarded children through reinforcement of other behaviors. *Journal of Applied Behavior Analysis* 7, 313-325.

Risley, T. R. (1968). The effects and side effects of punishing the autistic behaviors of a deviant child. *Journal of Applied Behavior Analysis* 1, 21-34.

Rogers-Warren, A. and Warren, S. F. (Eds). (1977). *Ecological Perspectives in Behavior Analysis*. Baltimore: University Park Press.

Rogers-Warren, A. K. (1984). Ecobehavioral analysis. *Education and Treatment of Children* 7, 283-303.

Schlinger, H. and Blakely, E. (1987). Function-altering effects of contingency-specifying stimuli. *The Behavior Analyst* 10, 41-45.

Schroeder, S. R. (1990). *Ecobehavioral Analysis and Developmental Disabilities*. New York: Springer-Verlag.

Schwartz, A. and Goldiamond, I. (1975). *Social Casework; A Behavioral Approach*. New York: Columbia University Press.

Skinner, B. F. (1938). *The Behavior of Organisms*. New York: Appleton-Century-Crofts.

Skinner, B. F. (1948). *Walden Two*. New York: Macmillan.

Skinner, B. F. (1953). *Science and Human Behavior*. New York: Macmillan.

Skinner, B. F. (1969). *Contingencies of Reinforcement: A Theoretical Analysis*. Englewood Cliffs: Prentice Hall.

Skinner, B. F. (1982). Contrived reinforcements. *The Behavior Analyst* 5, 3-8.

Stokes, T. F. and Baer, D. M. (1977). An implicit technology of generalization. *Journal of Applied Behavior Analysis* 10, 349-367.

Van Houten, R. and Rolinder, A. (1989). An analysis of several variables influencing the efficiency of flash card instruction. *Journal of Applied Behavior Analysis* 22, 111-118.

Vaughan, M. E. and Michael, J. L. (1982). Automatic reinforcement: an important but ignored concept. *Behaviorism* 10, 101-112.

Wahler, R. G. (1975). Some structural aspects of deviant child behavior. *Journal of Applied Behavior Analysis* 8, 27-42.

Wahler, R. G. (1980). The insular mother: her problems in parent-child treatment. *Journal of Applied Behavior Analysis* 13, 207-219.

Wahler, R. G. and Fox, J. J. (1981). Setting events in applied behavior analysis: Toward a conceptual and methodological expansion. *Journal of Applied Behavior Analysis* 14, 327-338.

Wahler, R. G. and Graves, M. G. (1983). Setting events in social networks: ally or enemy in child behavior therapy?. *Behavior Therapy* 14, 19-36.

Walters, R. G. and Walters, W. E. (1980). Decreasing self stimulatory behavior with physical exercise in a group of autistic boys. *Journal of Autism and Developmental Disabilities* 10, 379-387.

Willems, E. P. (1974). Behavioral technology and behavioral ecology. *Journal of Applied Behavior Analysis* 7, 151-166.

Willems, E. P. (1977). Steps toward an ecobehavioral technology. In A. Rogers-Warren and S. F. Warren (Eds). *Ecological Perspectives in Behavior Analysis*. Baltimore: University Park Press, pp 39-61.

Williams, C. D. (1959). The elimination of tantrum behavior by extinction procedures: case report. *Journal of Abnormal and Social Psychology* 59, 269.

Wolf, M. M. (1978). Social Validity: the case for subjective measurement or how applied behavior analysis is finding its heart. *Journal of Applied Behavior Analysis* 11, 203-214.

Woods, P. A. and Cullen, C. N. (1983). Determinants of staff behavior in long-term care. *Behavioural Psychotherapy* 11, 4-18.

Woods, P. A., Higson, P. J. and Tannahill, M. M. (1984). Token economy programme with chronic psychotic patients: the importance of direct measurement and objective evaluation for long-term maintenance. *Behavior Research and Therapy* 22, 41-51.

Zarkowska, E. and Clements, J. (1988). *Problem Behavior in People With Severe Learning Disabilities*. London: Croom Helm.

CHAPTER 4

Normalisation, Community Services and Challenging Behaviour

Sandy Toogood
University College of North Wales, Bangor and Clwyd Health Authority

Introduction

Normalisation, community services and, more recently, challenging behaviour are common expressions in modern day services. Each represents a major conceptual approach to the design and delivery of services for people who exhibit challenging behaviour. Yet the extent to which their real meanings are appreciated, and their implications therefore fully understood, is at best variable.

In this chapter the development, dissemination and content of normalisation theory is reviewed ahead of an examination of the concept of challenging behaviour and community respectively. Some of the implications normalisation has for community based services to people who display challenging behaviour are drawn out within the structure of the five essential accomplishments (O'Brien 1987). The importance of competency development is stressed and the resistance to the use of behavioural approaches discussed. Some recommendations are made for further discussion and analysis.

The development and dissemination of Normalisation theory

The Swedish and Danish formulations

It is widely accepted that normalisation originated in Denmark in 1959 with the inclusion of the statement into Danish law that the purpose of services was to '. . . create an existence for the mentally retarded as close to normal living conditions as possible' (Bank-Mikkelson, 1980; Wolfensberger, 1980a). The explicit intention of this inclusion was two fold. Firstly to make conditions of housing, education, work and leisure as near normal as possible for people with handicaps, and secondly to bring greater equality of rights, obligations and responsibilities under law. This was not to diminish, deny or ignore the special needs a handicapped person may have had but rather to specifically and beneficially alter such persons' relative position in society as a whole. This concept, popular because of its inherent simplicity, was adopted and elaborated upon by Nirje (1976) who later described the experience of being handicapped as threefold;

i)   *The mental retardation of the individual*; This means the cognitive handicap, the impairment in adaptive behaviour, the intellectual disability, with the repeated demands imposed by new experiences and complexities, with the hurdles of frustrations and failures, with the problems of patience and of understanding others.

ii) *The imposed or acquired retardation*; This is expressed in behavioral misfunctioning or underfunctioning due to possible deficiencies in the environment or the conditions of life created by society or due to unsatisfactory attitudes of parents, personnel, or people in general. Institutional poverty, nonexistent or unsatisfactory education and vocational training, lack of experiences and social contacts, the problems of understanding society etc. add to the original handicap.

iii) *The awareness of being handicapped*; This is the insight into being mentally retarded, expressed in possibly distorted self-concepts or defeated utterances or through defense mechanisms, closing in on inner sorrows. To assert yourself, in your own eyes or before your family and to confront society . . . might be difficult for anyone but the awareness of being handicapped brings a complicating factor the problem of understanding oneself. And in the end, even the retarded person has to manage as a private person and has to define himself before others in the circumstances of his life and existence (Nirje, 1980).

Nirje's formulation of normalisation retained the core of Bank-Mikkelson's simple and easily understood message or idea. His formulation was centrally concerned with reducing the burden of the *imposed* handicaps which, he argued, remained entirely open to cure. Once the imposed handicaps were remedied then other burdens associated with being handicapped would become easier to bear. Nirje's concentration upon the imposed handicaps led him to formulate normalisation primarily in terms of;

i)   routines of the day including access to privacy and activities,
ii) routines of the week including a place to live, go to school or to work,
iii) leisure time, including social interaction,
iv) the rhythm of year, including joining in various social customs according to the season.

67

Nirje's formulation also emphasised the importance of experiencing the changing roles in the life cycle of infanthood through to adulthood, of experiencing choice, relationships, and of enjoying the same economic patterns of life as non-handicapped citizens. Central to this formulation was the concept of personal choice, self determination and autonomy within a society of equal opportunity.

The Swedish formulation applied these principles to all persons, irrespective of the degree of their handicap, and suggested that when persons could not, or should not, continue to live within their family home then the alternatives provided must be of normal size and located within residential areas.

The North American formulation
The principles outlined above were re-formulated, extended, sociologicalised (Wolfensberger, 1980b) and disseminated internationally by Wolf Wolfensberger (Wolfensberger, 1972). Perrin & Nirje (1982, 1990), however, believe Wolfensberger's formulation to be a deviation from the original concept and not a reformulation, refinement or operationalisation of the principles on the basis of;

i)   Wolfensberger's diminution of personal autonomy in order to achieve conformity with values chosen by others,
ii) the resultant setting of different standards for people with handicaps and,
iii) Wolfensberger's reductionist approach, which it is alleged results in his being concerned with the appearance rather than the reality of normalisation.

Whether normalisation according to Wolfensberger is considered a re-formulation or a deviation from the Scandinavian principles it certainly included several important departures from that which had gone before. Firstly, it sought to universalise the principles so they could be applied to all classes of societally devalued persons. Secondly, it offered a definition of social deviance and located it in the context of time and the prevailing social culture. Thirdly, it attempted to establish a pattern of relationships between deviance, societal reaction, and systemic service responses. Fourthly, by subsuming many existing theories and practises in human services, it sought to place them in greater cohesion with one another and to establish a scientific basis for normalisation principles. Fifthly, Wolfensberger's formulation implicated the role of the unconscious in creating social deviance, thereby attaching greater importance to imagery and image juxtaposition with characteristics of deviance. Sixthly, it placed personal choice, regarding preference of lifestyle, beneath that which is culturally defined as appropriate. And lastly Wolfensberger's (re)formulation placed greater emphasis on personal competencies and gave consideration to both means and outcomes.

68

The theoretical basis of normalisation

Wolfensberger (1983, 1991) identified and described what he called the 'seven core themes of normalisation' which, he argued, occur at an individual, service system and societal level. The seven themes are briefly summarised for convenience in

---

FIGURE 1
SUMMARY OF THE SEVEN CORE THEMES OF NORMALISATION

The role of the unconscious
Human beings tend to function with a high degree of unconsciousness. This is true for much human activity in human services. In order to change (usually bad) things which happen to devalued persons other people first have to become conscious of the reality. Part of this reality has to do with societies' real (usually destructive) intentions which result in denied or repressed but real alternative functions for service systems.

Role expectancy and role circularity
The power of living up or down to the expectations of others is a major influence upon how an individual or group behaves. Low expectations of persons who are socially devalued lead to lower levels of attainment than would have otherwise been the case. This in turn reinforces the low expectations which were originally held.

The conservation corollary
The conservation corollary to the principle of normalisation is based upon the belief that negatively charged, devaluing characteristics perceived of a person or group have a multiplicative effect in the eyes of the observer. The removal of, or compensation for, one or more of the devaluing characteristics would therefore have a significant impact upon the likelihood of the person or group being attributed low or devalued status.
   In a similar way, image transfer may occur between individuals within a group of people with differing devaluing characteristics so that persons who individually would not be at risk of devaluation would become so by virtue of their, real or imagined, association with that group.
   The conservation corollary suggests that doing what is merely 'normal' may in fact contribute to deviancy making for persons who are at risk of devaluation. Services should therefore strive always for what is defined, by the prevailing social structure, as optimal.

The development model and personal competency enhancement
Persons frequently have real functional impairments which serve to render them less competent than other typical citizens. These functional impairments arise out of the handicapping condition itself and the combined effects of denied opportunities and experiences and poor or negative role expectancies. Normalisation requires that personal competencies be enhanced through, for example, the use of the developmental model.
   The developmental model presumes that all people have the ability to grow, it implies that high demands and expectations should be made and held and it recommends the use of the most powerful teaching techniques available to assist people in their growth.

The power of imitation
Imitation is one of the most powerful ways in which people learn. This is especially true for social behaviour. People accorded devalued status are frequently denied opportunities to learn from positive role models by virtue of being segregated and isolated from the places (and people) where such learning could be expected to occur. Congregation, in service settings, with other devalued citizens compounds the problem by exposing already devalued persons to further negative role models.
   Normalisation requires the fullest possible integration of devalued persons with the ordinary non-handicapped world so that exposure to positive role models is optimised.

The dynamics and relevance of social imagery
Symbolic image association, such as with animality, illness, death and so on, can adversely affect the role expectancies (see above) of a person so imaged. Normalisation requires that the social imaging of devalued persons be made as positive as possible in every aspect of their lives and associations.

The importance of personal social integration and valued social participation
People frequently attempt to place some distance between themselves and phenomena they find unpleasant, distasteful or unattractive. This is manifest in human terms through processes of social segregation of devalued persons from the mainstream of society. The consequences for devalued persons are manyfold, including the denial of normative experiences, the diminution of personal growth potential and attribution of additional negative images as a function of being segregated. In addition, wider society suffers as its tolerance for diversity diminishes.

Figure 1. Should the reader wish to investigate them further reference should be made to the PASSING manual (Wolfensberger & Thomas, 1983) or to Wolfensberger's (1991) publication, details of which are contained in the reference list.

The concept of deviance and the process of devaluation
Building on sociological concepts of role circularity and societal reaction to deviance (Emerson, 1990) Wolfensberger constructed a definition of deviance which he argued arose out of initial perceptions of differentness along one or more dimensions of identity, which when judged significant by others and valued negatively would lead to the ascribing of negative role images (Wolfensberger, 1980a). The sources of differentness were categorised by Wolfensberger as primarily inherent or acquired physical characteristics, overt or covert forms of behaviour and descent or lineage.

Wolfensberger's historical analysis of deviance led him to conclude that the casting of persons into deviant social roles correlated highly with systemic human service approaches - a manifestation indicative of the nature of societal reaction to deviance. Wolfensberger offered four broad categories of societal reaction to deviance;

i)   the destruction of deviancy,
ii) the protection of non-deviant persons from the deviant,
iii) the protection of deviant persons from the non-deviant,
iv) the reversal of deviancy through restoration, rehabilitation and reintegration.

Wolfensberger's summary definition of normalisation
It is the last of these four categories which defines normalisation according to Wolfensberger. Thus Wolfensberger's summary definition of normalisation became the *'utilisation of means which are as culturally normative as possible, in order to establish, enable or support behaviours, appearances, experiences and interpretations which are as culturally normative as possible.'* Wolfensberger essentially argued that since deviance was located with the perceivers of deviance then it could be reduced or eliminated by changing the perceptions and values of the perceiver whilst also minimising the differentness or stigmata which activate the process of devaluation. This conclusion is, of course, similar to Nirje's ideas about imposed handicaps being susceptible to cure.

Wolfensberger's later substitution of the term *Social Role Valorisation* arose out concerns regarding the widespread misunderstanding of the principles of normalisation (Wolfensberger, 1980b; Wolfensberger & Tullman, 1982). Wolfensberger sought a form of words which would both describe normalisation more accurately and stimulate more rigorous investigations of the topic. Thus a later definition of normalisation focused much more explicitly upon the creation and maintenance of valued social roles (Wolfensberger & Tullman, 1982; Wolfensberger & Thomas, 1983) which is reflected in the statement that the

70

ultimate goal of normalisation is '. . . *the creation support and defense of valued social roles for people who are at risk of devaluation*' (Wolfensberger 1983). This summary definition has since been revised to include '*the enablement, establishment, enhancement, maintenance, and/or defense of valued social roles for people - particularly those at value risk - by using, as much as possible, culturally valued means*' (Wolfensberger, 1991). In extending the summary definition Wolfensberger placed greater emphasis upon the role of others in the creation of valued social roles, included considerations of maintenance and reaffirmed the acceptance of the use of non-culturally valued means, where culturally valued means cannot be utilised, to obtain culturally valued outcomes.

Normalisation stated as the five service accomplishments
O'Brien's (1987) formulation of normalisation principles is well known throughout the UK. Whilst this formulation builds on Wolfensberger's theoretical construction of SRV, which is cited as complementary reading, it also represents something of a return to the original Scandinavian concept. Expressed as the five essential accomplishments of community presence, community participation, choice, competence and respect, it is, for example, much simpler and less scientific in its presentation and personal autonomy emerges with greater prominence.

The five essential accomplishments have been embraced and used in many policy documents throughout the UK. Because they are so well known they will be discussed in more detail later in this chapter to examine some of the implications normalisation has for services to people whose behaviour challenges services and communities.

Dissemination of normalisation within the UK
The dissemination of normalisation throughout the UK owes much to the work of Values Into Action (formerly The Campaign for People with Mental Handicaps) and others (see Emerson, 1990). Wolfensberger had systematised normalisation ideas much further than either Nirje or Bank-Mikkelson. In 1972 he published the first complete volume on the subject (Wolfensberger, 1972). The first version of *Program Analysis of Service Systems* (PASS) (Wolfensberger & Glenn, 1973) was reviewed and updated in 1975 (Wolfensberger & Glenn, 1975) and in 1983 *Program Analysis of Service Systems Implementing Normalisation Goals* (PASSING) was published (Wolfensberger & Thomas, 1983).

Both PASS and PASSING (PASS/ING) have served a dual function. The instruments were designed primarily as assessment tools to enable services to be evaluated against normalisation criteria. However, each instrument became a major vehicle for the dissemination and teaching of normalisation principles (Baldwin, 1985; Emerson and McGill, 1989). Moreover, as Emerson & McGill (1989) point out, PASS and PASSING also assumed the status of a blueprint for services based upon the principles of normalisation. Intensive 5-6 day PASS/ING workshops were

71

frequent throughout the 1980's. Participants were taught normalisation theory, and the structure of the instrument through lecture and simulations before embarking upon a practice evaluation of a selected service setting under the direction of experienced workshop leaders.

In contrast O'Brien produced a 'framework for accomplishment' (O'Brien & Lyle-O'Brien 1989a:1989b) rather than evaluation in the belief that planning desirable futures for people would cause normalisation to be seen and learned in a more positive and constructive light. Framework for accomplishment workshops are now run in parts of the UK and are seen as complementary to, rather than a substitute for, PASS and PASSING.

Summary

In its original Scandinavian form normalisation was a construct concerned essentially with extending individual rights and creating a more just society. Wolfensberger extended, scientificised and disseminated normalisation theory internationally. O'Brien later simplified the presentation of normalisation theory around personal futures planning.

Although there is much common ground, significant differences do exist in both content and emphasis, for example in relation to autonomy and competency, between the Scandinavian and the North American formulations of normalisation. Of the two it is the American formulations which have been most widely read, cited, and taught in the US and the UK (Flynn & Nitsch, 1980). For the sake of clarity the remainder of this chapter will, unless otherwise stated, discuss normalisation according to the North American formulation.

Defining challenging behaviour

Nowadays the term *challenging behaviour* is frequently used to label, describe or identify persons whose behaviour proves at times difficult for services, parents and communities to deal with. No doubt its popularity is accounted for in part by its apparent neutrality – at least for the moment. However, the concept of challenging behaviour in the everyday service world remains poorly defined and as a result some confusion is evident as to what in fact constitutes challenging behaviour.

Defining the challenge from the individual perspective

The King Edward's Hospital Fund publication on challenging behaviour (Blunden & Allen, 1987) adapted a definition of challenging behaviour previously offered by Emerson *et al.* (1987)

'. . . behaviour of such an intensity, frequency or duration that the physical safety of the person or others is placed in serious jeopardy or behaviour which is likely to seriously limit or delay [deny] access to, and use of, ordinary community facilities.'

Zarkowska & Clements (1988) suggest that behaviour may be regarded as problematic (challenging) if it satisfies one or more of the following criteria;

i)   The behaviour itself or its severity is inappropriate given a person's age and level of development.
ii) The behaviour is dangerous either to the person himself or to others.
iii) The behaviour constitutes a significant additional handicap for the person by interfering with the learning of new skills or by excluding the person from important learning opportunities.
iv) The behaviour causes significant stress to the lives of those who live and work with the person, and impairs the quality of their lives to an unreasonable degree.
v)   The behaviour is contrary to social norms.

And Towel (1987) referred to challenging behaviour as;

'. . . behaviour which is likely to be damaging to [the person] or others and/or seriously upsetting to other people with whom [the person comes] into contact'.

Emerson *et al.* describe challenging behaviour as occurring along three separate dimensions; intensity, frequency and duration. Behaviour may therefore be described as challenging if it occurs too often, for too long or too intensely - or any of these in combination. But to be defined as challenging the behaviour must function to threaten personal safety or significantly limit opportunities. Zarkowska & Clements (1988) use the term 'problem' rather than 'challenging'. Their definition is useful in that i) it adds more detail the possible range of negative effects that may result from the behaviour and ii) the behaviour is referenced to social norms and the individual's developmental level. Accordingly, some behaviour, such as severe self-injury, may be defined as challenging if it occurs at all whilst other behaviour may challenge services only when it occurs, for example, at the 'wrong' time, in the 'wrong' place or with the 'wrong' people. Behaviour might conceivably be defined as challenging when it proves difficult to elicit under the 'right' conditions, although in general challenging behaviour will be defined by observed behavioural excesses rather than deficits (Meyer & Evans, 1989).
     Challenging behaviour, at least as proposed by Emerson *et al.* is enduring. Emerson *et al.* complete their definition by stating that they would expect the person to have presented the pattern of behaviour for a considerable period of time. Challenging behaviour, they say, '. . . is not a transient phenomenon'.
     The above definitions are similar in that they avoid specific topographical or functional descriptions of behaviour concentrating instead upon the effect challenging behaviour is judged to have upon the life-style of the person exhibiting the behaviour and/or others. Whilst adequate in this sense they each omit a crucial element in the definition of challenging behaviour which is the capacity of others to deal effectively with it, that is, service and community competencies.

73

Defining the challenge from the service/community perspective

If, as Towel (1987) suggests, the term 'challenging behaviour' was chosen to focus the attention of service providers upon the challenges they must face in their attempts to provide a comprehensive pattern of locally based supports then the performance of services must be implicated somewhere in the definition of challenging behaviour.

People who challenge services are most often identified and labelled by those engaged to provide their support i.e., service staff. Identification and labelling may occur when the ordinary pattern of work is severely disrupted because;

– one service user consumes a disproportionate amount of service time and other resources, so that other demands go un-met
– there is undue invasion into out of work hours,
– conditions, arising out of an apparent inability to resolve a complex situation, lead to dysfunctional levels of stress.

In this context challenging behaviour describes behaviour which renders what might be considered the ordinary range of service supports relatively ineffective, or alternatively behaviour which places an unacceptable strain upon a service system and those employed within it. Indeed challenging behaviour is the most commonly cited reason for the breakdown of community living arrangements (Intagliata & Willer, 1982; Edgerton, 1981).

It follows that some service systems or programmes will be better equipped to deal with behavioural challenges than others. Behaviour which challenges one service system or programme may not necessarily challenge another to the same extent. It also follows that service systems can be challenged more, or less, by the same behaviour at different points in time e.g., as a function of staff turnover in a residential service or supported work programme.

Services and communities that demonstrate a considerable capacity for dealing effectively with difficult behaviour may be said to possess certain competencies over others which do not. The attachment of the label 'challenging' to certain behaviours may therefore be partially a function of where on a continuum of competency a particular service system finds itself at a given point in time. Thus, challenging behaviour may not be an absolute concept (Clwyd IST, 1990; Welsh Office, 1991) but rather one which interacts with the development of service competencies. This means, of course, that in a given geographical area the most problematic behaviour in terms of its frequency, duration and intensity may not in fact be the most challenging to services.

Combining the definition of challenging behaviour from the 'services/community' perspective and the 'individual' perspective should help to clarify the nature of the challenge in terms of the proper development of service systems, such that fewer behaviours function as barriers to community integration

74

and social participation for individual service users, without straining services systems to the point where they become dysfunctional. Thus, an alternative definition of challenging behaviour could be stated, in relation to the person's age and developmental level as;

> enduring patterns of behaviour which, at a given point in time, render what would be considred the ordinary range of services temporarily ineffective either as a function of the frequency, intensity or duration of the behaviour itself, or because of its negative consequences upon the life-style of the people concerned.

Negative consequences would, for example, include situations where the safety of the person or others is placed in jeopardy, or where developmental growth or access to the ordinary places and experiences of community life is severely limited through exclusion and other dysfunctional service/community responses.

Summary
Challenging behaviour has been defined primarily in terms of the enduring inhibitive effects it is observed to have upon peoples' lives. In this sense challenging behaviour exerts negative influences over the person's general quality of life and that of others close to them. However, it has been suggested that challenging behaviour may also be defined as function of where on a continuum of development a service system or community is in terms of its capacity to provide the range of supports necessary for an individual to obtain as normal a pattern of life as possible. In this sense challenging behaviour is a relative rather than absolute concept.

Community Based Services

Societies' interest in 'community' is much broader than the provision of mental health services (Wilmott, 1989) although its origins, which pre-date normalisation, lie very much in this general area e.g., Royal Commission on the Law Relating to Mental Illness and Mental Deficiency (Cmnd, 1957). The social policy of deinstitutionalisation, a process involving institutionalised and never institutionalised persons (Landesman & Butterfield, 1987) coincided with, and was not therefore a product of, the development and dissemination of normalisation theory (Wolfensberger, 1992). However, community provision and normalisation are often seen as synonymous because, notwithstanding Wolfensberger's (1992) proposition that 'phoney deinstitutionalisation' programmes are just as destructive as their predecessors, community provision tends to produce greater potential for the attainment of normalisation goals.

Thus far researchers have failed to agree upon a satisfactory definition of community based services. Assessing the effectiveness of community provision is therefore fraught with difficulties. However, the pattern of services of today is arguably different when compared with that of just ten years ago. A feature of the recent changes is the preference shown for supporting people in their own homes and the use of ordinary housing stock, dispersed across several neighbourhoods, as an alternative to, and a replacement for, congregate campus style hospital accommodation (see Felce, this volume). These types of services, along with a range of others, are collectively described in service shorthand as community services - *community services,* that is, as opposed to *institutional services.*

Landesman (1988), however, makes an important distinction between the structural and the functional aspects of service provision where structure refers, for example, to the physical design and location of services e.g., buildings, staffing arrangements, materials etc. whilst function describes what actually goes on i.e., interaction, engagement, types of activities and the context in which they occur. Thus, as Landesman argues, institutionalised community provision is perfectly possible where the structural components of community services remain intact yet the practices do not differ in any significant way from those of the institution. In a similar way Felce (1989) describes structure, orientation and procedure where structure refers to building location and design, staffing structure, staff roles etc. Orientation describes service competencies such as behavioural development, engagement and relationships. Procedure describes mechanisims used to obtain a range of service objectives such as individual programming, skills teaching, organisiation of the day etc. Thus in considering community in the context of service provision simply observing the physical pattern of provision is unlikely to be sufficient. Some attention also has to be given to what actually goes on.

Defining community

According to Wilmott (1989) the concept of community can be quite wide ranging. For example people will typically belong, not to one, but to several communities at the same time. Moreover, there are, Wilmott (1989) suggests, at least three different types of community; territorial communities, communities of interest and communities of attachment. Territorial communities are defined essentially by centres of population of various scales and sizes e.g., from a street to a nation. An interest community, on the other hand, is defined by the common interests or shared characteristics of its members. Territorial communities and interest communities are not mutually exclusive and either, or both, can function as a community of attachment. Attachment communities exist primarily as a function of the breadth and density of social relationships and the extent to which people feel a sense of identity with a place or a group.

Normalisation defines community in a more qualified way. After all large segregated institutions can function perfectly well as territorial communities of both interest and attachment. They do not however meet normalisation criteria. Wolfensberger (1975, 1983) introduced a generic, integrative, 'people and places' quality in his definition of the community suggesting it to be a geo-demographic area that has a sense of belonging together brought about by the presence of resources such that its members would not have to go elsewhere to have their basic needs met. But it could be argued that institutions function extremely well in this respect too. Normalisation, however, is concerned with the integration of societally devalued persons with non-devalued persons and it is in this respect that community is defined to exclude institutions.

According to normalisation theory community presence is important both as an end and as a means of obtaining other normalisation goals (see; seven core themes). For example community presence is viewed both as a way of maintaining society's tolerance for diversity and as an essential pre-condition for social integration and the forming of relationships. Arguments can be found in Wilmott's (1989) work for and against the importance of community presence in these respects. For example, Wilmott (1989) suggests that nowadays people spend more time 'privatised' in their own homes so that local (territorial) communities may no longer function as communities of attachment. Consequently people's work and other, often geographically distanced, relationships assume greater importance in this respect. Other work cited by Wilmott, however, suggests that superficial but regular interactions between the residents of a local area will encourage a sense of attachment with it (p14) which obviously bodes well for the development and maintenance of relationships.

Summary
Societies' interest in community provision is quite broad. The social policy of deinstitutionalisation pre-dates normalisation but the two are often seen as synonymous. Community in service terms is often used to describe patterns of service provision which are not institutional in their structural features but this tends to ignore the functional aspects i.e., what actually happens in so called community services. Wilmott (1989) defines three types of community; territorial, interest and attachment. However normalisation's concerns for the physical and social integration of devalued citizens result in a more qualified definition of community.

Normalisation and Community Services: Some implications for persons who exhibit challenging behaviour

Normalisation, community services and challenging behaviour are complex issues in their own right. Combining them serves only to add to their complexity. The development of behavioural competencies, whilst relevant to all people, is in my view particularly important in services for people who display challenging behaviour. This, and other normalisation outcomes will be discussed in the context of community provision. The framework of the five essential accomplishments (O'Brien, 1987) will be utilised before extending the discussion into other areas.

77

Community presence

In expressing community presence as 'the sharing of the ordinary places that define community life' O'Brien (1987) deals simultaneously with both the functional and the structural aspects of community provision in that the accomplishment describes *where* for example, people should live and work (structure) as well as *when, where and how* (function) people should spend their time and go about getting their various needs met. For people with severe/profound learning disabilities, whose behaviour challenges services, this means having all or most of their needs met in the same places, at the same times and by the same people as would be the case for any other citizen.

Community presence and community acceptance

Felce (this volume) argues a compelling case for why and how people with severe disabilities, including those who display challenging behaviour, should live in ordinary houses. Some people have already demonstrated their capacity to not only do this but also engage in productive work in integrated settings (Kings Fund, 1984, 1991). Strategies for inclusive education are now increasingly under discussion and the scope for community based recreational activities is becoming more clearly delineated (e.g., Wilcox & Bellamy, 1987).

However, these outcomes are not yet available for everyone and people who display very challenging behaviour remain amongst those most likely to be excluded (Edgerton, 1981; Intagliata & Willer, 1982). It is still common in the UK for people to be excluded from schools, training centres and even their own homes as a direct result of challenging behaviour. O'Brien (1987) suggests that without focused effort people *will* be segregated and deprived of opportunities to learn and to share. The requirement from the perspective of people who display challenging behaviour is clear. Opportunities must be provided for community living, work and education. Services and local communities need to direct their resources toward the creation and maintenance of supports that will enable these outcomes.

But as Kiernan (1991) points out beneficence, a concept borrowed from medical ethics for weighing the potential harms and goods from a given course of action, has to be appraised not only from the perspective of the individual who displays challenging behaviour but also from that of carers and other members of the community. Relying solely upon the 'rights' of people who display challenging behaviour to live in community settings, without reference to the needs of others, has proven to be unreliable as a means of ensuring continuity of provision let alone to facilitate the accomplishment of other normalisation goals. Services wishing to operationalise normalisation goals in relation to community presence will therefore need to attend to the development of behavioural competencies to bring about a greater convergence of the good for all concerned.

Highly competent services will be required to ensure that the benefits which accrue from community living arrangements consistently outweigh the harms for all concerned. Not only will services need to demonstrate considerable skill in working with challenging behaviour but, where personal responsibilities cannot be fully met by an individual, they must also be able to act prosthetically to make up the difference. How this is done (process or means) is highly relevant to image making and will therefore crucially affect the how the person, and the service, is viewed by others.

The value of community presence to people who display challenging behaviour can only be fully realised if detailed attention is paid to the establishment and maintenance of behaviour and appearances which defend and enhance valued social roles. To fully achieve this services must devise and operate strategies that support socially acceptable behaviour and minimise the negative effects of challenging behaviour.

Community participation
Community participation is defined by O'Brien (1987) as being part of a growing network of personal relationships that includes close friends. In Wilmott's (1989) terms this would amount to converting territorial communities into valued communities of interest and attachment. O'Brien suggests that without focused effort people with learning disabilities will have unusually small networks of people made up mainly of service staff and family. Anyone who has spent any time in services to people with learning disabilities can attest to the uncomfortable truth of this statement. Yet very few people with learning disabilities show total disinterest in others.

The premise that more and better relationships will develop in community settings is a basic tenet of normalisation theory. Some support for this can be found in the literature on deinstitutionalisation. For example, Landesman-Dwyer, Berkson & Romer (1979) reported that persons were more sociable when surrounded by others with a higher I.Q. thus, they argued isolating people from essential daily social contacts effectively reduced opportunities for people to develop relationships. Landesman-Dwyer & Berkson (1984) found that friendships and interacting with others was one of the most valued aspects of service user's lives and that for 21% of the population studied loneliness was a big problem. In spite of this Edgerton (1981) reported that most deinstitutionalised persons did not wish to return to institution. Saxby et al. (1986) investigated the extent and nature of social participation in the community of people with severe/profound learning disabilities, some of whom displayed very challenging behaviour, who were supported in services highly concerned with integration. They found that all ten people engaged in normative, purposeful activity whilst out and that nine out of the ten interacted successfully with other members of the public. A survey of local business people revealed largely favourable views concerning the appearance and behaviour of the service users. Despite this there was no indication that substantive relationships developed.

Normalisation theory suggests that people will tend to want to place some distance between themselves and phenomena they find unpleasant. Challenging behaviour is, by its own definition, likely to function as such a phenomenon both in terms of its enactment and how the person is perceived by others. People who scream, who are aggressive or self injurious are at times genuinely difficult to be with. The effect is reduced scope for the development of relationships. Normalisation requires that considerable effort be put to minimising negatively value charged forms of differentness through attending to both the appearances and behaviour of the individual concerned and the service supports which surround him/her. But is this enough? One example from my own work in community housing services which supports this interpretation concerns a young woman who had lived all of her life in the same neighbourhood as the then new community living arrangement was to be located (Felce & Toogood, 1988). She was quite well known about the community mainly because of her challenging behaviours and her odd, unattractive appearance. She was grossly overweight, her hair grew unevenly, she had no front teeth, she drooled and had obvious facial hair. She would remove all her clothing and remain naked for a great deal of time. As a result she wore one piece blue suits tied at the back. Because of her obesity and her tendency to sit down in the streets she used a wheelchair whilst out. She was part of a network of people, who were of roughly of her parents age, primarily as a function of their helping with her day to day care, she had no friends of her own age.

A multi-element plan which included weight loss, hair care, use of make up, regular exercise, skills teaching, communication training, housework, recreational activity, learning to stay dressed and learning to walk out was begun in her new home and at that of her parents. This work was far from easy and episodes of challenging behaviour, in and out of the house, sometimes worsened in intensity and included aggression, damage to property and disruption. As walking out increased so did sitting in the street. However, after about nine months the young lady, now a slender eight and a half stones, rarely stripped off her clothes and rarely sat in the street. Moderately high heeled shoes, tights, skirts, dresses, jeans and tee-shirts had replaced the one piece blue suits. Simple use of cosmetics removed the facial hair and enhanced the attractive features of her face. Her hair thickened, grew evenly and was styled. An unintended byproduct of higher shoes was a more upright posture.

Although she had changed little as a person she presented an altogether different picture of herself. The change in behaviour and appearance was such that one day, whilst out together, we were stopped for conversation by a near neighbour. Standing in the street, relaxed and comfortable, the neighbour enquired 'what happened to the fat girl who used to sit in the street, did she have to go away?'. The 'fat girl, who used to sit in the street' was in fact standing less than two feet away. That was ten years ago. Those initial gains have not only maintained but have developed over time. In November 1991 she and I were both, independently, present at a gathering of some 60-70 persons. She looked stunningly elegant and, despite her significant communication difficulties, was engaged socially by many people during the course of the evening. She now has glasses which enhance her appearance and wears her

80

hair in fashionable ringlets. However, although she is well known, and in a much more positive context than before, there are still relatively few people close to her, which serves to illustrate just how tough forming new and lasting relationships can be. Of all normalisation goals, those to do with relationships are probably the most difficult to achieve. Relationships cannot easily be engineered. How services are delivered, however, will exert some influence, helpful or otherwise, over the scope for their development.

Physical and social distance is a major barrier to the development of relationships. In working toward normalisation goals that have to do with relationships services will need to attend to many things including those aspects of appearance and behaviour (especially challenging behaviour) which may cause offense to others. In so doing some of the not inconsiderable barriers to relationship development may be weakened or removed. Part of this process will involve helping people to become socially competent e.g., learning to share, to wait, to smile, to greet etc. thereby promoting or enabling a greater degree of reciprocity within relationships. Contrary to what is often claimed sophisticated teaching does not produce robotic social responses. What it can do, however, is equip a person with more extensive means to i) create or capitalise upon naturally occurring opportunities, and ii) subsequently express themselves within the context of a given relationship. After all relationships built upon genuine mutuality are likely to last an awful lot longer than those which are not. Here again behavioural competencies are key.

Choice and personal autonomy
Choice, as defined by O'Brien (1987), is the experience of autonomy in matters both small and large. Choice covers a wide range of human activity e.g., where to go, what to do, how to look, who to live with etc. O'Brien (1987) argues that without focused effort to provide opportunities and support for decision making people will be passive, without a voice and unable to escape from undesirable situations.

The acceptable face of normalisation?
Whether or not choice exists as an expression of the 'free will' will not be discussed here. Suffice to say that a lot of people working in community settings believe that it does -and that it is important. Only rarely do people take issue with this statement of accomplishment - at least at a conscious level. Somehow the concept of choice seems to assimilate well with the often self defined liberalistic role and function of community services. For some normalisation simply means 'the accomplishment of choice' whilst for others the accomplishment of choice is *the* paramount issue.

A few cite 'choice' selectively, and rather cynically in my view, as a post-hoc rationale for non-interventionalism especially in relation to challenging behaviour. Such arguments are usually based upon on of two inter-related expressed positions i) the person is choosing to behave in this way and his right to choose must be respected, or ii) intervening means subjecting the person or behaviour to some form of external control, which is a violation of the person's right to choose. These positions ignore the fact that behaviour is likely to be under the control of external influences anyway, and that intervention is simply about the explicitness with which those controlling influences are identified and or changed in some way.

Choice and other accomplishments
In general the expression of choice presents no special difficulties whenever the expressed preference is i) consistent with what other people (especially carers) would choose, ii) perceived to be risk free and iii) unlikely to give rise to a conflict of interest. Should one or more of these conditions not be fully satisfied then it is highly likely that the 'choice' will be overruled in some way or other - explicitly or not.

Within normalisation theory problems arise when a person expresses a desire for a non or de-normalising option, that is, when accomplishing choice compromises one or more of the remaining accomplishments. Wolfensberger (1980b) suggests this would most likely occur as a function of deficits in education, training and/or experience resulting in an impaired ability to predict the consequences of a given course of action i.e. un-informed choice. Recognising that this could give rise to conflict and difficulties in the pursuit of normalisation goals Wolfensberger (1980b, p110-111) set out a way of dealing with inappropriate expressions of personal autonomy, summarised in Figure 2, which is consistent with normalisation principles.

What Wolfensberger offers is a structure or process for resolving difficulties not a universally applicable normalisation outcome. Generalised statements such as 'personal choice is paramount for all persons, on all issues, at all times' find no support here.

This is important, but often overlooked, evidence which should help to clarify what must be one of the most often and grossly misinterpreted aspects of normalisation. First and foremost normalisation theory does not conceptualise personal autonomy as 'all or nothing'. It recognises that all people have the capacity to decide on certain issues but not on others. This capacity may change over time and vary according to context. Normalisation recommends, therefore, that considerations around an 'inappropriate' expression of personal autonomy be person and issue specific, located in time and the context of the person's life. The process asks that the person's competency to decide on the issue be determined and that serious consideration be given to finding ways of enhancing personal competencies in the light of what may (or may not) have gone before. It asks that decision makers involve and inform the person as far as possible and suggests the use of independent representatives. It requires that decision makers become aware of what they propose, and that they set

FIGURE 2
WOLFENSBERGER'S APPROACH TO RESOLVING
PROBLEMS ASSOCIATED WITH INAPPROPRIATE CHOICES
(Abridged)

1. Determine the person's level or degree of understanding of the problem.

2. Apply the use of culturally normative informal influences to lead the person to the desired course of action (including long term reinforcement of desires responses p110) but avoid coercion until all social influences are exhausted.

3. Ascertain the degree of competency (especially for adults).

4. Where not competent, find someone who is responsible for the person under law or by virtue of their relationship.

5. For children, guardians may be used or appointed.

6. Determine what has and what can be done to embrace personal competency to a degree that would permit decision making.

7. For children coercive methods may be used but social influences should take priority.

8. Where adults are concerned, the importance of the issue should be determined in its own right and in the context of the person's life.

9. The person should be made as fully aware as possible of the intervention, its benefits if successful and its costs if it is not.

10. People in power (decision makers) should make themselves aware of infringements of rights and determine the parameters of acceptability.

11. The decision makers should also determine the duration of the state of affairs.

12. If all else fails, walk with the person and share their suffering with nothing more than a moral victory.

limits and time lines around any infringement of personal autonomy which they may agree.

There is an explicit recognition in normalisation theory that some important decisions may need to be 'traded off' against other important outcomes for the individual. Whilst the utilisation of normative influences is recommended coercion, although not defined, is not excluded from the range of possible tactics. Whether covert (i.e., undeclared) behavioural or ecological manipulations could or should be used to influence a person's 'choice' to engage in challenging behaviour would therefore be a matter of consideration within the overall structure of the decision making process.

Ultimately, if all else fails, Wolfensberger recommends that one should 'walk with the person . . . with nothing more than a moral victory'. Perhaps though, where challenging behaviour is concerned, he should have added something along the lines of 'if at first you don't succeed, try and try again'.

Current practice
Compare the proposed model to that which commonly applies in services to people who display challenging behaviour. Wolfensberger & Glenn (1975) state that only under exceptional circumstances should personal autonomy or rights be abridged and then only following assessment of competency (p28). They also state that 'long periods of total inactivity, peculiar sleep-waking cycles, excessive amounts of non-productive recreational activity, or highly idiosyncratic pursuits are devalued at any age' (p32). Yet over the years how many people living in highly resourced community services, that claim allegiance with normalisation principles, have been indirectly enabled by their carers to spend long periods of time in bed, to engage all day long in un-purposeful, stereotyped, or no activity at all, to be unnecessarily aggressive, destructive or self injurious? and how often has it been rationalised on the basis of choice?

The role of direct carers
Part, but by no means all, of the reason this state of affairs perpetuates lies in the, often unacknowledged, power of direct carer workers. By default a great deal of power is vested with direct carers, especially in the service context, to do or not to do for and on behalf of the service user. Too often direct carers are left to make these important decisions without insight or direction regarding the consequences of their (in)action. The contingencies that apply to direct care work in service settings seem even to permit the outright rejection of specific advice or managerial direction to implement behavioural programming.

Evidence of a profound learning disability coupled with seriously challenging behaviour would surely be sufficient grounds to consciously *consider* the temporary abridgment of a specific expression of autonomy, or the restriction of *certain* choices within defined parameters. Frequently, it seems not. Instead ad-hoc decisions go on being taken, often on the spot, many of which function to restrict autonomy, until the environment becomes so incoherent that breakdown occurs and major infringements of autonomy are the inevitable result.

Social environments that support choice
Paradoxically free choice within a wholly unstructured social environment can function to restrict the truest expressions of personal autonomy simply because the contingencies are too difficult to identify and manage. Explicit routines in some

community settings are vetoed, despite their functionality for most of us, because of their negative association with institutions. Yet flexible personalised routines, especially within group living situations, can enable choice to be expressed in many important ways e.g., initiative taking, choosing between a manageable number of options, learning through experience about a growing range of alternatives and about the consequences of (in)action. Similarly the avoidance of structured skills teaching, where the natural contingencies fail to teach, serves to diminish rather than enhance the opportunities a person may have to develop the necessary competencies for exercising personal autonomy.

Normalisation theory clearly supports the expression of personal autonomy in as many aspects of life as possible. Personal competencies will, among other things, determine the extent to which personal autonomy can be exercised. It therefore falls to services which aspire toward normalisation goals to assist in the development of those competencies.

Status, dignity and respect

Because so many aspects of normalisation overlap, conflict, function as ends and means to other accomplishments there is a real danger of repetition creeping into this text. The issues discussed under presence, participation, choice (and competence which is to follow), clearly have a bearing on the creation of valued social roles. In an effort to avoid repetition I propose to deal with the accomplishment of respect in a quite limited way. I want to establish one point, particularly in relation to challenging behaviour and community services, which is that behaviour matters a great deal.

Accomplishing respect through valued social roles
The accomplishment of respect is defined by O'Brien (1987) as having a valued place among a network of people and valued roles in community life. People generally fulfil a range of valued social roles e.g., worker, home owner, car driver, voter, student, consumer, contributor etc. The issue here is the extent to which people at risk of devaluation are seen by others to occupy the same range of valued roles, as opposed to being defined wholly in terms of their handicapping condition e.g., mentally handicapped, dangerous, nuisance, menace and so on.

The importance of behaviour and appearances
Normalisation theory states that images and ideas about people derive mainly from direct observation (deviance is in the eye of the beholder) and from real or imagined associations with other phenomena. Imagery is an extremely important part of normalisation theory and great importance is attached therein to behaviour and appearances (see summary definitions). The relevance of challenging behaviour to the societal process of devaluation should, therefore, not be underestimated.

85

According to normalisation theory labelling and the ascribing of negative social roles work hand in hand to produce physical and social distancing. How people are interpreted results from many things including groupings, proximity to other images of deviance, histories and labelling. However, Szivos (1992) cites research which shows that distantiation was influenced more by observed behaviour than by labels and that 'natural' labelling may in fact help people to be interpreted less negatively by others. Moreover, the visibility of a handicap can in some cases function as an 'explanation' for unusual behaviour and thereby elicit tolerance. Szivos reports that parents, not clients, believed that labels helped to ameliorate negative attitudes toward their offspring although the effect was weaker when aggressive behaviour was involved.

But whilst eliciting tolerance e.g., for diversity is one normalisation goal it is not the major goal of normalisation, even if it results in physical and social integration of some sort. Normalisation is unequivocal in stating its requirements as the establishment, enhancement, maintenance and/or defense of valued social roles. Minimising negatively valued forms of differentness, which includes challenging behaviour, is on the other hand a key normalisation goal. As such services seeking normalisation outcomes through the creation of valued social roles will need to develop and maintain effective ways of working with challenging behaviour which include changing the behaviour and mitigating its effects.

Competence

Competence is defined by O'Brien (1987) as the opportunity to perform functional and meaningful activities with whatever level or type of assistance that is required. Without focused effort, people with severe handicaps will be deprived of the expectations, opportunities, instruction and assistance, necessary for increased competency.

Other materials used in the teaching of normalisation (PASS/ING) reveal an unequivocal position regarding the development of personal competencies. Whilst personal competence is implicated in many of the PASS ratings explicit reference is made under the cluster of ratings 'Developmental Growth' (p39). In their introduction Wolfensberger & Glenn (1975) discuss the development of personal competencies both as a means of obtaining normalisation goals and as an outcome which is itself valued. In this context, they say, services pursuing normalisation goals should hold growth oriented expectations which are demanding, relentless, realistic yet supported by warmth and kindness. Such expectations should be mediated by direct tuition and instruction, therapies of various kinds and the presence (and use) of materials and devices which teach, facilitate or support behaviour and movement - including prosthetics and even automated operant environments! (p39). Further requirements are stated in the guidance for raters of R1143 Intensity of Relevant Programming (IRP) which is described as one of the most important issues in service delivery and the most important clinical (in contrast to systemic) rating in PASS (p40). There are three inter-related and equally important components of IRP;

i) a recognisable programme for developmental growth, which is
ii) relevant to the individual or group, and is
iii) intense in its content (challenging) and volume (the amount of time it occupies).

Intensity may also be assessed with reference to the use of modern equipment, technologies, therapies and procedures. Similar requirements are delineated in PASSING (Wolfensberger & Thomas, 1983) under the cluster of ratings [R23] Competency-Related Service Structured Activities and Other Uses of Time (p485-496) the arguments for which may be summarised thus;

i) The more skilful a person is the better able he will be to interact successfully with the non-handicapped world.
ii) Personal competency is a highly valued attribute, especially in Western societies. The more competent a person is the more likely he is to be esteemed by others.
iii) Higher levels of personal competence in some areas may function to compensate for potentially devaluing characteristics i.e., the deviancy/competency theory.
iv) It is what a great many services claim they exist to do - if they fail then they may actually inflict harm through supporting processes of non-development.

O'Brien & Tyne (1981) advocate the use of new teaching technologies to bring about changes in appearance and competence previously believed impossible. Stating that cure has an 'all or nothing' idea about it they argue for incremental change and describe normalisation not as something which is done to a person but as a principle which is useful for designing and delivering the services a person needs. As such normalisation avoids denying the needs people may have for additional help, it simply raises questions for those who deliver it.

Resistance to the accomplishment of competence
Given that the development of behavioural competencies is a key normalisation goal in and of itself, that it is cited as a major means of accomplishing other normalisation goals and that it is clear in its requirement for the use of the most powerful pedagogies available, why should there be such resistance to competency development in community based services?

The accomplishment of competency clearly exerts enormous influence over the potential to accomplish all other normalisation goals and has special relevance to persons who display seriously challenging behaviour. Yet in many community based services accomplishing competence, whilst undoubtedly the most thoroughly researched aspect of work with people who have learning disabilities and a central tenet of SRV, is the most controversial when it comes to implementation. It is truly ironic that the aspect of normalisation and service provision which has an empirically validated technology for its implementation should turn out to be the one which is given the least credence in services.

Reasons for this are, in the main, speculative but when arguments against intervention are based on normalisation they may be accounted for in terms of a partial adoption of normalisation principles. Some twelve years ago Flynn & Nitsch (1980) suggested that partial adoption of normalisation would be a most likely outcome. Despite careful treatment of the subject (e.g., Wolfensberger, and others same volume, 1980a; 1980b; 1980c) a complete and accurate explanation of partial adoption has proven elusive. It is unlikely that it will be obtained here. However, a few observations of factors which may have contributed to the poor uptake of a relatively well proven technology for the development of personal competencies are offered.

Partial adoption determined by normalisation teaching
Dissemination of normalisation in the UK has occurred mainly through written material (see Emerson, 1990; Flynn & Nitsch, 1980), workshops and short courses. A sizeable proportion of the published literature on normalisation, however, deals with global issues often at a societal/systems level. For a detailed account of normalisation requirements at a service system/individual level reference has to be made to either PASS or PASSING manuals the availability of which is tied closely to attendance of a workshop, and the accessibility of which is questionable. As a consequence learning about normalisation from written sources is likely to leave the reader with a rather better understanding of global rather than specific issues.

PASS and PASSING introductory workshops make use of experiential and theoretical formats for teaching normalisation i.e. presentation, simulation, practice evaluation and group conciliation of issues. However, ratings in PASS such as Intensity of Relevant Programming receive a disproportionately small amount of attention in relation to their importance. During introductory workshops IRP is usually rated only once, as part of the practice evaluation, and because practice sites are usually so weak in this area it is rated quickly e.g.,

Question:	Is there a programme?
Evidence:	No.
Conclusion:	If there isn't a programme then neither intensity nor relevance can be rated.
Rating:	Level 1

Thus, the most important clinical rating in PASS will often receive little more than two to three minutes out of the countless hours of the workshop. Moreover, IRP is often conciliated late into the session when people are tired and driven by the

88

goal to complete their evaluation rather than investigate an issue thoroughly. Hence participants inevitably fail to learn the significance of IRP but will remember normalisation as being concerned with physical and social integration. Shorter normalisation workshops have even greater problems in that they must cover the same material in less time. Issues therefore are necessarily presented and discussed more superficially.

Degree of fit with perceived role and function of services and the preferences of staff
The publicly declared role and function of services as expressed in service documentation will frequently claim some allegiance to normalisation principles - many cite the five essential accomplishments. But in reality how many service workers are made fully and properly aware of service intentions and the responsibilities they share in their fulfilment? In the absence of direction service workers will decide upon role and function for themselves. A rather extreme example of this involved residential service workers prohibiting access by responsible service managers and professionals to the house in which they worked. Their stated rationale was protection of service users from intrusive visits. But in defining and enacting their role as 'protectors' the service workers removed many key and normalisation consistent elements of service provision from the reach of the people they served including; access to the best available help and advice, access to resources and access to a source of protection from abuse. O'Brien & Tyne's (1981) statement that service users and staff will set the limit on how normative and valued the results of hard and creative work will be has both a positive and negative connotation.

In a similar way behavioural interventions are often refused or sabotaged by direct care workers, in spite of guidance or direction from their managers or the interests of the client, on the basis of a narrow interpretation of normalisation. Whether these are genuinely held, if misinformed, views or whether they are post-hoc rationalisations for behaviour otherwise motivated is not known. What has been shown is that progress made by service users is not a powerful determinant of staff behaviour (Woods & Cullen, 1983). As long as the perceived aversiveness of the demands made upon staff in operationalising recommended intervention strategies remain more powerful than the aversiveness associated with tolerating challenging behaviour little progress will be made. This has implications for training, as a method of reducing the aversiveness of task difficulty for staff, in the same way that training might be recommended to reduce task difficulty for service users.

Hangover from the early days of communitisation
Resistance to the application of teaching technologies, particularly in community living arrangements, may also be the result of a hang over from the early days in the community movement. Efforts to stimulate interest in community housing as a real

89

alternative to institutional care led, with some support from normalisation theory, to wholesale blaming of institutions for all the ills which befell their occupants - including the eliciting of challenging behaviour. Blaming institutions resulted in two implicitly held beliefs;

i) structural interpretations of institutions; the provision of housing alone would resolve all the harms inflicted by institutions.
ii) functional interpretations of institutions; community based alternatives would need to do the opposite of institutions - in every respect.

So, for example, as institutions were rigid in their routines then routine had no place in community based settings, and as institutions were the first hosts to behaviour modification then behavioural approaches also had no place in community settings. A case of throwing out the baby with the bath water?

Current emphasis upon rights and personal autonomy in a culture of professional safety and protectionism
Very recent years have seen the public vilification of social workers and allied professions in regard to the work they undertake on societies behalf. This, coupled with legislation and case law in the UK which confers greater rights and protection of potentially vulnerable service users, a key normalisation outcome, has resulted partly in a culture of fear where non-interventionism, especially if the client can be blamed (e.g., for his own self injury) may be considered a safer option for professionals and carers alike. There are certainly examples of non-normalising, competency reducing, service options being selected e.g., secure accommodation over more risky but competency enhancing community placements, on the basis of professional safety rather client interest.

The early presentation and subsequent mythology that surrounds behaviourism
This chapter opened by outlining the development and dissemination of normalisation theory. Throughout the same period rapid developments were being made, building upon the earlier work of B. F. Skinner (1953), in the field of behavioural psychology. Behaviour modification began to reach services toward the end of the 1960's. During the 1970's it became an established, if rather rare, component of service provision. The established belief that people with learning disabilities were not capable of learning was, however, beginning to be challenged (Kiernan, 1991). The 1980's produced a huge volume of research under the rubric of Applied Behaviour Analysis (ABA) and the division of opinion regarding the use of aversive procedures (see Sturmey *et al.* this volume) seems set to belong to the 1990's.
     Interestingly behaviour modification was seen as an important and acceptable way of obtaining normalisation goals such that a chapter (Roos, 1972) was included

in Wolfensberger's 1972 publication. Flynn & Nitsch (1980) also recognised the potential behavioural theory held as a major means of obtaining normalisation goals rather, than as an opponent or alternative to it. Their call for a rapprochement of behavioural theory and normalisation, citing clear advantages to both, was to be echoed years later by Emerson & McGill, (1989) in a an excellent discussion of the supposed values technology dichotomy.

However, the legacy of the sometimes clumsy and *apparently* inhumane approaches to the early applications of behaviour modification seem to have stuck. Nowadays opponents to the behavioural approach, both academic and in services, speak of behaviourism as being cold and mechanistic, stripping people of the very qualities that make them human (Wolfensberger, 1992; see also chapters by Sturmey, Ricketts & Goza and by Jones & McCaughy, this volume). Yet applied behaviour analysis and normalisation theory share many areas of common interest. Both are concerned with the betterment of society (c.f. Baer, Wolf & Risley, 1968) and socially important behaviour. Kazdin (1977), for example defined the concept of social validity in ABA in the following three ways;

i) the behaviour to be changed should be socially important to the client and others,
ii) the means used to change behaviour should be socially acceptable, and
iii) the effect of the intervention (changed behaviour) should be socially important to the client and others.

What seems to be at the root of the problem is not so much a conflict between basic values or intentions as a differential concern with empiricism.

The rise of the non-aversive movement
Flynn & Nitsch (1980) were quick to spot the commonalities between the development in ABA of social validity and normalisation theory but for a long time there was a wholesale failure to capitalise on opportunities. However, there is some evidence of a middle ground beginning to emerge with, for example the recently published works of LaVigna & Donellan (1986), Donnellan *et al.* (1988) on non-aversive approaches, McGee *et al.* (1987), McGee & Menolascino (1991) on Gentle Teaching, Training in Systematic Instruction (Gold, 1980), Cognitive Counselling (Lovett 1985) and Durrand's (1990) functional communication training. Other useful texts such as those by Meyer & Evans (1989) and Evans & Meyer (1985) and a range of volumes on supported employment (e.g., Gardner *et al.* 1988; Rusch, 1990) all seek to marry values with technology (see also discussion of Gentle Teaching by Jones & McCaughy, this volume). Some approaches seem to be more palatable in services than others, all are rightly the subject of further debate regarding their utility etc. But this should be a debate framed positively in the quest for workable solutions to complex problems not the polarised, vitriolic and

personalised debacle we sometimes witness. There is, as yet, still a great deal to be learned in the field of applied behaviour analysis (Butterfield, 1990).

Normalisation and aversive conditioning
The current debate regarding the use of aversive procedures has become polarised (see Sturmey *et al.*, this volume). However, normalisation theory can be interpreted in such a way that it does not align itself with one camp or another. Normalisation says services should use the most powerful pedagogies available and that *as far as possible* use should be made of the most culturally valued means. However, the theory of normalisation recognises that sometimes unusual means may need to be traded off against other important normalisation goals (O'Brien & Tyne, 1981). This calls for careful balancing of means and ends on an individual basis.

While the aversives debate rages on, it is sobering to reflect upon the findings of Oliver *et al.* (1987) that of the 596 identified cases of self injury in the south east of England only 2% had any form of written psychological treatment programme. Whilst the issue of non-aversive treatments is of obvious interest to us in the UK, the current major issue here has to be access to the most effective, preferably non-aversive, psychological treatments.

Conclusions
In scratching at the surface of these issues it is hoped that a few points will have been confirmed in the mind of the reader as worthy of further discussion and analysis. For example, the extent to which concepts such as normalisation, community services and challenging behaviour have, in spite of the many expert writings on the subjects, remained relatively poorly defined in the service world will be of concern to academics, trainers and service managers alike.

Alternatively consideration might be given *within services* to one, or more, of a range of specific issues such as the relative understatement of competency development in the mainstream interpretation of normalisation theory, or the relationship between competency development, choice making and other normalisation goals. The false dichotomy that exists between applied behaviour analysis and normalisation theory warrants further consideration as does the scope normalisation might have for developing and extending the concept of social validity in applied behaviour analysis. The reader may be tempted to contemplate on ways of diminishing the chasm that exists between academic and applied work, perhaps by addressing functional modalities and incentives for the translation of theory into practice, and for its maintenance over time.

The way forward
The way forward is signposted, indicating, for example, the need for better definitions of normalisation within services, the development of transferable

technologies for the implementation of normalisation goals and a fuller, more accurate definition of the role and function of community services themselves.

This may be conceptualised the second generation of change within the community movement, as such it may need to be managed in the context of organisational change. This will require a twin track approach comprising visionary but sensitive management coupled with more and better focused teaching and training of both normalisation and behavioural methods, delivered in the specific context within which they are intended to be applied.

Competency development and choice making
In preparing this chapter an attempt has been made to highlight the importance of competency development as defined i) explicitly in normalisation theory, ii) as a means of obtaining other normalisation goals and iii) as a means of ensuring continuity of placement in the community over time. I have suggested that competency development is a crucial aspect of service provision, which has special relevance to people who display challenging behaviour, and that there is proven technology available for its accomplishment. Yet there is considerable and widespread resistance to its application in community based services which is often argued on ideological grounds. This may be a function of a deliberate partial adoption of normalisation theory, an incomplete appreciation of normalisation principles or incompatibility with the perceived role and function of services.

The role and function of services
Clarifying the role and function of services, especially in terms of competency development, will be crucial if change is to occur. Service managers will, for example, need to state much more explicitly what it is services exist to do (outcomes), and be clear about how those things are done (processes). This will include specifying clearly, and in some detail, the roles and responsibilities individuals and groups have in relation to service goals. In a residential programme,for example, it would include being explicit about how a household is run, about the routines and rhythms of the day and the week, about how opportunities are planned, skills are taught and use is made of ordinary community facilities. Moreover, a coherent framework for accurately monitoring these service performances will be needed. There is a huge literature which describes, guides and supports these types of service activities.

Training
Operational guidelines will need the support of good training which is person and context specific. The workshop model of training should therefore be reserved for consciousness raising. Other training models, which make full use our knowledge from behavioural theory, should be applied to the teaching of specific work skills (see Anderson, 1987). The volume of such training needs to be substantially

93

increased (Mittler, 1987) within and across service programmes so that the density of trained staff reaches the critical mass necessary to achieve change (Landesman-Dwyer & Knowles, 1987).

Management of a second generation of organisational change
Training alone is unlikely to be enough. Given that services are provided from within an organisational framework reference to the literature on the management of organisational change (e.g., Beckhard & Harris, 1987) might prove fruitful. We are, I believe, now facing the second generation of change in the community movement. The first, primarily structural (changing buildings, locations and to a certain extent values and expectations) is partly achieved. Now whilst persevering with the first we must engage with the second, the technological phase of change, the functional aspects of service provision, those concerned with behaviour, interactions and engagement. In so doing we must be careful not to 'throw out the baby with the bath water' in terms of the means used.

The current social policy of deinstitutionalisation has provided a unique, and possibly time limited, opportunity to do something worthwhile for a small number of seriously disadvantaged people. To capitalise on this opportunity 'values' will have to marry with, or produce, a 'technology' for their realisation, or face becoming a destructive waste of peoples' lives. The larger society has given services a clear mandate to provide community based services on its behalf. Society has its own interests in seeing that the job is done well. It has set the parameters and provided the resources. If services do not get it reasonably right there is a real risk of a backlash of opinion regarding the feasibility and desirability of community provision. Indeed it has been suggested that the future of the community care initiative for people with learning disabilities could rest crucially upon services developing the capacity to serve those who display challenging behaviours, and that such service provision might serve as a bench mark for assessing the quality of a larger service system (Towel, 1987). Beneficence for all will require a high degree of service competency. Services need to demonstrate the feasibility, not just the fundamental rightness, of community provision.

Breaking the mythologies which surround behaviourism
The various emotive mythologies which surround behaviourism, such as 'mechanistic' and 'dehumanising', need to be dispelled if they are to be accepted more fully into community service provision. Applied behaviour analysis has come a long way in recent years and has much to offer. However, the discipline has, to a large extent, failed to market its product successfully where it has huge potential; in services to people who present with challenging behaviour.

The current taxonomy of approaches such as cognitive, behavioural, ecological, psychoanalytical etc. is perhaps in itself a major inhibitor to their take up in services. An alternative would be unaligned presentation of material more suited to

94

its audience. Unaligned, carefully packaged descriptions of procedures, without extensive theoretical underpinnings, would have two advantages in the service world. Firstly, it would increase the probability of acceptance, functionally defined procedures would be more likely to be seen as 'safe' procedures if they were underpinned with, and supported by, organisational structures themselves shot through with values. Secondly it would encourage the actual use of the procedures rather than a relabelling of existing practices which has often been the case, for example, with Gentle Teaching. Academic critique would remain largely where it is now, within academic circles.

Final remarks

Let us not forget the serious nature of challenging behaviour. We know challenging behaviour predicts community placement failure (Intagliata & Willer, 1982), we know challenging behaviour predicts stress for carers (Pahl & Quine, 1984) we know challenging behaviour predicts isolation, segregation and institutional placement (Edgerton, 1981), we know challenging behaviour predicts abuse (Rusch *et al.*, 1986). In a few extreme cases we know it can even threaten life. The onus is with us.

References

Anderson, S. R. (1987). The management of staff behaviour in residential treatment facilities: A review of training techniques. In J. Hogg and P. Mittler (eds.), *Staff Training in Mental Handicap*. Croom Helm: London.

Baer, D. M, Wolf M. M. and Risley. T. R. (1968). Some current dimensions of applied behavior analysis. *Journal of Applied Behaviour Analysis* 1, 91–97.

Baldwin, S. (1985). Sheep in wolf's clothing: Impact of normalisation teaching on human services and service providers. *International Journal of Rehabilitation Research* 8, 131–142.

BankMikkelson, N. E. (1980). Denmark. In *Normalisation, Social Integration and Community Services* (ed. R. J. Flynn and K. E. Nitsch). Proed: Austin, Texas.

Beckhard, R and Harris, R. T. (1987). *Organisational Transitions: Managing Complex Change.* Addison Wesley: Massachusetts.

Blunden, R. and Allen, D. (Eds) (1987). Facing the challenge: an ordinary life for people with learning difficulties and challenging behaviour. King's Fund Centre, London.

Butterfield, E. C. (1990). The compassion of distinguishing punishing behavioral treatment from aversive treatment. *American Journal of Mental Retardation* 95, 137-141.

Cmnd 169 (1957). *Royal Commission on the Law Relating to Mental Illness and Mental Health.* HMSO: London.

Clwyd Health Authority (1990) *Operational Policy for the Intensive Support Team.* Broughton Hospital. Clwyd.

Donnellan, A. M., LaVigna, G. W., NegriShoultz, N. and Fassbender, L. L. (1988). *Progress Without Punishment: Effective Approaches for Learners with Behavior Problems.* Teachers' College Press: New York.

Durrand, V. M. (1990) *Severe Behavior Problems: A Functional Communication Approach.* Guilford: New York.

Edgerton, R. B. (1981). Crime, deviance and normalisation reconsidered. In *Deinstitutionalisation and Community Adjustment of Mentally Retarded People.* Monograph 4. AMMD. Washington.

Emerson, E and McGill, P. (1989). Normalisation and applied behaviour analysis: Values and technology in services for people with learning difficulties. *Behavioural Psychotherapy* 17, 101–117.

Emerson, E. (1990). What is normalisation? In H. Brown and H. Smith (eds.), *Normalisation: A Reader for the 1990's.* Routledge: London.

Emerson, E., Barrett, S., Bell, C., Cummings, R., McCool, C., Toogood, A. and Mansell, J. (1987). *Developing Services for People with Severe Learning Difficulties and Challenging Behaviour.* CAPSC. University of Kent: Canterbury.

Evans, I. M. and Meyer, L. H. (1985). *An Educative Approach to Behaviour Problems: A Practical Decision Model for Interventions with Severely Handicapped Learners.* Brookes: Baltimore.

Felce, D. and Toogood, S. (1988). *Close to Home.* BIMH Publications: Kidderminster.

Felce, D. (1989). *The Andover Project: Summary Report of a DHSS Funded Research Project.* BIMH Publications: Kidderminster.

Flynn, R. J. and Nitsch, K. E. (1980). Normalisation: Accomplishments to date and future priorities. In J. F. Flynn and K. E. Nitsch (eds.), *Normalisation, Social Integration and Community Services.* Proed: Austin, Texas.

Gardner, J. F., Chapman, M. S., Donaldson, G. and Jacobson, S. G. (1988). *Toward Supported Employment: A Process for Planned Change.* Brookes: Baltimore.

Gold, M. (1980). *Try Another Way.* Research Press: Champaign. Illinois.

Intagliata, J. and Willer, B. (1982). Reinstitutionalisation of mentally retarded persons successfully placed into family care and group homes. *American Journal of Mental Deficiency* 87, 39–43.

Kazdin, A. E. (1977). Assessing the clinical or applied importance of behaviour change through social validation. *Behavior Modification* 1, 427–452.

Kiernan, C. (1991). Professional ethics: Behaviour analysis and normalisation. In B. Remmington (ed.), *The Challenge of Severe Mental handicap: A Behaviour Analytic Approach.* Wiley: Chichester.

King's Fund Centre. (1984) *An Ordinary Working Life. Vocational Services for People Mental Handicap.* King's Fund Publishing Office: London.

King's Fund Centre. (1991). *Meeting the Challenge: Some UK Perspectives on Community Services for People with Learning Difficulties and Challenging Behaviour.* (ed. D. Allen and S Staite). King's Fund Publishing Office: London.

Landesman, S. (1988). Preventing institutionalisation in the community. In M. P. Janicki, M. W. Krauss and M. M. Seltzer (eds.), *Community Residences for Persons with Developmental Disabilities; Here to Stay.* Brookes: Baltimore.

Landesman-Dwyer, S. and Knowles, M. (1987). Ecological analysis of staff training in residential settings. In J. Hogg and P. Mittler (eds.), *Staff Training in Mental Handicap.* Croom Helm: London.

Landesman-Dwyer, S., Berkson, G. and Romer, D. (1979). Affiliation and friendship of mentally retarded residents in group homes. *American Journal of Mental Deficiency.* 83, 571–580.

Landesman, S and Butterfield, E. (1987). Normalisation and deinstitutionalisation of mentally retarded individuals. *American Psychologist* 42, 809–816.

Landesman-Dwyer, S. and Berkson, G. (1984). Friendships and social behaviour. In J. Wortis (eds.), *Mental Retardation and Developmental Disabilities.* Plenum Press: New York.

LaVigna, G. and Donnellan, A. M. (1986) *Alternatives to Punishment: Solving Behavior Problems with Non-Aversive Strategies.* Irvington: New York.

Lovett, H. (1985). *Cognitive Counselling and Persons with Special Needs.* Praeger: New York.

McGee, J. J., Menolascino, F. J., Hobbs, D. C. and Menousek, P. E. (1987). *Gentle Teaching: A Nonaversive Approach to Helping Persons with Mental Retardation.* Human Sciences Press: New York.

McGee, J. J. and Menolascino, F. J. (1991) *Beyond Gentle Teaching: A Nonaversive Approach to Helping Those in Need.* Plenum Press: New York.

Meyer, L. H. and Evans, I. M. (1989). *Nonaversive Intervention for Behavior Problems: A Manual for Home and Community.* Brookes: Baltimore.

Mittler, P. (1987). Staff training in mental handicap. In J. Hogg and P. Mittler (eds.), *Staff Training in Mental Handicap.* Croom Helm: London.

Nirje, B. (1976). The normalisation principle. In R. Kugel and A. Shearer (eds.), *Changing Patterns in Residential Services for the Mentally Retarded.* President's Committee on Mental Retardation: Washington.

Nirje, B. (1980). The normalisation principle. In J. F. Flynn and K. E. Nitsch *Normalisation, Social Integration and Community Services*. Proed: Austin, Texas

O'Brien, J. (1987). A guide to lifestyle planning: Using the activities catalog to integrate services and natural support systems. In *A Comprehensive Guide to the Activities Catalog; An Alternative Curriculum for Youth and Adults with Severe Disabilities*. (ed. B. Wilcox and G. T. Bellamy). Brookes: Baltimore.

O'Brien, J. and Lyle-O'Brien, C. (1989a). *Framework for Accomplishment: A Workshop for People Developing Better Services*. Responsive Systems Associates: Lithonia, Georgia.

O'Brien, J. and Lyle-O'Brien, C. (1989b). *Framework for Accomplishment:Human Service Program Design*. Responsive Systems Associates: Lithonia, Georgia.

O'Brien, J. and Tyne, A. (1981). *The Principle of Normalisation a Foundation for Effective Services*. Campaign for Mentally Handicapped People: London.

Oliver, C., Murphy, G. H. and Corbett, J. A. (1987). Self injurious behaviour in people with a mental handicap. *Journal of Mental Deficiency Research* 31, 147-162.

Pahl, J. and Quine, L. (1984). *Families with Mentally Handicapped Children*. HSRU. University of Kent: Canterbury.

Perrin, B and Nirje, B. (1982). Setting the record straight: A critique of some frequent misconceptions of the normalisation principle. *Australia and New Zealand Journal of Developmental Disabilities* 11, 69-74.

Perrin, B. and Nirje, B. (1990). Setting the record straight: A critique of some frequent misconceptions of the normalisation principle. In A. Brechin and J. Walmsley (eds.), *Making Connections: Reflecting on the Lives and Experiences of People with Learning Difficulties*. Hodder and Stoughton: London.

Roos, P. (1972). Reconciling behavior modification procedures with normalisation. In W. Wolfensberger (ed.), *The Principle of Normalisation in Human Services*. National Institute on Mental Retardation: Toronto.

Rusch, F. R. (1990). *Supported Employment: Methods, Models and Issues*. Sycamore Publishing Co: Sycamore IL.

Rusch, R. G., Hall, J. C. and Griffin, H. C. (1986). Abuse provoking characteristics of institutionalised mentally retarded individuals. *American Journal of Mental Deficiency* 90, 618–624.

Saxby, H., Thomas, M., Felce, D. and de Kock, U. (1986). The use of shops, cafes and public houses by severely and profoundly mentally handicapped adults. *The British Journal of Mental Subnormality* 32, 69-81.

Skinner, B. F. (1953). *Science and Human Behavior*. MacMillan: New York.

Szivos, S. (1992). Labelling: A path to stigmatization or to increased understanding and awareness? *Clinical Psychology Forum* 39, 26.

Towel, D. (1987). Foreword. In R. Blunden and D. Allen (eds.), Facing the challenge: *An Ordinary Life for People with Learning Difficulties and Challenging Behaviour*. King's Fund Publishing Office: London.

Welsh Office, (1991) *Challenges and Responses a Report on Services in Support of Adults with Mental Handicaps with Exceptionally Challenging Behaviours, Mental Illnesses or who Offend*. The All Wales Advisory Panel on the Development of Services for people with Mental Handicaps. Cardiff.

Wilcox, B and Bellamy, G. T. (1987). *The Activities Catalog: An Alternative Curriculum for Youth and Adults with Severe Disabilities*. Brookes: Baltimore.

Wilmott, P. (1989). *Community Initiatives: Patterns and Prospects*. Policy Studies Institute: London.

Wolfensberger, W. (1972). *The Principle of Normalisation in Human Services*. National Institute on Mental Retardation: Toronto.

Wolfensberger, W. (1975). *The Origin and Nature of Our Institutional Models*. Human Policy Press: Syracuse.

Wolfensberger, W. (1980a). A brief overview of the principle of normalisation. In J. F. Flynn and K. E. Nitsch (eds.), *Normalisation, Social Integration and Community Services*. Proed: Austin, Texas.

Wolfensberger, W. (1980b). The definition of normalisation: Update, problems, disagreements and misunderstandings. In J. F. Flynn and K. E. Nitsch (eds.), *Normalisation, Social Integration and Community Services*. Proed: Austin, Texas.

Wolfensberger, W. (1980c). Research, empiricism and the principle of normalisation. In J. F. Flynn and K. E. Nitsch (eds.), *Normalisation, Social Integration and Community Services*. Proed: Austin, Texas.

Wolfensberger, W. (1983). Social role valorization: A proposed new term for the principle of normalisation. *Mental Retardation* 21, 234239.

Wolfensberger, W. (1991). *A Brief Introduction to Social Role Valorization as a HighOrder Concept for Structuring Human Services*. Syracuse Universirty: Syracuse.

Wolfensberger, W. (1992). Deinstitutionalization policy: How it is made, by whom and why. *Clinical Psychology Forum* 39, 711.

Wolfensberger, W. and Glenn, L. (1973). *Program Analysis of Service Systems: Vol 1 Handbook*. National Institute on Mental Retardation: Toronto.

Wolfensberger, W. and Glenn, L. (1973). *Program Analysis of Service Systems Vol 2. Field Manual*. National Institute on Mental Retardation: Toronto.

Wolfensberger, W. and Glenn, L. (1975). *Program Analysis of Service Systems*. National Institute on Mental Retardation: Toronto.

Wolfensberger, W. and Thomas, S. (1983). *Program Analysis of Service Systems Implementation of Normalisation Goals*. National Institute on Mental Retardation: Toronto.

Wolfensberger, W. and Tullman, S. (1982). A brief outline of the principle of normalisation. *Rehabilitation Psychology* 27, 131-145.

Woods, P. and Cullen, C. (1983). Determinants of staff behaviour in long term care. *Behavioural Psychotherapy* 11, 417.

Zarkowska, E. and Clements, J. (1988). *Problem Behaviour in People with Severe Learning Difficulties: A Practical Guide to a Constructional Approach*. Croom Helm: London.

CHAPTER 5

A Review of the Aversives Debate: An American Perspective

Peter Sturmey
Abilene State School, Texas
and
Robert W. Rickets and Amanda Goza
Southwest Institute for Developmental Disabilities, Abilene, Texas, USA

Introduction

During the past ten years the field of intellectual disabilities has been witness to an explosive debate regarding the use of restrictive procedures to treat challenging behaviours in persons with intellectual disabilities. This chapter will examine the ideological and empirical aspects of this debate from the standpoint of the American experience. We will begin by outlining the nature and impact of the debate and examining how, for example, the language and terminology used has led to increased confusion and divisiveness. A number of illustrative case studies will be described in order to highlight the extreme ways in which the debate has impacted on the field of intellectual disabilities. Finally, organisational responses are described and future directions are suggested.

The Nature of the Debate

Severe cases of self-injury or aggression frequently result in significant physical damage such that identification of effective treatment interventions is crucial. The propriety and efficacy of various interventions, however, is highly controversial (Guess, Helmstetter, Turnbull, & Knowlton, 1987; Mulick & Kedesdy, 1988). For example, strong objections to the use of aversive procedures in the treatment of self-injurious behaviour (SIB) have been raised, in spite of their effectiveness in reducing these life-threatening behaviours. Their use has consequently become a highly debatable and often inflammatory issue (Repp & Singh, 1990). The use of psychotropic medication (Aman & Singh, 1986) and other restraint procedures

(McDonnell & Sturmey, this volume) has raised similar issues. Currently, these issues are some of the most frequently discussed topics in the United States in the field of intellectual disabilities (Matson & Taras, 1989; National Institutes of Health, 1989). The resultant controversy involves parents, advocates, researchers, clinicians, and lawyers. These groups have become polarized in their views, with one group comprised of individuals who support a judicious and well regulated use of aversive procedures and the other comprised of persons who advocate a complete ban of aversive techniques (Goza, Ricketts & Perkins, in press; Singh, Lloyd & Kendall, 1990).

The debate has occurred on several different levels including scientific, ethical, moral, and legal (Sherman, 1991) and to some extent it is because of this that the debate has become so heated. For example, while many professionals (e.g., psychologists) address the issues from a scientific base, others may be viewing the issues from an ideological stance (Mulick, 1988). As noted by Axelrod (1990), 'such a debate should not exist within a discipline committed to the scientific method; the data speak for themselves. Yet, the debate does exist in books, in newsletters, in journal articles, and at professional conferences. The data may speak for themselves, but this is irrelevant if professionals fail to attend to them'. Of course, it is not simply that some professionals fail to attend to the data, but that there are a host of non-professionals for whom the data are completely irrelevant to the argument.

The result is that no consensus regarding the use of restrictive procedures has been arrived at. Indeed, the issues of great significance to one group (e.g., advocates) may not even be recognized by the other (e.g., professionals). For example, it is not an uncommon experience for the propriety of a behavioural programme to be questioned. A psychologist will immediately bring forth data to support the efficacy of the programme. Unbeknownst to the psychologist however, is that the efficacy of the program is not in question, rather it may be that there is a philosophical opposition to the use of the procedures, and data regarding efficacy are of no significance, even given a life-threatening situation.

The seeds for the current controversy were planted more than 30 years ago concurrent with the emergence of the field of applied behaviour analysis. It was at that time that applied behaviour analysis was viewed as a science which could address large societal problems in addition to specific problems of individuals. Following this early period, constraints on the use of applied behaviour analysis were enacted during an era of heightened emphasis on individual's civil rights in the 1970's. This emphasis on individual and constitutional rights served as the catalyst for the current controversy which is characterized by strong political and legal activity, and moral, ethical, and ideological confusion (Schroeder, Oldenquist, & Rojahn, 1990).

The emotional intensity of the debate has at times been extreme as evidenced by the negative rhetoric which has permeated the issues. Schroeder & Schroeder (1989) report several examples including one where a presenter at a state-wide workshop gave the following definition of punishment. 'Punishment is like trying to teach a cat to 'woof' like a dog. First, you shampoo it, get it all dried off, fluffed up, and perfumed. Then you put it in a trash can, throw in a lighted match, and it goes 'woof'!' Another comment came from an invited speaker during a presentation before a Developmental Disabilities Planning Council where it was stated that 'permitting punishment is like living in Berlin and ignoring a nuclear holocaust.'

Personal attacks on professionals are not unknown either. While speaking at a National conference on the aversives controversy one very highly respected and nationally prominent professional began to cry while relating his own experience with being harassed, and stopped speaking momentarily to regain his composure. Similarly, another well respected professional has ceased working with persons with intellectual disabilities altogether due to the 'punishing nature' of interactions he has had with persons who advocate banning aversive techniques.

However, the negative impact of this kind of behaviour extends well beyond the immediate effects upon the professionals themselves. It has clearly been counterproductive, polarizing the field into 'aversive' and 'positive' camps where professionals are all but forced to align themselves with one of the two dichotomous positions. The result is that professional expertise and integrity are then compromised in the eyes of persons in the opposing camp. This is routinely demonstrated in employment listings advertised in national professional publications which seek individuals who are, for example, 'committed to positive approaches'. Thus, the implication is that anyone who believes that punishment procedures may sometimes be appropriate is automatically disqualified, presumably because their professional skills or ethical/moral standards are somehow less than desirable.

The plethora of issues which permeate the debate are reflected in a recent book (Repp & Singh, 1990). As noted in the introductory chapter of this book, 'What started off as a simple question of whether to use aversive procedures in any therapeutic intervention for serious behaviour problems has grown, by now, into a large set of philosophical, ethical, legal, and empirical questions' (Singh *et al.*, 1990). Some of the questions cited by Singh *et al.* (1990) include the following:

* Do we have good scientific evidence to show that either procedure, aversive or nonaversive, is more effective than the other?
* Are all procedures, aversive or nonaversive, always effective?
* Is it moral to deny an individual with intellectual disabilities access to effective intervention? Does the proscription of aversive procedures restrict the rights of individuals to effective treatment?
* Does a functional analysis of the problem behaviour invariably indicate that the most effective treatment of choice will be nonaversive?
* What do we do when caregivers charged with the treatment of an individual are given unlimited resources and, even using these resources (e.g., bringing in the

best experts on nonaversive intervention), are not successful in altering the individual's life-threatening behaviour?

* Should we advocate a complete ban on the use of any procedure that can be considered to be aversive to an individual? Are these procedures unnatural processes such that we do not use them with persons who are not handicapped?

* Is it possible to have an aversive-free society?

These and many other questions comprise the aversives controversy. Of course, the response to these questions vary widely, and consensus has been reached on none. For example, Donnellan & LaVigna (1990) state that 'positive alternatives are rendering the traditional use of punishment obsolete', and that 'the position that punishment/aversives are necessary . . . is conceptually untenable'. Conversely, it has been noted that even the people who oppose the use of aversive procedures rigorously utilize a wide array of punishers against professionals who disagree with the non-aversive position. 'Perhaps that is the lesson in all of this. Sometimes changing human behavior without invoking punishment practices may be impossible' (Axelrod, 1990).

If nonaversive techniques presently exist to treat such disorders effectively, as has been suggested (LaVigna & Donnellan, 1986), then a ban on aversive procedures might be warranted. Otherwise, promoting a ban of aversive procedures will result in persons with intellectual disabilities not being provided with the services they need (O'Brien, 1989).

Our task is to develop a public policy that is founded upon a positive ideology, while fully utilizing the knowledge base of the behavioural and biological sciences (Mulick & Kedesdy, 1988). Therefore, for resolution to occur, there must be a marriage of values and technology. 'Values without technology often produces unuseful rhetoric. Technology without values can easily lead to inappropriate applications. Procedures should meld high ethical standards with the most advanced behavioral technology available' (Schroeder, Oldenquist, & Rojahn 1990).

Definitional Issues
The terminology and language used in the debate remains ambiguous. For example, to date there has not been an adequate definition of an aversive procedure (Alberto & Andrews, 1991; Starin, 1991). Are all punishment procedures aversive? If so, does this mean that verbal reprimands, for example, should be disallowed? Further, even such presumably 'positive' procedures such as differential reinforcement of other behaviour (DRO) and differential reinforcement of low rates of behaviour (DRL) have been shown to be procedures that are functionally punishment techniques (Rolider & Van Houten, 1990). Yet, DRO and DRL are procedures which are advanced by those opposed to aversives as 'strategies that can be used to effectively eliminate problem behavior without punishment' (Donnellan & LaVigna, 1990).

Further, it would seem that whether or not any particular technique is aversive or punishing is highly idiosyncratic. For example, it has clearly been shown that mechanical restraint may in fact be reinforcing (Favell, McGimsey & Jones, 1978). Similarly, it has been observed that even with such presumably aversive procedures as shock, not all individuals react in such a manner as to indicate that the stimulus is painful or creates discomfort (Ricketts, Goza, & Matese, 1992). Thus, the distinction between aversive and non-aversive is not only blurred, but is also quite fluid, varying both between and within individuals across time and setting.

The selection of the term 'punishment' by Skinner was perhaps an unfortunate one. In everyday language it has connotations of revenge, retribution, criminality and humiliation. Yulevitch & Axelrod (1983) note that the synonyms of 'punishment' in Roget's Thesaurus include 'execution, killing, decapitation, hanging, strangulation, electrocution, stowing, impailment, flaying, burning, massacre, mass murder, purge, genocide, slaughter'. This history of the use of the term 'punishment' can be said to have two distinct roots within psychology: the notion of punishment as an aversive stimulus and the functional definition of punishment (Walters & Grusec, 1977). The notion of punishment as an aversive stimulus essentially relies on the subjective experience of an observer; the observer assumes that the stimulus s/he experiences as aversive is also aversive to others. With non-verbal organisms the experience of aversiveness is difficult to determine. The observer has to rely on observations of escape-avoidance or emotional behaviours. (However, it should be noted that some apparently intensely aversive stimuli may actually inhibit the development of escape behaviours.) The inference that a consequence which reduces a behaviour is experienced as an aversive stimulus is just that - an inference. On the other hand, however, the functional definition of punishment is the approach most closely associated with radical behaviourism. Here a punisher is defined as the consequence of a behaviour which reduces the future probability of that behaviour. No reference to subjective experience is made (Azrin & Holtz, 1966). These two traditions of defining punishment differ in that the former emphasizes the *process* of behaviour change whereas the latter emphasizes the *product* of behaviour change.

Much debate has resulted from the use of different definitions of the terms punishment. Many of the anti-aversive camp emphasize the subjective experience of pain, whereas many of the right to treatment camp emphasize the product of behaviour change.

At first sight the distinction between punishment - and reinforcement-based procedures is readily apparent. Contingent praise and tokens are surely reinforcement procedures? Surely contingent slaps and shouts are punishment procedures? Much of the traditional exposition of these principles has been based upon labelling certain procedures as punishment or reinforcement procedures. However, changes in one behaviour do not occur in isolation: if one behaviour increases somewhere else another behaviour decreases. It thus becomes

103

difficult to classify any procedure simply as a reinforcement or punishment procedure. Yulevitch & Axelrod (1983) have argued strongly that the distinction between reinforcement and punishment has neither conceptual nor empirical foundations.

In some debates it is suggested that punishment is more likely to lead to undesirable side-effects than reinforcement. Punishment can certainly be associated with undesirable side effects including emotional behaviours such as fear, aggression (including imitative aggression), escape avoidance, response substitution, facilitation of the target response, and generalized suppression of behaviour (Newsom, Favell, & Rincover, 1983). However, punishment may also be accompanied by a variety of desirable side effects including prosocial behaviour, positive emotional behaviours such as smiling, laughing and calmness, and increased adaptive responses such as learning, play and attending (Newsom et al., 1983; Ricketts et al., 1992). In a similar vein, although reinforcement procedures are often accompanied by desirable effects they may also be accompanied by negative effects. Balsom & Bondy (1983) identified the following reported negative side effects of reward: elicited responses such as aggression, ritualistic or stereotyped responding, suppression of the target behaviour and excessive approach responses to the reinforcing agent; other desirable behaviours may decrease; generalization may be poor; alternative responses, such as lying and cheating, may be induced by a reinforcer, the effects may be transient; and, inappropriate imitation of reinforcement techniques may develop (Balsom & Bondy, 1985; Cowdry, Iwata & Pace, 1990; Epstein, 1985; Matson & Taras, 1989). Whether reinforcement or punishment procedures produce different patterns of side effects is an empirical question which has not yet been resolved. What is clear is that *both* procedures can produce both positive and negative side-effects in a way which is not yet readily predictable.

Case Studies
At first sight the aversive debate is primarily a technical one. It appears to revolve around pure and academic questions such as treatment efficiency, treatment side effects, and so on. This is simply one facet of the debate. Indeed, some may view the technical aspects of treatment as a small pawn in a larger ideological battle. In this section we illustrate other aspects of the debate on restrictive procedures by a number of case studies.

The case of BRI
The Behavior Research Institute (BRI) was a facility for approximately 60 children and adults aged 13 to 39 from Massachusetts, New York, New Jersey, Delaware, Maryland and Wyoming. Students had intellectual disabilities such as autism and/or mental retardation and extreme behaviour disorders. Its director was Matthew Israel, Ph.D., a behavioural psychologist. Fees in 1986 were approximately $87,000 per

year (*The Providence Journal*, December 2, 1986). Thus, BRI had an annual income of the order of several million dollars in 1986.

In July 1985 Vincent Milletich, a 22 year old student with autism at BRI, died of asphyxiation while receiving an aversive behavioural programme which consisted of a helmet playing loud, white noise (*Taunton Daily Gazette*, December 13, 1986). The subsequent autopsy did not relate the student's death to his treatment. No charges were filed against BRI.

On September 26, 1985 Mary Kay Leonard, Director of the Office for Children (OFC), issued an order prohibiting the use of all aversive treatments, prohibited the admission of any new students and attempted to strip BRI of its license (*Taunton Daily Gazette*, December 13, 1986). Leonard's order stated that '*an emergency situation* exists at the Group Care Facility of BRI and that BRI's *failure to comply* with the applicable statutes and regulations endangers the life, health and safety of children in BRI Group Care Facility'. This was not explicitly related to the recent death at BRI. BRI was also ordered to notify all parents of the imminent closure. Fifteen students were removed from BRI by their funding states. Thus, BRI probably lost 25% of its income precipitously. Staff were laid off and two of its seven homes were closed (*Providence Journal*, December 2, 1986). BRI filed a $15,000,000 lawsuit against the OFC.

On December 18, 1985, BRI and the parents of Janine C. successfully petitioned Judge Rosenberg's court to reinstitute a previous behaviour programme consisting of physical aversives and contingent food. It was found that removal of the programme had been followed by a life threatening deterioration of the child's behaviour. As a result of this, the regression of Janine's behaviour was reversed and she made rapid progress in eliminating her self-abusive behaviour (BRI *et al.* vs. Mary Kay Leonard, June 4, 1986 Findings).

At about this time, December 1985, the Association for Severely Handicapped Persons Boston conference adopted a resolution to find local and respectful alternatives for BRI students.

On January 22, 1986 BRI and five parents petitioned the court for restitution of aversive programming for five more students. Despite the observed regression in the behaviour of all five children, some to a life threatening degree, and despite the improvements observed in Janine C. at this time, OFC opposed this but gave no explanation to the court. The finding document states that 'Not one scintilla of affirmative evidence was offered at these guardianship hearings by OFC, even though the agency was requested by the Court to produce any reasonable available alternative treatments which might be adopted'. Resumption of the aversive programmes was ordered and results similar to those of Janine C. were found.

An appeal to a higher court on the 7th and 8th of February 1986 by OFC was subsequently quashed on March 5, 1986. Back at the lower court on March 7, 1986 all parties were convened by the judge to address emergency treatment for eighteen more students. All parties agreed to enter into a process in which a team of

105

professionals and parents would develop behaviour programmes for these students. Although it had been explicitly agreed that the team could develop behaviour programmes at variance with Leonard's order of September 1986, Leonard issued a further order on April 24, 1986 to restrict the teams options for aversives to 'ignore', 'no', and 'token fines'. Subsequently, four days of extended testimony took place.

On June 4, 1986, Judge Rotenberg issued his findings. These revealed the following: All expert witnesses and parents supported the aversive programming at BRI, which was effective. Matthew Israel was supported as an appropriate person to direct BRI. Leonard's order in September 1985 had caused a major regression for many of the children and increased staff injuries; restitution of the aversive programmes benefited the children. The OFC had acted improperly in several ways. First, prior to relicensing BRI in September 1985 the OFC had commissioned a report to evaluate BRI from expert consultants which was highly favorable to BRI. Yet, twenty-six days after receiving this report OFC ordered termination of BRI's aversive programmes. When this report was presented to the court it had been tampered with. The word 'DRAFT' had been stamped on every page one day after BRI and the parents had requested the document from OFC under the Massachusetts freedom of information legislation. No other report existed. Second, the court found that Mary Leonard was not qualified to make treatment decisions - she was in fact an attorney and that after she had issued her order of September 1985 she panicked. She subsequently set up a panel to evaluate BRI, claiming the panel to be objective. The children's parents objected to the panel and blocked access to the children's records. The court found that the panel did not even interview the students. The judge ordered restitution of all of BRI's programming to protect the children (BRI et al. vs. Leonard, June 4, 1986 Findings). On November 6, 1986 Rotenberg awarded $580,704 in legal fees to BRI and its parents against OFC and Leonard personally. This was the second highest attorneys fee judgement in Massachusetts at that time (*The Sun Chronicle,* November 7, 1986). BRI and the parents did not get the $15,000,000 it filed for in damages.

In 1990 a bill, *An Act to Protect Disabled Persons,* was presented to the Commonwealth of Massachusetts, a state where many BRI clients lived, to ban any procedure designed to cause pain, such as hitting, pinching or electric shock. This 1990 Act was defeated. Another bill has been presented in 1992.

As a footnote to this incident, it is worth noting that this account of the BRI case is based only upon documents currently in the public domain. The situation was probably more complex and subtle than portrayed here. The role of different personalities, and the efforts of lobbyists behind the scene are not clearly documented even though these are probably key elements in this story.

Skinner misrepresented

In September 1987, B. F. Skinner was interviewed on videotape by Dr. Marcia Smith, a psychologist for Community Services for Autistic Adults and Children

106

(CSAAC), concerning his views on punishment. The videotape of this interview was shown at the CSAAC conference. Skinner subsequently published a statement in the *APA Monitor* stating that his interview had been edited '. . . to make it appear he was opposed to the use of all aversives.' Skinner wrote that the tape, which was being sold, 'omits certain significant statements. . . . The tape also gives the impression that I oppose the use of punishment under all circumstances. That is not my view.' He asked that the tape no longer be sold (*IARET Newsletter*, Fall, 1988, pp. 3-4).

Subsequently, Skinner published a statement. In it he wrote: 'I am frequently said to be opposed to all forms of punishment, and I should like to make the following correction. Punishment is usually to the advantage of the punisher, but there are exceptions, and they can sometimes be justified. Some autistic children, for example, will seriously injure themselves or engage in other excessive behavior unless changed or restrained. . . . If brief and harmless aversive stimuli, made precisely contingent on self-destructive or other excessive behavior, suppresses the behavior and makes the children free to develop in other ways, I believe it can be justified. . . . To remain satisfied with punishment without exploring nonpunitive alternatives is the real mistake.' (*IARET Newsletter*, Fall 1988, p. 4 - a full account can be found in Griffin, Paisey, Stark & Emerson, 1988).

There is one final addendum to Skinner's position on aversives. On March 8, 1989 Skinner wrote a lobby letter to oppose proposed legislation put before the legislature of the Commonwealth of Massachusetts to make the use of aversives illegal in Massachusetts.

Misquotation in secondary sources
A common criticism directed at professionals who support the non-aversive position is that they have taken quotations from scientific articles out of context in order to give the impression of empirical support for their position. Goza *et al.*, (in press) addressed this issue by assessing the social validity of references made to scientific articles in support of the 'depersonalization hypothesis', namely, that aversives tend to depersonalize individuals receiving these treatments. The study focused on references made to journal articles in a monograph by Guess *et al.*, (1987). Three groups were surveyed in this study: (a) psychologists working with individuals with intellectual disabilities (Group I, $n = 53$); (b) selected professionals with expertise in the area of self-injurious behaviour and in the use of behaviour modification techniques with individuals with intellectual disabilities (Group II, $n = 7$); and, (c) three of the six primary authors of the journal articles that were selected for the present study (Group III).

Results indicate that the authors of the monograph were not completely accurate in their references to the six articles. Sixty percent of the respondents from Group I, 71% of Group II respondents, and two of the three respondents from Group III rated the citations made in the monograph as inaccurate. In addition, over half of Group I

107

respondents and all respondents from Groups II and III rated the articles as non-supportive of the depersonalization hypothesis for which they were cited. These findings suggest that in at least some instances, the authors of the monograph had used references selectively and incorrectly in support of their views. This study emphasizes the importance of critical reading of secondary sources which argue strongly in favor of one position. Further, this study indicates the need for operationally defined hypotheses which may be examined empirically.

The misleading use of language
A major part of the aversive debate relates to language and the different emphases placed by different camps within the aversive debate. A mild form of this problem is illustrated by the use of language to misrepresent behavioural procedures incorporated within procedures which are presented as non-aversive procedures. Thompson (1990) notes how removing a food tray becomes 'meal interruption' rather than time out and how aversive components of gentle teaching are named 'protecting' rather than response interruption (see Jones & McCaughey, this volume).

Sometimes, other than the use of language, it is difficult to see the distinction between programmes labelled 'non-aversive' and those which use aversive procedures. For example, Israel (*letter dated 4-03-89*) notes that, in some of the residential facilities developed as alternatives to BRI, procedures such as response blocking, restraining a student and physically redirecting a student, which could be done quite forcefully, are neither admitted or recorded, since blocking and redirection are 'non-aversive'. In another 'non-aversive' programme, Israel notes that the following procedures were used: two to four person takedown, locked room seclusion or 'time-out', and water squirt.

Misrepresentation of data
The credibility of the non-aversive position has been seriously undermined by what appears to be examples of either fraud or serious misrepresentation of the actual data within academic articles. Berkman & Meyer (1988) reported treatment of self-abuse and vomiting in a 45 year old man by 'going all out non-aversively'. In this paper Berkman & Meyer state that efforts to control this individual's self-injurious behaviour 'included a daily dosage of 1200 mg of Thorazine throughout the time period reported here' (1988, p. 78). In 1990 unpublished data were obtained from Dr. Meyer during her cross-examination as an expert witness in Michigan. The data showed: (l) the daily dose of Thorazine varied from 0 to 1600 mg. daily; (2) data had been suppressed during a drug holiday; and (3) the implementation of the 'all out non-aversive' program was closely correlated with medication dosage. Thus, the outcomes could simply relate to the sedating properties of Thorazine (Israel, *letter dated* 5-01-91). To date the *Journal for Persons with Severe Handicaps* has not yet printed any retraction or comment.

Perhaps the most curious and paradoxical incident comes from the following report of the behaviour of Dr. John McGee, advocate for non-aversive, gentle teaching (Linscheid, Meinhold & Mulick, 1990). They state:

'We recently reviewed a videotape (CTN, 1989) of Dr. McGee conducting a gentle teaching session in which he clearly and apparently purposefully stuck his finger into the client's eye. Not surprisingly, immediately after the act the client became more compliant' (see Jones & McCaughey, this volume).

The Coldwater Studies

Controversy relating to restrictive procedures has not only been related to the use of behavioural procedures. Sentiments against drugs, especially those prescribed for challenging behaviours, has been strong. Court cases in the United States have found that the abuse of medication may occur when it is used without alternative or adjunctive treatments, when medication is used for the convenience of staff and when global sedation is used in place of active programming. Serious side-effects, such as tardive dyskinesia, may result from chronic neuroleptic therapy, and other side-effects, such as sedation, may interfere with learning and adaptive behaviour. This general anti-drug sentiment has lead to rigorous monitoring and auditing of psychotropic medication in the United States (see above). This has probably reduced the prevalence of psychotropic medication substantially in residential facilities in the United States from between 50% to 65% in the 1970's to about 20% to 30% in the early 1990's. In contrast the prevalencce of psychotropic medication in Great Britain continues to remain much higher (Clarke, Kelly, Thinn & Corbett, 1990) as it is unchecked by legal constraints or external monitoring.

Aman & Singh (1986) reviewed seven studies by Breuning and his colleagues in the early and mid 1980's. These studies, five of which were apparently well controlled, showed that antipsychotic drugs interfered with learning and adaptive behaviour in persons with intellectual disabilities. Aman & Singh (1986) criticize these studies as being limited in their generality since they selected subjects who were not responsive to medication, used very high doses of medication typical of their use as antipsychotics, and because these studies appeared to be set up to deny the use of medication in any circumstances. Aman & Singh contrast the rather clear results of the Coldwater studies with others in the literature which show a far more varied relationship between psychotropic medication and adaptive behaviour. Subsequently, the National Institute of Mental Health (NIMH) investigated Breuning's work in the Coldwater studies. They unanimously found that he knowingly, wilfully and repeatedly engaged in fraudulant practices and concluded that the research had not been carried out and that he added authors' names to papers. Breuning strongly disagreed with the findings of the NIMH panel (Matson, 1988).

Organisational Responses

Human Rights Committees

As can be seen from the above case studies, the recent debate on restrictive procedures has given greatest attention to behavioural procedures although other intrusive procedures such as mechanical restraint and psychoactive medication have also received attention. Following the *Wyatt v. Stickney* case in 1972, human rights committees were set up in many institutional settings in the United States (Spreat & Lanzi, 1989). Recently these committees have also dealt with intrusive procedures and human rights issues in community services as well as in institutional settings (Nord, Wieseler & Hanson, 1991).

Spreat & Lanzi (1989) surveyed 284 public residential facilities as to the composition and function of their human rights committees. The return rate was 77%. Almost 98% had a human rights committee. Most members were facility staff (39%), parents (14%), outside professionals (12%), and advocates (10%). The common issues monitored were safety (89%), appropriate consent (79%), continuing review (78%), and clinical appropriateness (65%). Many restrictive/aversive procedures *required* the consent of a human rights committee. Nord *et al.* (1991) compared the rates and types of restrictive procedures in both public residential facilities and licensed community-based services in Minnesota. They found that submissions to human rights committees were made for 11% of persons in public residential facilities and 6% of persons in community services.

Human rights committees are commonly concerned with many restrictive procedures, other than behavioural treatments. Consent for psychotropic medication and personal and mechanical restraints is commonly considered especially with regard to client safety, and access to the least restrictive treatment. These concerns and oversight have probably been responsible for a massive reduction in the use of psychotropic medication in the United States.

Position Statements

Many professional and advocacy organizations have now promulgated position statements delineating their stance on the use of aversive or restrictive procedures. Some of these organizations include the Association for Behavior Analysis: International (ABA), the American Association on Mental Retardation (AAMR), and The Association for Persons with Severe Handicaps (TASH). A summary of the issues addressed by the position statements is contained in Table 1.

As noted in this table, there is considerable variation in the areas addressed. It is clear that each organization is concerned with ensuring the protection of client rights and freedom from harm. However, TASH is the only one which clearly calls for the cessation of procedures utilizing aversive stimuli, which are not defined, and for a cessation to the use of chemical restraint. The AAMR statement calls for the elimination of 'inhumane aversive procedures'. It is unclear whether this means that all aversive procedures are inhumane and should therefore be eliminated, or that only some aversive procedures are inhumane and that only this segment of aversives should be eliminated. It would seem to be the latter, but the statement is poorly articulated.

Standard	ABA	Organisation AAMR	TASH
Ensure Protection of client rights/Protection from harm	Yes	Yes	Yes
Ensures procedures are free from chemical restraint			Yes
Ensures procedures are free from aversive stimuli			Yes
Provision of therapeutic environment	Yes		
Client participation in program development	Yes		
Peer review	Yes		
Human Rights Committee review	Yes		
Treatment by a competent professional	Yes		
Ensure program teaches functional behaviours	Yes		
Ensures ongoing behavioural assessment	Yes		
Promotes research		Yes	
Promotes integration of client into community settings		Yes	Yes

Table 1

In general, the major difference between the statements seems to be one of how the issue is approached. AAMR and TASH both take what is primarily a philosophical approach, simply stating that inhumane or unethical procedures should not be utilized. However, a definition of these procedures is not forthcoming.

111

Conversly, ABA is unique in that its position statement attempts to operationalize the process by which individuals can be ensured of receiving effective treatment while protecting them from harm. Notably, ABA is the only organization which specifically states that intervention procedures should be designed by competent professionals, and undergo human rights committee and peer review. Further, they emphasize the need to conduct adequate behavioural assessments throughout programme development and implementation. The statement by ABA would seem to place the burden of choice upon local peer review and human rights committees, while requiring that certain minimal professional standards be maintained.

Guidelines for the use of restrictive procedures
The assurance of safe, effective treatment is a goal common to all human service agencies (Christian, Luce, & Larsson, 1992) and is a particularly important issue in facilities serving persons with intellectual disabilities. The client's right to effective treatment must be carefully weighed against his or her right to the most appropriate, least intrusive intervention (Feldman, 1991). Facilities in which clients with intellectual disabilities exhibit maladaptive behaviours normally develop written guidelines to govern the management of these inappropriate behaviours in order to ensure that the clients' rights are protected. Important issues addressed in these policies include record keeping, data collection, consent issues, staff training and qualifications, protection of clients' rights, and programme review, implementation, and monitoring. In addition, they specifically address the use of intrusive procedures including time-out rooms, physical restraints, psychoactive medications, and the application of painful or noxious stimuli (Nord et al., 1991; Spreat & Lanzi, 1989). The following examination of the content of each of these policies is based on United States federal regulations set forth by the Health Care Financing Administration to govern the use of behavioural and restrictive procedures in facilities serving individuals with intellectual disabilities (Federal Register, 1988).

Record keeping and data collection
The purpose of a record keeping system is to provide documentation of the client's health care, active treatment, social information, and protection of the client's rights. For behavioural objectives, data documented in measurable terms to show progress, regression, or no change is essential information which offers staff guidance for programme implementation, change, or deletion. While there is no one 'right' frequency for reporting progress, there should be a schedule for each person based on his or her active treatment programme and which provides staff with sufficient progress information to make informed treatment decisions.

Consent
Policies should mandate that the facility seek consent from the individual and inform the individual of his or her right to refuse treatment before initiating any

112

intrusive procedure. Informed consent implies that the individual giving consent is competent to evaluate the risks, benefits, and alternatives of the treatment. For individuals who are minors or who are legally incompetent to make informed decisions concerning treatment but have no appointed legal guardian, informed consent may be obtained from the legal guardian, parent, or someone or some agency appointed in accordance with the law to act as a representative of the individual's interests.

Staff training and qualifications
The facility's policies should specify the staff members who may authorize the use of specified interventions, and a means of monitoring and controlling the use of interventions. They should specify the training required for employees who work with clients and the skills and techniques staff must be able to demonstrate to administer interventions to manage the inappropriate behaviour of clients.

Rights protection
Policies should be developed to ensure that clients are not subjected to physical, verbal, sexual, or psychological abuse or punishment. A definition of 'punishment' is not provided. However, it is probable that these regulations did not intend to restrict the use of aversive stimuli *per se* but rather intended to restrict the use of physical force, pain and verbal abuse as retribution by staff. They should further confirm that clients should be free from unnecessary drugs, physical restraints, and other restrictive or intrusive procedures and are provided active treatment to reduce dependency on these procedures.

Individual programme plan
The use of systematic interventions to manage inappropriate client behaviour should be incorporated into a programme plan specific to that individual. In general, the behaviour therapy programme should specify the following: (1) the behaviour therapy techniques to be used, (2) the schedule for use of the techniques, (3) the person(s) responsible for the programme, (4) the type of data and frequency of data collection necessary to be able to evaluate progress toward the desired objectives, (5) the inappropriate behaviour(s) targeted by the programme, and (6) provisions for the appropriate expression of behaviour and the replacement of inappropriate behaviour with behaviour that is adaptive or appropriate (Federal Register, 1988, Part 484.440, p 20499).

Intrusive procedures
In addition to the policies mentioned above, specific conditions are placed on the use of intrusive procedures such as time-out, restraint, application of noxious stimuli, and use of psychoactive medication. These requirements should be designed

to ensure that a client's rights and safety are not compromised when receiving intrusive behavioural or medical treatment.

Time out rooms
Time-out room guidelines should specifically address the conditions under which the procedure may be used, the amount of supervision required while the procedure is in effect, how the room should be secured, the maximum length of time the procedure may be used, protection of client's safety while in the time-out room, and record keeping required. According to United States federal regulations, time-out room procedures may only be used if: (1) the placement is a part of an approved systematic programme (emergency placement is not allowed), (2) the client is under the direct constant visual supervision of designated staff while in the time-out room, and (3) the door to the room must be shut manually or by a mechanism requiring constant physical pressure from a staff member to keep the mechanism engaged and which will allow immediate entry when disengaged. Clients placed in time-out rooms must be protected from hazardous conditions such as sharp corners and objects, uncovered light fixtures, and unprotected electrical outlets. Placement of a client in a time-out room must not exceed one hour, and a record of time-out activities must be kept (Federal Register, 1988, Part 483.450, p. 20500).

Physical restraint
Similarly, The facility's guidelines should address the conditions under which restraint may be employed and for what length of time, authorization required to initiate restraint, client safety and comfort while in restraint, and record keeping required. Federal regulations mandate that a facility may employ physical restraints only: (1) as an integral part of an individual programme plan that is intended to lead to less restrictive means of managing and eliminating the target behaviour, (2) as an emergency measure if absolutely necessary to protect the client or others from injury; or (3) as a health-related protection prescribed by a physicain if absolutely necessary during a specific medical or surgical procedure, or if absolutely necessary for client protection during the time that a medical condition exists.

Authorisations to use or extend restraints as an emergency measure must be in effect no longer than 12 consecutive hours and obtained as soon as the client is restrained or stable. The facility must not issue orders for restraint on a standing or 'as needed' basis. A client placed in restraint must be checked at least every 30 minutes by staff trained in the use of restraints and released from the restraint as quickly as possible. Restraints should cause the least discomfort possible and should not cause physical injury to the client. Opportunities for motion and exercise must be provided for a period of not less than 10 minutes during each two-hour period in which restraint is employed, and the individual should be allowed bathroom privileges at least once every two hours. In addition, the individual should receive all regularly prescribed medications, meals, and fluids while in

114

restraint. A record of all restraint activity must be kept (Federal Register, 1988, Part 483.450, p 20501).

Psychoactive Medication
Professional standards require that drugs used for control of inappropriate behaviour be used only as an integral part of the client's individual programme plan designed to lead to the reduction and eventual elimination of the behaviours targeted with the medication. Approval by the client's interdisciplinary team should be sought, and the team should determine that the harmful effects of the behaviour clearly outweigh the potentially harmful effects of the drug before drug therapy is initiated. Psychoactive medications should be monitored closely and routinely as dictated by a predetermined schedule for effectiveness and adverse side effects. Withdrawal from the drug should be attempted periodically (at least annually, for example) unless clinical evidence indicates that to do so would be countertherapeutic.

Painful and noxious stimuli
Virtually all professionals agree that the application of painful or noxious stimuli should be reserved for use as a last resort, when documentation shows that consistently implemented positive reinforcement methods have failed and that to withhold the procedure would be detrimental to the health of the individual or others (Iwata, 1988; Feldman, 1991). In order to assure that the procedures do not result in physical or mental harm to the health and safety of the client, programmes involving painful or noxious stimuli should be continuously monitored for effectiveness and side-effects by professional staff.

Monitoring
The facility's policies should specify a timetable (at least annually, for example) by which the individual programme plan must be reviewed and revised, as appropriate. In order to adequately review behaviour therapy programmes, the facility should designate and use a specially constituted committee or committees to assure that treatments are consistent with professional and societal standards of care (Christian *et al.*, 1992). These committees should consist of members of facility staff, parents, legal guardians, clients (as appropriate), qualified persons who have either experience or training in current behaviour modification techniques and/or psychoactive medication, and persons not affiliated with the facility. The functions of the committee(s) are: (1) to review, approve, and monitor individual behaviour therapy programmes and any other programmes that involve risks to client protection and rights, (2) to ensure that the written informed consent of the client, parents, or legal guardian is obtained prior to implementation of these programmes, and (3) to review, monitor, and make recommendations about the facility's practices and programmes as they relate to control of

inappropriate behaviour (particularly through intrusive means), protection of client rights and property, and any other areas that the committee believes need to be addressed.

Christian *et al.,* (1992) identify two types of committees which are designed to ensure the rights of clients receiving behavioural treatments. The first of these, the peer review committee, is designed to assess if professional standards of care are being met for the individual receiving treatment and the behaviour being treated. It is therefore essential that each member of a peer review committee be familiar with the professional standard of care for the behaviour(s) being reviewed. HRC's, on the other hand, are designed to assess the societal standard of care, as mandated by the laws and regulations governing the facility, and therefore should include a broad range of interest groups including lawyers, physicians, clergy, client guardians, psychologist, and educators. 'In short, the HRC is concerned with the legal safety of service programming - namely, *how clients can receive effective treatment without infringing on their consitutional right to be free from unnecessarily restrictive treatment'* (p.357).

Elements of a formal behaviour therapy plan
In order to ensure that the client is receiving the least intrusive appropriate intervention when behaviour therapy is prescribed, a heirarchy of acceptable interventions should be determined which ranges from least to most restrictive or intrusive. This categorization should be based on both the level of expertise required to properly conduct the procedure and the cost to the individual incurred by its implementation. The system should require that less intrusive procedures be considered and/or tried and found to be inappropriate or ineffective before a more restrictive procedure is implemented.

When selecting a behavioural intervention, the professional in charge should consider the following factors: (1) the severity of the behaviour to be reduced, (2) the degree of expertise of the staff or consultants available, (3) the cost to the individual, (4) the resources required to implement the procedure successfully, (5) the individual's behaviour treatment history, and (6) the operant, environmental, and physiological variables which may be associated with occurrence or non-occurrence of the maladaptive behaviour (i.e., a functional analysis).

Highly intrusive procedures such as locked room time-out, restraint, presentation of painful or noxious stimuli, and the use of psychoactive medication require review by human rights and behaviour therapy committees. Use of such procedures should be integrated into an individual programme plan designed to gradually decrease dependency on the procedure to control the maladaptive behaviour. Objectives for progression of the programme should be included in the programme plan in precise behavioural terms which specify the behaviour targeted by the intervention, the criterion for progression, the target date for progression, and the procedure or medication to be used.

When submitted for approval from a behaviour therapy or human rights committee, programmes should be accompanied by written proof of informed consent from the individual or the appropriate party. In addition, the programme should include information relevant to the development of the programme such as data indicating past effectiveness of behavioural interventions and results of evaluations seeking the motivation of the target behaviour.

Federal Inspections of Care

Federal inspections of care (IOC's) are conducted annually by the state's Department of Health, and are followed by a post-audit visit to determine if noted deficiencies have been corrected. An IOC may also be conducted to respond to specific complaints of abuse, neglect, etc. In addition, the Department of Health may conduct impromptu IOC's with no forewarning. In these instances, the IOC team may go directly to the living areas, present identification, and conduct a review. It is anticipated that this type of unscheduled audit will become more common in response to the suspicion that facilities are preparing for scheduled IOC's. The IOC review team includes at least one registered nurse and other appropriate health and social-services personnel. At least one team member must be a Qualified Mental Retardation Professional. A physician must be available to the team for consultation.

In order to conduct a review at a facility, the IOC team first selects a representative sample of individuals from that facility's population, and each team member is assigned to a particular group of individuals. The auditor begins by reviewing the record of each individual to determine if the individual's programme plan is being carried out. He or she then conducts a direct observation of the individual to determine if what staff know and do with the individual is consistent with what the individual's programme plan directs. Following direct observation the auditor conducts interviews with staff to obtain any further information necessary to make compliance decisions. The auditor also observes the preparation and administration of medications in order to detect errors. Finally, all areas of the facility serving individuals, including those not represented by individuals in the sample, are visited to determine if all areas are providing services in the manner required by federal regulations, meeting physical environment requirements, and proactively asserting and protecting individual rights. Following this on-site review the team meets to determine if the facility is in compliance with federal regulations, and a list of deficiencies are made and presented to the facility. The facility is generally required to make corrections within a specified length of time. Depending upon the severity and extent of the deficiencies noted the facility may lose its federal funding, causing the state to fund the facility, until corrections are satisfactorily made.

Thus, it can be seen that detailed guidelines have been drawn up and acted upon which in theory provide protection for clients. It is perhaps better to acknowledge

117

the potential use of aversive procedures and have mechanisms to control and limit their use, than to risk their covert use which may occur if they are banned.

Concluding Remarks
The wide range of intrusive and aversive procedures which are used with people with intellectual disabilities have raised numerous concerns. Increasing public concern has led to closer public scrutiny within the United States. This has led to a massive bureaucracy of local, state and federal regulation with accompanying commitment of resources both to protect the rights of persons with intellectual disabilities and to ensure effective treatments. This can be seen in numerous differences between the services in the United States and Great Britain. In the United States this regulation has lead to a massive reduction in psychotropic medication, fully documented use of behaviour therapy programmes and clearly scheduled active treatment rarely found in Great Britain.

Increasing public concern is not without many costs. Many services in the USA are driven by the fear of litigation or loss of funding. A substantial part of the mass of paperwork is unnecessary other than for the purpose of meeting standards required by monitoring. A broader cost has been the intense politicisation of treatment decisions: To use extreme treatment programmes may require court approval.

Doubtless, the debate on intrusive procedures is with us for many years to come. Many of the issues discussed here will reemerge within different contexts. The future may see research into more vigorous pursuit of procedures apparently based on reinforcement, which are of greater acceptability as well as efficacy. A second area of importance may be the application of staff management procedures to reduce the dependence upon restrictive procedures and foster the use of effective, more acceptable alternatives (Myers, Richards, & Huff, 1991).

References
Alberto, P., and Andrews, D. (1991). Are moral considerations sufficient for selecting nonaversive interventions?: A review of Repp and Singh's *Perspectives on the use of nonaversive and aversive interventions for persons with developmental disabilities.* The Behavior Analyst, 14, 219-224.

Aman, M. G., and Singh, N. N. (1986). A critical appraisal of recent drug research in mental retardation: The Coldwater studies. *Journal of Mental Deficiency Research,* 30, 203-216.

Axelrod, S. (1990). Myths that (mis)guide our profession. In A.C. Repp and N.N. Singh (Eds.), *Perspectives on the use of nonaversive and aversive interventions for persons with developmental disabilities* (pp. 59-72). Sycamore, Illinois: Sycamore.

Azrin, N. H. and Holtz, W. C. (1966). Punishment. In: W. K. Honig. (Ed.) *Operant behavior: Areas of research and application.* New York: Appleton-Century-Crofts.

Balsom, P. D., and Bondy, A. S. (1983). The negative side-effects of reward. *Journal of Applied Behavior Analysis,* 16, 283-296.

Balsom, P. D., and Bondy, A. S. (1985). Reward induced response covariation: Side effects revisited. *Journal of Applied Behavior Analysis,* 18, 79-80.

Berkman, K. and Meyer, L. (1988). Alternative strategies and multiple outcomes in the remediation of severe self-injury: Going 'allout' nonaversively. *Journal of the Association for the Severely Handicapped*, 13, 76-86.

Christian, W. P., Luce, S. C., and Larsson, E. V. (1992). Peer review and human rights committees. In J. K. Luiselli, J. L. Matson, and N. N. Singh (Eds.), *Self-injurious behavior: Analysis, assessment, and treatment* (pp. 352-366). New York: Springer-Verlag New York, Inc.

Clarke, D. J., Kelley, S., Thinn, K. & Corbett, J. A. (1990). Psychotropic drugs and mental retardation: 1. Disabilities and the prescription of drugs for behaviour and for epilepsy in three residential settings. *Journal of Mental Deficiency Research*, 34, 385–395.

Cowdery, G. E., Iwata, B. A., and Pace, G. A. (1990). Effects and side effects of DRO as a treatment for self-injurious behavior. *Journal of Applied Behavior Analysis*, 23, 497-506.

Donnellan, A. M., and LaVigna, G. W. (1990). Myths about punishment. In A.C. Repp and N.N. Singh (Eds.), *Perspectives on the use of nonaversive and aversive interventions for persons with developmental disabilities* (pp. 33-57). Sycamore, Illinois: Sycamore.

Epstein, R. (1985). The positive side effects of reinforcement: A commentary on Balsom and Bondy (1983). *Journal of Applied Behavior Analysis*, 18, 73-77.

Favell, J. E., McGimsey, J. F., and Jones, M. L. (1978). The use of physical restraint in the treatment of self-injury and as positive reinforcement. *Journal of Applied Behavior Analysis*, 11, 225-242.

Federal Register (1988). *Department of Health and Human Services: Health Care Finances Administration* (42 CFR).

Feldman, M. A. (1991). Balancing freedom from harm and right to treatment for persons with developmental disabilities. In A. Repp and N. Singh (Eds.), *Perspectives on the use of nonaversive and aversive interventions for persons with developmental disabilities* (pp. 261-271). Sycamore, Illinois: Sycamore Publishing Company.

Goza, A. B., Ricketts, R. W., and Perkins, T. S. (in press). The social validity of an argument supporting a ban on aversive procedures. *Journal of Intellectual Disability Research*.

Griffin, J. C., Paisey, T. J., Stark, M. T. and Emerson, J. H. (1988). B. F. Skinner's position on aversive treatment. *American Journal of Mental Deficiency*, 93, 104-105.

Guess, D., Helmstetter, E., Turnbull, H. R., and Knowlton, S. (1987). *Use of aversive procedures with persons who are disabled: An historical review and critical analysis.* Seattle, Washington: The Association for Persons with Severe Handicaps.

Iwata, B. A. (1988). The development and adoption of controversial default technologies. *The Behavior Analyst*, 11, 149-157.

Linscheid, T. R., Meinhold, P. M., and Mulick, J. A. (1990). Gentle teaching? *The Behavior Therapist*, 13, 32.

Matson, J. L. (1988). Editorial: A retraction. *Research in Developmental Disabilities*, 9, 1-2.

Matson, J. L., and Taras, M. (1989). A 20 year review of punishment and alternative methods to treat problem behaviors in developmentally delayed persons. *Research in Developmental Disabilities*, 10, 85-104.

Mulick, J.A. (1988). *Aversives in behavior therapy: When science and public policy clash.* Paper presented at the 112th meeting of the American Association on Mental Retardation, Washington, D.C.

Mulick, J. A., and Kedesdy, J. H. (1988). Self-injurious behavior, its treatment, and normalization. *Mental Retardation*, 26, 223-229.

Myers, A, M., Richards, T., and Huff, J. (1991). Program report: 'Time-in': A two year project for the reduction of severe maladaptive behaviors in a center for persons with developmental disabilities. *Behavioral Residential Treatment*, 6, 119-144.

National Institutes of Health Consensus Development Conference Statement (1989). *Treatment of destructive behaviors in persons with developmental disabilities*, 7, Bethesda, MD: NICHD.

Newsom, C., Favell, J. E., and Rincover, A. (1983). Side effects of punishment. In: S. Axelrod and J. Apsche (Eds.) *The effects of punishment on human behavior.* New York: Academic. (pp 285- 315).

Nord, G., Wieseler, N. A., and Hanson, R. H. (1991). Aversive procedures: The Minnesota experience. *Behavioral Residential Treatment*, 6, 197-205.

O'Brien, F. (1989). Punishment for people with developmental disabilities. In E. Cipani (Ed.), *The Treatment of Severe Behavior Disorders* (pp. 37-58). Washington, D.C.: American Association on Mental Retardation.

119

Repp, A. C., and Singh, N. N. (1990). *Perspectives on the use of nonaversive and aversive interventions for persons with developmental disabilities.* Sycamore, Illinois: Sycamore Publishing Company.

Ricketts, R. W., Goza, A. B., and Matese, M. (1992). Case study: Effects of naltrexone and SIBIS on self-injury. *Behavioural Residential Treatment, 7,* 315–326.

Rolider, A., and Van Houton, R. (1990). The role of reinforcement in reducing inappropriate behavior: Some myths and misconceptions. In A. C. Repp and N. N. Singh (Eds.), *Perspectives on the use of nonaversive and aversive interventions for persons with developmental disabilities* (pp. 119-127). Sycamore, Illinois: Sycamore Publishing Company.

Schroeder, S. R., Oldenquist, A., and Rojahn, J. (1990). A conceptual framework for judging the humaneness and effectiveness of behavioral treatment. In A.C. Repp and N.N. Singh (Eds.), *Perspectives on the use of nonaversive and aversive interventions for persons with developmental disabilities* (pp. 103-118). Sycamore, Illinois: Sycamore Publishing Company.

Schroeder, S. R., and Schroeder, C. S. (1989). Guest editorial: The role of the AAMR in the aversives controversy. *Mental Retardation, 27,* iii-v.

Sherman, R. A. (1991). Aversives, fundamental rights, and the courts. *The Behavior Analyst, 14,* 197-206.

Singh, N. N., Lloyd, J. W., and Kendall, K. A. (1990). Nonaversive and aversive interventions: Introduction. In A.C. Repp and N.N. Singh (Eds.), *Perspectives on the use of nonaversive and aversive interventions for persons with developmental disabilities* (pp. 3-16). Sycamore, Illinois: Sycamore Publishing Company.

Spreat, S., and Lanzi, F. (1989). Role of human rights committees in the review of restrictive/aversive behavior modification procedures: A national survey. *Mental Retardation, 27,* 375-382.

Starin, S. (1991). 'Nonaversive' behavior managment: A misnomer. *The Behavior Analyst, 14,* 207-209.

Thompson, T. (1990). The Humpty Dumpty world of 'aversive' interventions. *Journal of the Association for Persons with Severe Handicaps, 15,* 136-139.

Walters, G. C., and Grusec, J. E. (1977). Punishment. San Francisco: Freeman.

Yulevitch, L. and Axelrod, S. (1983). Punishment: A concept that is no longer necessary. In: M. Hersen, R. M. Eisler, and P. M.Miller (Eds.) *Progress in Behavior Modification,* Volume 14.

Wyatt v Stickney, 344 F. Suppl. 387 (M.D. Ala. 1972).

CHAPTER 6

Ordinary Housing: A Necessary Context for Meeting Service Philosophy and Providing an Effective Therapeutic Environment

David Felce
Mental Handicap in Wales: Applied Research Unit

Introduction

Policies on the provision of residential services to people with severe intellectual disability generally have become increasingly firm in their embrace of an ordinary life model (King's Fund, 1980). Living in ordinary housing, locally within the communities where individuals have their ties and associations, is accepted as a critical condition for promoting integration, development of skills and experiences, keeping a broad range of opportunities available and sustaining people's social networks. As will be elucidated in greater detail later, such outcomes are now seen as central to the judgement of whether a service can be regarded as effective. One which separates users from the outside world, does nothing to widen experience or improve skills, narrows or takes away opportunities for everyday activity and inhibits social relationships can surely only be seen as of poor quality, far removed from any claim to being effective. Yet, despite widespread demonstration that such deficiencies are the norm in long-stay hospital services, the traditional solution of specialist institutional care for people with challenging behaviour is still put forward as an option. The onus still rests on proving the feasibility of community alternatives. The field has seemingly failed to realise that an effective service can only be provided to people with severe learning difficulties and challenging behaviour, as to others, through an ordinary housing, community-based model. This chapter addresses why the ordinary housing model has positive advantages for providing an effective service. It also analyses what is required to make such services work; the specialism that is a necessary ingredient for success.

121

The main question posed in relation to community services has been whether they can cope with people with severe intellectual disability and severely challenging behaviour. Would it prove feasible to accommodate such people in ordinary housing in close proximity to the general public? While ordinary housing is part of the required service design, a simple ordinary housing model is, in itself, not a sufficient condition for a high quality service. A systematic approach to organising the daily environment and one-to-one programming is also needed. People with severe intellectual disability and challenging behaviour do have conspicuous problems which are out of the ordinary and, in this respect, a specialist response or specialism is required. In my view, the field has been slow to define the nature of that specialism and learn how to develop it within mainstream service models. Possibly, the controversy concerning the relative merits of hospital or community-based care for people with challenging behaviours has obscured the analysis of what service features and working methods are required for the design of effective service provision. I will therefore seek to address such an analysis in this chapter.

It is not difficult to understand why the feasibility of an ordinary housing prescription for specialist provision is questioned. Many people with severe learning difficulties and challenging behaviours have lived and continue to live in traditional institutions (DHSS, 1971; Harris & Russell, 1989; Kushlick & Cox, 1973; Oliver, Murphy & Corbett, 1987). Challenging behaviours are, however, not unique to institutional provision. They are a major contributor to stress experienced by the parents of children with severe learning difficulties (Hubert, 1991; Quine & Pahl, 1985) and are one of the main factors in parents deciding to seek residential placement for their son or daughter (Tausig, 1985). The presence of challenging behaviours is commonly cited among the reasons for first admission to institutional care & for readmission following community placement breakdown (Hemming, 1982; Pagel & Whitling, 1978; Sternlicht & Deutsch, 1972; Sutter, Meyeda, Call, Yanagi & Yee, 1980). A recent survey by Mencap London Division (1989) found that 77% of those identified as having severe behaviour problems and receiving residential services were living in hospitals and that many local authorities were unsure about how they could provide for them.

People with challenging behaviour represent a particularly vulnerable group at risk from exclusion from families, communities and ordinary settings (Lakin, Hill, Hauber, Bruininks & Heal, 1983; Scheerenberger, 1981) (see Toogood, this volume). Moreover, the proposition that effective specialist treatment is delivered within hospitals is not well grounded. The Mencap survey quoted above went on to describe hospital conditions as poor, with individuals receiving little in the way of daycare or activity, and with about 60% maintained on medication prescribed for their behaviour. A widespread picture of deprivation in institutions emerges from the research literature: low levels of staff-initiated contact with individuals, low levels of resident engagement with their material or social world, isolation from the community and the general public, and poor personal development. Residents pass the bulk of their time in inactivity, engagement in challenging behaviours, or trivial occupation (e.g., Beail, 1985; Bratt & Johnston, 1988; Felce, Kushlick & Mansell, 1980; Felce, de Kock & Repp, 1986, Hemming, Lavender & Pill, 1981; Landesman, 1987; Morris, 1969; Oswin, 1971, 1978; Rawlings, 1985; Thomas, Felce, de Kock, Saxby & Repp, 1986). There is little evidence of skill improvement over time (e.g., Conroy, Efthimiou & Lemanowicz, 1982; Smith, Glossop & Kushlick, 1980). Residents have few contacts with the outside world either through community visits or family and friendship contacts (e.g., de Kock, Saxby, Thomas & Felce, 1988; Felce, Lunt & Kushlick, 1980; Firth & Short, 1987). Despite the rhetoric about the concentration of professional treatment expertise, people are unlikely to receive psychological or other therapeutically-based help for their challenging behaviours (Griffin, Williams, Stark, Altmeyer & Mason, 1986; Griffin, Ricketts, Williams, Locke, Altmeyer & Stark, 1987; Oliver, Murphy & Corbett, 1987). Moreover, it would be hard to believe that treatment effects would outweigh the impoverishment of the therapeutic environment. Further, research has also demonstrated the high proportion of people with challenging behaviour who receive psychoactive medication of dubious therapeutic value over extensive periods of time and/or are restrained (Altmeyer, Locke, Griffin, Ricketts, Williams, Mason & Stark, 1987; Gadow & Poling, 1988; Oliver, Murphy & Corbett, 1987; Singh & Millichamp, 1985; Stone, Alvarez, Ellman, Hom & White, 1989).

Much of the available evidence points to the chronicity of challenging behaviour and the failure to bring about change over time (Eyman, Borthwick & Miller, 1981; Hill & Bruininks, 1984). Moreover, people with severely challenging behaviour rarely present just one form of challenge; the presence of multiple problem behaviours is common (Felce, Lowe & de Paiva, in press). A capacity to contain people with challenging behaviour in 'specialist' segregated settings does exist, albeit with resort to restrictive measures. However, one can hardly conclude that existing services are specialist in the sense of delivering effective treatment and a high quality of life. The low level of treatment effect, despite long-term administration of psychoactive medication, undermines the credibility of a blanket psychiatric interpretation of challenging behaviour. It also suggests the need for a broader analysis of the nature of the required specialism. It is not enough to plan settings with a high and close involvement of psychiatrically oriented medical and nursing specialists, or any other professional grouping for that matter, and consider that a specialist service has been designed.

The chronicity of challenging behaviours also implies that intuitive caring, as found in a good number of families, community residential settings or hospitals, does not generally lead to their resolution. It is, on this basis, clear that individuals with severe problem behaviours do present a special challenge and that service support has to contain a matching degree of specialism. However, it is also clear that we can have little complacency over our ability to organise such specialist support currently. A fundamental review of the nature of needs in this area and of service design to meet need is necessary and the remainder of this chapter is an attempt at such an analysis.

The nature of need and of specialism

The assessment of individual need is generally taken as the basis for designing appropriate services. Before exploring the nature of the needs of this client group, I want to introduce a distinction relating to the use of the word need. I think the notion of need should reflect a sense of outcome: the ends or situations which people want to accomplish. In this sense, one can consider that there are many major, near universal, needs which all people, including those with handicaps, share. Fulfilment, stimulation, a sense of belonging, companionship, purpose, something to do, choice and control and other similar outcomes are commonly agreed as important aspects of life. There is a tendency for need in relation to clients of services to be defined not in this way but in terms of the receipt of particular services. A person may be said, for example, to need speech therapy, or psychotherapy or drug stabilisation. This is a narrow definition of need and may more correctly be seen as the description of a service response to need. No-one really needs psychotherapy for example; it is the consequences of it that they hope to achieve: perhaps to gain a greater sense of self-worth. If the person's real needs are assumed or implied and remain unstated, there are clear dangers that they may be overlooked or oversimplified. There is also the danger that the service is given an easy route by which to lay claim to excellence. Extending the example, if it provides psychotherapy, it is meeting need, even if no improvement to the self-worth of its users occurs.

People with special difficulties are often referred to as having special needs. In the sense of need meaning outcome or accomplishment, this may not be a useful formulation. The desired outcomes in general terms may be no different for a person with or without challenging behaviour; that is, behavioural development, constructive pursuit, community and social integration, etc. What may be special are the ways of helping a person with special difficulties achieve such outcomes. Again, one finds the descriptor, special, more appropriately referring to service processes, or specialism, rather than to need or outcome. Another related problem is that people with special difficulties have a particular vulnerability to their needs being associated solely with their difficulties; they become people with *only* special needs. This risk is present whenever people are defined by a single pathological characteristic, such as having severely challenging behaviour. The notion of special need brings with it the implication that overcoming the problems which define special need constitute the most pressing issue for the person's welfare. This may not be so. For example, as frequent contact as possible with those nearest and dearest to the person may be far more central to an individual's quality of life than resolution of occasional aggressive outbursts.

124

Traditional definition of specialism

The similar categorisation of a group of people who are said to have similar needs on the basis that they share a common diagnosis or pathological characteristic, underpins the traditional definition of specialism, which focuses on the delivery of specialist treatment. Key features of the traditional design specification for specialist services are the greater than average establishment of professional therapeutic staff and the grouping together of clients defined by a narrow set of pathological characteristics. The congregation of clients is linked to the concentration of specialist staff and therefore the implied intensity of treatment. Indeed, in some proposals for specialist units for people with severe learning difficulties and severely challenging behaviour, the grouping of people in order to serve them better and the establishment of professionally qualified staff may be the only distinctive features of the service design. Otherwise, buildings, locations, staff roles and the like may be similar to those in forms of care which are accepted as having a decidedly poor track record. Rarely are the issues of staff competencies, working methods and treatment intensity addressed explicitly.

A model defined by a narrow specification of need and the mustering of specialist treatment to meet need without regard to a wider set of outcomes can be acceptable, as in the case of acute medical intervention. The key determinants in this model are the seriousness and pervasive nature of the pathology, the short period of dislocation from ordinary living associated with effective acute treatment, and the complexity of effective treatment which means that it has to be organised around the practicalities of delivery rather than the individual concerns of the recipient, in a centralised rather than peripatetic form. Moreover, the focus of treatment has to be related to a phenomenon that is environmentally independent so that the character of the person's natural environment is largely irrelevant to treatment success. Critically, these conditions do not apply in relation to people with severe learning difficulties and severely challenging behaviour. There is a considerable literature which establishes the link between individual behaviour and the natural environment (see for example the content of several applied psychology journals). The chronicity of challenging behaviour and of severe learning difficulties indicates that specialist treatment certainly has to be sustained, if not life long. No professional treatment is sufficiently powerful to make a major impact on outcome via an acute modality. Nor is it clear that treatment complexity requires centralisation. An alternative model of needs assessment and service design would seem more appropriate.

Moving towards a needs-led definition of specialism

It is unlikely that a service response designed to meet a narrow definition of need will coincidentally allow the achievement of a wider spectrum of desirable outcomes. The major needs of people as people, whatever their disability or extent of additional problems, must therefore be central to service design. The true specialism of the service lies in its ability to achieve such a broad range of fundamental human needs consistent with a decent quality of life for a client group with particular difficulties. This requires a service design which can bring together what is required for a decent quality of life with those special processes necessary to effective work with people who have particular pathological conditions (see Figure 1). The challenge for service design is to produce an environmental and social context which provides the opportunities and supports for a decent ordinary life as well as the capability to deliver individually designed remedial programmes. The overall service formulation has to be one in which what is determined or done with regard to the special problems of individuals is compatible with their more general needs. Any service formulation which compromises the achievement of one set of needs in order to achieve another is inherently underachieving.

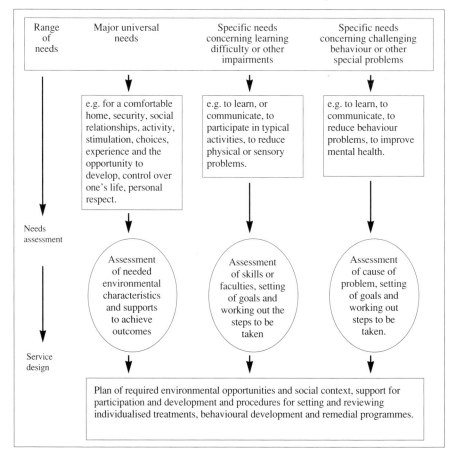

Figure 1. Model relating breadth of individual needs to service design

126

Defining need: the contribution of service philosophy

Since the 1960s, there has been a considerable movement to re-evaluate the place that people with severe or profound intellectual disability occupy in our society. The growing catalogue of criticism of institutional care referred to earlier was made all the more lamentable by the better understanding being reached of the potential for learning, behavioural development and positive contribution among people with even the most severe disabilities (e.g., Berkson & Landesman-Dwyer, 1977). New principles based on a consideration of the needs of people have set a frame of reference to think about service design (DHSS, 1971; Jay Committee, 1979; Welsh Office, 1983). The principle of normalisation (Wolfensberger, 1972), subsequently elaborated as social role valorisation (Wolfensberger, 1983), has had widespread influence as a means of examining need and understanding some of the factors which may determine the place people with disabilities have in society. Moreover, in recent years, there has been a concerted call for quality of life to be the dominant criterion for judging the adequacy of service design (Heal & Chadsey-Rusch, 1985; Landesman, 1986; Schalock, 1990).

Blunden (1988) suggested a framework for addressing quality of life which employed four dimensions: Physical, Material, Social and Cognitive well-being. Physical well-being may be summarised as an absence of morbidity. Material well-being may be seen in terms of having an adequate level of income, decent home and sufficient personal possessions to lead a reasonable quality of existence. The attempt to capture what is meant by a decent quality of life from a social and cultural perspective is fraught with difficulties and no criteria are universally agreed. However, there is a surprising degree of overlap (see Figure 2) between principles to guide services articulated in the government policy *Better Service for the Mentally Handicapped* (DHSS, 1971) and the notion of *Five Essential Service Accomplishments* said by O'Brien (1987) to provide an operational definition of the *Principle of Normalisation*; surprising in that these perspectives might be considered to represent poles of conservative and progressive ideology. One can perhaps assume, therefore, that there is now fairly widespread agreement that a quality of life which current services would aspire to achieve would include as outcomes for their users: (a) a typical level of participation in community settings, (b) a typical network of friendships and frequency of social activities, (c) growth in skills and experience; the best use of skills and the achievement of the maximum level of independence and participation in day-to-day activity, (d) breadth of opportunities and the exercise of choice, and (e) positive status and respect conferred by others. Cognitive well-being is also multifaceted and would include a good self-image, satisfaction with lifestyle, relationships and activities, 'happiness' and positive mental health status. If such a framework is going to be taken seriously as a guiding theme of what services ought to achieve, then it has to be considered at every stage of service design.

Selected principles from *Better Services for the Mentally Handicapped* (DHSS, 1971)	Five essential service accomplishments (consistent with the *Principle of Normalisation*) (O'Brien, 1987)
Mentally handicapped people should not be segregated from the general life of the local community	Community Presence – living in a local community and using its amenities
Mentally handicapped people should not be segregated from other people of similar age . . . and should normally maintain links with families after leaving home	Community Participation – possession of a range of relationships with friends, family, peers, colleagues and the like, variety and extensiveness of social life
Families should have help to maintain a normal social life	As above
Each handicapped person should develop to their maximum capacity and exercise all skills acquired	Competence – development of abilities, experience and independence in all aspects of everyday life
Mentally handicapped people should maintain as near normal a life as handicap permits	Choice – the exercise of independence and the conduct of life with due allowance for personal preferences
	Respect – opportunities to fulfill a number of socially valued roles worth of the respect of others

Figure 2. Principles concerned with the quality of services: Overlap between longstanding government policy and the principle of normalisation

Understanding challenging behaviour: analysing specialism

The nature of specialism in services for people with severely challenging behaviour might logically be based in an understanding of the causes of such behaviours, and it is this area that is examined next. Baumeister (1978) and Carr (1977) have identified a variety of possible aetiologies for stereotypic and self-injurious behaviours. In a more recent paper consolidating known theory, Baumeister (1989) suggests seven causative possibilities for challenging behaviours: (a) developmental stage, (b) psychodynamic motivation, (c) organic or neurological abnormality, (d) neural oscillator functioning, (e) homeostasis, (f) communicative function or (g) conditioning.

Developmental theory suggests that challenging behaviours are an exaggeration of those that are normal in early development, particularly at transition points. Individuals with the most severe or profound handicaps who achieve little developmental progress are seen as trapped within a stage of development for which challenging behaviour is characteristic. Perseverance of the behaviours may account for their exaggerated form. Although this account is speculative, as prospective studies tracing the onset and development of challenging behaviours have not been conducted, it does emphasise a common observation; namely, the inverse relationship between the presence of adaptive and aberrant behaviours. On the basis of developmental theory then, services for people with challenging behaviour should pay special attention to the developmental opportunities and supports available to individuals. This is very much in line with priorities that should be pursued anyway in the light of people's severity of intellectual disability. Exposure to the full character and range of normal experiences is necessary at the same or greater intensity which other people have when they learn. Particular emphasis on the intensity, clarity, and sequencing of skill teaching can help to advance development beyond infantile patterns of behaviour.

Psychodynamic interpretations of challenging behaviour have emphasised the difficulties an individual may experience in distinguishing their 'self' from the external world or in tracing their 'ego boundaries'. Challenging behaviour may reflect 'repression', 'hysteria' or 'guilt'. In general, such terms are difficult to operationalise and, therefore, it is hard to test such theory. However, psychodynamic theory has focused attention on the possible impact of severe disruption to normal mother-infant interactions on later development. Individuals may have experienced trauma or deprivation of 'mothering' through early separation and institutionalisation or through emotional rejection or abuse. The association of behaviour with emotional development is also implied. The reversal of the damage caused by rejection, trauma and abuse would suggest that a specialist service was able to offer a secure and accepting environment at the very minimum, one which maintains positive relationships with the person and a positive interpretation of the person despite the challenge of their behaviour (see Jones & McCaughey, this volume). A reliance on punitive control and restriction has no place in a definition of specialism which seeks to ensure that the consequences of possible traumatising experience in the past are not carried into the future. The social milieu of the setting is vital; one which seeks to promote self-expression and understand limited communication, as well as offer practical support for people with limited independence, may very well minimise frustration and emotional disruption.

The *organic/neurological hypothesis* states that challenging behaviours result from disordered physiological or neurological processes. Where certain clinical syndromes are associated with characteristic behaviour, the presence of a biologically determined link is a reasonable inference. Psychiatry has regularly interpreted challenging behaviour as a sympton of an underlying disorder. More recently, specific models of neurochemical imbalance have been developed (Cataldo & Harris, 1982; Oliver & Head, 1990). The biological basis for some challenging behaviour emphasises the value of skilled medical assessment and intervention. Differential diagnosis, not only to identify organic or neurochemical causation, but also to distinguish internal from environmental causes, is clearly a matter for professional specialism, which will span several medical and psychological disciplines. A specialist service will need sufficient competent professional input.

The *neural oscillator theory* is also an organic model of behaviour. Although lacking a well-developed theoretical basis, it has been articulated to account for the highly rhythmic production of stereotypic behaviour and its intra-response consistency, as if an internal 'switch' turns the behaviour on and off. Its main implication for a specialist service concerns the programming and sequencing of alternative activities.

The remaining three causal hypotheses are particularly useful as constructs to explain mechanisms by which behaviour may be influenced by environmental conditions or events. The *homeostasis or arousal theory* states that people seek an optimal level of stimulation, probably for survival reasons. When understimulated, a person may engage in various behaviours, such as stereotypy, to increase their arousal state. Similarly, when overstimulated, a person may engage in the same or other types of behaviour to decrease arousal state. The *communication theory* states that challenging behaviours have communicative intent; that is, they function as elementary, although socially unacceptable, means of communication. Several studies, for example, have shown that persons who engage in stereotypy or self-injury stop these behaviours when taught alternative ways to communicate their desire to receive the same consequences that their challenging behaviour was producing (Carr and Durand, 1985; Donnellan, Mirenda, Mesaros and Fassbender, 1984). The *conditioning theory* states that challenging behaviours are learned and maintained through positive reinforcement (i.e. the response produces an event that reinforces the behaviour) or negative reinforcement (i.e. the response removes an aversive event and is thereby reinforced). The communication theory can be viewed as representing a subset of the conditioning theory and may be subsumed under it. The central tenet of the communication theory is that, as in the conditioning theory, the function of the behaviour can be understood in terms of its antecedents and consequences.

A service which aspires to sustained behavioural change and development must, according to these theories, combine a number of competencies. Effective teaching of independence skills and social behaviours provides the individual with a variety of appropriate means of environmental control which can have the same function as their challenging behaviour and therefore supplant it. Teaching a wide range of adaptive behaviours also gives the person alternative ways to gain stimulation. Skilled behavioural analysis is a necessary complementary component: to identify the functions of challenging behaviour which can guide positive behavioural programming to re-educate the person to behave differently (see Oliver & Head, this volume). At the most basic level, the setting should provide an appropriate level of positive stimulation, such as opportunities for activity, and an absence of aversive stimulation, such as unpleasant smells, noise or chaotic circumstance, so that the individual does not have to resort to challenging behaviour to adjust for gross deficiences or excesses in ambient stimulation.

A synthesis of universal needs and special requirements: the design brief

Adults with severe learning difficulties require lifelong support for the achievement of a broad range of universal human accomplishments, and the services which contribute to their support have to be designed to promote such ends. People with severely challenging behaviours are no exception; they share a similar range of fundamental needs but have characteristics which call upon a particular degree of expertise from those who support them. Figure 3 summarises some of the considerations which have come out of the analysis of the previous two sections. Those which relate to general considerations for a decent quality of life are made specific to the province of a residential service and focus particularly on material and social well being. Moreover, what is striking is that the special requirements that are relevant to helping people with challenging behaviour are desirable characteristics for any service for people with severe intellectual disability with or without challenging behaviour: inclusion in the mainstream, access to ordinary activities, a positive, secure and stimulating environment, skilled teaching and skilled behavioural analysis and positive programming with access to skilled medical intervention and a range of psychological and therapeutic advice.

Why is ordinary housing vital to an effective service?

The arguments in favour of ordinary housing for people with severely challenging behaviour are, of course, similar to those for people without such behaviours. If clients are to engage in and develop skills relevant to a broad range of normal activities, they must be exposed to a corresponding range of normal opportunities. A major deficit of many existing residential services lies in the poverty of the domestic environment which severely constrains how residents can spend their time. The location of settings away from town or suburban centres used by the rest of the population creates obstacles to such activities as shopping, eating out and using community leisure facilities, clubs and associations. When physical proximity is achieved, the size of facility may still attenuate the real opportunities available to each person.

Ordinary housing establishes conditions of life for people with disabilities that are familiar to us all, and have stood the test of time for the great majority of the population. Ordinary housing provides the context and opportunities which match the goals of ordinary living and development. Smallness of scale not only provides

Universal requirements	Special requirements
A permanent home	Secure and stimulating environment
A base in the community and a place to entertain visitors	Inclusion and access to ordinary opportunities
Support to access community activities – shopping – clubs – amenities	Skilled teaching: – development – skills to replace function of challenging behaviour – alternative stimulation
Support to develop social networks – family – friends – acquaintances	– with access to professional advice
Support to conduct a wide range of activities – personal – household – social – leisure	Skilled behavioural analysis and positive programming – with access to professional advice
Support to develop greater experience and competence	Skilled medical help to identify organic or neurochemical problems
A place to make one's own and support to exercise choice and control	

Figure 3. Design brief for a residential service taking account of universal and special requirements.

the size of residential groupings which are normative for our society, but is also linked to the ease with which service effort can be individually tailored. There is evidence from a number of studies that achievement of small staff:resident working groups has a beneficial effect on staff:resident interaction and resident participation in activity (Felce, Repp, Thomas, Ager and Blunden, 1991; Harris, Viet, Allen and Chinsky, 1974).

Ordinary housing is also a metaphor for the expected standards concerned with the design, furnishings and level of appointments or equipment in the environment.

Critically, providing constructive occupation is central to goals of ordinary living, development and social and community integration. Good service design will, therefore, ensure a well equipped home with the usual variety of rooms devoted to different functions of life and an adequate material environment such as the majority of people take for granted.

The ordinary housing metaphor extends to the location of residences within typical residential communities. Location is important in two ways: proximity to immediate family and any existing wider friendship networks, and proximity to the community amenities of the town or suburban centre. Distance is clearly an obstacle to frequency of contact or frequency of amenity use. Once problems arising from sheer physical distance have been removed, the frequency of community use and family/friendship contact is open to influence by many other factors. Small size of residence promotes the opportunity for individual or small group trips to the community, a characteristic which may be important to personal integration and acceptance (see Saxby, Thomas, Felce and de Kock, 1986). The use of well furnished ordinary housing gives residents the opportunity to receive visitors and offer reasonable comfort, privacy and hospitality.

In summary, given the goals of ordinary living, as normal a lifestyle as possible, community integration and typical behavioural development, the ordinary housing model of provision is necessary to service effectiveness. There seem to be no reasons why larger than normative groupings would be advantageous, or why a lower standard of material enrichment or a deviation from typical domestic design would enhance objectives. Critically, location in the community close to both amenities and social ties is an overriding determinant of the opportunity for integration of all kinds. However, a distinction has to be drawn between necessary and sufficient conditions for an effective service. The above suggests that an ordinary housing community-based model is necessary for an effective service, but it does not state that an effective service will be provided merely by specifying that it will be small in size, use ordinary housing and be located in the community. Such factors have not been found to guarantee high quality and attention to other aspects of service design is required (Felce, 1988; Landesman, 1988)

Designing an ordinary housing service to be effective

Figure 3 illustrates the centrality of opportunity, stimulation, support to engage in typical daily living activities, skill-teaching and behavioural development in the day to day (or even minute by minute) functioning of an effective residential setting. The key issue is, therefore, how to design the setting so that these characteristics are established and maintained. In other words, we need to make sure that the opportunities inherent in the ordinary housing model are translated into participation and development in practice. Figure 4 summarises what we have learnt about other necessary factors in the design of better residential services in the last two decades.

133

Orientation or Operational Policy

- ❏ models inherited from the past: ──────▶ ❏ ordinary life, habilitative model
  custodial, asylum, medical or 'hotel'

- ❏ job definition: nursing or caring ──────▶ ❏ job definition: role to support and
  (plus domestic and catering staff,   motivate participation and independence
  works department support and   (no domestic or catering staff, works
  central supply)   department support or central supply)

Staff Performance

- ❏ low rates of interaction ──────▶ ❏ increase rates of interaction

- ❏ untherapeutic quality distribution ──────▶ ❏ define a model for routine interaction
  and timing of interaction   and train staff to deliver support
                                                according to need and to encourage
                                                participation and independence

- ❏ low implementation of individual ──────▶ ❏ develop systems for the implementation
  programmes   of individual programmes

- ❏ difficult setting for the use of ──────▶ ❏ conducive setting for the use of
  professional expertise   professional expertise

Organisation of Activity

- ❏ inadequate level of activity ──────▶ ❏ offer activity – all people, all times
                                              (develop the natural source of
                                              functional activity in the setting)

- ❏ inadequate day-to-day planning of ──────▶ ❏ develop a method for activity planning
  activity and staff : client assignment   and for working out staff : client
  (who does what with whom)   assignments throughout the day

Monitoring, Management and Training

- ❏ undeveloped management systems ──────▶ ❏ incorporate quality indicators within
  related to quality of life outcomes;   working methods
  (no monitoring of quality –
  management not related to effective   ❏ establish such indicators and working
  procedures –   methods as key issues for managerial
  non-specific training)   attention

                                             ❏ develop specific training

Figure 4. Improving the design of residential services.

134

Change in Orientation, Operational Policy and the Role of staff

Many services do not have an orientation or operational policy consistent with an up-to-date philosophy. Objectives, service practices and service structures are inherited from past, outmoded models. Traditional services have design features which can be easily understood in terms of the delivery of custodial care, asylum, or traditionally organised medical care, but which cannot be reconciled against the kinds of objectives summarised in the previous sections. The definition of the staff job as concerned with nursing or caring fits such models. Associated 'hotel' services, such as domestic and catering staff, works department support and centralised supply of food and other goods, promote efficiency of operation of these outmoded models. However, such features are counterproductive to goals of ordinary living, integration, participation and development. Moreover, because service design characteristics appropriate to past models continue to constrain opportunities for client participation and development, staff skills which are relevant to new ways of working inevitably stay underdeveloped.

Service redesign must, therefore, be thorough and comprehensive. The implications of the goals of ordinary living and habilitation must inform service operation, organisation and structure. In particular, a new job definition is required; one which sees the role of staff to support and motivate resident participation and development across a wide range of ordinary activities. There is no place for 'hotel' services (domestic and catering staff, works department support and central supply) as these remove many opportunities for residents to be involved in cleaning, tidying, household upkeep, cooking, shopping and similar activities. If staff are employed to do activities for residents, or if services use processes which preclude resident involvement, or if staff see their job in terms of caring - doing things for people but without giving them the opportunity, help and encouragement to join in - participation, development and integration are bound to suffer.

Changes in Staff Performance

Staffing is clearly an important resource: what staff do and how they do it is central to an analysis of what services accomplish. Many studies have shown rates of interaction between staff and residents to be disappointingly low (e.g., Burg, Reid & Lattimore, 1979; Cullen, Burton, Watts & Thomas, 1983; Hemming, Lavender & Pill, 1981; Montegar, Reid, Madsen & Ewell, 1977; Moores & Grant, 1976; Rawlings, 1985; Wright, Abbas & Meredith, 1974). Individuals can typically expect contact from staff for no more than about 5% of the time, with interactions occurring at a rate of only about two per hour and lasting for 30 seconds or less. Such levels of interaction are clearly insufficient to support people with severe or profound learning difficulties in any reasonable quality of existence. Of particular concern is that those individuals, who might reasonably be expected to require more intense staff intervention, have been found to receive the least (Raynes, 1980). Clients with higher levels of maladaptive behaviour, and lower levels of

135

independence and adaptive behaviour, receive fewer positive interactions (Grant & Moores, 1977) and less informative speech (Pratt, Bumstead, & Raynes, 1976) from staff.

Further, one cannot assume that when interaction does occur it is necessarily directed towards growth of resident experience and personal development; much may even maintain dependency. Oswin (1978) studied 223 profoundly multiply handicapped children in eight mental handicap hospitals, and found that a child might typically receive an average of one hour of physical care, but only 5 minutes of 'mothering' attention (cuddling, play, talking) in a 10-hour period. Repp, Barton & Brulle (1981, 1982) showed that staff most often interacted conversationally with residents, and least often used forms of structured help which were most effective in enabling residents to do activities successfully. Further, Warren & Mondy (1971) suggested that the way staff gave attention to residents could conceivably maintain their challenging behaviour.

In summary, it would seem that desirable staff performance is neither intuitive nor guaranteed by the effects it might have on resident behaviour (Repp, Felce & de Kock, 1987, Woods & Cullen, 1983). Opportunities for development and a good quality of life are unlikely to occur naturally for people with the most severe handicaps. Clearly, there is a need to train staff how to interact with residents in ways which are most likely to achieve desirable objectives. If staff are to interact with residents, not only more, but in ways that are helpful to and supportive of their involvement in the activities of ordinary life, a clear model for how they are to do this must be part of the service design.

My colleagues and I developed one possible model in our work on housing services for people with severe or profound intellectual disability, including those with challenging behaviour, in Winchester District. The role of staff in helping residents to be involved in every aspect of day-to-day life was central to the definition of their job. Put another way, staff were to do nothing independently of residents. This emphasis created the context for staff to be with individuals during virtually all of their time on duty. High rates of interaction were a likely consequence and this line of reasoning is confirmed by research which shows higher rates of interaction occurring when staff work on their own with individuals or small groups of clients (Felce, Repp, Thomas, Ager & Blunden, 1991). Second, a model for staff interaction was devised to try to make it more likely that (a) intensity of support would vary appropriately according to individual ability, (b) effective supportive strategies would be used, and (c) the distribution of staff attention would provide a constructive motivational climate (Figure 5). Three strategies are combined in the model. A hierarchy of graduated guidance provides a simple procedure by which staff can give residents the support necessary to be involved in activity to the extent of their abilities. Staff can tell the person what to do, show them (if more help is required), prompt them (again if more help still is required) or if necessary physically assist or guide them. The skills of task analysis enable staff to simplify and sequence activity so that what residents are expected to do can also be adjusted to their abilities. Combined, the graduated guidance hierarchy and task analysis techniques can ensure that support is matched to differing individual abilities and that individuals can participate to the limit of their independent abilities. The third element assumes that how staff distribute their attention will determine the general motivational climate of the setting. The model looks for the bulk of attention to be given to residents when they are appropriately engaged in activity. In this way, participating in the routine of ordinary living is encouraged. The success of the model is illustrated in related evaluation studies (see Felce, de Kock & Repp, 1986; Felce, Saxby, de Kock, Repp, Ager & Blunden, 1987; Felce, 1989).

Antecedent	Behaviour	Consequence
❏ Ask ❏ Instruct ❏ Show ❏ Prompt ❏ Guide	Small steps (Use Task Analysis to judge appriopriate size of task)	❏ Attention and ❏ Praise for Participation
Fade level of help for development		Shape behaviour for development

Figure 5. Model for routine support and motivation.

Such a model also has heuristic appeal when considering the environmental influences on challenging behaviour. Efficiency and function are two important concepts in environmental explanations of behaviour. Behaviours which most consistently produce a given consequence in a certain situation, with least effort, will be those that are repeated. The hierarchy of graduated assistance which staff are to give people in the model is related to the notion of efficiency. The giving of greater help can lower the response difficulty of appropriate ways of achieving

137

stimulation or a given social or environmental function, so that appropriate behaviours become no more difficult to do than existing challenging behaviours the person may already do. The hierarchy of assistance also approximates a graduated guidance procedure for responding to escape motivated challenging behaviours. If the model is followed through with some determination, the individual is not allowed to escape participation in activity, but is given increasing assistance to carry out the task in the appropriate way. Thus, the appropriate response to the task may be established as the more efficient route to gaining escape from its demands (when the task is done, the demand to do it is over). The model of interaction also makes attention contingent on appropriate participation in general. From the point of view of any challenging behaviours reinforced by attention, the model establishes a generalised differential reinforcement of incompatible behaviour contingency.

Implementation of Individual Programmes
Another commonly reported problem in staff performance is the low rate of implementation of individualised programmes (e.g., Ferguson & Cullari, 1983). Although specification of individual programmes has conventionally been seen as requiring professional competence, the small numbers of therapists, psychologists or doctors in ratio to the overall client group has made the use of a triadic model commonly accepted, whereby such professionals deliver their expertise through more prevalent mediators rather than in direct work with clients (Tharp & Wetzel, 1969). There is a recognition that frontline staff have to be involved in the design and implementation of individual programmes if such programming is to become anything more than a marginal affair. This has led to a considerable effort to develop systematic procedures for a range of individual programming activity, with clear practical guidance available to staff on how to design and implement a variety of programmes.

One can expect a specialist service to establish working methods for assessing individual need and for devising and implementing programmes. One function is individual programme planning, sometimes also referred to as life planning, shared action planning and the like. Its purpose is the regular identification and review of priority goals and desired service action to be taken on behalf of the individual. Methods for individual plan review have been developed and described in practical terms by several authors (e.g., Blunden, Evans & Humphreys, 1987; Brechin & Swain, 1986; Jenkins, Felce, Toogood, Mansell & de Kock, 1988).

Systems for the implementation of individualised teaching programmes have also been developed to provide a service with a basic working method. Many developmental checklists exist in order to help staff identify teaching objectives (e.g., Felce, Jenkins, de Kock & Mansell, 1986; Jeffree & Cheseldine, 1982; Kiernan & Jones, 1982; White & East, 1983; Williams, 1986) and systematic methods for constructing and implementing teaching programmes have been described in practical terms (e.g., Chamberlain, Eysenk, Hill & Wallis, 1984;

McBrien & Foxen, 1981; Mansell, Felce, Jenkins, Flight & Dell, 1986; Shearer, Billingsley, Frohman, Hilliard, Johnson & Shearer, 1972). Opportunity planning (Toogood, Jenkins, Felce & de Kock, 1983) also provides a simple means for structuring the implementation of a wide range of goals. Considerable efforts have also been directed towards describing behavioural analysis and modification technology in practical 'how to do it' terms, and to devising training courses so that the professional competence of psychologists in this area is transferred to frontline staff. For example, McBrien & Felce (1992) set out a systematic guide to behavioural programming. The specific focus of such working methods also allows for short practical staff training courses to be effective, and many of the approaches cited have developed training materials.

It is important to emphasise that these attempts to describeworking methods systematically across a variety of individual programming concerns does not replace the professional role. Rather, the attainment of a general understanding and basic competence in goal planning, behavioural development and other therapeutic approaches creates a well informed and high quality workforce that is more receptive to and can better use professional advice. The practical nature of these working systems means that staff can acquire a common format and set of procedures to guide their performance. This facilitates communication with professionals, families or other settings who also adopt similar approaches. The activity chart formats used to specify teaching (see Mansell, Felce, Jenkins, Flight & Dell, 1986) can also provide a conduit for professional advisors to prescribe physiotherapy exercises, speech therapy or psychology programmes and the like for staff to implement, a process not very different in principle to a doctor writing a prescription for an individual's medical programme.

Organisation of activity
Activity planning and allocation of staff to duties present common problems in many services. Often, there is no specific method of ensuring that staff are deployed effectively. Research has shown that this aspect of service operation is vital if the best return from the investment in staff is to be gained. Mansell, Felce, Jenkins & de Kock, (1982) and Cataldo & Risley (1972) have shown that increasing numbers of staff can result in decreasing returns in terms of interaction with clients unless staff are given clear and separate assignments. Harris, Viet, Allen & Chinsky (1974) and Felce, Repp, Thomas, Ager & Blunden (1991) have also shown the desirability of staff working separately with small groups of clients. Staff having a clear idea of what they are going to do, and with whom, makes good common sense. At the same time, it is equally important to ensure that all residents are catered for, with at least one available source of activity for each person and a member of staff identified as having the responsibility to help that person spend their time constuctively occupied.

The organisation of any competent setting has to aspire to provide each person with an option for constructive activity at all times. The following extract from an operational policy from Winchester District illustrates this commitment:

'Staff will provide each person living in the home with access to at least one activity at any time of the waking day. Activities will be carefully planned and sequenced to avoid time spent by clients passively waiting for the next event. Each activity will be organised to ensure that: materials are arranged so that the client can get to them and use them; developmentally appropriate help and encouragement is readily available from staff; the activity is appropriate to the chronological age of the client; a range of activity is available for every single client each week (including activities outside the home which bring people living in the house into contact with other citizens and integrate them into the local community); priority is given to organising housework activities in which clients can participate (rather than providing 'occupational' activities with pre-school toys).'

Providing constructive occupation is central to goals of ordinary living, development and social and community integration. Good service design will, therefore, ensure a well equipped home, an adequate material environment such as the majority of people take for granted, and no limitation of access to activity areas or particular activities. A high quality specialist service will safeguard the health and safety of residents by offering appropriate support and supervision rather than by restricting the availability of or access to activities or equipment. A well designed service will, therefore, establish a method for day-to-day activity planning and for working out staff responsibilities for residents throughout the day.

A method of activity planning which avoids imposing a standard repetitive routine has been described by Felce & de Kock (1983), Mansell, Felce, Jenkins, de Kock & Toogood (1987) and Brown & Brown (1987). The approach combines a weekly 'calendar' of regular household tasks, social and community engagements and individual appointments with a means by which staff could communicate changes and additions to the normal routine. Each oncoming shift decides who is to be responsible for each resident, what activities they are to do (referring to the 'calendar'), and how individual programmes are to be fitted in. The responsibility of staff for particular residents can be planned to change during the shift, as can the mix of residents involved in activities. The plan allows variety and change in what staff and residents do, while ensuring that there is also some organising force behind what needs to be done. Other methods for addressing the organisation of activities are also available. Cragg & Garvey (1990) have produced an illustrated activity menu, which can not only prompt staff to think about the breadth of possible activities available, but can also be used to facilitate choice by residents of what each might want to do. Wilcox & Bellamy (1987) and Bellamy & Stern (1985) also describe a systematic approach to planning activity in a model staffed housing service.

Developing supportive monitoring, management and staff training

In the absence of systematic definitions of working methods and goals, management approaches relative to the area of quality are an underdeveloped part of service design and operation. The definition of clear quality objectives and staff procedures is a starting point to the ability to build review, personnel development and positive management into the service. It is also important to recognise that these three entities are interconnected. Monitoring underscores the orientation and philosophy of the service: what is monitored by management is viewed as important by staff. Monitoring and performance feedback have been shown to be useful management approaches in their own right (see Anderson, 1987). The approach of quality circles or quality action groups (Blunden & Beyer, 1987), as ways of organising peer, consumer and management review, also depends on the ability to define desired outcomes operationally and draw up practical methods for measuring attainment. Training, if it is to be focused and specific and, hence, arguably more likely to affect performance, has also to arise out of a clear understanding of aims and methods as well as a review of current practice (see Scally & Beyer, 1991). Moreover, there is considerable evidence that training has to be matched to the organisational requirements of the setting and that managerial attention has to be given to its subsequent implementation for it to be effective in changing how staff work (Hogg & Mittler, 1987).

There are obvious advantages if performance monitoring can be built into the way staff work. By way of example, services developed for adults with the most severe learning difficulties and challenging behaviour (Felce, 1989, 1991) followed the procedures for individual programme planning (Jenkins, Felce, Toogood, Mansell & de Kock, 1988), activity planning (Felce & de Kock, 1983; Mansell, Felce, Jenkins, de Kock & Toogood, 1987), and skill teaching (Mansell, Felce, Jenkins, Flight & Dell, 1986) referred to above. All provide methods and proforma for the regular recording of what is achieved. Thus, for each resident, there was regular information on the achievement of individual plan goals, the extent of participation in household, leisure and community activities, the range and frequency of social contacts and on the implementation and success rate of teaching programmes.

Conclusions

Designing an effective service is a matter of attending to the detail of its orientation, structure and working methods. Research shows and commentators have argued that there are no short cuts to the provision of a high quality service; high quality can not be assured simply by the correct determination of a few key variables such as the size, design and staffing make-up of the residence (Balla, 1976; Felce, 1988; 1989;

Landesman-Dwyer, 1981: Landesman, 1988). I have made great play in the above that factors central to how staff do their job - how the job is defined, how staff interact with residents, methods for organising activity, methods for the implementation of a range of individual programmes, methods of monitoring - are crucial to the effectiveness of the service in enabling people with the most severe intellectual disabilities to share the kinds of accomplishment now commonly set out in service philosophy.

Another theme has been that local, community-based, ordinary housing is a necessary condition for an effective service. I think that I have argued sufficiently above that this would ideally be so if an ordinary housing formulation was indeed feasible. Three research and development projects have attempted to address the question of feasibility in a systematic way. Data on the Andover Project in Winchester Health District and on the NIMROD scheme in Cardiff have been summarised by Felce, Lowe & de Paiva (in press). They show that these services unquestionably catered for people with severe intellectual disabilities and severely challenging behaviour and provided a quality of service better than a number of more traditional hospitals or larger community units. The work of the Special Development Team in South East Thames Region in relocating a number of the most handicapped and difficult people from institutional to community placements reinforces these findings (Emerson, 1990; Mansell & Beasley, 1990). Ordinary housing can be a feasible option for a great many people currently categorised as severely challenging as long as the effort put into the design of these early demonstration projects is repeated. Indeed, it is to be hoped that improvements in service design can be achieved so that the issue of community residence for people with challenging behaviour can become accepted without question. However, I think that such improvements will only arise if further detailed attention is given to the kinds of factors I have discussed in this chapter.

References

Altmeyer, B. K., Locke, B. J., Griffin, J. C., Ricketts, R. W., Williams, D. E., Mason, M. and Stark, M. T. (1987). Treatment strategies for self-injurious behavior in a large service delivery network. *American Journal of Mental Deficiency*, 91, 333-340.

Anderson, S. R. (1987). The management of staff behaviour in residential treatment facilities: A review of training techniques. In J. Hogg and P. Mittler (Eds) *Staff Training in Mental Handicap*. London: Croom Helm.

Balla, D. (1976). Relationship of institution size to quality of care: A review of the literature. *American Journal of Mental Deficiency*, 81, 117-124.

Baumeister, A. A. (1978). Origins and control of stereotyped movements. In C. E. Meyers (Ed.) *Quality Of Life In Severely And Profoundly Mentally Retarded People: Research Foundations For Improvement*. Washington D.C.: American Association on Mental Deficiency.

Baumeister, A. A. (1989). *Causes of severe maladaptive behaviour in persons with severe mental retardation: A review of hypotheses*. Presentation given to the National Institutes of Health, Bethesda, Maryland.

Beail, N. (1985). The nature of interactions between nursing staff and profoundly multiply handicapped children. *Child: Care, Health and Development*, 11, 113-129.

Bellamy, G. T. and Stern, A. J. (1985). *Neighborhood Living Model Operations Manual*. Eugene: Center on Human Development, University of Oregon.

Berkson, G. and Landesman-Dwyer, S. (1977). Behavioral research on severe and profound mental retardation (1955-1974). *American Journal of Mental Deficiency*, 81, 428-454.

Blunden, R. (1988). Programmatic features of quality services. In M. P. Janicki, M. W. Krauss and M. M. Seltzer (Eds). *Community residences for persons with developmental disabilities: Here to stay*. Baltimore: Paul H. Brookes.

Blunden, R. and Beyer, S. (1987). Pursuing quality: A practical approach. In L. Ward (Ed) *Getting Better All The Time?: Issues and Strategies for Ensuring Quality in Community Services for People with Mental Handicap*. London: King' s Fund Centre.

Blunden, R., Evans, G. and Humphreys, S. (1987). *Planning with individuals: An outline guide*. Cardiff: Mental Handicap in Wales: Applied Research Unit.

Bratt, A. and Johnston, R. (1988). Changes in lifestyle for young adults with profound handicaps following discharge from hospital care into a' second generation' housing project. *Mental Handicap Research*, 1, 49-74.

Brechin, A. and Swain, J. (1986). Shared Action Planning: A skills workbook. In *Mental Handicap: Patterns for Living*. Milton Keynes: Open University Press.

Brown, H. and Brown, V. (1987). *Bringing People Back Home: Participation in Everyday Activities*. Brighton: Pavilion Publishing.

Burg, M. M., Reid, D. H. and Lattimore, J. (1979). Use of a self-recording and supervision program to change institutional staff behavior. *Journal of Applied Behavior Analysis*, 12, 363-375.

Carr, E. G. (1977). The motivation of self-injurious behavior: A review of some hypotheses. *Psychological Bulletin*, 84, 800-816.

Carr, E. G. and Durand, V. M. (1985). Reducing behavior problems through functional communication training. *Journal of Applied Behavior Analysis*, 18, 111-126.

Cataldo, M. F. and Harris, C. J. (1982). The biological basis for self-injury in the mentally retarded. *Analysis and Intervention in Developmental Disabilities*, 2, 21-39.

Cataldo, M. F. and Risley, T. R. (1972). *The organisation of group care environments: The infant day care center*. Paper presented at American Psychological Association, Honolulu.

Chamberlain, P., Eysenck, A., Hill, P. and Wallis, J. (1984). *Skills Teaching Education Programme*. Southsea: STEP Publications.

Conroy, J., Efthimiou, J. and Lemanowicz, J. (1982). A matched comparison of the developmental growth of institutionalized and deinstitutionalized mentally retarded clients. *American Journal of Mental Deficiency*, 86, 581-587.

Cragg, R. and Garvey, K. (1990). *What's on? A comprehensive menu of ordinary living activities for adults*. Birmingham: R. J. Cragg.

Cullen, C., Burton, M., Watts, S. and Thomas, M. (1983). A preliminary report of interactions in a mental handicap institution. *Behaviour Research and Therapy*, 21, 579-583.

de Kock, U., Saxby, H., Thomas, M. and Felce, D. (1988). Community and family contact: An evaluation of small community homes for adults. *Mental Handicap Research*, 1, 127-140.

Department of Health and Social Security (DHSS) (1971). *Better Services for the Mentally Handicapped*. London: HMSO.

Donnellan, A. M., Mirenda, P. L., Mesaros, R. A. and Fassbender, L. L. (1984). Analysing the communicative functions of aberrant behavior. *Journal of the Association for Persons with Severe Handicaps*, 3, 201-212.

Emerson, E. (1990). Designing individualised community-based placements as an alternative to institutions for people with a severe mental handicap and severe behaviour problem. In W. Fraser (Ed.) *Key issues in mental retardation research*. London: Routledge.

Eyman, R. K., Borthwick, S. A. and Miller, C. (1981). Trends in maladaptive behavior of mentally retarded persons placed in community and institutional settings. *American Journal of Mental Deficiency*, 85, 473-477.

Felce, D. (1988). Behavioral and social climate in community group residences. In M. P. Janicki, M. W. Krauss and M. M. Seltzer (Eds). *Community residences for persons with developmental disabilities: Here to stay*. Baltimore: Paul H. Brookes.

143

Felce, D. (1989). *Staffed housing for adults with severe and profound mental handicaps: the Andover Project*. Kidderminster: BIMH Publications.

Felce, D. (1991). Using behavioural principles in the development of effective housing services for adults with severe or profound mental handicaps. In R. Remington (Ed). *The challenge of severe mental handicap: A behaviour analytic approach*. Chichester: John Wiley and Sons.

Felce, D. and de Kock, U. (1983). *Planning Client Activity: A Handbook*. University of Southampton: Health Care Evaluation Research Team.

Felce, D., de Kock, U. and Repp, A. (1986). An eco-behavioral analysis of small community-based houses and traditional large hospitals for severely and profoundly mentally handicapped adults. *Applied Research in Mental Retardation*, 7, 393-408.

Felce, D., Jenkins, J., de Kock, U and Mansell, J. (1986). *The Bereweeke skill-teaching system: goal-setting checklist for adults*. Windsor: National Foundation for Educational Research/Nelson Publishing Company.

Felce, D., Kushlick, S. and Mansell, J. (1980). Evaluation of alternative residential facilities for the severely mentally handicapped in Wessex: Client engagement. *Advances in Behaviour Research and Therapy*, 3, 13-18.

Felce, D., Lowe, K. and de Paiva, S. (in press). Ordinary housing for people with severe mental handicaps and challenging behaviours. In E. Emerson, P. McGill and J. Mansell (eds) *Severe Learning Disabilities and Challenging Behaviour: Designing Quality Services*. London: Chapman and Hall.

Felce, D., Lunt, B. and Kushlick, A. (1980). Evaluation of alternative residential facilities for the severely mentally handicapped in Wessex: Family contact. *Advances in Behaviour Research and Therapy*, 3, 19-23.

Felce, D., Repp, A. C., Thomas, M., Ager, A. and Blunden, R. (1991). The relationship of staff:client ratios, interactions and residential placement. *Research in Developmental Disabilities*, 12, 315-331.

Felce, D., Saxby, H., de Kock, U., Repp, A., Ager, A. and Blunden, R. (1987). To what behaviors do attending adults respond?: A replication. *American Journal of Mental Deficiency*, 91, 5, 496-504.

Ferguson, D. G. and Cullari, S. (1983). Behavior modification in facilities for the mentally retarded: Problems with the development and implementation of training programs. In S. E. Breuning, J. L. Matson and R.P. Barrett (Eds) *Advances in Mental Retardation and Developmental Disabilities* Vol. 1. Greenwich: JAI Press Inc.

Firth, H. and Short, D. (1987). A move from hospital to community: evaluation of community contacts. *Child: Care, Health and Development*, 13, 341-354.

Gadow, K. D. and Poling, A. G. (1988). *Pharmacotherapy and mental retardation*. Boston: Little, Brown and Co.

Grant, G. W. B. and Moores, B. (1977). Resident characteristics and staff behavior in two hospitals for mentally retarded adults. *American Journal of Mental Deficiency*, 82, 259-265.

Griffin, J. C., Ricketts, R. W., Williams, D. E., Loche, B. J., Altmeyer, B. K. and Stark, M. T. (1987). A community survey of self-injurious behavior among developmentally disabled children and adolescents. *Hospital and Community Psychiatry*, 38, 959–963.

Griffin, J. C., Williams, D. E., Stark, M. T., Altmeyer, B. K. and Mason, M. (1986) Self-injurious behavior: A state-wide prevalence survey of the extent and circumstances. *Applied Research in Mental Retardation*, 7, 105-116.

Harris, P. and Russell, O. (1989). *The prevalence of aggressive behaviour among people with learning difficulties (mental handicap) in a single health district: Interim report*. University of Bristol: Norah Fry Research Centre.

Harris, J. M., Veit, S. W., Allen, G. J. and Chinsky, J. M. (1974). Aide-resident ratio and ward population density as mediators of social interaction. *American Journal of Mental Deficiency*, 79, 320-326.

Heal, L. W. and Chadsey-Rusch, J. (1985). The lifestyle satisfaction scale (LSS): Assessing individual's satisfaction with residence, community setting, and associated services. *Applied Research in Mental Retardation*, 6, 475-490.

Hemming, H. (1982). Mentally handicapped adults returned to large institutions after transfers to new small units. *British Journal of Mental Subnormality*, 28, 13-28.

Hemming, J., Lavender, T. and Pill, R. (1981). Quality of life of mentally retarded adults transferred from large institutions to new small units. *American Journal of Mental Deficiency*, 86, 157-169.

Hill, B. K. and Bruininks, R. H. (1984). Maladaptive behaviour of mentally retarded individuals in residential facilities. *American Journal of Mental Deficiency*, 88, 380-387.

Hogg, J. and Mittler, P. (1987). *Staff training in mental handicap*. London: Croom Helm.

Hubert, J. (1991). *Home-bound*. London: King's Fund Centre.

Jay Committee (1979). *Report of the Committee of Enquiry into Mental Handicap Nursing and Care*. London: HMSO.

Jeffree, D. and Cheseldine, S. (1982). *Pathways to Independence*. Sevenoaks, Hodder and Stoughton Educational.

Jenkins, J., Felce, D., Toogood, S., Mansell, J. and de Kock, U. (1988) *Individual Programme Planning*. Kidderminster: BIMH Publications.

Kiernan, C. C. and Jones, M. (1982). *Behaviour Assessment Battery*. Windsor: NFER-Nelson Publishing Co.

King's Fund (1980). *An ordinary life: Comprehensive locally-based residential services for mentally handicapped people*. London: King's Fund Centre.

Kushlick, A., and Cox, G. R. (1973). The epidemiology of mental handicap. *Developmental Medicine and Child Neurology*, 15, 748-759.

Lakin, K. C., Hill, B. K., Hauber, F. A., Bruininks, R. H. and Heal, L. W. (1983). New admissions and readmissions to a national sample of public residential facilities. *American Journal of Mental Deficiency*, 88, 13-20.

Landesman, S. (1986). Quality of life and personal life satisfaction: Definition and measurement issues. *Mental Retardation*, 24, 141-143.

Landesman, S. (1987). The changing structure and function of institutions: A search for optimal group care environments. In S. Landesman and P. Vietze (Eds) *Living environments and mental retardation*. Washington D.C.: American Association on Mental Deficiency.

Landesman, S. (1988). Preventing 'institutionalisation' in the community. In M. P. Janicki, M. W. Krauss and M. M. Seltzer (Eds). *Community residences for persons with developmental disabilities: Here to stay*. Baltimore: Paul H. Brookes.

Landesman-Dwyer, S. (1981). Living in the community. *American Journal of Mental Deficiency*, 86, 223-234.

McBrien, J. and Felce, D. (1992). *Working with people who have severe learning difficulties and challenging behaviour: A practical handbook on the behavioural approach*. Kidderminster: BIMH Publications.

McBrien, J. and Foxen, T (1981). *The EDY in-service course for mental handicap practitioners: Training staff in behavioural methods*. Manchester: Manchester University Press.

Mansell, J., Felce, D., Jenkins, J. and de Kock, U. (1982). Increasing staff ratios in an activity with severely mentally handicapped people. *British Journal of Mental Subnormality*, 28, 97-99.

Mansell, J., Felce, D., Jenkins, J., Flight, C. and Dell, D. (1986, 2nd edition revision). *The Bereweeke Skill-teaching System: Handbook*. Windsor: NFER-Nelson Publishing Co.

Mansell, J., Felce, D., Jenkins, J., de Kock, U. and Toogood, S. (1987). *Developing Staffed Housing for People with Mental Handicaps*. Tunbridge Wells: Costello.

Mansell, J. and Beasley, F. (1990). Severe mental handicap and problem behaviour: Evaluating transfer from institutions to community care. In W. Fraser (Ed.) *Key issues in mental retardation research*. London: Routledge.

Mencap London Division (1989). *The challenge: Research into services and support for people who have a severe mental handicap and a severe behaviour disorder*. London: Mencap.

Montegar, C. A., Reid, D. H., Madsen, C. H. and Ewell, M. D. (1977). Increasing institutional staff-to-resident interactions through in-service training and supervisor approval. *Behaviour Therapy*, 8, 533-540.

Moores, B. and Grant, G. W. B. (1976). On the nature and incidence of staff-patient interactions in hospitals for the mentally handicapped. *International Journal of Nursing Studies*, 13, 69-81.

Morris, P. (1969). *Put Away*. London: Routledge and Kegan-Paul.

O'Brien, J. (1987). A guide to life-style planning. In B. Wilcox and G. T. Bellamy (Eds) *The Activities Catalog: An Alternative Curriculum for Youth and Adults with Severe Disabilities*. Baltimore: Paul H. Brookes Publishing Co.

Oliver, C. and Head, D. (1990). Self-injurious behaviour in people with learning disabilities: determinants and interventions. *International Review of Psychiatry*, 2, 101-115.

145

Oliver, C., Murphy, G. H. and Corbett, J. A. (1987). Self-injurious behaviour in people with mental handicap: a total population study. *Journal of Mental Deficiency Research*, 31, 147-162.

Oswin, M. (1971). *The Empty Hours*. Harmondsworth: Penguin.

Oswin, M. (1978). *Children Living in Long-stay Hospitals*. London: Heineman.

Pagel, S. E. and Whitling, C. A. (1978). Readmissions to a state hospital for mentally retarded persons: reasons for community placement failure. *Mental Retardation*, 16, 164-166.

Quine, L. and Pahl, J. (1985). Examining the causes of stress in families with mentally handicapped children. *British Journal of Social Work*, 15, 501-517.

Pratt, M. W., Bumstead, D. C. and Raynes, N. V. (1976). Attendant staff speech to the institutionalized retarded: Language as a measure of the quality of care. *Child Psychology and Psychiatry*, 17, 133-143.

Rawlings, S. (1985). Behaviour and skills of severely retarded adults in hospitals and small residential homes. *British Journal of Psychiatry*, 146, 358-366.

Raynes, N. (1980). The less you've got the less you get: Functional grouping, a cause for concern. *Mental Retardation*, 18, 217-220.

Repp, A. C., Barton, L. E. and Brulle, A. R. (1981). Correspondence between effectiveness and staff use of instructions for severely retarded persons. *Applied Research in Mental Retardation*, 2, 237-245.

Repp, A. C., Barton, L. E. and Brulle, A. R. (1982). Naturalistic studies of mentally retarded persons V: The effects of staff instructions on student responding. *Applied Research in Mental Retardation*, 3, 55-65.

Repp, A. C., Felce, D. and de Kock, U. (1987). Observational studies of staff working with mentally retarded persons: A review. *Research in Developmental Disabilities*, 8, 331-350.

Saxby, H., Thomas, M., Felce, D. and de Kock, U. (1986). The use of shops, cafes and public houses by severely and profoundly mentally handicapped adults. *British Journal of Mental Subnormality*, 32, 69-81.

Scally, M. and Beyer, S. (1991). *An evaluation of an individual service development planning system*. Cardiff: Mental Handicap in Wales: Applied Research Unit.

Schalock, R. L. (1990). *Quality of life: Perspectives and issues*. Washington D.C.: American Association on Mental Retardation.

Scheerenberger, R. C. (1981). Deinstitutionalization: Trends and difficulties. In R. C. Bruininks, C. E. Meyers, B. B. Sigford and K. C. Lakin (Eds) *Deinstitutionalization and community adjustment of mentallly retarded people*. Washington D.C.: American Association on Mental Deficiency.

Shearer, D., Billingsley, J., Frohman, A., Hilliard, J., Johnson, F. and Shearer, M. (1972). *The Portage Guide to Early Education*. Windsor: NFER-Nelson Publishing Co.

Singh, N. N. and Millichamp, C. J. (1985). Pharmacological treatment of self-injurious behaviour in mentally retarded persons. *Journal of Autism and Developmental Disorders*, 15, 257-267.

Smith, J., Glossop, C. and Kushlick, A. (1980). Evaluation of alternative residential facilities for the severely mentally handicapped in Wessex: Client progress. *Advances in Behaviour Research and Therapy*, 3, 5-11.

Sternlicht, M. and Deutsch, M. R. (1972). *Personality Development and Social Behavior in the Mentally Retarded*. Lexington, MA: D.C. Heath.

Stone, R. K., Alvarez, W. F., Ellman, G., Hom, A. C. and White, J. F. (1989). Prevalence and prediction of psychotropic drug use in California Developmental Centers. *American Journal of Mental retardation*, 93, 627-632.

Sutter, P., Mayeda, T., Call, T., Yanagi, G. and Yee, S. (1980). Comparison of successful and unsuccessful community-placed mentally retarded persons. *American Journal of Mental Deficiency*, 85, 262-267.

Tausig, M. (1985). Factors in family decision-making about placement for developmentally disabled individuals. *American Journal of Mental Deficiency*, 89, 352-361.

Tharp, R. G. and Wetzel, R. J. (1969). *Behavior modification in the natural environment*. New York: Academic Press.

Thomas, M., Felce, D., de Kock, U., Saxby, H. and Repp, A. (1986). The activity of staff and of severely and profoundly mentally handicapped adults in residential settings of different sizes. *British Journal of Mental Subnormality*, 32, 82-92.

Toogood, S., Jenkins, J., Felce, D., and de Kock, U. (1983). *Opportunity Plans.* University of Southampton: Health Care Evaluation Research Team.

Warren, S. A. and Mondy, L. W. (1971). To what behaviors do attending adults respond? *American Journal of Mental Deficiency,* 75, 449-455.

Welsh Office (1983). *All Wales Strategy for the Development of Services for Mentally Handicapped People.* Cardiff: Welsh Office.

White, M. and East, K. (1983). *The Wessex Revised Portage Language Checklist.* Windsor: NFER-Nelson Publishing Co.

Wilcox, B. and Bellamy, G. T. (1987). *The Activities Catalog: An Alternative Curriculum for Youth and Adults with Severe Disabilities.* Baltimore: Paul H. Brookes Publishing Co.

Williams, C. (1986). *The STAR Profile: Social training achievement record.* Kidderminster: BIMH Publications.

Wolfensberger, W. (1972). *Normalization: The Principle of Normalization in Human Services.* Toronto: National Institute of Mental Retardation.

Wolfensberger, W. (1983). Social role valorization: a proposed new term for the principle of normalization. *Mental Retardation,* 21, 234-239.

Woods, P. A. and Cullen, C. (1983). Determinants of staff behaviour in long-term care. *Behavioural Psychotherapy,* 11, 4-17.

Wright, E. C., Abbas, K. A. and Meredith, C. (1974). A study of the interactions between nursing staff and profoundly retarded children. *British Journal of Mental Subnormality,* 20, 38.

CHAPTER 7

Managing Violent and Aggressive Behaviour: Towards Better Practice

Andrew Mcdonnell
University of Birmingham, UK
and
Peter Sturmey
Abilene State School, Texas, USA

Introduction

Aggression and violence have remained a major topic of concern for many years in services for people with intellectual disabilities. These behaviours are stigmatising and present a devalued image of the person to the general public and to carers. Maladaptive behaviours in general and extra personal maladaptive behaviours in particular have been implicated in the breakdown of family placements (Rousey, Blacher & Haunerman, 1990; Sherman, 1988), placement in more restrictive settings such as institutions (Borthwick-Duffy, Eyman & White, 1987; Black, Cohn, Small & Cites, 1985; Hill & Bruininks, 1984), breakdown of community placements and subsequent readmission (Lakin, Hill, Hauber, Bruininks & Heal, 1983) and reduced chance of discharge (James, 1986). Aggressive and violent behaviours give rise to injury to carers and peers (Hill & Spreat, 1987) and may in some circumstances be associated with high staff turnover and lower job satisfaction. These behaviours may result in injury to the client themselves through attempts to restrain them and may provoke physical abuse from carers (Rusch, Hall & Griffin, 1986). The need for advice and training on how to manage these behaviours and for carers to defend themselves non-violently, whilst also ensuring clients safety has been recognised (Rusch *et al.*, 1986). Indeed, existing training courses are not placing enough emphasis on methods of preventing and coping with difficult behaviour (Mittler, 1987).

Qualitative differences in violence and aggression

Research on violence and aggression among people with intellectual disabilities has tended to reflect quantitative rather than its qualitative aspects (see Murphy & Holland, this volume). A number of studies have investigated violent incidents using global categories such as physical violence (Tutton *et al.*, 1990), physical assault, and aggression towards others defined as striking another person (Spengler *et al.*, 1990). Whilst the literature has concentrated on violent incidents, there is little or no data on the nature of these incidents.

Reed (1990) reported data on 11 clients gathered from interviewing care staff about incidents where some form of tissue damage had occurred. The most common classes of behaviour were: hitting/punching, scratching/pinching and kicking. There was only one incident reported which involved the use of a weapon. A problem with this study for the present purpose was that a number of the categories were clustered together such as scratching and pinching and hitting and punching. Other categories such as slapping, pulling clothing and hair and throwing objects were not included. The areas of the body which received injury were also not specified. McDonnell, Dearden & Richens (1991b) have speculated that the physical nature of violent incidents is dependent on the situation and the nature of the population studied. They maintain that it is relatively uncommon for people with intellectual disabilities to fight in the same manner as a 'hardened streetfighter'. Intuitively, the use of weapons is quite rare, as is punching and kicking when compared to hair pulling, biting and the grabbing of clothing. However, the authors only cited anecdotal data to support these claims.

This lack of data is a little surprising given the concerns about managing these behaviours. If the assumption that there are qualitative differences in violent incidents between people with intellectual disabilities and other populations is correct, then content of training should reflect this difference (McDonnell *et al.*, 1991a). Future research is also needed into the nature of violent and aggressive behaviours. More evidence of behaviours which staff and carers perceive as 'challenging' requires further investigation.

The effects of violence and aggression on carestaff

Although there is an extensive literature on the epidemiology of violence and aggression (Jacobsen, 1982a, 1982b; James, 1986; Hill & Bruininks, 1984; Lakin, Hill, Hauber, Bruininks & Heal, 1983; Spengler, Gilman & LaBorde, 1990; Tutton, Wynne-Wilson & Piachaud, 1990), little has been written on the experiences of staff. However, a study of psychiatric nurses by Basque & Merhige (1980) reported staff experiences of verbal abuse/threats, patients destroying property and physically and abusing staff. The proportions of staff experiencing these behaviours on a daily basis were 34%, 16% and 8% respectively and on an annual basis were 99%, 97% and 90% respectively. Haller & Deluty (1988) maintain that assaults on staff in psychiatric settings are on the increase although they cited primarily 'soft' data to justify this claim.

Hill & Spreat (1987) reported that some 30% of staff injuries in a University-operated residential facility were due to the use of physical restraint. Injuries to staff were much more likely to occur during emergency, personal restraint, whereas planned, mechanical restraint was much safer. Although the data is a little scant, the largest proportion of injuries to staff in psychiatric settings appear to be related to the use of seclusion and restraint procedures (Haller & Deluty, 1988). No studies were located which examined violence and aggression to parents or other family members.

Most of the available literature has emphasised violent behaviours, probably since they are easier to observe and remember, than threatening behaviours and because they can result in direct costs to facilities in compensation and lost staff time (Hill & Spreat, 1987). Although somewhat more subtle than physical assaults upon others, the importance of threatening behaviours has largely been ignored in this literature. While tissue damage may not occur in incidents involving threats, it is likely that the fear engendered by a threat from a client is just as psychologically damaging. This fear of violence is probably much more common than the violence itself.

It is difficult to extrapolate from these data. Care staff do experience assault although it is surprisingly difficult to provide a quantitative estimate. Some evidence for the frequency of assaultive and threatening behaviour may be provided by the finding that surveys of the training needs of care staff frequently identify dealing with violent and aggressive behaviours as a relatively high priority.

Current intervention practices

Aggressive and violent behaviours have received considerable attention in the treatment literature. Although behavioural treatments have predominated in the research literature (for reviews see Lennox, Milenberger, Spengler & Erfanian, 1988; Lundervold & Bourland, 1988), there is evidence that the implementation of behavioural programmes in routine settings is at best patchy. For example, Oliver, Murphy & Corbett (1987) found that only 2% of people within one Regional Health Authority who self-injured, to the extent of causing themselves tissue damage, had a current written behavioural programme. Thus, in service settings carers have to routinely cope with aggressive and violent behaviours in the absence of effective behavioural treatments. Even high staffing ratios in community homes may not have dramatic effects on major challenging behaviours (Emerson, Beasley, Offord & Mansell, 1992). People with intellectual disabilities and challenging behaviours may often have exhibited these behaviours for most of their lives; changing these behaviours may require lifelong strategies. Therefore, it is not suprising that a wide range of other procedures to manage or prevent the behaviour occurring and to protect others are commonly used. These include pharmacotherapy, inter-personal strategies (such as 'talking down' an aggressive person), personal and mechanical restraint and seclusion.

In the rest of this chapter we review a range of preventative and management strategies. These include procedures such as physical and mechanical restraint for dealing with aggressive and violent behaviours. Seclusion will not be reviewed in this chapter, as it is the contention of the authors that this procedure has no place in services for people with intellectual disabilities. We also review the literature with respect to training carers and policies and guidelines in this area.

Interpersonal Skills

Interpersonal skills in dealing with a violent or potentially violent client are often recognised as important when attempting to reduce the likelihood of injury or damage occurring (DHSS, 1976; COHSE, 1977; Department of Health and Welsh Office, 1990; DHSS, 1988). Equally, it is often recognised that inappropriate social behaviour from carers can elicit or maintain aggressive behaviours. In the following section we briefly review some important aspects of interpersonal skills related to managing aggression and violence among people with intellectual disabilities.

The most often cited principle is to *remain calm* (DHSS, 1976; COHSE, 1977; McDonnell, Dearden & Richens, 1991b). This can be achieved by 'speaking slowly and quietly to the client'. Furthermore staff are recommended to 'breath normally and to avoid tensing their arms or gritting their teeth'. However, Davies (1989) maintains that this is not always the best strategy. Rather, he recommends that the carer should attempt to match his or her degree of arousal with the client's. Similarly, Breakwell (1989) advocates that 'The assailant who shouts is shouted at: calm intensity is greeted with equal intensity'. Another active procedure was recommended by Willis & LaVigna (1985) which they called 'stimulus change'. This involves breaking a behavioural chain by the introduction of a novel stimulus or altering stimulus conditions. Thus, if a client is assaulting a member of staff they could 'go completely limp, drop to the ground and play dead'. It is further suggested that other novel stimuli might include 'singing, jumping up and down, giving a ridiculous instruction, telling all the other clients to jump up and down, laughing hysterically'. Willis & LaVigna (1985) acknowledge that with repeated usage these methods can become ineffective. However, no data are cited to support these assertions. It is possible that such reactions might serve to arouse some individuals to assault staff and clients or may be reinforcing to others, particularly where clients are not engaged in regular daily activities.

Should a person maintain *eye contact* with a client who is becoming aggressive or violent? Direct eye contact is a physiologically arousing phenomenon (Mehrabian, 1972) and prolonged staring is also a signal of attack (Argyle, 1986). Gaze has also been interpreted as a sign that one person likes another (Mehrabian, 1969). Generally, most eye contact tends to be intermittent rather than continuous. When faced with a person who is angry or upset, maintaining eye contact has been

151

advocated by some authors (Craft & Berry, 1985), but not by others (Breakwell, 1989). Eye contact prior to an instruction may also be used as an antecedent for compliance which is often an important element in managing an incident (Van Houten *et al.*, 1982). However, such a method can clearly be a double edged sword and depends greatly on individual differences.

If a client is becoming disturbed or agitated, how should the individual be *spoken* to by carers. In contrast to advice to 'remain calm' some authors have advocated raising their voices to maintain control of the situation. Stewart (1978) advised carers who approach a person who shows signs of becoming aggressive to 'raise your voice to be heard if the patient is very noisy, but do not give any indications of being aggressive yourself'. This may be difficult as when a person speaks loudly they may often show non-verbal signs of arousal (Argyle, 1986). It has been suggested that raising a person's voice will help to de-escalate a potentially violent situation. Thus, Craft & Berry (1985) recommended that if two residents were fighting that 'surprises and noise level are useful. A sudden arrival may daunt fighters; a quiet voice or sudden shout of "What's this?" may surprise them'. Advice like this appears to be based almost entirely on anecdotal evidence.

Personal space refers to 'the area individuals maintain around themselves into which others cannot intrude without arousing discomfort' (Hayduk, 1983). There are clear rules which govern the space surrounding the body that people require in every day social interactions. Hall (1966) demonstrated that between four and twelve feet is the normal social distances for an interaction whereas more intimate personal distances range from one and a half to four feet. People who stand in close proximity to individuals have been rated as friendly, extroverted, dominant or aggressive (Patterson & Sechrest, 1970). Therefore, how close people stand to others can affect their perception of danger or threat. These social distances can vary with different groups of people. For example, Kinzel (1970) demonstrated that violent prisoners prefer larger interpersonal spaces than non-violent prisoners. Similarly, disruptive adolescents also maintain larger interpersonal spaces than a group of non-violent controls (Newman & Pollack, 1973).

Touch is used to communicate both warmth and dominance (Major & Heslin, 1982). Argyle (1986) states that 'The most basic meaning of touch is that an interpersonal bond is being offered or being established, rather like a direct glance or a shift to greater proximity'. When a person is involved in a violent situation very little advice has been given directly about touching individuals. A person may attempt to touch an individual who is angry or upset to communicate warmth and empathy. However, this form of touch may not be *perceived* by the recipient in this manner (see Jones & McCaughey, this volume). McDonnell *et al.* (1991b) advised that initially carers should avoid touching clients who are aroused or angry, although they may choose to do this at a later stage. When being physically restrained a person is being touched, and interpersonal spaces which are much smaller than usually are experienced by both client and staff. Thus, during the management of an incident both staff and client may feel highly vulnerable due in part to the small interpersonal distances.

Social psychological research has demonstrated that a variety of postures can communicate much information to an observer. Some *postures* may have particular connotations. For example Mehrabian (1969) found that the placing of arms on a person hips is often negatively construed by observers. McDonnell *et al.*, (1991b) recommend that a carer should adopt a relaxed posture when confronted by an aggressive individual. In contrast Powers (1987) recommended postures commonly employed in the martial arts, that nurses could adopt when approached by potentially violent clients. Powers maintained that such defensive postures would provide maximum stability and balance to the individual. No mention of the threat such a posture might engender was made.

It is notable that very few empirical studies were found which explicitly compared or evaluated alternative interpersonal strategies. There is a lack of a coherent theoretical framework, which leads to advice which is often contradictory. A good example of this is the advice by some authors to *remain calm* (McDonnell *et al.*, 1991b; DHSS 1976, 1988) compared the reactions which are presumably more *arousing* (Willis & LaVigna, 1985; Davies, 1989; Breakwell, 1989). This deficiency is exacerbated further by a lack of empirical research, it is striking that nearly all of the research cited in this section appears to be based on anecdotal evidence.

Restraint

The use of physical and mechanical restraints are likely to be viewed negatively by people in general and are often carried out reluctantly by carers. This negative view may arise from several sources. First, restrictive treatments, and especially those which involved forced or restrictive environments. Second, these treatments present devaluing images of the client. Third, they involve violation of personal space usual for everyday social interaction. There is also a risk of injury to staff, especially during unplanned restraint (Hill & Spreat, 1987) and of course injury to the client. This latter issue has been highlighted on the literature with older adults both in relation to the immediate risk of mechanical injury but also in relation to the health risks associated with the use of chronic mechanical restraints. These include, bone demineralisation, and shortening of tendons and malformation of limbs. Behavioural effects of chronic restraint also include reduced interaction with the environment, and the possibility the access to restraints might become highly reinforcing, and may facilitate the development of escape-avoidance behaviour. Finally, carestaff may well face allegations of client abuse associated with the use of restraint. Thus, the use of restraint should be approached with caution in order to protect the client and carer alike.

In this chapter we are concerned with the management of aggression and violence rather than its treatment by behavioural methods. It should be noted that a variety of behavioural interventions involve restraints of various forms of contingent restraint (e.g., Edwards, 1974) overlap may also occur with some procedures such as overcorrection, required relaxation and in-chair time out. Thus, in this section we are concerned with the emergency application of non-violent methods of restraint. It should be noted, however, that the routine application of restraint procedures contingent upon aggressive and violent behaviours may, in effect, function as a behavioural intervention.

Physical restraint procedures
In this section we describe a variety of methods of physical restraint. Many of these methods come from recommended packages of how to handle incidents and, thus, often involve both methods of physical restraint and recommendation on interpersonal skills.

Harvey & Schepers (1977) proposed a restraint procedure to use with people with intellectual disabilities which they referred to as the *two person take down*:

'Two staff members, operating as a team, approach the resident from the sides, grasp the wrists on each hand at the joint and follow immediately by grasping the upper arm above the elbow. They push down on the wrist and pull up on the upper arm and place each of the resident's arms behind his back. Staff directions are maintain this hold throughout the entire procedure, do not switch hands or you will lose control of the resident. After the arms are secure behind the resident each staff member places one foot behind the resident's feet and pulls the resident off balance and to the floor. As soon as the resident is close to the floor one staff member steps over the resident and the other staff member comes behind the resident thus rolling the resident on his front maintain the hold on the arms of the resident throughout these steps. The final step in securing the resident is for one member of staff to sit on the residents upper legs, just above the knees to prevent kicking'.

In an attempt to evaluate this procedure the method was task analysed and carried out slowly by trained martial artists at the University of Birmingham. We found that in four attempts it was almost impossible to lower the person face down without the individual reporting pain in their shoulders and in one case receiving a facial injury. It was also difficult to avoid hitting the person's face on the floor. This method also relies on the use of physical pain by means of armlocks. It is also relatively easy to break an arm or dislocate a shoulder in the event of any hurried movements. This is especially so if a member of staff loses his or her balance and falls forward with the person. Similarly, restraining a person face down on a floor does not enhance dignity and respect for the individual concerned.

154

Anders (1983), a U.S. military nurse, suggested throwing a blanket over an individual to distract the person. He then recommended the following restraint procedure:

'One of the staff members in front of the patient should reach down between the legs and secure posteriorly in a rotating movement. If four staff members are available for the takedown another should approach the patient from the side and secure the other leg. The arms are restrained by the other two staff members. All of these movement should be made simultaneously. Once the extremities have been secured the patient should be gently lowered to the floor in a face down position'.

Anders (1983) then made recommendations for transporting the individual:

'If four individuals are available for the takedown two can each take a leg. If only three persons are available, one can carry the legs by standing inside the legs. The patient will be carried by lifting the legs from the quadracept region.'

The author then recommended that the person be restrained on their back by means of four leather manacles attached to the wrists and ankles. Although photographs did accompany the descriptions it is difficult to replicate this procedure from the information in the article alone.

Another restraint procedure is suggested by Powers (1987):

'To blanket a patient's limb (arm or leg) for restraint purposes, take the proper stance and then place your hands in front and back of limb. Your hands should grip the limb with a pincer like grip using the thumb and middle finger. This type of grip provided much greater control then gripping with all five fingers. This is because the force of the grip is concentrated rather than being displaced.'

Powers (1987) did not provide evidence for his assertion that a 'pincer like grip' is more effective. This would intuitively seem less effective than using all four fingers and a thumb. Powers (1987) then provides further advice for escorting clients:

'You must first blanket the upper arm with your right hand over the biceps and left hand at the triceps just above the elbow. Simultaneously, you will slide your right hand down the patient's forearm and will take a pincer grip between the hand and wrist joint. Take the slack out of the arm by pulling the hand close to your centre. When walking away with a patient from the escort position, always stay half a step behind to maintain control'.

Penningroth (1975) recommended the use of one or more mattresses to help restrain individuals in mental health settings. Penningroth states that:

'once the patient is pinned in a corner, or against a wall by one or more mattresses, other staff can reach around and seize the patient's limbs. The patient may than be pulled forcefully forward so that he falls face down on the floor with the mattress cushioning the impact. Whenever possible use patients clothing rather than his limbs to restrain him. If limbs have to be grasped, they should be held near a major joint to reduce leverage and the possibility of fracture'

It is possible that too much pressure could be used by care staff when leaning on these mattresses, potentially leading to asphyxiation or damage to the client's cranium caused by pressing against a wall.

Reid (1973) described a four person physical restraint procedure for use by nursing staff as follows:

'If the patient makes a dash for it grab him firmly around both arms, one staff on each side and hold firmly with both hands. Back the patient into a wall, a bed, or anything solid, even the floor if the patient can be lowered there. If the patient is unable to walk where you wish to take him, another team member must pick up the patient's legs from the side, close to the hips and hold them firmly together close to the team member's body. The fourth staff member places one hand under the patients chin and one hand at the back of the patients head; this prevents bites or the head being used as a battering ram, injuring the patient himself and or the staff.'

In our attempts to replicate this procedure, we have found that holding an individual's head in such a manner could lead to serious neck and spinal injuries should one of the staff members slip or lose their balance.

Some articles provide scant details of restraint methods. Lion, Levenberg & Strang (1972) briefly described another restraint procedure.

'For an average man four nursing staff are adequate. One man can monopolize the patient's attention while the other members encircle the patient and, altogether, push or pull him off balance. Each member concentrates on immobilizing an extremity'.

This procedure is difficult to replicate as its description is vague and imprecise. There is clearly a risk to the client and staff involved when trying to push or pull someone off balance, particularly in an area which may be filled with household furniture.

The Tyne and Wear Autistic Society (1990) developed a physical restraint procedure using a duvet. They emphasise that this procedure is to be used in conjunction with behavioural principles. The procedure involves two adults wrapping and restraining the child in the duvet for a maximum of 2 minutes. Release is contingent upon the person being relaxed. The procedure incorporates a number of desirable behavioural principles (e.g., response contingent release, turning the child's face away from any interesting activities during restraint returning the child back to the previous activity etc.). The procedure document is also notable since it includes recommendations on the reporting and documenting use of the procedure.

A non-violent method of physical restraint has been developed for people with intellectual disabilities (McDonnell, et al., 1991a; 1991b; 1991c). This method does not involve the use of painful armlocks or holds and it requires only two staff to implement the method. The first step should be to attempt protect yourself and avoid physical contact.

'Firstly, you should (if possible) place your hands in front of you at right angles to your body. This protects you hair and your eyes, as the client moves towards you twist your hands, taking care to keep your hands raised'.

Only if this fails should restraint be used. The restraint procedure is then described in detail as follows:

'You should then grab the clients forearm, and place your own forearm in a slightly upwards movement into the clients armpit. Both staff and client are now facing in the same direction. At this point you should request help from a second member of staff, who should approach from the clients rear. Placing themselves in the same position on the opposite side of the client'.

The care staff should not struggle with a client. While care staff should retain control the aim should not be to drag the client to a chair and restrain them. They recommend the 'two step rule', that

'For every step forward you make with the client you should take two steps backwards. This procedure is carried out at a slow pace until the client can be sat in a chair. This can be achieved by backing the client into the chair, which gently buckles their knees.'

The restraint method in a chair requires nothing more than human bodyweight.

'You and your colleagues place the client's forearms on the arms of the chair, you then place your forearm in the crook of the client's elbow joint. Most crucially you must use your bodyweight when restraining the client and not brute strength. This can be achieved by bending your knees (keeping your head up) and placing your forearm at a ninety degree angle into the bent arm of the client. You then lean forward onto the clients arm joint pushing your bodyweight into the back of the chair'.

This restraint method has been successfully taught to care staff in a large hospital for people with intellectual disabilities (McDonnell, 1988). The main advantage of this particular method of restraint is that is avoids painful and dangerous locks and maintains the dignity and respect for the client in comparison to other restraint methods. The social acceptability of this procedure was assessed in a recent study using a sample of young people who rated three video-tapes of restraint procedures. One video tape showed the above procedure while the other two showed a person being restrained on the floor (Harvey & Schepers, 1977; Lefensky *et al.*, 1978). The chair method was rated as more acceptable (McDonnell, Sturmey & Dearden, (in press). This study also serves as an illustration that a methodology can be used to evaluate the acceptability of restraint and other physical management procedures.

General restraint guidelines
In the United Kingdom a number of concerned bodies have published guidelines about physical restraint procedures. The Department of Health circular HD76 (11) makes the following recommendation:

'As a general principle clothing rather than limbs should be held to effect restraint and if limbs have to be grasped they should be held near a major joint in order to reduce the danger of fracture or dislocation. Every effect should be made to safeguard the patient's vulnerable areas, for example, the neck, throat, chest or abdomen. A patient . . . should, when possible, not be gripped by the head, throat or fingers. A bearhug from behind to pinion the arms to the side is valuable and it is better to grip the legs together above the knee and around the calves rather than separately. If the patient is brought to the ground, . . . staff lie with their weight across his legs and trunk and thus immobilise him . . . when a patient is biting, the hair may have to be firmly held'.

Thus, these recommendations refer to general principles to be used, making allowances for differences from one situation to another, rather than a series of steps to be followed in a set order.

Reviewing these recommendations on physical restraint we have been struck by a number of features. First, none of these procedures have been evaluated for their effectiveness, with respect to containing the incident effectively, injury to carers or clients, or the acceptability of the procedures to the general public, carers or clients.

Our recent research has begun to address the issue of social validity of restraint procedures with people with intellectual disabilities. Second, the descriptions of many of the procedures were often imprecise such that it was not possible to replicate these procedures. The use of photographs, line drawings and videotape may help here. However, it should be noted that presentation of information in symbolic formats (e.g., written and verbal presentation) and iconic formats (e.g., pictures, videotape, role play etc.) may well be insufficient on their own to enable carers to effectively gain these skills (Milne, 1986). Further different formats of written or graphic information vary substantially in their effectiveness in imparting knowledge and skill (Hartley, 1985). Third, it should be noted that these procedures vary substantially in the numbers of carers (two to four) and equipment (chairs, blankets, mattresses etc.) needed. Sometimes carers have to face aggression and violence alone and need to defend themselves against assaults or escape from holds and grips without assistance. The matters have generally been neglected but some preliminary advice may be found (McDonnell *et al.*, 1991a; 1991b; 1991c).

Staff Training, Policies and Guidelines
As we have seen in the preceding sections care staff often have to deal with aggressive or potentially aggressive situations. Individual treatment plans, local and national policies all require that carestaff carry out the range of skills discussed above competently. Indeed the Department of Health and Social Security circular HD 76 (11) offers protection to staff for their actions *providing that they are consistent with the staff training they have received*. HC 76 (11) also requires management to carry out and monitor and effective programme of staff training as well as maintain, disseminate and monitor local policies and guidelines. Failure of management to comply with these service standards has been put forward by unions as a major contribution to continued assaults on staff (COHSE, 1977).

Staff training
Staff training is a relatively common activity in services for people with intellectual disabilities. This form of service delivery has become known as the triadic or pyramidal method of service delivery (for reviews see Bernstein, 1982, 1984; Milne, 1986). Two rationales are usually offered for this approach. Firstly, there is an efficiency argument. This advocates the dissemination of skills to all care staff. This has been implicitly acknowledged by the DHSS circulars and documents which require widespread staff training, not only training for staff working with high risk groups (DHSS, 1976; 1988). Second, the behaviour of carers may inadvertently contribute to the maintenance of aggression and violence and/or could be changed to reduce these behaviours doubtless, this is why the area of interpersonal skills has been so frequently identified as an area for concern.

Thus, a number of reports have attempted to describe and evaluate courses of staff training.

Fein, Garreri & Hansen, (1981) describe a two-day training workshop for nursing staff. The course was divided into eight units and involved a total of 11.5 teaching hours. The workshop involved 21 participants and three instructors. The course content included describing assaultive behaviour, staff reactions to assault, physical restraint, seclusion, methods of avoiding attacks (such as hair pulling, choking, kicking, chair attacks, and physical blows), and how to record incidents. Teaching methods included the use of role play, group discussions and lectures by the instructors.

Only one post-outcome measure was reported. This was a fourteen item multiple choice questionnaire based on fourteen competencies which summarised the course content. The authors found an increase from 57% to 87% correct responses at post-test on a sample of 36 course participants. The participants completed a course evaluation questionnaire and appeared to find the course useful particularly those aspects of evasive self defence. In this study no follow-up or measures of skill acquisition retention and generalization were reported. This is particularly concerning as participants were taught ten methods of evasive self defence in only $2^1/_2$ hours.

Infantino & Musingo (1985) examined the injury data of staff in a state psychiatric hospital over a two year period. The criterion used included injuries to staff requiring medical attention, time off work or financial compensation. The staff with training worked in different parts of the hospital along with staff without training, only one member of staff out of 32 (3%) had reportedly been assaulted compared to 24 out of 65 (37%) untrained staff. However, the authors highlight the problems of using a non-random sample of staff in this study, therefore, the differences could be due to the selection criterion used for training rather than the training itself. Gertz (1980) reported a reduction of violent incidences from 174 during the year prior to training to 117 during the year after training. In these studies there is no method of accurately judging how representative the samples were. There is also the difficulty of interpreting incident data, especially when incidents may be under-reported (Lion *et al.*, 1981). It is possible that staff may be more reticent to report injuries or more tolerant of aggression following training.

Gilbert (1988) described some of the procedures employed in the control and restraint course run by the Home Office. He described the course as being based on 'the martial arts, particularly the wrist locks in Aikido'. Gilbert also suggested in the article that the retention rate of material was not great. He stated that 'I can remember about six of the twenty different ways I was shown to extricate myself when grabbed in various parts of the anatomy'. The author did cite outcome data for the training procedures at Moss Side Hospital in Liverpool, staff and client injury rates apparently reduced although no data were presented. Steyn, (1978) reported the outcome of a training course which dealt with avoidance methods and physical restraint in a Canadian psychiatric hospital. No course measures appear to have been taken except reported reductions in incident data and staff injury rates.

McDonnell (1988) evaluated a two day training course conducted for care staff in day care and hospital settings in the management of violence and aggression. The training included aspects of the law, exercises which attempted to emphasize the variation in the qualitative differences in aggression and violence experienced by carers in a variety of settings, a behavioural model of violence, management skills, including, non-violent methods of removing fingers from clothing or hair, the grabbing of wrists and strangulation, (McDonnell et al., 1991b) and a non-violent method of physical restraint (see section on physical restraint). Pre- and Post-measures included a multiple choice knowledge test, a self-rating confidence questionnaire and behavioural ratings of a role play test which included physical restraint. It was found that at the end of the two day course staff could competently carry out a simple restraint procedure. There were also statistically significant increases in staff knowledge and self-confidence from the baseline measures. At four month follow-up the knowledge test scores were still significantly different from the baseline scores, however, self-confidence scores had decreased from the post-training levels. No behavioural test of the restraint procedure was conducted at the follow-up. The lack of a matched control group and a long-term follow-up makes it difficult to assess the impact of the effects of this type of training. There were also no behavioural measures of skill generalization to the workplace.

Most research to date on staff training has emphasised the immediate acquisition of skills and knowledge rather than on the maintenance of high quality staff performance over an extensive period of time. This is a common finding elsewhere in services for people with intellectual disabilities. The most promising strategies to maintain staff and parent behaviours over long periods of time have involved the identification of corrects staff performances and given them regular feedback and/or consequences on the basis of their performance either through self or external monitoring. Feedback can be given verbally or in written format and can take the form of scores of the proportion of possible correct performances and, the use of positive monitoring, which identifies staff correct performance and suggests areas for action.

Glynn, Bowen, Marshall & Banzett (1989) evaluated the introduction of a heirachical procedure to reduce the use of seclusion. A hierarchy of least-to-most restrictive interventions were developed. The lower level was the use of a *quiet area* in which residents were required to sit quietly for 15 to 120 minutes. They could leave the area after they had been quiet for 2 consecutive minutes. Clients who did not go the quiet area when requested were placed in a *quiet room* the door of which was secured. They were placed there for at least 15 minutes which extended to 30 minutes if they did not comply. Again clients were required to be calm for two minutes before they were released from the quiet room. Glynn *et al.*, reported that three quarters of incidents resulted only in the quiet area and a quarter in the quiet room. They suggested the promotion of alternative to seclusion was effective in minimising seclusion.

Some of the studies have shown that training courses can increase knowledge, staff confidence and change behaviour in role play situations. Some evidence is also available to suggest that staff training may reduce subsequent aggression and violence. However, most of the studies were compromised by lack of follow-up, lack of demonstration of generalisation, and inattention to experimental control. In particular, insufficient attention has been paid to ecology of staff training (Georigades & Phillamore, 1975; Woods & Cullen, 1983) and organisation context of this kind of work (Praill & Baldwin, 1988). More emphasis is needed on how staff should be trained. In particular should staff be trained in large groups from the same setting, as opposed to individual members of staff from a variety of settings? The latter could conceivably dilute the skills taught to a dangerous and unacceptable degree. Whereas the former my lead to a more effective disemination of these skills. Clearly staff training should not on its own be regarded as a panacea, merely a necessary, but not sufficient, condition for changing staff and client behaviour (Cullen, 1987).

Policies and Guidelines

Adequate policies and guidelines on aggression and violence and related matters such as restraint, seclusion, time out and staff training. Indeed many such guidelines are mandated by good practice and the Department of Health (DHSS, 1976; 1988; Department of Health and the Welsh Office, 1990). Such policies and guidelines are important in order to specify good and unacceptable practices, to reduce the use of seclusion and promote non-restrictive alternatives, to promote staff training and to protect clients and staff from abuse and injury. Policies and guidelines should also be adequately formulated as they may form the basis of disciplinary action against staff.

The recently published *Code of Practice* for the Mental health Act (1983) devotes an entire chapter to client's who present management difficulties (Department of Health and Welsh Office, 1990). They discuss the kinds of behaviour which may need management, the possible causes of aggression and violence, prevention, restraint, training and the use of medication. They recommend that incidents should, as far as possible, be dealt with by non-physical methods. They recommend that prior to the use of physical restraint that assistance should be sought, one member of the team should assume control, agreement should be sought from the client to stop the behaviour, explanation should be given of the consequences of non-compliance and other clients should be asked to leave the room. If these methods are ineffective the following steps should be taken: look for weapons, assign specific roles to staff, fewer, well briefed staff rather than a large number of staff should be used. It then instructs, 'aim at restraining arms and legs from behind if possible, see to immobilize swiftly and safely', explain actions to the client and attempt to enlist voluntary control from the client, avoid neck holds and excessive weight on stomach and neck, do not slap, kick or punch. It finally adds that any restraint must be 'reasonable in the circumstances'. It must be the minimum necessary to deal with the harm that needs to be 'prevented'. Whilst this report is more comprehensive than much advice on offer, the advice on restraint can be queried in a number of ways. Firstly, it is imprecise on a number of points - terms such as 'a large number of staff', 'where possible', 'avoid' are imprecise. Secondly, its recommendation to use restraint from behind may be impractical for some staff and may lead to injuries to the staff member's head if the client headbutts backwards. Finally, although it states 'do not slap, kick or punch', it does not exclude other behaviours such as; headbutting, biting and elbowing.

Policies and guidelines have often been judged to be inadequate in a number of ways (Gurguis, 1978). Firstly, they often contain a number of vague statements such as, 'adequate' staffing levels, exhortations that 'the degree of force should be the minimum required to control the violence,' etc. Such non-operationalized statements, because of their imprecision, can permit a wide range of unacceptable practices. Second, policies, in order to be effective in changing carers' behaviour should be readily available and accessible to them. It is not unusual to find services which have no policies in these areas or which only have long standing 'draft' policies, yet to be finalised. Policies and guidelines may also be effectively inaccessible to carers if they are locked in filing cabinets, if staff are not trained in their use during their induction or if they are not regularly retrained in their use. Policies and guidelines may also be effectively inaccessible to staff if they are written in incomprehensible, obscure English or if they are excessively long. A recent review of staff training materials, commonly used in services for people with intellectual disabilities, found that many materials were written in unnecessarily difficult English (Sturmey, 1990). This can reduce comprehension, recall, satisfaction and speed to find information (c.f. McGaw & Sturmey, 1989).

The management are often reluctant to introduce policies and guidelines since they may have important resource implications which may be difficult or impossible to provide (for example, relating to staff training, monitoring of staff performance, maintaining the physical environment, staffing levels etc.). Unions may also oppose guidelines which clearly specify what staff must do and, by implication, what behaviours will necessarily require disciplinary action. This behavioural trap - the avoidance of negative consequences for both staff and management if adequate policies remain undeveloped - may often be the cause to adequate policies not being developed or adhered to.

Towards Better Practice
Management of violent and aggressive behaviours in people with intellectual disabilities impinges upon a broad range of issues. These include not only the methods of recording and managing a particular incident but also a wide rage of organisational and managerial issues such as monitoring staff behaviour, policies and guidelines, staff training, the design of buildings, the behaviour of middle and senior managers and the role of external agencies such as the Department of Health and the Mental Health Act Commission. Thus, the management of violent and aggressive behaviours raises issues which permeate entire organisational networks. In concluding this chapter we would like to highlight four issues: the importance of preventative strategies, empirical evaluation of current practices, neglected issues, the ecology of managing violence and aggression and families.

Preventative strategies
The majority of the literature emphasises methods of dealing with and recording individual incidents such as developing better methods of restraint, monitoring seclusion more effectively. It is our conclusion that greater emphasis should be placed upon prevention in both research and services. Whilst many policies and guidelines dutifully acknowledge the importance of these issues, services rarely adhere to these guidelines: where are the units for people with violent and aggressive behaviours where all staff are routinely trained, monitored and retrained as a matter of course? Where are the services which, as a matter of course, provide high levels of engagement as part of their strategy on violence and aggression? Where are the managers who routinely ensure that all staff have access to policies, monitor these policies and actively remedy deficiencies?

In Figure 1 we illustrate the relative importance of *Prevention* to intervention as an inverted pyramid where most effort and resources and placed in preventative strategies. In this model greatest emphasis is placed on general strategies aimed at prevention of violence and aggression. This includes strategies carried out by staff such as maintaining high engagement environments, removing unnecessary environmental restrictions (including both unnecessary physical and social restrictions) and maintaining an individual programme plan system which will provide an individually tailored intervention strategy which is regularly monitored and evaluated. Preventative strategies which involve management staff include providing and monitoring comprehensive staff training, providing and monitoring adequate and accessible policies and guidelines and monitoring staff adherence to both preventative strategies, policies and guidelines. We contend that if a more active effort was made in this area and the effectiveness of these strategies was actively monitored and evaluated then actual incidents of violence and aggression would decrease and lead to a reduced need to invest resources in other, more restrictive strategies.

164

PREVENTION
High levels of engagement
Reduced environment restrictions
Individual programme plans system
Staff training
Staff monitoring
Clear policies and guidelines

DIFFUSION
Specific IPP's
Interpersonal skills
Differential reinforcement of other behaviour
Management of antecedents

AVOIDANCE
Non-violent self-protection
Stepping away
Escape from being held
Removing other clients

INTERMITTENT RESTRAINTS
Intermittent personal restraint
Intermittent mechanical restraint
Intermittent pharmacological restraint

HIGHLY RESTRICTIVE PRACTICES
Seclusion
Continual personal restraint
Continual mechanical restraint

Figure 1

The next level involves *Diffusion* of potential or actual incidents. This could include IPP's specifically planned to reduce violence and aggression in individuals identified at risk for these behaviours or who actively exhibit them. Diffusion would incorporate the use of interpersonal skills, provision of activities, differential reinforcement of other behaviours, the identification of antecedents for the target behaviour and individually tailored non-restrictive behavioural programme based on a functional analysis (see Woods and Blewitt, this volume).

Avoidance refers to strategies for dealing with incidents which are non-violent. These include methods of avoiding assault, methods of escape from being held and protecting other clients and staff by removing them from ongoing incidents. As discussed above, these methods should be not only be effective but also safe, non-painful and non-devaluing.

The penultimate level of intervention refers to *intermittent restraints* which includes intermittent personal, mechanical and pharmacological restraint. Finally, *Highly Restrictive Practices* include seclusion and continual restraint.

Under this model the majority of effort is invested into preventative strategies on a regular basis and would form the majority of routine management practices. When these strategies fail management procedures move onto the next restrictive level of management. Management of the problem does not proceed automatically, immediately to those strategies which are identified as more restrictive. Before proceeding onto the next level of restrictive practice it should be ensured that the previous level of management has in fact been implemented. (Since many organisations fail to implement preventative strategies routinely that most effort should go into remediation of this area.) When individuals are admitted on an emergency basis and more restrictive practices are used initially the person's IPP should be designed in order to actively reduce the use of these restrictive practices and move up the pyramid to less restrictive practices.

Empirical evaluation

A second theme which has recurred throughout this chapter is that many areas of current practice have not been subject to even minimally acceptable evaluation. Empirical evaluation plays an important role in protecting clients and staff from practices which are ineffective or even counter-productive. Empirical evaluation can also play a role in resolving the blatantly contradictory advice which is preferred to staff in a frankly profligate manner. The development of sound management strategies will also ultimately enhance the credibility of professionals who provide advice on these matters.

Considerable emphasis is now placed on the development of alternatives to restrictive practices which are both effective *and* acceptable (See Figure 2).

Figure 2 represents some speculations about management procedures. Treatments acceptable are those which present dignified images of the client, which do not restrict their movement, and which do not involve removal of access to everyday behaviour and everyday things such as food, clothing and activities (Morgan, 1989). Whilst some procedures may be effective, they may not be acceptable in the management of violence and aggression - these might include continual seclusion, excessive medication and assaults on clients. Physical restraint procedures which require the use of armlock etc. (Harvey & Schepers, 1977) may

	UNACCEPTABLE	ACCEPTABLE
EFFECTIVE	Seclusion Restraint using locks Excessive medication Assaults on clients	Talking calmly to clients Non-violent restraint
INEFFECTIVE	Denial of privileges Staring at clients	Excessive cups of tea Ignoring clients

Figure 2

also be effective but not acceptable. Some procedures may be acceptable but ineffective for example continually offering cups of tea or sweets to clients in the hope that they might calm down. Finally, some strategies may be both ineffective and unacceptable (e.g., the intermittent denial of privileges).

Future evaluations of management procedures should attend to both *effectiveness* and *acceptability*. Treatment acceptability becomes an especially important consideration in evaluation as there is a strong danger of developing procedures which are effective but unacceptable or in ignoring procedures which are equally effective but more acceptable. Figure 2 represents speculations by the authors about these procedures. Further research into these two dimensions is urgently needed.

Empirical evaluation has also been extensively applied to the management of individual cases. However, this approach has been mainly restricted to the use of behavioural methods of intervention. The collection of routine data on at risk clients should be seen as good practice in any approach to the management of violence and aggression. Thus, empirical evaluation should be routinely applied to individual cases where seclusion, pharmacotherapy, restraint or any other form of management is to be evaluated. In this way clients will be protected from ineffective or deleterious treatments and practitioners will receive better feedback on their own behaviour.

Neglected issues

The literature on violence and aggression in people with intellectual disabilities is patchy and contains many important omissions (see Murphy & Holland, this volume). The majority of this literature refers to institutional settings and care staff in the National Health Service. This presumably reflects the higher prevalences of

167

violence and aggression in these areas. It may be that as services for more people, including people with violent and aggressive behaviours, are progressively transferred to Social Services and the voluntary sector that greater interest will be shown in those settings.

Two neglected groups of individuals in this literature are parents and professionals. In family settings violent and aggressive behaviours are not uncommon as shown in prevalence studies of community registers (Jacobsen, 1990) and are related to family stress and breakdown of family placement (Rousey *et al.*, 1990). Some progress has been made in research with families, especially relating to surveys of families with young children with intellectual disabilities. However, little attention has been paid to the management strategies parents use and to families with adult children with intellectual disabilities.

Professional groups such as psychiatrists, clinical psychologists, social workers etc. are often called for help for this client group. Few studies, if any, have addressed their behaviour in the management of these clients, their relationships with staff, parents and managers, and the coverage of the service they provide for this client group. In the same way as compliance has been highlighted as an important issue for care staff managers (see below) it would be interesting to develop standards of good practice and investigate compliance by professional staff. Similarly, issues such as the frequency of experience with these problems related stress and coping strategies could also be investigated.

Ecology of management strategies

The management of violent and aggressive behaviours is a complex matter which requires an analysis which goes beyond the individual client, ward or staff training event. Several reviews have highlighted the importance of considering a wide range of factors beyond the immediate invention, referring variously to organisational climate, organisational barriers to intervention (Cullen, 1987; Georigadeis & Phillimore, 1975; Praill & Baldwin, 1988). Undoubtedly these are important considerations. However, they should not detract from the possibility that developing more effective interventions may, on its own, lead to the desired behavioural change. Thus, developing more effective methods of staff training can lead to increased changes in staff behaviour by references to a competent behavioural analysis of staff behaviour without any direct reference to 'organisational constraints' (Milne, 1986).

Conclusion

Despite the advances in behavioural intervention strategies over the last two decades comparatively little research emphasis has been placed on how to manage these violent and aggressive behaviours when they occur. Although preventative strategies based on positive approaches such as alternatives to punishment (LaVigna & Donnellan, 1986) do appear to show promise, it is likely that people will always be confronted with situations which require them to manage violent and aggressive behaviours. Similarly, there is some evidence that approaches that are based on teaching positive skills may initially increase behavioural disturbances (Weld & Evans, 1990). Therefore, effective and socially valid management strategies are essential for successful intervention work. However, the lack of research into both verbal and physical management strategies is extremely concerning. Staff training in the management of violence and aggression may provide some of the answers, but only if setting conditions such as clear and precise policies (McDonnell *et al.*, 1991a) are provided by services. If in future services for people with challenging behaviours are to become 'community based and integrated' (Donnellen, LaVigna, Zambito & Thevdt, 1985) much more emphasis will need to be placed by professionals into managing violent and aggressive behaviours if we are literally to 'face the challenge'.

References

Anders, R. (1983). Management of violent patients. *Critical Care Update*, January, 41-47.

Argyle, M. (1986). *Social Interaction.* London: Methuen.

Basque, L. O. and Merhige, J. (1980), Nurses' experience with dangerous behaviour: Implication for training. *The Journal of Continuing Education in Nursing,* 11, 47-50.

Bernstein, G. S. (1982). Training of behavior change agents: A conceptual review. *Behavior Therapy,* 13, 1-23.

Bernstein, G. S. (1984). Training of behavior change agents. *Progress in Behavior Modification,* 17, 167-199.

Black, M. M., Cohn, J. F., Small, M. W. and Cities, L. S. (1985). Individual and family factors associated with risk of institutionalisation of mentally retarded adults. *American Journal of Mental Deficiency,* 90, 271-276.

Borthwick-Duffy, S. A., Eyman, R. K. and White, J. F. (1987). Client characteristics and residential placement patterns. *American Journal of Mental Deficiency,* 92, 24-30.

Breakwell, G. (1989). *Facing Physical Violence.* Leicester: British Psychological Society.

COHSE. (1977). *The management of violent or potentially violent patients: report of a special working party offering information advice and guidance to COHSE members.*

Craft, M. and Berry, I. (1985). The role of the professinal in aggression an dstrategies of coping. In: M. Craft, J. Bricknell, and J. Hollins (Eds.) *Mental Handicap: A multidisciplinary Approach,* London: Balliere Tindall.

Cullen, C. (1987). Nurse training and institutional contraints. In: J. Hogg and P. Mittler, (Eds.). *Staff Training in Mental Handicap.* Bechenham: Croom Helm.

Davies, W. (1989). The prevention of assault on professional helpers. In: K. Howells and C. Hollin (Eds.). *Clinical Approaches to Violence,* Chichester: Wiley.

Department of Health and Welsh Office, (1990). Code of Practice: Mental Health Act 1983. London: HMSO.

DHSS. (1976). *The management of violent or potentially violent, hospital patients.* HC(76)11, London: HMSO.

DHSS. (1988). Violence to staff: Report of the DHSS advisory committee on violence to staff. London: HMSO.

Donnellan, A. M., LaVigna, G. W., Zambito, J. and Thevdt, J. (1985). A time limited intensive intervention program model to support community placement for persons with severe behavior problems. *Journal of the Association for Persons with Severe Handicaps*, 10, 123-131.

Edwards, K. A. (1974). Physical restraint as time-out in therapy. *Psychology Record*, 24, 393-397.

Emerson, E., Beasley, F., Offord, G. and Mansell, J. (1992). An evaluation of hospital based specialized staffed housing for people with seriously challenging behaviours. *Journal of Intellectual Disability Research*, 36, 291-307.

Fein, B. A., Gareri, E., and Hansen, P. (1981). Teaching styles to cope with patient violence. *Journal of Continuing Education in Journal*, 12, 7-11.

Gertz, B. (1980). Training for prevention of assaultive behavior in a psychiatric setting. *Hospital and Community Psychiatry*, 31, 628-630.

Georigades, N. J. and Phillimore, L. (1975). The myth of the hero innovator and alternative strategies for organisational change. In: C. C. Kiernan and F. P. Woodward (Eds.). *Behavior Modification with the Severely Retarded*. New York: Associated Scientific Publishers.

Gilbert, P. (1988). Exercising some restraint. *Social Work Today*, 30, 16-18.

Glynn, S. M., Bowen, L. L., Marshall, B. D. and Banzett, L. K. (1989). Compliance with less restrictive aggression-control procedures. *Hospital and Community Psychiatry*, 40, 82-84.

Gurguis, E. F. (1978). Management of disturbed patients. An alternative to the one of mechanical restraints. *The Journal of Clinical Psychiatry*, 20, 295-230.

Hall, E. T. (1966). *The Hidden Dimension*. New York: Doubleday.

Haller, R. M. and Deluty, R. H. (1988). Assaults on staff by psychiatric in-patients: A critical review. *British Journal of Psychiatry*, 152, 174-179.

Hartley, J. R. (1985). *Designing Institutional Text*. (Second Edition). London: Kegan Paul.

Harvey, E. R. and Schepers, J. (1977). Physical control techniques and defensive holds for use with aggressive retarded adults. *Mental Retardation*, 15, 29-31.

Hayduk, L. A. (1983). Personal space: Where we stand now. *Psychological Bulletin*, 94, 293-335.

Hodgkinson, P. (1985). The use of seclusion. *Medical Science and Law*, 25, 215-222.

Hill, B. K. and Bruininks. R. H. (1984). Maladaptive behavior of mentally retarded individuals in residential facilities. *American Journal of Mental Deficiency*, 88, 380-387.

Hill, J. and Spreat, S. (1987), Staff injury rates associated with the implementation of contingent restraint. *Mental Retardation*, 25, 141-145.

Infantino, J. A, and Musingo, S. (1985). Assaults and injuries among staff with and without training in aggression control techniques. *Hospital and Community Psychiatry*, 36, 1312-1314.

Jacobsen, J. W. (1982a). Problem behavior and psychiatric impairment in a developmentally disabled population 1: Behavior frequency. *Applied Research in Mental Retardation*, 3, 121-139.

Jacobsen, J. W. (1982b). Problem behavior and psychiatric impairment within a developmentally disabled population 2: Behavior severity. *Appplied Research in Mental Retardation*, 3, 369-381.

Jacobsen, J. W. (1990). Assessing the prevalence of psychiatric disorders in a developmentally disabled population. In: D. Alex and I. Judd (Eds.) *Assessment of Behavior Problems in Person with Mental Retardation Lining in the Community*. Rockville, Maryland NIMH/NICHHD.

James, D. H. (1986). Psychiatric and Behavioural disorders among older severely mentally handicapped patients. *Journal of Mental Deficiency Research*, 30, 341-345.

Kinzel, A. F. (1970). Body buffer zones in violent prisoners. *American Journal of Psychiatry*, 127, 59-64.

Lakin, K. C., Hill, B. K., Hauber, F. A., Bruininks, R. H. and Heal, L. W. (1983). New admissions and readmissions to a national sample of public residential facilties. *American Journal of Mental Deficiency*, 88, 13-20.

LaVigna, G. W, and Donnellan, A. M. (1986). *Alternatives to Punishment*, New York, Irvington Press

Lefensky, B., De Palma, B. T. and Lociercero, D. (1978) Management of violent behaviors. *Perspectives in Psychiatric Care*, 16, 212–217.

Lennox, D. B., Miltenberger, R. G., Spengler, P. and Erfanian, N. (1988). Decelerative treatment practices with persons who have mental retardation: A review of the literature. *American Journal of Mental Retardation*, 92, 492-501.

Lion, J. R., Levenberg, L. B. and Strang, R. E. (1972). Restraining the violent patient. *Journal of Psychiatric Nursing and Mental Health Services*. 32, 497-498.

Lion, J. R., Snyder, W. and Merrill, G. L. (1981). Under-reporting of assaults on staff in a state hospital. *Hospital and Community Psychiatry*, 32, 497-498.

Lundervold, D. and Bourland, G. (1988). Quantitive analysis of treatment of aggression, self-injury, and property destruction. *Behavior Modification*, 12, 590-617.

Major, B. and Heslin, R. (1982). Perceptions of same sex and cross sex touching: it's better to give than to receive. *Journal of Nonverbal behaviour*, 6, 148-162.

McGaw, S. and Sturmey, P. (1989). The effects of text readability and summary exercise on parental knowledge of behavior therapy: the Portage parent readings. *Educational Psychology*, 9, 127-132.

McDonnell, A. A. (1988). An investigation of a two day staff training course in the management of violence and aggression in a mental handicap hospital. Unpublished MSc Thesis, University of Birmingham.

McDonnell, A. A., Dearden, B. and Richens, A. (1991a). Staff training in the management of violence and aggression. 1: Setting up a staff training system *Mental Handicap*, 19, 73-76.

McDonnell, A. A., Dearden, B. and Richens, A. (1991b). Staff training in the management of violence and aggression. 2: Avoidance and escape principles. *Mental Handicap*, 19, 109-112.

McDonnell, A. A., Dearden, B. and Richens, A. (1991c). Staff training in the management of violence and aggression. 3: Physical restraint. *Mental Handicap*, 19, 151-154.

McDonnell, A. A., Sturmey, P. S, Dearden, R. L. (in press). The acceptability of physical restraint procedures. *Behavioural Psychotherapy*.

Mehrabian, A. (1969). Significance of posture and position in the communication of attitude and status relationships. *Psychological Bulletin*, 71, 359-372.

Mehrabian, A. (1972). *Nonverbal Communication*, Chicago and New York: Aldine-Atherton.

Milne, D. (1986). *Training Nurses as Behaviour Therapists*. London: Croom Helm.

Mittler, P. (1987). Staff development: Changing needs and service contexts in Britain. In J. Hogg and P. Mittler (Eds.). *Staff Training in Mental Handicap*, Beckenham: Croom Helm.

Morgan, R. L. (1989). Judgements of restrictiveness, social acceptability, and image: Review of reseaerch on procedures to decrease behavior. *American Journal on Mental Retardation*, 94, 121-133.

Newman, R. C. and Pollack, D. (1973). Proxemics in deviant adolescents. *Journal of Consulting and Clinical Psychology*, 40, 6-8.

Oliver, C., Murphy, G. and Corbett, J. (1987). Self-injurious behaviour in people with a mental handicap: A total population study. *Journal of Mental Deficiency Research*, 31, 147-162.

Patterson, M. L. and Sechrest, L. B. (1970). Interpersonal distance and impression formation. *Journal of Personality*, 38, 161-166.

Penningroth, P. (1975). Control of violence in a mental health setting. *American Journal of Nursing*, 75, 606-609.

Powers, T. (1987). Professional survival tips: Defensive tactics for dealing with the uncooperative patient. *Peripatetic Nursing Quarterly*, 3, 59-66.

Praill, T. and Baldwin, S. (1988). Beyond hero-innovation: Real change in unreal systems. *Behavioural Psychotherapy*, 16, 1-14.

Reed, J. R. (1990). Identification and description of adults with mental handicaps showing physical aggressive behaviours. *Mental Handicap Research*, 3, 126-136.

Reid, J. A. (1973). Controlling the fight/flight patient. *Canadian Nurse*, 69, 30-34.

Rousey, A. B., Blacher, J. B. and Hauneman, R. A. (1990). Predictors of out of home placement of children with severe handicaps: A cross-sectional analysis. *American Journal on Mental Retardation*, 94, 522-531.

Rusch, R. G., Hall, J. C. and Griffin, H. C. (1986). Abuse-provoking characteristics of institutionalised mentally retarded individuals. *American Journal of Mental Deficiency*, 90, 618-624.

Sherman, B. R. (1988). Predictors of the descision to place developmentally disabled family members in residential care. *American Journal of Mental Deficiency*, 92, 344-351.

Spengler, P., Gilman, B. and La Borde, R. (1990). Frequency and types of incidents occurring in urban-based group homes. *Journal of Mental Deficiency Research*, 34, 371-378.

Steyn, L. R. (1978). A positive approach to negative behaviour. *Canadian Nurse*, 74, 45-50.

Stewart, A. T. (1978). Handling the aggressive patient. *Perspectives in Psychiatric Care*.

Sturmey, P. (1990). Goal planning manuals: Their readability, human interest and content. *Mental Handicap Research*, 3, 70-80.

Sturmey, P. and Crisp, A. G. (1990). Organizing staff to provide individual teaching in a group: A critical review of room management and related procedures. *Australia and New Zealand Journal of Developmental Disabilities,* 15, 127-142.

Tutton, C., Wynne-Wilson, S. and Piachaud, J. (1990). Rating management difficulty: A study into the prevalance and severity of difficult behaviour displayed by residents in a large residential hospital for the mentally handicapped. *Journal of Mental Deficiency Research,* 34, 325-329.

Tyne and Wear Autistic Society (1990). Thornhill Park School Duvet Technique Thornhill Park School, 21, Thornhill Park, Sunderland, U.K.: Unpublished manuscript.

Van Houten, R., Nau, P. A., Mackenzie-Keating, S. E. Sameoto, D. and Colevecchia, B. (1982). An analysis of some variables influencing the effectiveness of reprimand. *Journal of Applied Behavior Analysis,* 15, 65–83.

Weld, E. and Evans, I. (1990). The effects of part versus whole teaching strategies on skill acquistion and excess behaviour. *American Journal of Mental Retardation,* 94, 377-386.

Willis, T. J. and LaVigna, G. W. (1985). *Emergency Management Guidelines.* Los Angeles: Institute for Applied Behaviour Analysis.

Woods, P. and Cullen, C. (1983). Determinants of staff behaviour in long term care. *Behavioural Psychotherapy,* 11, 4-18.

CHAPTER 8

All You Need is Love?
Common Misunderstandings
of Gentle Teaching

Robert S. P. Jones
and
Renee E. McCaughey
University College of North Wales, Bangor

'Gentle teaching is the first step in creating feelings of companionship; a set of strategies that encourages unconditional valuing and human engagement; an approach that calls for mutual transformation; an ongoing way of interacting; a prelude to a psychology of interdependence' (McGee & Menolascino, 1991)

'Gentle teaching is a scientifically unverified treatment approach which, while sounding humane, caring and ethical, is essentially no more than a set of behavioral principles packaged with a heavy dose of old-time patent-medicine showmanship' (Linscheid, Meinhold & Mulick, 1990)

Introduction

Gentle teaching is a controversial approach to working with individuals with challenging behaviour which has become increasingly popular over the last decade. The phrase 'gentle teaching' first appeared in professional journals in 1985 (McGee, 1985a; 1985b; 1985c) but the ideas behind the approach can be traced to earlier publications by the same authors. In 1983 Frank Menolascino and John McGee published a paper in *The Journal of Psychiatric Treatment and Evaluation* which probably marks the first clear expression of these ideas. Earlier papers in the late 1970's and early 1980's had dealt with the medical and emotional aspects of the care of people with autism and intellectual disabilities (McGee, 1979; McGee & Hitzing, 1978; Menolascino & Egger, 1978; Menolascino & McGee, 1981; Stark, Baker, Menousek & McGee, 1981) but the 1983 paper was the first to suggest that an emphasis on the posture or attitude of the caregiver and on the importance of 'human engagement' were central to the effective reduction of challenging behaviour (Menolascino & McGee, 1983). Although almost exclusively known in relation to services for people with intellectual disabilities, the philosophy of gentle teaching has a broader origin. Many of the ideas underlying this approach are based in liberation theology (Boff & Boff, 1987) and the ideological basis of gentle teaching draws heavily on such concepts as interdependence (Unger, 1984), conscientisation (Freire, 1970; 1972) and systemic theory (Bateson, 1951). McGee & Menolascino (1991), have commented that the origin of these ideas. . .

'evolved from our work among marginalised people in the Americas. The slum dwellers of north eastern Brazil taught us much, for in the Third World interdependence is a necessary way of life, where absolute poverty drives people to help or seek help from one another and where the people recognise that a culture of life and a culture of death are posed in an omnipresent battle. This struggle necessarily rejects domination and seeks freedom, not just for self, but for all. In working among the children of prostitutes and thousands of other street children in a city called Juazeiro, it became clear that education and psychology need to reach out to those in pain, and that this act not only helps to liberate the other person, but frees those who are working with others.' (McGee & Menolascino, 1991)

In the early and mid 1980's these ideas attracted little attention and it was only with the advent of the intense and bitter debate surrounding the use of aversive procedures which raged in the U.S.A. from the mid 1980's that gentle teaching became both popular and increasingly controversial. Although there is some evidence that the intensity of this debate is passing, the aversives issue continues to engender some of the most contentious and emotive invective of any aspect of service provision to people with intellectual disabilities. Many recent reviews are available (Butterfield, 1990, Guess, Helmstetter, Turnbull & Knowlton, 1986; Guess, Turnbull & Helmstetter, 1990; Mulick, 1990; Mulick & Kedesdy, 1988; Repp & Singh, 1990; Sturmey et al., this volume). At the height of the aversives debate in 1987, two publications appeared which helped to present gentle teaching as the definitive non-aversive approach. McGee, Menousek & Hobbs contributed a chapter to a book on community integration (Taylor, Bicker & Knoll, 1987) in which they presented gentle teaching as an alternative to punishment techniques, and McGee, Menolascino, Hobbs & Menousek published the book *Gentle Teaching* which portrayed the gentle teaching approach as being in almost direct opposition to the use of aversive procedures. The scene was set for the controversy to begin. Mudford (1985), who had seen a pre-publication copy of the book, published a searing criticism of the text and the next six years saw a host of publications which either heavily endorsed this approach (e.g., Brandon, 1989a, 1989b, 1990; Butler, 1990; Kelley & Stone, 1989) or heavily criticised it (e.g., Barrera & Teodoro, 1990;

Jones, Singh & Kendall, 1990; Jones, Singh & Kendall, 1991; Linscheid, Meinhold & Mulick, 1990; Turnbull, 1990).

At the present time, many services claim to be influenced by the philosophy of gentle teaching and to have organised their service provision in keeping with this philosophy. It is the position of the present authors that a number of service providers, direct-care staff and professionals have misunderstood many of the central concepts and that what passes for 'gentle teaching' in some services seriously misrepresents the philosophy of this approach.

This chapter will begin by presenting an outline of gentle teaching and an examination of some of the techniques used in its implementation. Core themes in the definition of gentle teaching are discussed and some of the responses to gentle teaching from the perspective both of direct-care staff and professionals are examined. Finally some future directions are discussed.

Definition

Although the main points behind the philosophy of gentle teaching are continually reiterated and explored throughout the literature, it can be very difficult to find a clear statement defining gentle teaching. Jones & McCaughey (1992) suggest that 'gentle teaching can be defined as a non-aversive method of reducing challenging behavior which aims to teach bonding and interdependence through gentleness, respect, and solidarity' (Jones & McCaughey, 1992).

Techniques. There are a number of specific techniques which are used in gentle teaching. McGee, Menousek & Hobbs (1987) state that although these procedures are identical to many behavioural interventions they should be seen within an overall ideological framework and that the techniques are meaningless without this 'humanizing and liberating posture'. They are not prescribed as a rigid set of procedures but rather as a group of techniques from which the caregiver can select the most appropriate strategy.

A central issue in the interaction between a caregiver and a learner is that often this interaction occurs while a task is being taught. This is different in emphasis to the traditional task-instruction session in that the task is regarded primarily as a 'vehicle' or a 'bridge across which interactions gain their meaning' (McGee, 1985a). In other words the value of the task itself is of little importance when compared to the use of that task as a method of teaching the rewarding value of human presence and participation.

McGee (1985b) outlines nine specific techniques which he has adapted from the experience of working with 'over 600 persons with both mental retardation and severe behavioural problems'. He emphasises that although these techniques are not new and have been used by other care givers for years, 'what is new is that mixtures of these techniques enable us to avoid using punishment and, more importantly, teach interactional control which leads to bonding'.

Ignore-Redirect-Reward. This technique is used when a learner is engaging in some kind of inappropriate behaviour. Caregivers are instructed not to speak to or look at the learners as they engage in maladaptive behaviours, but to attempt to redirect them to the task at hand. The caregiver is therefore aiming to reduce the inappropriate behaviour and to maximise opportunities for reward teaching by directing the learner's attention back to the task being completed.

Interrupt-Ignore-Redirect-Reward. This technique is similar to the one above except that it is used on occasions when the challenging behaviour is more severe and could result in injury either to the learner or teacher. McGee suggests that caregivers should intervene during an episode of challenging behaviour in the least conspicuous manner in order to protect themselves, the learner and others. Interruption should be used as a last resort and should be carried out in a 'gentle, respectful, and minimal manner'. Examples would be the teacher placing an arm on a hard surface to cushion the fall of a client's head, or the teacher redirecting the learner's arm as the learner begins to hit out.

Environmental Control. This involves organising the physical setting in such a way that maladaptive behaviours are less likely to occur. For example, if the caregiver is aware that the learner tends to become distressed and aggressive when he/she is in a noisy and crowded environment, then it would be appropriate to organise sessions in a quiet area with only the caregiver and learner present. There are many other factors which could be taken into account in organising the physical setting; for example, access to doors, seating arrangements, levels of heat and light, safety precautions etc.

Stimulus Control. This involves organising a task such that maladaptive behaviours are less likely to occur and the chances of success are increased. For example, if the teacher chooses a task which is too difficult and makes no attempt to modify the presentation, then the opportunities for reward and reinforcement will be reduced and the learner will be more likely to engage in challenging or inappropriate behaviours. It is therefore necessary to consider factors such as the presentation of the task, the age appropriateness of the task and the positioning of materials etc.

Errorless Learning. This strategy requires the teacher to break tasks down into smaller units in order to help the learner master the skill while avoiding failure. In this way, the caregiver can use the task to create opportunities for teaching the value of reward, human presence and interaction.

Shaping and Fading. Shaping involves the gradual building up of complex skills from simpler, easier steps. This may initially involve the caregivers in assisting and redirecting the learner. In order to avoid overdependence on the caregiver, however,

McGee advises that they remove the external assistance and reward as rapidly as possible so that the person will remain on-task without becoming overdependent on prompting from the caregiver.

Teaching Quietly. This involves using verbal instructions as little as possible in order to maximise the rewarding aspects of verbal interactions, and a gradual increase in the use of language by the caregiver as the reward-learning takes hold. For example, rather than using verbal instructions exclusively, the caregiver can use gestures or signs in order to help the learner respond correctly.

Assistance Envelope. To facilitate learning, the caregiver is advised to assist the learner in order to ensure success, and increase opportunities for administering reward. The degree of assistance should decrease systematically over time, yet remain flexible enough to allow redirection or reward-teaching. Here there is obvious overlap with some of the techniques suggested earlier.

Reward Envelope. McGee advises that the teaching process should include a sufficient degree of reward-teaching 'to ensure that the person learns the power of verbal and tactile praise' (1985b). Again, caregivers are advised to systematically and rapidly decrease the degree of reward but to 'be ready at any given time to offer higher degrees of reward for the purpose of redirection'. Again the concept of reward envelope overlaps with earlier techniques.

McGee stresses that it is not necessary for caregivers to use each of these techniques in a systematic order but that they should base their teaching on their own judgement of the moment-to-moment changes in the learner's behaviour. Indeed one of the defining characteristics of gentle teaching according to McGee is that a rigid, menu-like approach to programming is unlikely to be flexible enough to meet the needs of a highly demanding and challenging client group. Thus . . . 'gentle teaching techniques are not 'recipes' which guarantee the effective teaching and management of mentally retarded individuals with severe behavioural/ emotional problems. They comprise a group of techniques which are effective in various combinations and which lead to interactional control.' (McGee, 1985b).

Gentle Teaching in Action
McGee (1985c) describes several case examples of the use of gentle teaching with individuals displaying various problem behaviours such as verbal and physical aggression, verbal hostility, personality disorder, and depression. One of these cases describes an intervention to reduce the severe aggressive behaviour of Ronald, a 27-year-old man with profound intellectual disability. McGee (1985c) stated that on admission to the gentle teaching programme Ronald was restrained in hand cuffs and leg irons and had an open wound on his forehead as a result of frequent

headbanging. This man had a history of institutional placement dating over 20 years and had reduced educational and vocational experiences due to his non-compliant and aggressive behaviours. McGee describes the intervention used as follows:

'Initial goals focused on bonding and the teaching of reward. Task demands were initially minimal and easy. He was requested to assemble up to five three-piece tasks before (being) allowed a short break . . . . Verbal praise and physical contact was provided for on-task responses. As on-task responding increased task demands increased in number and difficulty. Breaks were faded to short pauses (30-40 secs) seated at his work table while more work materials were presented or a new task was prepared'.

McGee (1985c) went on to describe how an individual package of techniques drawn from the list illustrated above was used to deal with Ronald's severe aggressive responses. It was noted that he would slap, hit and kick caregivers and engage in a variety of non-compliant and aggressive responses. Environmental control was programmed by using a table to separate the client and caregiver thereby reducing the chances of hitting or kicking. Where possible caregivers would interrupt a sequence of aggression by removing objects, blocking hits or head bangs and redirecting him to the task. If his behaviour escalated the client would typically sit on the floor. If this occurred table and chairs were moved away to limit injury from contact with these objects. The use of other gentle teaching techniques is illustrated in this extract from the case study:

'Eye contact and attention were avoided even though he was on the floor. When he approached or reached out for the materials he was praised and assisted in returning to the task . . . As teaching continued progress was noted in several areas. Increased success on work tasks lead to increased independence on the tasks performed as well as increased complexity of the task learned . . . By attending to Ronald and providing verbal and tactile reward on his way to the work table, inappropriate behaviours were reduced to zero by the third week. Most importantly, he became closely bonded to his daily caregivers, smiling frequently and responding appropriately to interactions' (McGee, 1985c).

Core Issues in Gentle Teaching

Even a cursory reading of the gentle teaching literature reveals inconsistencies and apparent contradictions which make a clear understanding of the approach quite difficult. It is clear, for example, that although the proponents of gentle teaching seem to wish to distance themselves from behaviourism, the techniques and the case study described earlier would not be out of place in many mainstream behavioural textbooks. In addition, there are apparent contradictions in instructions given to 'teach quietly' and to 'talk continuously' to clients. In addition it is difficult to equate the unconditional valuing and use of human reward with the use of contingent reinforcement described above. Thus, McGee, Menousek & Hobbs (1987) recommend that caregivers 'do not speak to or look at people as they engage in maladaptive behaviors'. In contrast, McGee (1990a) stresses the importance of the caregiver providing 'encouraging words, gazes, pats on the back and smiles. These signals are given unconditionally and are not related to any current behaviors whether adaptive or maladaptive'. Perhaps the most dramatic inconsistency in the gentle teaching literature concerns the concept of bonding. Although popular in earlier formulations of gentle teaching, the concept of bonding has all but disappeared from later reformulations. The reasons for this are complex (see Jones & McCaughey, 1992, for a fuller discussion) but may be due to an over-identification with mother-infant bonding (Bowlby, 1982; Matas, Arend & Sroufe, 1978) which seemed to detract from the importance of equitable staff/client relationships. Despite these inconsistencies, however, it is possible to determine some central core issues which have withstood the theoretical developments of the last few years. As it is presently formulated, there are four interacting core themes which characterise gentle teaching. Each of these themes forms a component part of 'a psychology of human interdependence' which is regarded as being concerned . . . 'with the whole being - mind, body, emotions, and spirit - not just observable behavior, but also the inner nature of the human condition' (McGee & Menolascino, 1991).

1) *Unconditional Valuing.* Gentle teaching. . . 'places unconditional valuing at the centre of the caregiving and therapeutic process. It does not wait for those who are marginalized to earn reward, but offers valuing without question and with the hope of transformation. It puts aside compliance as a central purpose and replaces it with the establishment of feelings of companionship' (McGee & Menolascino, 1991).

It is difficult to define unconditional valuing precisely, but there are clear parallels with other theoretical perspectives. For example, there are apparent similarities with the non-aversive use of behavioural approaches, especially non-contingent reinforcement (Bradshaw & Szabadi, 1988; Cataldo, Ward, Russo & Riordan, 1986; Ney, 1973; Tierney, McGuire & Walton, 1979). McGee & Menolascino (1991), however, attempt to distance gentle teaching from the non-aversive movement in behaviourism: 'The challenge is not to find non-aversive behavioral techniques, but to formulate and put into practice a psychology of interdependence that goes against the grain of modifying the other and asks for mutual change. This presents a major challenge to parents, professionals and advocates. It requires an awakening of our values and putting them into practice in the most difficult situations' (McGee & Menolascino, 1991). There are also apparent similarities with humanistic psychology and particularly with the humanistic concept of 'unconditional positive regard' (Rogers, 1961). Similarly, however, McGee & Menolascino (1991) draw distinctions between gentle teaching

179

and humanistic psychology: 'A psychology of interdependence calls for a different perspective than what is typically seen in caregiving. Humanistic psychology speaks of the glory of individualism and the striving for personal peak experiences. Interdependence, even though it facilitates and honors self-development, goes beyond the walls of the person and calls for the pursuit of social justice' (McGee & Menolascino, 1991). Thus gentle teaching seeks to put aside compliance as a central concept and relegate it to a secondary position behind 'unconditional valuing'.

2) *Returning Value.* Unlike many other person-centred approaches, gentle teaching aims to teach people who are marginalized not only that human presence can be safe and secure, but also that human interaction is reciprocal in nature and that people can be taught the process of reciprocity. 'Love given does not necessarily mean love returned. A parent can pour love and affection on a child and still see that child withdraw or become violent. For many vulnerable people, such as those with autism, we have to literally teach the reciprocation of valuing' (McGee & Menolascino, 1991). Thus, learning to return value to others is a central part of gentle teaching: 'This is meant to encourage and teach the person to return and initiate value-giving towards others. It is as significant as any valuing that the caregiver conveys. Like value-giving, these interactions need to be elicited from the person in a spirit of companionship, avoiding force or a condescending attitude. They initially depend on our seeking them from the person' (McGee & Menolascino, 1991).

The proponents of gentle teaching use the rather unwieldy phrase *'reciprocity eliciting'* to describe this process. Reciprocity eliciting is said to refer to 'any interaction on the part of the caregiver that has as its expressed purpose the evocation of the expression of valuing on the part of the person towards the caregiver' (McGee & Menolascino, 1991).

3) *Mutual Change.* In outlining an approach aimed at improving the relationship between caregiver and client, McGee and his colleagues infer that successful relationships require input and commitment from both parties and that successful relationships are rarely one-sided. In this way, gentle teaching is targeted at caregivers as well as individuals with intellectual disabilities. Thus McGee regards the development of solidarity between the carer and the learner as being of prime importance in maintaining dignity and respect for an individual. 'A posture of solidarity accepts the inherent dignity of each person as a human being' (McGee, Menolascino, *et al.*, 1987).

Similarly, McGee (1990a) has stated that gentle teaching 'asks caregivers to give not only high frequency, non-contingent valuing, but also to elicit it. Quantitative and qualitative dyadic change can result. Emerging data suggests the approach is capable of transforming individuals with severe behavioural problems' (McGee, 1990a). According to McGee (1990a) '. . . gentle teaching sees dyadic, or two-way, change as critical - in order to lessen aggression, self-injury or stereotyped behaviour, both the caregiver and the mentally handicapped person must mutually undergo change. Gentle teaching aims to create bonded relationships within which this change occurs'.

4) *Engagement*. One of the most common misunderstandings of gentle teaching is that caregivers do not need to constantly engage their clients and that somehow gentle teaching offers individuals the 'choice' to engage in aberrant behaviour if they so wish. A similar misunderstanding has also been noted in relation to social role valorisation theory (Baldwin, 1985; Toogood, this volume).

In fact, the importance of engagement has been stressed in all the formulations of gentle teaching. McGee has argued strongly against the 'all-you-need-is-love' approach to service provision and asserts that gentle teaching implies 'structure and discipline' and that 'in using the phrase gentle teaching we do not wish to imply an attitude that fosters pity or low expectations. Although not blatantly or consciously cruel, such a posture also leads to human subjugation.' (McGee, Menousek & Hobbs, 1987). Perhaps the most dramatic evidence for the importance of engagement in recent formulations of gentle teaching can be found in the book *Beyond Gentle Teaching* (McGee & Menousek, 1991). Here ten pages are devoted to the discussion of engagement as a central part of the gentle teaching process. The following quotation is illustrative: 'In essence, as we seek to bring about participation, day-to-day activities serve as the structure within which engagement occurs, such as when the mother invites the child to wash dishes with her, when the father helps the child clean his bedroom, when the teacher sits with the student, or when the group home worker goes shopping with the resident' (McGee & Menouseck, 1991).

This emphasis on engagement may be one of the most important components of gentle teaching given the continuing concern at the lack of staff intervention with persons displaying challenging behaviour (Jones *et al.*, 1991).

For example, LaVigna & Donnellan (1986) have argued that the greatest sin committed against people with intellectual disability is the 'sin of omission'. These authors argue 'that some of the greatest abuses against learners in our mental health/education delivery systems come not from inappropriate utilization of behavioral intervention but from the lack of application of such technology in situations that clearly warrant it'. LaVigna & Donnellan (1986) go on to describe programmes which . . . 'make no legitimate demands on a particular learner because to do so requires programming, intervention, and staff effort. Thus, many learners in schools and other institutions are allowed to languish because this is easier for staff'. Similarly, in a study by Oliver, Murphy & Corbett (1987), it was found that of 596 people who had displayed self-injurious behaviour in the previous four months, only two per cent were enrolled on formal psychological treatment programmes.

181

The issue of engagement relates closely to staffing issues. McGee (1989) reporting data on staff characteristics gathered over a five year period in the Nebraska programme, stated that the attributes which characterised the best gentle teachers were a 'sense of humour', 'a sense of 'playful optimism' and a 'flexible approach'. McGee reported that these characteristics were more relevant than attributes such as the number of years experience of working with people with intellectual disabilities, professional background, or accumulated years of service. These characteristics are not unique to gentle teachers, and may be desirable in all direct-care staff (see Jones & McCaughey, 1992 for a discussion of similar attributes in relation to behaviourally oriented direct-care staff). What may be true, however, is that these attributes are not only desirable but *essential* for the implementation of gentle teaching. In our experience the gentle teaching approach requires a particular kind of staff member - intelligent, articulate, flexible in attitude, highly motivated, adequately supervised and with a clear, long-term vision. In the hands of poorly motivated, untrained, apathetic and highly-stressed staff, gentle teaching can appear to provide a rationale for the all-too-pervasive attitude of neglect which passes for service provision in the field of intellectual disabilities. Many of the practices carried out in the name of gentle teaching are a travesty of its basic message. Yet the gentle teaching movement itself must bear some responsibility for this due to the confusing, jargon-filled and often contradictory ways in which the principles of gentle teaching have been articulated.

Responses to Gentle Teaching
Responses to gentle teaching can broadly be divided into two: (1) Largely positive responses from front line staff working with people with challenging behaviour and intellectual disability and (2) Largely negative responses from professionals, primarily from within the behavioural community working with the same population.

Positive Responses.
There can be little doubt that gentle teaching is very popular with many front line staff. The reasons for this popularity seems to be a result of a number of factors:

1) *The use of language.* The gentle teaching literature abounds with warm, comforting words which have an intuitive appeal to many staff. Words like 'gentle', 'valuing', 'bonding', 'solidarity' and 'warmth' convey an image of kindly benevolence which can lead to the adoption of the entire gentle teaching 'package' through methods which are familiar to advertising and marketing experts. An irony here is that a deeper reading of the gentle teaching literature reveals a consistent and pervasive use of jargon, obscure phraseology and 'psychobabble' which almost borders on the gratuitous (Conneally, 1989; Jones, 1990). One reason why this has not detracted from the popularity of gentle teaching is that, until quite recently,

access to original material written by McGee and colleagues had been very difficult since 'the purveyors of gentle teaching have not chosen to publish their work in any of the standard peer-reviewed journals' (Bailey, 1992) and that published literature on gentle teaching has to 'be culled from a wide variety of books and professional journals derived from three continents' (Cuvo, 1992). Thus, until recently, many direct-care staff have only had access to 'second-hand' literature describing the ideas behind gentle teaching from the perspective of the commentator. Perhaps inevitably, these commentators added their own interpretation to the theory and this may have coloured the acceptance of gentle teaching by staff. For example the commentaries by Brandon (1989a; 1989b; 1990) emphasised the importance of solidarity between carer and learner and outlined the relationship between gentle teaching and social role valorisation (normalisation). The need for a structured and systematic approach and the importance of engagement were, however, largely ignored.

2) *Non-interventionism.* A second reason for the popularity of gentle teaching is that superficially it may seem to justify a 'non-interventionist' attitude to working with people with challenging behaviour. 'All you need is love' seemed to be the way forward and gentle teaching appeared to supply the philosophical base for 'allowing' the clients to behave as they wished. Similar service deficits have also been caused by a misunderstanding of the basic tenets of social role valorisation (Baldwin, 1985). One of the present authors (RJ) has visited a number of services where the phrase 'gentle teaching' was used to explain the absence of careful record keeping, high levels of client disengagement, sloppy professional behaviour and a management attitude which fostered paternalism and low expectations. This is clearly not what the proponents of gentle teaching have intended in their writings and workshops but the point remains that many service personnel have implemented a version of gentle teaching which has done little to enhance the quality of life of the service users involved.

3) *Packaging and marketing.* Anyone who has attended a gentle teaching workshop run by professionals from the University of Nebraska cannot but be impressed by the charismatic performance of the presenters. Videotapes show the presenters working with people displaying extreme challenging behaviour while the use of professional audio-visual aids enhances the presentation. Questions from the floor are encouraged and the audience is invited to talk about case examples and how the theory might be applied in their own work environment. Delegates are presented with a folder to take away which contains copies of the overheads used and throughout the presentation a professional and relaxed atmosphere is created. When this is allied to the undoubted sincerity and commitment of the presenters it is not surprising that many staff return from these workshops with an almost evangelical desire to 'do' gentle teaching. This may be especially true for staff who have

183

previously attended staff training in behavioural methods which may not have been as carefully marketed or presented and which may have involved presentations from professionals who appeared divorced from the day-to-day realities of working with clients displaying challenging behaviour. Issues related to scientific validation or objective data analysis may take second place to a persuasive presentation. 'Most providers, advocates, parents and staff are not well versed in scientific method and do not bring a critical eye to the discussion. As citizens primarily concerned with the health and welfare of these developmentally disabled persons, they are easily persuaded by someone with a message of doom and revelation. When a Professor from a major university sounds the alarm and uses terms like "torture" who wouldn't sit up and listen?' (Bailey, 1992).

4) *Staff motivation.* A criticism of behaviourism is that it has only recently begun to address the chronicity and variability of severe challenging behaviour. Up to the late 1980's readers of mainstream behavioural literature could have been forgiven for assuming that challenging behaviour could be explained by the same simple, orderly, rules of environmental control which governed less complex forms of behaviour. The influences of physiological variables (Oliver & Head, this volume), verbal behaviour (Jones, Williams & Lowe, in press) and setting conditions (Woods & Blewitt, this volume) as well as the difficulties often encountered in obtaining a clear functional analysis (Owens & MacKinnon, this volume) are phenomena which are only slowly finding acceptance in the behavioural literature. Frequently, staff who undertake training in behavioural approaches are presented with a philosophy and methodology which suggests that dramatic and enduring improvements in challenging behaviour can be obtained by applying behavioural principles obtained from work with infra-human species in laboratory settings or from work with human subjects with mild challenging behaviours in highly controlled and well staffed demonstration projects. The chronicity and intractability of, for example, severe self-injurious behaviour appears to be rarely mentioned in staff training workshops. The inevitable disappointment which is experienced when the behavioural skills which have been taught on these courses fail to effect long lasting positive changes in client behaviour is often compounded by the fact that failure is either overtly or covertly attributed to the inability of staff to implement the procedures correctly. Once again, it is not surprising that direct-care staff may find more appeal in an alternative approach which appears to acknowledge the difficulty and chronicity of challenging behaviour and which suggests that the attitude and long-term commitment of the caregiver can be of central importance. Barrera & Teodoro (1990) have phrased the issue as follows:

'Much of gentle teaching's appeal seems to be based on not whether it works . . . but instead on its ability to help caregivers cope with and accept the chronic and seemingly intractable traits of their charges. Caregivers are taught to make attitudinal changes and lifelong commitments, i.e., true parental or therapist bonds, seemingly sharing many of the attributes of positive healing and palliative care. These life choices presumably reduce the daily stress of dealing with problem behaviors and the guilt of inefficiency and defeat, and thus strengthen acceptance of disabling conditions with some dignity and self-respect. Apparently, these commitments can be reinforced by even minute signs of social responsiveness, even in the absence of therapeutic behavioral changes, because they justify in the caregivers' perceptions their new faith. For much of gentle teaching, the question of whether it works or not is thus meaningless, and it is not surprising that in the face of negative treatment results some caregivers will reply that it does not really matter, while others will argue that it does *appear* to work'.

This concept of a long-term commitment is reiterated frequently by the proponents of gentle teaching. At a workshop attended by the first author, McGee (1989) stated that 'you have to work with your whole body - your hands and your heart and your soul to be a caregiver'. Similarly, staff are reminded that they have 'a difficult and long road to journey' (McGee & Melonascino, 1991) and that 'if it were easy there would be few behavior problems. Our belief in the dignity of the human condition is what sustains us in good times *and* hard times' (McGee & Menolascino, 1991).

Thus, for a variety of reasons, a philosophy of care with little evidence of effectiveness, which emphasises how difficult and intractable challenging behaviour can be, and which seems to demand a long-term commitment from caregivers, can paradoxically appear both appealing and motivating and become popular with direct-care staff.

Negative Responses.
At the same time that gentle teaching was enjoying growing popularity with many direct-care staff it was widely criticised by professionals from within the behavioural perspective. Barrera & Teodoro (1990) have summarised the position as follows:

'We have sneered at gentle teaching's ungentle criticisms of behaviorism and of the scientific principles of lawfully determined behavior, and we have shunned it as biased, unscientific, and naive. We also have conducted revisionistic armchair analysis of gentle teaching, dismissing it more often than not as a mere recombinant of positive reinforcement, manual guidance, prompting, and extinction'.

The criticisms of gentle teaching have centred on a number of issues:

185

(1) *Gentle teaching and applied behavioural analysis.*
The proponents of gentle teaching have maintained a sustained and vitriolic attack on behaviourism. The first chapter of the book entitled *Gentle Teaching* (McGee, Menolascino, *et al.*, 1987) is devoted to arguing against the use of punishment techniques in the reduction of challenging behaviour. The authors certainly do not mince their words in attacking those who have employed such practices. For example, readers are informed that:

> 'Like torturers, some behavior modifiers are trained in the nuances of pain and punishment . . . Torturers are protected by authoritarian governments and behavior modifiers are protected by human rights committees . . . The end result of both torture and punishment is the same - creation of the feeling that the 'programmer' is omnipotent and omniscient and a reduction of the person to a state of total mortification, humiliation and degradation' (McGee, Menolascino, *et al.*, 1987).

Given the strength of this language, it is rather unfortunate to find that, as pointed out by Mudford (1985), the chapter contains inaccurate information concerning the work of several researchers. For example, it is stated that 'strange practices such as squirting ammonia in the face . . . are periodically introduced as innovative practices' (McGee, Menolascino, *et al.*, 1987). A number of references are cited in support of this assertion (Gross, Berier, & Drabman, 1982; Reilich, Spooner, & Rose, 1984; Tanner & Zeiler, 1975). However, as Mudford (1985) points out, none of these references refer to the squirting of ammonia in the face. In fact, two of the papers involved the use of a water mist sprayed in the learner's face (Gross *et al.*, 1982; Reilich *et al.*, 1984), and the third involved placing a crushed ammonia capsule under the learner's nose (Tanner & Zeiler, 1975). It is particularly unfortunate that the allegation concerning the squirting of ammonia was repeated and exaggerated in a series of articles by David Brandon in which he stated that the use of ammonia spray was '*common* (our emphasis), especially in the United States' (1989a) and that in one hospital in Western Ontario the use of ammonia sprays was 'fairly common' (1990). The only evidence presented to back up these assertions was a reference to McGee's book.

There are many other examples of inaccurate and unfair reporting in McGee's writings. This has led Mudford (1985) to assert that 'the ill researched, vitriolic attack on mainstream behavior analysts . . . is definitely incorrect and possibly libellous'. On the other hand, behaviourists have responded by criticising McGee personally (Linscheid, Meinhold & Mulick, 1990) and the gentle teaching movement itself (Turnbull, 1990; Mudford, 1985). Turnbull (1990) dismisses gentle teaching as 'unimpressive' and Linscheid *et al.*, (1990) state that 'gentle teaching should be thought of as no more than another example of pop-therapy' and claim that during a gentle teaching session McGee 'clearly and apparently purposefully stuck his finger into the client's eye'.

Jones *et al.*, (1991) have suggested that this extreme polarisation does little to advance either cause and raises serious questions about the objectivity of the protagonists of both approaches. They have stated that . . . 'what is perhaps most ironic is how frequently behaviourists claim that gentle teaching is both identical to behaviourism *and* ineffective without apparently being aware what this statement says about the efficacy of behavioural procedures'.

(2) *Gentle teaching is ineffective.*

The proponents of gentle teaching have made wide-ranging and extravagant claims regarding its effectiveness. McGee (1985c) reported that gentle teaching had been used successfully with over 600 learners at the Nebraska Psychiatric Institute and other venues including, group homes, sheltered workshops and the learner's own home. The client group included individuals with mild and severe intellectual disability exhibiting problems such as aggression and self-injurious behavior, as well as learners diagnosed as depressed or schizophrenic. Elsewhere McGee had quoted extremely impressive outcome data for this client group. 'Only 13% were reported to require additional treatment at the facility, and 5% returned twice. These figures suggest that gentle teaching is a powerful treatment approach because the average stay at the facility was only 28 days' (Jordan *et al.*, 1989). Despite these claims, it is extremely difficult to find objective, scientific evidence as to the effectiveness of gentle teaching. A number of anecdotal accounts of successful outcomes have appeared in the literature (Butler, 1990; Kelley & Stone, 1989) but as with McGee's claims these have been characterised by a lack of objective data gathering, no baseline or control conditions and inadequate follow-up measures. It is clear that the learners in these studies showed significant decreases in challenging behaviour. What is not clear, however, is whether these reductions were because of, unrelated to, or despite the gentle teaching intervention. On the other hand a number of more scientifically controlled studies have appeared which showed gentle teaching to have little or no effect (Barrera & Teodoro, 1990; Jordan, Singh & Repp, 1989; Paisey, Whitney & Moore, 1989).

More recently, a small number of studies with objective methodologies have found gentle teaching to be successful in some cases (Jones, Singh & Kendall, 1990; Jones, Singh & Kendall, 1991; McGee, 1990b; McGee & Gonzalez, 1990). These studies are discussed in detail by McCaughey & Jones (1992) who concluded that . . . 'the effectiveness of gentle teaching has yet to be adequately researched but initial investigations suggest a mixed success with a minority of studies reporting some reductions in challenging behaviour. It is therefore premature either to abandon gentle teaching completely, or to accept it uncritically without further scientific evaluation assessing its potential as an approach in the treatment of severe challenging behaviour. A first step in this endeavour will necessitate the proponents

187

of gentle teaching providing operational definitions of the central concepts which are thought to underlie this approach'.

3) *Gentle teaching could be aversive.* Physical danger is always a possibility during gentle teaching. 'Julie Stone has been working full time on gentle teaching with staff in a school since Tuesday of last week. She will be staying till Friday. That's nine straight days for her. *Her hands and arms are a terrible mess - scars and wounds from scratching and gouging* (our emphasis). Her family is wondering what's up and when I look I have no choice but to feel the same. But it's working . . .' (Kelley & Stone, 1989). Not only could there be a potential for danger to staff who attempt to implement gentle teaching, there may also be a danger to learners. McGee's own writings seem to bear this out. For example, McGee (1985b) states that at the beginning of the process of gentle teaching '. . . the person will display behaviours which obviously indicate that the person does not want anything to do with the caregiver - screaming, hitting, biting, kicking, scratching, avoiding, etc.' Unless the caregiver is both highly motivated and highly trained this scenario may be dangerous to both parties. A number of authors have suggested that gentle teaching may be an aversive strategy to some learners depending upon their motivation for engaging in challenging behaviour (Emerson 1990; Jones *et al.*, 1991). Although McGee quite rightly emphasises the communicative basis of challenging behaviour, he fails to adequately distinguish between the different functions which challenging behaviour may serve (see Owens & MacKinnon, this volume). McGee and his colleagues emphasise the fact that insufficient attention has been paid to the assessment of the role of dyadic relationships in the analysis of challenging behaviour. While this emphasis may be justified, it is unfortunate that this form of analysis is their only attempt to investigate the motivational dynamics underlying an individual's challenging behaviour. Not only is there sufficient evidence to suggest that the lack of a full functional analysis reduces the probability of treatment effectiveness (Jones, 1989), it is also possible that in some cases a premature intervention may actually be dangerous to the learner. To take self-injurious behaviour as an example, there is evidence to suggest that self-injury may occur as a consequence of frontal lobe epilepsy (Geyde, 1989) or as a response to pain resulting from any number of untreated medical conditions (Gunsett, Mulick, Fernald & Martin, 1989). Although the proponents of gentle teaching seem aware of the recent research on functional analysis, indeed the key papers are well summarised in McGee, 1990b and in McGee & Gonzalez (1990), there seems to be no attempt to include such an analysis prior to implementing gentle teaching. Finally, there are some suggestions that even a successful gentle teaching intervention could itself lead to the development of new inappropriate behaviours. Both Kelley & Stone (1989) and Butler (1990) point to the development of novel challenging behaviours during gentle teaching interventions. Interestingly this phenomenon has also been reported

in the behavioural literature as occurring in some cases during differential reinforcement procedures (Jones, 1991).

Future Directions

The gentle teaching approach has raised a number of issues which touch at the heart of service provision for learners with challenging behaviour and intellectual disabilities. The first of these concern the differing responses to gentle teaching outlined above. It seems obvious that there is a great deal of misinformation surrounding this approach and that the combination of heated debate, arrogance and ignorance which are found elsewhere in service provision are also relevant to gentle teaching. The suggestion from the present authors that it may be productive for the proponents of both gentle teaching and applied behavioral analysis 'to recognise that much can profitably be gained from adopting some of the positive aspects of the other's approach' (Jones & McCaughey, 1992) has already drawn a strongly negative response from some American behaviourists (Bailey, 1992; Cuvo, 1992) and it seems likely that similar responses will be evoked on this side of the Atlantic. In contrast, our attempts to emphasise engagement and functional analysis as important aspects of gentle teaching (Jones et al., 1991) have drawn similar negative responses from some individuals who regard themselves as gentle teachers. We make the same request to those who are passionate advocates of the gentle teaching movement as we do to those who are passionately opposed to it: Please read the gentle teaching literature!

A second issue concerns the available evidence on the effectiveness of gentle teaching. Although the majority of studies have reported a lack of success, some more recent studies suggest that *at least in some circumstances* gentle teaching can effect reductions in challenging behaviour. We need to regard gentle teaching as a package of interventions rather than as a single intervention. Like any therapeutic package, it is composed of a number of components and some components may be necessary, some may be neutral and some may actually reduce its effectiveness. This suggests some interesting lines of future research: For example, are there components of gentle teaching (e.g., bonding) which in and of themselves will lead to therapeutic success or is the whole 'package' necessary? Are there particular learner characteristics which are predictive of therapeutic success? As a first step, however, we need to go beyond the small scale and time-limited nature of much of the studies undertaken so far and move towards an analysis of why specific treatments work for some individuals and seem to be ineffective for others (Jones, 1991). As with almost all other therapeutic interventions, it seems likely that there will be some learners who will benefit from a gentle teaching approach just as there will be some who will not. Future researchers will need to address more complicated issues concerning treatment effectiveness rather than attempting to answer the basic question of whether or not gentle teaching 'works' (McCaughey & Jones, 1992).

The methodology of research studies could profitably move away from single-case reversal designs towards the use of multiple baseline or group designs, allowing sufficient time (measured in months rather than days) in each phase for therapeutic effects to become established. (The very short times given to experimental observation has been a particular criticism of some of the early experimental attempts to externally assess gentle teaching.) It would also be useful to monitor any response co-variation effects by measuring a range of collateral behaviours, including the concurrent monitoring of additional appropriate and inappropriate behaviours (Jones & McCaughey, 1990). It may be of particular interest to monitor behaviours which might be associated with increases in 'interdependence'. These might include increases in 'eye contact', 'friendly comments', and 'turn taking' (McGee & Gonzalez, 1990). In this context, the use of a detailed functional analysis will be important in establishing whether gentle teaching is more effective with behaviour maintained by one function (e.g., attention) rather than another (e.g., self stimulation).

Finally, we may wish to conduct the type of revisionist armchair analysis suggested by Barrera & Teodoro (1990) and speculate as to whether there really is something unique about gentle teaching or whether it is merely a cleverly repackaged version of well-known behavioural principles. What is clear, however, is that the combination of value-based interventions, high staff motivation, a clear vision and a determined will to succeed allied to powerful and experimentally validated behavioural procedures may represent one of the most forceful techniques yet developed. In the final analysis it doesn't matter what its called - if it works we should seek to know why.

Service Implications.

Although it is likely that the arguments for and against the use of gentle teaching will continue for some time, already many services have adopted some of the basic philosophical ideas into their service practice.

A number of factors should be considered by any service attempting to adopt these principles:

* Gentle teaching has a wide focus and directs service providers to look beyond the simple reduction of challenging behaviours towards an analysis of the entire environment in which a learner exists. This focus may be essential for the successful implementation of gentle teaching and needs to be emphasised. Gentle teaching is not just about being nice to people.

* Gentle teaching requires fundamental changes in staff as well as learners. Management issues such as staff supervision, motivation and burnout are extremely important in any service to persons with intellectual disability but may be central to gentle teaching.

* Gentle teaching implies engagement. Again, it is not sufficient merely to be nice to people. In addition to tolerance, warmth, and affection gentle teaching implies 'structure and discipline' (McGee, Menousek & Hobbs, 1987). Individuals need sufficient programming to ensure that their behaviours are not ignored but rather redirected, that sufficient learning of new skills are programmed to prevent the future occurrence of challenging behaviour, and that staff are actively engaged in ongoing interactions with all learners.

* Although not mentioned by McGee, it is would seem essential that a thorough functional analysis be carried out for each individual learner before any decisions are made regarding which treatment strategy to implement in cases of challenging behaviour. In this way, the risk of employing procedures that appear gentle but which could be aversive or potentially dangerous will be reduced.

* Although there is some limited evidence of treatment effectiveness (McCaughey & Jones, 1992), the present status of gentle teaching is equivocal as regards experimental validity. This suggests that for the present at least, gentle teaching should be regarded as an ideology rather than a method of proven effectiveness, much in the same way as the theory of social role valorisation is regarded at present.

* Finally, the proponents of gentle teaching themselves must take some responsibility for the increasing numbers of services which, while still using the name 'gentle teaching', have departed from the basic concepts and are providing less than optimum environments for people with intellectual disabilities. Clear guidelines, operational definitions and the public refutation of shoddy services may be necessary if gentle teaching is to survive as a treatment beyond this first decade. Unless this responsibility is accepted then gentle teaching could become a name for the archives rather than a viable treatment option for people with intellectual disabilities and challenging behaviour.

References

Bailey, J. S. (1992). Gentle teaching: Trying to win friends and influence people with euphemism, methapor, smoke and mirrors. *Journal of Applied Behavior Analysis*, 25, 879–883.

Baldwin, S. (1985). Sheep in wolf's clothing: Impact of normalisation teaching on human services and service providers. *International Journal of Rehabilitation Research* 8, 131-142.

Barrera, F. J., and Teodoro, G. M. (1990). Flash bonding or cold fusion? A case analysis of gentle teaching. In A. C. Repp and N. N. Singh (Eds.), *Current perspectives on the use of aversive and non-aversive interventions with developmentally disabled persons*. Sycamore, IL: Sycamore Publishing Co.

Bateson, G. (1951). Information and codification: A philosophical approach. In J. Ruesch and G. Bateson (Eds.), *Communication: The Social Matrix of Psychiatry*. New York: Norton and Company.

Boff, L. and Boff, C. (1987). *Introduction to a Theology of Liberation*. Maryknoll, NY: Orbis Books.

Bowlby, J. (1982). *Attachment and loss: Volume 1 attachment* (2nd Ed.). New York: Basic Books.

Bradshaw, C. M., and Szabadi, E. (1988). Quantitative analysis of human operant behavior. In G. Davey, and C. Cullen (Eds)., *Human operant conditioning and behavior modification*. New York: Wiley.

Brandon, D. (1989a). The gentle way to work with mental handicap. *Social Work Today* 20, 14-15.

Brandon, D. (1989b). How gentle teaching can liberate us all. *Community Living* 2, 9-10.

Brandon, D. (1990). Gentle teaching. *Nursing Times* 86, 62-63.

Butler, B. (1990). Gentle teaching in practice. *Frontline*, 90, 13-14.

Butterfield, E. C. (1990). The compassion of distinguishing punishing behavioral treatment from aversive treatment. *American Journal on Mental Retardation* 95, 137-141.

Cataldo, M. F., Ward, E. M., Russo, D. C., and Riordan, M. (1986). Compliance and correlated problem behavior in children: Effects of contingent and non-contingent reinforcement. *Analysis and Intervention in Developmental Disabilities* 6, 265-282.

Conneally, S. (1989). Gentle teaching. *The Irish Psychologist* 16, 5-6.

Cuvo, A.J. (1992). Gentle teaching: On the one hand . . . but on the other hand. *Journal of Applied Behavior Analysis*, 25, 873–877.

Emerson, E. (1990). Some challenges presented by severe self-injurious behaviour. *Mental Handicap* 18, 92-98.

Freire, P. (1970). *Cultural Action for Freedom*. London: Penguin Books.

Freire, P. (1972). *Pedagogy of the Oppressed*. London: Penguin Books.

Geyde, A. (1989). Extreme self-injury attributed to frontal lobe seizures. *American Journal on Mental Retardation* 94, 20-26.

Gross, A. M., Berier, E. S., and Drabman, R. S. (1982). Reduction of aggressive behavior in a retarded boy using a water squirt. *Journal of Behavior Therapy and Experimental Psychiatry* 13, 95-98.

Guess, D., Helmstetter, E., Turnbull, H. R., III, and Knowlton, S. (1986). U*se of aversive procedures with persons who are disabled: An historical review and critical analysis* (Monograph). Seattle: The Association for Persons With Severe Handicaps.

Guess, D., Turnbull, H. R., III, and Helmstetter, E. (1990). Science, paradigms and values: A response to Mulick. *American Journal on Mental Retardation* 95, 157-163.

Gunsett, R. P., Mulick, J. A., Fernald, W. B., and Martin, J. L. (1989). Indications for medical screening prior to behavioral programming for severely and profoundly mentally retarded clients. *Journal of Autism and Developmental Disorders* 19, 167-172.

Jones, R. S. P. (1989). Operant procedures in the treatment of self-injurious behaviour in people with a mental handicap. *Irish Journal of Psychology* 10, 100-110.

Jones, R. S. P. (1990). Gentle teaching: Behaviourism at its best? *Community Living* 3, 9-10.

Jones, R. S. P. (1991). Reducing inappropriate behaviour using non-aversive procedures: Evaluating differential reinforcement schedules. In B. Remington (Ed.), *The challenge of severe mental handicap: A behaviour analytic approach*. Chichester: Wiley.

Jones, R. S. P., McCaughey, R. E., and Connell, E. M. (1991). The philosophy and practice of gentle teaching: Implications for mental handicap services. *The Irish Journal of Psychology* 12, 1-16.

Jones, R. S. P., and McCaughey, R. E. (1992). Gentle Teaching and Applied Behavior Analysis: A critical review. *Journal of Applied Behavior Analysis*, 25, 853–867.

Jones, R. S. P., Williams, H., and Lowe, C. F. (In Press). Verbal self-regulation. In I. Fleming and B. S. Kroese (Eds). *People with learning difficulties and challenging behaviour: A sourcebook*. Manchester: Manchester University Press.

Jones, L. J., Singh, N. N., and Kendall, K. A. (1990). Effects of gentle teaching and alternative treatments on self-injury. In A. C. Repp and N. N. Singh (Eds.), *Current perspectives on the use of aversive and non-aversive interventions with developmentally disabled persons*. Sycamore, IL: Sycamore Publishing Co.

Jones, L. J., Singh, N. N., and Kendall, K. A. (1991). Comparative effects of gentle teaching and visual screening on self-injurious behavior. *Journal of Mental Deficiency Research* 35, 37-47.

Jordan, J., Singh, N. N., and Repp, A. C. (1989). An evaluation of gentle teaching and visual screening in the reduction of stereotypy. *Journal of Applied Behavior Analysis* 22, 9-22.

Kelley, B., and Stone, J. (1989). Gentle teaching in the classroom. *Entourage* 4, 15-19.

LaVigna, G. W. and Donnellan, A. M. (1986). *Alternatives to Punishment: Solving Behavior Problems with Non-aversive Strategies*. Irvington: New York.

Linscheid, T. R., Meinhold, P. M. and Mulick, J. A. (1990). Gentle teaching? *Behavior Therapist* 13, 32.
Matas, L, Arend, R, and Sroufe, L. A. (1978). Continuity of adaptation in the second year: The relationship between quality of attachment and later competent functioning. *Child Development* 49, 547-556.
McCaughey, R. E., and Jones, R. S. P. (1992). The effectiveness of Gentle Teaching. *Mental Handicap* 20, 7-14.
McGee, J. J. (1979). *The Needs of Autistic Persons and their Families.* Omaha, NE: Nebraska Chapter of the National Society for Autistic Children.
McGee, J. J. (1985a). Bonding as the goal of teaching. *Mental Handicap in New Zealand* 9, (4), 5-10.
McGee, J. J. (1985b). Gentle teaching. *Mental Handicap in New Zealand* 9, (3), 13-24.
McGee, J. J. (1985c). Examples of the use of gentle teaching. *Mental Handicap in New Zealand* 9, (4), 11-20.
McGee, J. J. (1989, March) *Gentle teaching:* A three day workshop presented to the Mental Handicap Group of the Psychological Society of Ireland, Galway City, Ireland.
McGee, J. J. (1990a). Gentle Teaching: The basic tenet. *Mental Handicap Nursing* 86, 68-72.
McGee, J. J. (1990b). Towards a psychology of interdependence: A preliminary study of the effects of gentle teaching in 15 persons with severe behavioral disorders and their caregivers. In A. Dosen, A. Van Gennep, G. J. Zwanikken. (Eds.) (1990). *Treatment of mental illness and behavioral disorder in the mentally retarded.* Proceedings of the International Congress, May 3rd and 4th 1990 Amsterdam, the Netherlands. Leiden, the Netherlands: Logon Publications
McGee,J. J., and Gonzalez, L. (1990). Gentle teaching and the practice of human interdependence: A preliminary group study of 15 persons with severe behavioural disorders and their caregivers. In A. C. Repp and N. N. Singh (Eds.), *Current perspectives on the use of aversive and non-aversive interventions with developmentally disabled persons.* Sycamore, IL: Sycamore Publishing Co.
McGee, J. J., and Hitzing, W. (1978). *The Continuum of Residental Services: A Critical Analysis.* Proceedings of the Symosium on Residential Services. Arlington, TX: National Association for Retarded Citizens.
McGee, J. J., and Menolascino, F. J. (1991). Beyond gentle teaching: A nonaversive approach to helping those in need. New York: Plenum Press.
McGee, J. J., Menolascino, F. J., Hobbs, D. C., and Menousek, P. E. (1987). *Gentle teaching: A non-aversive approach to helping persons with mental retardation.* New York: Human Sciences Press.
McGee, J. J., Menousek, P. E., and Hobbs, D. C. (1987) Gentle teaching: An alternative to punishment for people with challenging behaviors. In S. J. Taylor, D. Bicker, J. Knoll (Eds.), *Community integration for people with severe learning disabilities.* New York: Teachers College Press.
Menolascino, F., and Egger, M. L. (1978). *Medical Dimensions of Mental Retardation.* Lincoln, NE: University of Nebraska Press.
Menolascino, F., and McGee, J. J. (1981). The new institutions: Last ditch arguments. *Mental Retardation* 19, 215-220.
Menolascino, F. J., and McGee, J. J. (1983). Persons with severe mental retardation and behavioural challenges: From disconnectedness to human engagement. *The Journal of Psychiatric Treatment and Evaluation* 5, 187-193.
Mudford, O. C. (1985). Treatment selection in behaviour reduction: Gentle teaching versus the least intrusive treatment model. *Australia and New Zealand Journal of Developmental Disabilities* 10, 265-270.
Mulick, J. A. (1990). The ideology and science of punishment in mental retardation. *American Journal on Mental Retardation* 95, 142-156.
Mulick, J. A., and Kedesdy, J. H. (1988). Self-injurious behavior, its treatment, and normalization. *Mental Retardation* 26, 223-229.
Ney, P. G. (1973). Effect of contingent and non-contingent reinforcement on the behavior of an autistic child. *Journal of Autism and Childhood Schizophrenia* 3, 115-127.
Oliver, C., Murphy, G. H., and Corbett, J. A. (1987). Self- injurious behaviour in people with mental handicap: A total population study. *Journal of Mental Deficiency Research,* 31 147-162.
Paisey, T. J., Whitney, R. B., and Moore, J. (1989). Person-treatment interactions across nonaversive response-deceleration procedures for self-injury: A case study of effects and side effects. *Behavioral-Residential-Treatment* 4, 69-88.

Reilich, L. L., Spooner, F., and Rose, T. L. (1984). The effects of contingent water mist on the stereotypic responding of a severely handicapped adolescent. *Journal of Behavior Therapy and Experimental Psychiatry* 15, 165-170.

Repp, A. C., and Singh, N. N. (Eds.). (1990) *Current perspectives on the use of aversive and non-aversive interventions with developmentally disabled persons.* Sycamore, IL: Sycamore publishing Co.

Repp, A. C., Felce, D., and Barton, L. E. (1988). Basing the treatment of stereotypic and self-injurious behaviours on hypotheses of their causes. *Journal of Applied Behaviour Analysis* 21, 281-289.

Rogers, C. R. (1961). *On becoming a person: A therapist's view of psychotherapy.* Boston: Houghton Mifflin.

Stark, J., Baker, D., Menousek, P., and McGee, J. J. (1981). Behavioral programming for the severely mentally retarded/behaviorally impaired. In K. Lynch, W. Kiernan, and J. Stark (Eds.), *Prevocational and vocational education for special needs youth.* Baltimore: Paul H. Brookes Publishers.

Tanner, B., and Zeiler, M., (1975). Punishment of self-injurious behavior using aromatic ammonia as the aversive stimulus. *Journal of Applied Behavior Analysis* 8, 55-57.

Taylor, S. J., Bicker, D., and Knoll J. (1987) *Community Integration for People with Severe Learning Disabilities.* New York: Teachers College Press.

Tierney, I. R., McGuire, R. J., and Walton, H. J. (1979). Reduction of stereotyped body-rocking using variable reinforcement: Practical and theoretical implications. *Journal of Mental Deficiency Research* 23, 175-185.

Turnbull, J. (1990). Gentle Teaching: The emperor's new clothes? *Mental Handicap Nursing* 86, 64-68

Unger, R. M. (1984). *Passion: An Essay on Personality.* New York: Free Press.

Woods, P. A., and Cullen, C. (1983). Determinants of staff behaviour in long-term care. *Behavioural Psychotherapy* 11, 4-17.

CHAPTER 9

Challenging Behaviour, Psychiatric Disorders and the Law

Glynis Murphy
Institute of Psychiatry, London
and
Tony Holland
University of Cambridge

Introduction

People with intellectual disabilities are sometimes accused of offending against the law. Offending behaviour is almost always challenging behaviour (though the reverse is not necessarily true) and it may be associated with psychiatric disorders. In this chapter, we consider what is known about people with intellectual disabilities who offend and what can be offered to them in the way of interventions to increase the likelihood that they will live an ordinary life.

Historical perspective

Historically, both in England and in the USA, there have been special legal provisions for people with psychiatric disorders who are convicted of breaking the law. Walker & McCabe (1968) note that even in the thirteenth century people considered to be insane were pardonned by the King for crimes such as arson and murder (though probably not for lesser crimes, such as theft). By the seventeenth century, people considered insane could be sent to hospitals, such as the Bethlem, following relatively minor crimes (Forshaw & Rollins, 1990), though they more frequently went to prison (Walker & McCabe, 1968). It was not until 1800, however, with the famous case of Hadfield, who fired a pistol at King George III, that a special verdict of 'not guilty because of insanity' entered the statutes, with subsequent detention of such people in hospital (the Bethlem, in Hadfield's case). The trial of McNaughton (1843) and the McNaughton rules specifying the grounds for such a verdict followed later (Walker & McCabe, 1968;

Forshaw & Rollins, 1990) and similar rules were adopted in the USA in the late 1800's (Quen, 1990).

By the thirteenth century 'idiocy and madness' were differentiated (Walker & McCabe, 1968, p. 25) and people with intellectual disabilities were also sometimes pardonned for crimes. Walker mentions a thirteenth century case of a man in prison as a result of theft, who was considered to be an 'idiot' and 'not to blame' and whose case was therefore referred to the King (p 25). By the sixteenth century there were crude methods of testing whether people could manage their own affairs;

'He who shall be said to be a(n) . . . Idiot from birth is such a person who cannot account or number twenty pence, nor can tell who was his Father or Mother, nor how old he is etc, so as it may appear that he hath no understanding of Reason what shall be for his Profit or what for his Loss' (Fitzherbert, 1567, quoted by Walker & McCabe, 1968).

By the 1600's, people were certainly acquitted of crimes on the basis of cognitive difficulties (e.g., the case of Francis Tims, of the Parish of Stepney, who stole a silver cup, quoted by Walker & McCabe, 1968 p 37) and some people dealt with under the later McNaughton rules (of 1843) were probably disabled by intellectual disabilities rather than by 'insanity' *per se* (for example, the case of Atkinson, described by Forshaw & Rollins, 1990). It was not, however, until the 1913 Mental Deficiency Act that people in the UK with 'arrested or incomplete development of mind', who were convicted of an imprisonable offence, were commonly committed to institutions (Walker & McCabe, 1973) and in the two years just after the end of the First World War, 133 (1919) and 183 (1920) people were ordered to institutions, following convictions, under the Mental Deficiency Act (see Table 4, page 74 of Walker & McCabe 1973).

Despite the fact that during the early 1900s more sophisticated methods of assessing intellectual ability became available, there was no formal requirement for these tests to be used to determine whether a person was or was not an 'idiot, imbecile etc.' under the Mental Deficiency Act, and the Board of Control did not consider that this was a necessary part of the assessment when considering whether someone had 'arrested or incomplete development of mind'. Thus it is likely that many people detained who were considered `mentally deficient' were probably on the borderline in terms of ability.

In the UK, the perceived need for the segregation of people with 'mental deficiency' led to the establishment of large institutions ('colonies') which were eventually taken over by the new nationalised health service in 1948 and became hospitals. Although the majority of people with an intellectual disability continued to live outside hospital it was only with the advent of the Government White Paper 'Better Services for the Mentally Handicapped' (1971) that there developed a real commitment to change for those already incarcerated.

Following the Percy Commission, some of the problems of the 1913 Mental Deficiency Act were eliminated by the 1959 Mental Health Act (MHA), which named specific 'disorders and disabilities of mind' including Mental Illness, Psychopathic Disorder and Mental Subnormality and Severe Mental Subnormality. In the definitions given for the categories of mental subnormality and severe mental subnormality evidence of significant and severe impairment of intelligence and social functioning, respectively, were required, thus moving away from the previous concept of 'mental deficiency'. With improved treatment for mental illness the emphasis of the 1959 Act was on the 'right to treatment' leading to discharge from hospital. However, particularly in the case of those detained under categories other than mental illness, 'treatment' easily became long term residential care.

In 1983 a new MHA came into force which further refined the definition of what had been 'Mental Subnormality' and 'Severe Mental Subnormality' (Gostin, 1985) and the terms were changed to 'Mental Impairment' and 'Severe Mental Impairment'. It became necessary for the person to have, in addition to the previous criteria, evidence of 'abnormally aggressive and seriously irresponsible conduct' if s/he were to meet the criteria for the 'mental disorder' of 'mental impairment' or 'severe mental impairment' under the new Act. This change appropriately narrowed the criteria, which allowed compulsory detention in hospital for treatment, to those people with a developmental intellectual disability who might also have mental health or psychological needs.

During the height of the Eugenics movement, in the early 1900's, particularly in the USA, it was thought that a disproportionate number of people with 'mental deficiency' (as well as those with psychiatric disorders or alcohol-related difficulties) committed criminal offences, as this extract shows:

'there is no investigator who denies the fearful role played by mental deficiency in the production of vice, crime and delinquency . . . not all criminals are feeble-minded, but all feeble-minded are at least potential criminals' (Terman, 1916, quoted by Craft, 1984).

Early analyses of the 'abilities' of convicted people sentenced to prison tended to confirm the prejudices of those in the Eugenicist camp (as discussed in Woodward, 1955; Coid, 1984; Craft, 1984). Such analyses were based on extremely poor data (e.g., literacy levels, rather than less biased measures of intellectual functioning) and recent findings in the USA and UK have suggested that there is little or no over-representation within prison populations (see below under Intellectual Disabilities and Offending Behaviour).

Association between intellectual disabilities, challenging behaviour and psychiatric disorder

In order to try to understand the relationship between learning disability and the presence of challenging behaviour and/or psychiatric disorder it is important to be clear about the terms used and their definitions.

Intellectual Disabilities

By definition, 2-3% of the general population will score more than two standard deviations below the population mean for I.Q., assuming a normal distribution. The true prevalence of mild intellectual disabilities is therefore usually quoted as about 2-3%. Within the educational system people with such difficulties may be identifiable (because of, e.g., poor literacy and numeracy skills), but after leaving school many will blend with the rest of the general population so that the administrative prevalence of mild intellectual disabilities reduces by about 75% at the end of schooling (Richardson & Koller, 1985). Those still in touch with services in adulthood generally have intellectual disabilities and social functioning deficits, sometimes in combination with mental health needs and/or challenging behaviour.

More severe disabilities associated with an I.Q. below 50 are estimated to occur in 3 to 4 per 1,000 children (Alberman, 1984) and are frequently associated with biological causes (Roberts, 1987). Most of these children will continue to need special services even in adulthood and the administrative prevalence will differ little from true prevalence in adulthood. Very few will ever be charged with offences against the law, though some will show challenging behaviour.

Challenging behaviour

'Challenging behaviour' refers to behaviour which challenges the services. Severely challenging behaviour is defined by Emerson *et al.,* (1988) as:

'behaviour of such an intensity, frequency or duration that the physical safety of the person or others is likely to be placed in serious jeopardy, or behaviour which is likely to seriously limit or delay access to and use of ordinary community facilities'.

This is a descriptive term and does not in itself imply an understanding of the factors which have contributed to the behaviour. Such factors will include biological, environmental and other variables (see below under Assessment and Treatment). Most studies which have adopted the term challenging behaviour report that aggressive behaviour is the most commonly recognised challenge (Emerson *et al.,* 1988; Murphy *et al.,* 1991). The precise prevalence of challenging behaviour within a population will depend on a variety of issues:

i) The definition employed.
ii) The services surveyed.
iii) The manner by which services are surveyed (e.g., by post/telephone/visits/etc.).
iv) The period of time specified as relevant.
v) The quality of service provision.

The definition adopted has a major effect on the resultant estimate of prevalence and it is clear from a number of studies that service personnel have difficulty agreeing on 'caseness', even with concrete definitions (Oliver *et al.*, 1987). Figures from Jacobsen's New York studies are often quoted as evidence of the prevalence of challenging behaviour amongst people with intellectual disabilities but as the figures result from multiple personnel applying unspecified definitions the figures are probably extremely unreliable (Jacobsen, 1982). More reliable are figures from some careful British studies. These demonstrated that, for example, the prevalence of self-injurious behaviour sufficient to produce tissue damage was 12% amongst people with intellectual disabilities resident in hospital but only 3% amongst adults with intellectual disabilities in the community (Oliver *et al.*, 1987); that the prevalence of aggressive behaviour including physical violence and verbal threats, was 10% in adult day facilities, and 38% in mental handicap hospitals (Harris & Russell, 1990). According to Qureshi & Alborz (1992) an average Health District of 220,000 people can expect to need to provide special services for 42 people with seriously challenging behaviour at any one time.

Where the variation of challenging behaviour has been examined in conjunction with levels of intellectual functioning, it has appeared that the majority of challenging behaviours are more common amongst people with profound or severe disabilities than amongst those with moderate or mild disabilities (e.g., Eyman & Call, 1977). This fits well with the recent research on the functions of challenging behaviour (eg, Carr & Durand, 1985), since both communicative and sensory stimulation functions can be expected to be more common within populations with little or no alternative modes of expression, especially when this is combined with higher rates of sensory impairment and immobility (Hogg & Sebba, 1986).

Particular challenging behaviours are thought to be relatively more frequent amongst people with mild intellectual disabilities than amongst more disabled groups. Eyman & Call, 1977, for example, demonstrated that 'hostile/abusive language', 'rebelliousness', and 'untrustworthiness' (as measured by the ABS, Part II) were all more commonly encountered amongst more-able than less-able people. However, this does not imply that a large proportion of people with mild intellectual disabilities display such behaviour since a brief consideration of the relative prevalence of mild intellectual disabilities (2-3 per 100) as compared to that for more severe intellectual disabilities (3-4 per 1,000) immediately indicates that most people with mild disabilities display no challenging behaviour whatsoever or it would be impossible for the majority of them to 'disappear' into the general population after leaving school.

Mild intellectual disabilities are known to be 28 times as common amongst families where the bread-winner has an unskilled manual job as in families where the bread-winner has a professional or managerial job (Richardson, 1981) and this differentiates children with mild intellectual disabilities from those with severe/profound intellectual disabilities, where there is a much less strong social class trend (Tizard, 1974). The family conditions which produce later behaviour disturbance in people with mild intellectual disabilities appear to be those of disorganisation and conflict (Nihira et al., 1980; Frost, 1984) and instability or discontinuities in care-taking (Stein & Susser, 1960; Richardson et al., 1985a). The effect of these conditions within the family appears to be long-lasting, with considerable evidence of continuity in behavioural difficulties over 10 to 20 years (Richardson et al., 1985b).

Psychiatric Disorder

Psychiatric disorder is a general term for a number of different groups of mental disorders with specific diagnostic criteria. It is therefore very different from the more general term 'challenging behaviour'. The International Classification of Diseases (ICD-9) provides a section on mental disorders which includes organic, psychotic, neurotic and personality disorders and mental retardation, with definitions being given for each category. It is important to note that the term mental illness is not synonymous with the term psychiatric disorder. The latter includes the variety of disorders named in the ICD-9 while 'mental illness' (psychotic disorders) refers to schizophrenia, different types of affective disorders (e.g., manic depressive psychosis etc.), and other forms of psychiatric illness characterised by mental state abnormalities. The 'diagnostic' approach recognises that particular disorders can be identified by specific characteristics and, especially in the case of specific mental illnesses, they have a particular aetiology and response to specific treatments. Such an approach is complementary to a 'functional' perspective and may be crucial at times because of the implications for treatment. For example, ignoring the fact that a person who had committed arson (a 'challenging behaviour') was suffering from a psychotic illness at the time would result in the failure to treat a highly treatable disorder.

The use of defined criteria for diagnosing mental disorders is not only essential from a treatment and management perspective but is also essential for epidemiological research. The application of such defined criteria to a population of people with intellectual disabilities is possible but in the case of mental illnesses specific problems arise. The diagnosis of well recognised mental illnesses such as schizophrenia depends upon the person concerned being able to give a description of their mental state as specific phenomena are characteristic of specific disorders. For example, third person auditory hallucinations, passivity feelings and delusional perception, are likely to be indicative of schizophrenia. If a person's level of language development is limited they may not be able to experience such phenomena or at least not be able to describe them. In the case of affective disorders, such as manic depressive psychosis, this is less of a problem as associated biological features of sleep and appetite disturbance, impaired concentration and agitation may still occur, making the diagnosis possible.

As with studies of the prevalence rates of challenging behaviour in people with intellectual disabilities, there are problems with epidemiological studies of psychiatric disorders due to variations in definitions and diagnosis. Some studies have reported consistently high rates of psychiatric disorder (this includes mental illness, neurotic and personality disorders etc.) of between 25% and 40% in people with intellectual disabilities (Rutter *et al.*, 1970; Corbett, 1979; Reid *et al.*, 1978, Lund, 1985). The presentation of any of the forms of psychiatric disorder may be associated with the presentation of problem behaviour and thus may meet the criteria for 'challenging behaviour'.

In the U.K. there have been a number of hospital based studies which have looked specifically at the rates of psychiatric or mental illness in a population of people in mental handicap hospitals. Rates of schizophrenia are reported to be as high as 3% (c.f. life-time prevalence in the non-mentally handicapped population of 1%) and of affective disorder of between 1% and 4% (Reid, 1972; Wright, 1982). Clearly, though, hospital-based studies will produce far higher prevalence figures for these disorders than community-based studies and because of the difficulty of distinguishing between true and administrative prevalence in adults with mild intellectual disabilities, community-based studies would present major base rate problems.

Challenging behaviour and psychiatric disorder
The extent of overlap between 'challenging behaviour' and psychiatric disorder is uncertain. There has been considerable confusion over terms and different criteria have been used in the various studies. In some surveys, it has been asserted that there is a major overlap (Jacobsen, 1982) while in others there is reported to be very little (Leudar & Fraser, 1987). Some of the reasons for this disagreement are clear:

(i) Some surveys (e.g., that of Jacobson and colleagues) report 'psychiatric' illness amongst people with severe/profound intellectual disabilities. Diagnosis in this group is likely to be unreliable (Reid, 1982; Holland & Murphy, 1990).
(ii) Challenging behaviour can be incorrectly taken as indicative of a psychiatric disorder.
(iii) In some cases, the definitions of psychiatric disorder and of challenging behaviour are loosely applied or not specified.

The likelihood is, of course, that there is some overlap and it is probable, though not inevitable, that a higher proportion of people with mild intellectual disabilities, who are also suffering from psychiatric disorders, show challenging behaviours than the proportion of people with mild intellectual disabilities and no psychiatric disorders. However, it is also clear that it is perfectly possible to engage in seriously challenging behaviour and not suffer from a psychiatric illness, (for example, the young man described by Clare *et al.*, 1992). It is also possible to suffer from a psychiatric illness, such as severe depression but not be considered to display challenging behaviour (unless withdrawal, for example, be considered challenging), just as it is possible to engage in seriously challenging behaviour and also have a psychiatric illness (for example, Mr. S. in Murphy & Clare, 1991).

Intellectual disabilities and offending behaviour

Early studies of prison populations which suggested a link between intellectual disabilities and criminal behaviour (see Historical Perspective above) were based on extremely poor data and recent prison surveys have suggested that there is little or no over-representation of people with intellectual disabilities in prison (MacAchron, 1979; Gunn *et al.*, 1991). However, the fact that some people are diverted through the hospital system means that any links between intellectual disabilities and offending can only be properly investigated by total population studies. A recent investigation of this kind, of a birth cohort in Sweden, has suggested that offending rates are somewhat higher amongst people who attended special education classes in childhood, though the effects of sociological disadvantage and poverty later in life might explain the effect (Hodgins, 1992). People with intellectual disabilities are certainly thought to be over-represented amongst people wrongly convicted of crimes (Gudjonsson & MacKeith 1988; Perske, 1991) and this has led in England to special provision for people with intellectual disabilities when they are initially arrested by police (see below).

When a person with intellectual disabilities engages in a challenging behaviour of a potentially criminal nature staff are often reluctant to call the police (Carson, 1989). The police (and hence the Criminal Justice System) are usually only involved if the person is relatively able and are not always called even then. So, for example, if someone with profound disabilities attacks a member of staff, it is unlikely that the police will be called, If they are called, it is unlikely that the police will proceed or if they do, that the Crown Prosecution Service will wish to prosecute as it is rarely seen to be 'in the public interest' unless the offence is particularly serious.

If a person has no speech and comprehends only a few single words/simple commands, then even if the actus reus (criminal act) requirement of law could be satisfied, that of mens rea (criminal intent) could not (similarly, children of normal ability, less than 10 years of age are not held to be 'criminally responsible'). In the

USA this is termed the 'culpability' requirement and those people with intellectual disabilities who can be shown to be not 'culpable' cannot be convicted and the same is true in other parts of Europe (Lund, 1990; Rasch, 1990). Consequently, the people with intellectual disabilities who find themselves in the Criminal Justice System are generally those with mild intellectual disabilities (i.e. with IQs between 50 and 70), both in Britain and the USA. It seems likely that the presence of intellectual disabilities in defendants often goes undetected, however, and in the USA (McAfee & Gural, 1988) it is still possible to be sentenced to death despite 'mental retardation' (McAfee & Gural, 1988; Perske, 1991; Calnen & Blackman, 1992).

Many of the more seriously challenging behaviours, such as violent attacks on others, arson, sexual assaults, can be considered as criminal offences, while others (such as self-injurious and stereotyped behaviour) do not fall within the jurisdiction of the Law. Whether a person with intellectual disabilities is taken for questioning and whether they are charged with an offence depends in part on the police (Thomas, 1989) and on their estimate of the likelihood of conviction. The police, in turn, will be aware that the Crown Prosecution Service will only proceed if the likelihood of conviction is over 70%. In practice, this means that the police are far more likely to proceed if the person confesses or if there are eye-witness accounts or forensic evidence available.

People with intellectual disabilities are more vulnerable on arrest and during police questioning. Clare & Gudjonsson (1991) have demonstrated that they have a very poor understanding of the police caution and Notice to Detained Persons, even when these are read to them. The Home Office is currently allowing a new caution and Notice to be tested which it is hoped will be clearer for adults both with and without an intellectual disability (Clare, personal communication). During questioning, the raised probability of people with intellectual disabilities confessing erroneously due to high acquiescence and suggestibility is also now recognised (Clare & Gudjonsson, in press) and under the Police and Criminal Evidence (PACE) Act of 1984, people suspected of having intellectual disabilities can only be interviewed with an 'appropriate' adult present (e.g., a social worker or relative).

There are, at present, no reliable data available on the total number of crimes committed in the UK (as opposed to the number reported to the police), so the proportion attributable to people with intellectual disabilities is also unknown. Those people with disabilities who are eventually convicted of crimes in the UK may go to prison or they may receive probation orders or conditional discharges or they may be detained in hospitals under the Mental Health Act. It is thought that very few people with intellectual disabilities are sent to prison in the UK (Gunn et al., 1991) but little is known about the numbers receiving probation orders or conditional discharges. However, there have been a number of examinations of people detained, following Court convictions, under the Mental Health Acts of 1959 and 1983, under the category of 'subnormality'/'severe subnormality' (1959 Act) or 'impairment'/'severe impairment' (1983 Act). These studies have led to a number of erroneous conclusions about people with intellectual disabilities who offend (Lund, 1990).

Walker & McCabe (1968, 1973) investigated a 90% sample of all hospital orders made under the Mental Health Act 1959 between April 1963 and March 1964. They estimated that, at that time, only about 1 in 200 of convicted offenders (excluding motoring offences) were subject to detention under the Mental Health Act. Of the 969 male offenders in their sample, 330 (i.e., approximately one-third) were classified under 'subnormality' or 'severe subnormality' (265 men and 65 men respectively). A further 409 were classified as having schizophrenia, of whom an unknown but probably fairly small percentage may also have had intellectual disabilities; 120 were classified as having a personality disorder and a proportion of these men would also have had a intellectual disabilities; the remaining 72 had depressive illnesses and 38 were unclassified as regards diagnoses. For those labelled 'subnormal', i.e., labelled as having intellectual disabilities, 53% of the crimes they committed were acquisitive (e.g., theft), 27% sexual (ranging from rape to inappropriate undressing), 5% arson and 4% personal violence. The equivalent figures for people labelled as 'severely subnormal' were 49% acquisitive, 31% sexual, 3% arson and 5% crimes of personal violence.

Walker & McCabe's study is often quoted as evidence that people with intellectual disabilities commit proportionately more sexual offences and arson than other mentally disordered offenders. Walker & McCabe considered their figures supported this since two-thirds of all the 'sexual' crimes and half of the arson offences were committed by the male offenders classified under subnormality/severe subnormality (one-third of the total group). It has sometimes been taken to mean that people with intellectual disabilities commit more arson and sexual offences than any other people and both this assertion and that of Walker & McCabe require some discussion.

First, it is important to note that classifications under the MHA may be unreliable: although standardised measures of intelligence should be employed for the classification of mental impairment and severe mental impairment they may not always be used. Parker showed that 60% of people classified as 'severely subnormal' and 54% of those classified 'subnormal' were incorrectly classified (Parker, 1974, quoted by Craft 1985). Therefore, some people with intellectual disabilities may be classified elsewhere, even if they do not have added psychiatric disorders and vice versa.

Secondly, it is essential to consider the process by which people may eventually come to be detained under the Mental Health Act following conviction in Court (Figure 1 and Gunn, 1984). At the simplest level, it is well known that only a very small proportion of all sexual crimes are reported to the police. From that small proportion reported and the even smaller proportion which eventually reach the court, only a small percentage are committed by offenders considered by the Court to be 'mentally disordered', so very little can be concluded about whether the slight over-representation of people with intellectual disabilities amongst this latter group means anything (for example, they may be more easily described by witnesses, they may be less sophisticated at evading the Law, they may be more likely to be wrongly convicted, etc.). Similarly, for the crime of arson, it is thought that the majority of malicious fire-setting is for financial gain (see below) and since it is unlikely that people with intellectual disabilities could benefit financially from fire-setting (since they are unlikely to own insured buildings), it seems improbable that people with intellectual disabilities are more likely to set fires than other people. It is possible, however, that of the 'malicious' fires set by mentally disordered people, those with intellectual disabilities may be somewhat over-represented (see below under arson).

Subsequent to Walker & McCabe's study, the number of people classified as 'subnormal' and sent to hospital by Courts reduced dramatically, from over 300 each year in the 1960's to less than a 100 by 1977 and this was all the more remarkable given the concurrent increase in the numbers of indictable offences (Robertson, 1981; Parker & Tennant, 1979). Robertson suggests that this may be partly a result of the reduction in hospital places over this period and partly a function of the reluctance of doctors to place the more-able person in a hospital setting as hospitals became increasingly reserved for more disabled individuals (Robertson, 1981). Certainly, by 1974, less than 2% of mental handicap admissions were people sent from the Courts (Parker & Tennant, 1979) and few of the offences committed by people so admitted were trivial (Kearns, 1988), suggesting that trivial offences were dealt with by other means.

Recent Home Office statistics for restricted mentally disordered offenders, such as those people detained under section 37/41 of the Mental Health Act, indicate that people with 'mental impairment'/'severe mental impairment' form a minority of all restricted mentally disordered offenders: only 13% of all those so detained in 1986 and only 6% of new admissions in 1986 were classified under some form of mental impairment (Home Office, 1988). However, Home Office statistics do not provide a very detailed breakdown of the figures for unrestricted mentally disordered offenders (e.g., they do not specify the offences of those classified under mental impairment).

Black has recently attempted to produce a more complete picture of people with intellectual disabilities who offend against the Law and are sentenced to hospital in Scotland (Black, 1990). She commented that there were few points in the legal process at which useful information was being collected with respect to people with intellectual disabilities. Of those 44 people detained in three Scottish hospitals for people with intellectual disabilities since 1984, however, two had been detained following firesetting, 15 following aggressive assaults on others, eight for seriously irresponsible behaviour, one for indecency and the remainder for miscellaneous offences.

Court procedure

Within any country, laws provide a framework for the determination of the limits of acceptable and unacceptable behaviour. If a person steps outside these limits, and is caught doing so, there are powers, usually exercised by the Police, to have the 'facts of the case' tested in Court and sentence determined. In the UK, there are criminal and civic laws which specifically identify those 'under disability', with intellectual disabilities and those with mental impairment (see Gunn, 1990 for review) and the same is true in the USA (Sadoff, 1990) and Europe (Rasch, 1990). If challenging behaviour leads to prosecution, those wishing to assist the person concerned will have to take Court procedure into account and to recognise that Magistrates and Judges have to consider a number of factors in determining a particular course of action (including the protection of the public).

There are several points at which the Court itself, or solicitors acting for a person with intellectual disabilities, may wish to seek special advice (see Figure 1). The defence may be concerned about the reliability of confession evidence, or may wish to use the presence of learning disabilities as mitigation prior to sentencing. The defence can also put to the Court that a person is 'under disability' and therefore 'unfit to Plead' (Criminal Procedure (Insanity) Act, 1964). The test for fitness to plead is somewhat rigorous (being able to instruct your lawyer, understanding the proceedings in Court, knowing the difference between being Guilty or Not Guilty, and being able to challenge a member of the Jury) and the consequences of being found unfit, as the Law stood until 1992, were serious as the person had to be detained until he/she became 'fit to plead' and the facts of the case were not heard until then. For people 'under disability' due to intellectual disabilities, it was possible they would never be fit to plead and this sometimes led to prolonged detention of essentially untried persons (Grubin, 1991). The recent adjustments to this law (in 1991) have improved this situation since the facts of the case now have to be tried first (Letts, 1991).

If a person before the Court has a mental disorder, or is suspected of having a mental disorder, the MHA (1983) allows for their detention for assessment and/or treatment (Gostin, 1985). Where treatment is considered appropriate this has to be in a hospital or a registered 'mental nursing home'. For the different Sections in the MHA there are particular criteria which have to be met and in the majority of Sections the person has to have one of the four named mental disorders (see section on Historical Perspectives above) and there also are criteria about the necessity of treatment. The strength of such an Act is that a Court, after hearing the facts of case, if the person is found guilty, can direct that they receive treatment (which might reduce their risk of re-offending) rather than a prison sentence. The main disadvantage is that the period of detention is primarily determined by the 'Responsible Medical Officer', and in the case of Restriction Orders (Section 37/41) by the Home Secretary. Although there is the right of appeal after certain periods of time loss of liberty, albeit in a hospital, can be for a longer period than if a person

206

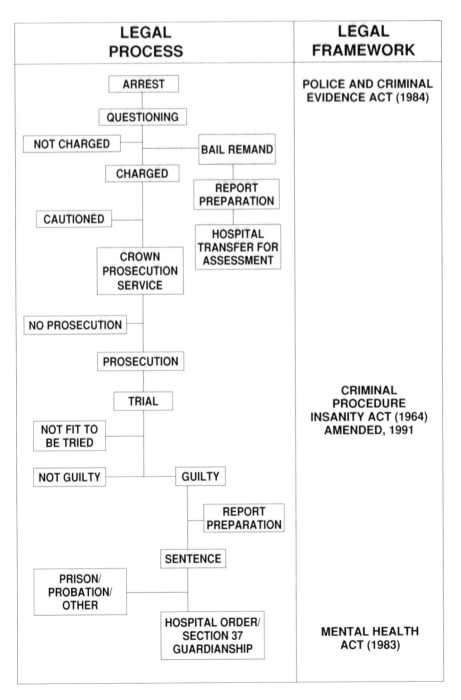

LEGAL PROCESS	LEGAL FRAMEWORK
ARREST	POLICE AND CRIMINAL EVIDENCE ACT (1984)
QUESTIONING	
NOT CHARGED — BAIL REMAND	
CHARGED	
REPORT PREPARATION	
CAUTIONED	
HOSPITAL TRANSFER FOR ASSESSMENT	
CROWN PROSECUTION SERVICE	
NO PROSECUTION	
PROSECUTION	
TRIAL	CRIMINAL PROCEDURE INSANITY ACT (1964) AMENDED, 1991
NOT FIT TO BE TRIED	
NOT GUILTY — GUILTY	
REPORT PREPARATION	
SENTENCE	
PRISON/ PROBATION/ OTHER	
HOSPITAL ORDER/ SECTION 37 GUARDIANSHIP	MENTAL HEALTH ACT (1983)

had received a prison sentence and it appears to be particularly long for people with intellectual disabilities (Robertson, 1981).

The 1983 MHA Act does provide the opportunity for guardianship orders to be made (Gunn, 1984; Gostin, 1985), which require the person to be resident at a particular address, but as yet the order is relatively rarely employed (in 1984, for example, only 10 guardianship orders were made, according to Home Office statistics, compared to a total of 819 hospital orders - Home Office Statistical Bulletin, 1985). Guardianship Orders, however, may provide a useful statutory framework around which to build a package of care within a community setting. Alternatively, Courts may exercise their powers to fine, conditionally discharge, or place on probation orders and the last of these can be subject to conditions such as having to live at a particular place and co-operate with a a proposed course of treatment. The person has to consent to this and the probation officer has the power to recall the person to Court if they do not comply with the conditions. This course of action can sometimes provide a useful statutory framework for providing some structure and support to a person who might otherwise re-offend.

Where challenging behaviour and psychiatric disorder contribute to offending the Criminal Justice System can provide both safeguards for the individual and society and a structure whereby a person who requires help can receive it, but it is not without its difficulties and care needs to be taken to consider the pros and cons of any given course of action which might be suggested to a Court.

Assessment and treatment

Within criminology, there have been disputes over both definitions and theories of crime. Hollin considers that the three most commonly accepted definitions of crime, those arising from the consensus view, the conflict view and the interactionist view, can be linked to the three main sets of theories of crime: classical and positivist theories, radical criminology theory and labelling theory (Hollin, 1989). The belief that offending can be reduced by providing assessment and treatment of psychological and/or psychiatric difficulties fits within the consensus view of crime and would be classified by Hollin as falling within positivist theories of crime.

Within the prison service there has been relatively little assessment and/or treatment available in the UK. The Government is now under pressure to improve the mental health services within prisons (particularly since the suicide rate in prison is so high) and to provide treatment for sex offenders in prison. It is unlikely, however, that these facilities will be rapidly provided and even more unlikely that they will have much impact on the population of people with intellectual disabilities who are detained more often in hospitals than prisons.

In contrast, if people offend against the law and are sentenced to hospital for six months or more under the Mental Health Act 1983 then the court has to be satisfied that treatment in hospital is likely to alleviate or prevent deterioration in the condition (Gunn, 1984; Gostin, 1985). The difficulty of providing effective treatment for people classified under psychopathy has led Grounds to argue that restriction orders of indeterminate length, under the Mental Health Act, should not be employed (Grounds, 1987). Robertson has also argued that detention under Section 60 of the Mental Health Act 1959 or Section 37 of the Mental Health Act 1983 would become unnecessary given adequate provision for supervision in the community for people with intellectual disabilities (Robertson, 1981). Be this as it may, between 50 and 100 new hospital orders (with and without restrictions) appear to be made by the courts each year for people with intellectual disabilities (Robertson, 1989). The total number of people detained with restrictions under mental impairment/severe mental impairment was 249 in 1984 (Home Office Statistics, 1985) so that it is likely that currently around 1,000 people in total are detained with and without restrictions in hospitals after conviction for criminal offences and categorised as having some kind of intellectual disability. In addition, there are some classified as 'unfit to plead' with 'mental impairment'/'severe mental impairment' (51 people according to Home Office Statistical Bulletin of 1985, though for these people there cannot be said to have been a conviction for an offence, since the facts of their cases were never heard).

What kinds of assessments and treatments are offered to people with intellectual disability detained in hospitals and can any firm conclusions be drawn about the effectiveness of such treatments? Recently, over half of the people with restrictions on discharge (i.e. mainly those detained under Section 37/41), classified under 'mental impairment'/'severe mental impairment', have been sent to Special Hospitals (such as Moss Side, now renamed Ashworth South, or Rampton Hospital) - Robertson, 1989. A larger proportion of those sentenced to hospital without restriction orders probably go to local hospitals and/or Regional Secure Services.

The assessment and treatment available in hospitals will depend to a large extent on where a person resides. In one recent study of a British Special Hospital for people without intellectual disabilities by Dell & Robertson (1988), 89% of the men, detained under the category mental illness, were receiving psychotropic medication and only 8% were receiving 'non-physical treatments' (such as psychotherapy, social skills training or sex education) while of those under the category psychopathic disorder, far fewer received medication (14%) but more received other treatments (for example, 14% were having 'psychotherapy', 13% group therapy, 3% social skills training). No equivalent figures are available for a Special Hospital with large numbers of people with intellectual disabilities but it seems likely that, for the majority of people in such an environment, specific psychological assessments and treatments will rarely be provided. Even so, some would argue that 'being there' is the treatment, although it is difficult to envisage what help being locked up with other people with similar difficulties and no specific treatments could provide, apart from perhaps increased maturity (which is well-established as an important factor in criminal offending).

It is, therefore, instructive to consider the results of studies which have followed up people released from Special Hospitals, in order to answer the question of whether their propensity to commit offences has waned or not. One of the first large-scale releases of 'criminally insane' offenders occurred in the USA as a result of a judicial decision in the case of Baxtrom (Steadman & Halfon, 1971). Following this, 969 people were discharged from two large institutions where they had spent, on average, the previous 13 years of their lives. It transpired that both the reconviction and re-admission to hospital rates were remarkably low (Steadman & Halfon, 1971; McGarry, 1971) but one possible reason for this was the increased age of the residents, since age is strongly related to criminal offending.

British studies of mentally disordered offenders released from Special Hospitals also tend to show relatively low reconviction rates for serious crimes. In addition, they report better outcome for those who were older, those who were well supervised in the community, those classified as mentally ill rather than psychopathic and poorer outcome for those with longer records of previous convictions (Tong & MacKay, 1958; Gathercole et al., 1968; Bowden, 1981; Black, 1982). Few of these investigators apart from Robertson, 1981, made specific comments about people with intellectual disabilities. Those who did commented that they had a relatively poorer outcome overall than people who had been classified under 'mental illness'. Robertson's study involved a 15-year follow-up of the people identified in Walker & McCabe's classic examination of crime and insanity in England (between 1963 and 1964) and sent to local psychiatric hospitals under Section 60 of the Mental Health Act 1959. For those with intellectual disabilities, he found that, for both men and women, only 3-4% committed further serious violent offences (grevious bodily harm/wounding, manslaughter, rape) though a great many men and women commited larceny (54% and 50%) during the 15-year period of the follow-up. As in other studies, previous offences were the best predictors of future offending. In terms of the differences between the men originally classified as mentally ill and those classified as having intellectual disabilities (comparisons for women were not possible because of small numbers), Robertson reported that the most overwhelming differences were that of age (the latter groups being about 10 years younger than the former) and previous hospitalisation (more of the 'mentally ill' had been previously hospitalised). Compared to those with 'psychopathic disorder', men with intellectual disabilities had fewer reconvictions.

The assessment and treatment provided in hospitals other than Special Hospitals varies greatly. Detention under hospital orders in large, locked, under-staffed facilities, such as wards of general psychiatric or mental handicap hospitals, is likely to be associated with little or no active treatment apart from psychotropic medication. A number of special facilities exist, however, where at least some other forms of assessment and treatment may be offered (e.g., Denkowski et al., 1983a; Denkowski et al., 1983b; Day, 1988; Murphy et al., 1991). Some of these are medium secure facilities and in many cases the main form of treatment is a token economy, often involving identical conditions for all clients with relatively little individualised treatment (Denkowski et al., 1983b; Day, 1988) and ceasing when the client leaves the service. Presumably, the assumption behind such treatment is that the client has been insufficiently reinforced for pro-social behaviours in the past and that all that is required to return him to the 'straight and narrow' is a relatively brief period of training in adaptive behaviours. In judging the efficacy of such an approach, adequate follow-up of clients leaving the service is essential since high re-conviction rates or re-admissions might suggest an inadequate analysis of the underlying problem. Denkowski et al. provide very little follow-up data but Day (1988) claims that, at six month follow-up, 85% of previous residents were 'well-adjusted' or 'reasonably well-adjusted', this decreasing to 70% at one year. Similar programmes involving token economies for people with mild intellectual disabilities and major challenging behaviours, who are not necessarily all offenders, report similar levels of success at follow-up (Fidura et al., 1987; Sandford et al., 1987).

A more productive approach considers each client individually and designs assessment and treatment procedures to meet the person's needs (e.g., Murphy & Clare, 1991; Holland & Murphy, 1990). Such an approach requires the development of hypotheses about the psychiatric and psychological factors which have contributed to offending behaviour. The nature of the behaviour itself may give very few clues as to the causative factors. Psychiatric and psychological approaches share certain common features but theoretically are very different (see Holland & Murphy, 1990).

Psychiatric Assessment and Treatment

Challenging behaviour whether it results in offending or not can be seen as the result of an interaction between factors from both within and from outside the person. In any given person on any particular occasion the relative importance of factors may vary. The purpose of assessment is to identify these factors and to attempt to change or modify them during the intervention phase on the understanding that such a change will reduce the likelihood of similar behaviour occurring again. Detailed history taking from a variety of sources, client interview, neurological and chromosomal investigations, observational and psychometric data provide the basis for the decision making. From the psychiatric point of view, it is considered necessary to determine the cause of intellectual disabilities, to carry out a thorough mental state examination to identify mental experiences characteristic of mental illness or affective disorder, and to identify other disorders such as sensory impairments, epilepsy and dementia.

The role of specific investigations of chromosomal abnormalities or brain pathology in this context is easily misunderstood. At times, such underlying disorders may not have direct relevance to offending but at other times there may be clear links. For example, the recognition that a person who has been charged with

211

shop-lifting for food has Prader-Willi Syndrome would be very significant in understanding that offence (Holland, 1991). For families and carers, the knowledge that this person has an abnormality of appetite control and thus seeks out food helps identify the need for a particular management strategy. Furthermore, the knowledge that this syndrome is related to an abnormality of chromosome 15 (Ledbetter *et al.*, 1981) is often very helpful in allowing families and carers to develop a more understanding approach to the person's constant over-eating.

Day (1988) in his follow-up study of 20 people with intellectual disabilities who had been admitted to a secure unit, reported that 45% had additional disorders such as mental illness and similar figures have been found in other services (Murphy *et al.*, 1991) so that psychiatric issues need to be considered for a large proportion of offenders in facilities for people with intellectual disabilities.

People with intellectual disabilities also have an increased risk of mental illness (see above), epilepsy (Corbett & Pond, 1979), sensory impairments (Ellis, 1986) and social impairment (Shah *et al.*, 1982). These factors may be relevant to offending and may be treatable, thus reducing the likelihood of re-offending. In some cases, the links with challenging behaviour may be complex: in the case of epilepsy, for example, a detailed assessment of the presence and type of seizures and their temporal relationship to the challenging behaviour will be required (Fenwick, 1986).

The process of history taking, mental state and physical examination and investigation has as its purpose the identification of symptoms and signs characteristic of particular problems which in turn have implications for treatment. Such a process is not limited to the identification of particular neurological or psychiatric pathology but includes the identification of, for example, bereavement, the effects of other life events and the role of past and present life experiences, such as previous sexual and physical abuse. As with other models of assessment, the purpose is to enable the development of some valid and reliable understanding as to why a particular behaviour occurs, with a particular person in a particular place.

For more serious offences, the development of a model which allows some statement about future risk of offending may be of particular importance. In this context the diagnosis of, for example, a mental illness does not only allow immediate treatment but it may also allow some more appropriate long-term management strategy to be developed. Holland & Murphy (1990) gave an example of Mr. L. who had been convicted of indecent assault. The identification of a severe mental illness and the demonstration that his propensity to difficult behaviour (and thus offending) was closely linked to the presence of an abnormal mental state had major implications for his management within a community setting. When well, he could lead a relatively independent life but when his mental state deteriorated, there was a significant risk of offending and on these occasions temporary restriction of his freedom would have been appropriate.

The particular difficulties of diagnosing psychiatric disorder in people with intellectual disabilities means that the effects of treatment need to be especially

212

carefully monitored. Neuroleptic medication may be of value if it is established that an additional mental illness is present but the use of such medication carries with it the possibility of side-effects such as movement disorders (Gualtieri *et al.*, 1986). There is no place for medication unless it is prescribed on the basis of a defined hypothesis (e.g., the diagnosis of schizophrenia) with careful evaluation.

The use of a psychiatric diagnostic approach complements the psychological treatments discussed below. It should not be assumed that all those convicted of a particular offence (such as arson) share a common reason for their behaviour. The reasons can be very diverse and therefore require individual assessment and very different approaches if the propensity to similar behaviour in the future can be reduced.

Psychological assessment and treatment
Psychological assessments and treatments for people with intellectual disabilities who offend have to combine the more traditional operant approaches (Murphy & Oliver, 1987; Zarkowksa & Clements, 1988; Donnellan *et al.*, 1988) with more broadly based approaches from cognitive-behavioural psychology. The latter have often been developed for more able populations and frequently require adaptations for people with poor literacy skills and/or cognitive difficulties. The techniques employed will be described under three illustrative headings: violent and aggressive behaviour; sexual offending and arson.

Violent and aggressive behaviour
Verbal abuse and/or physical violence may be maintained by its operant consequences and, if so, can be commonly construed as escape or attention-maintained (Carr & Durand, 1985) or maintained by other consequences. In these circumstances, it may be possible to determine the operant function of the behaviour by the use of analogue conditions or naturalistic observations (Murphy & Oliver, 1987; Slifer *et al.*, 1986) as long as the behaviour is neither too severe nor too infrequent. Logical operant treatment programmes (involving e.g., DRO, DRC, extinction, etc.) may then be feasible (Murphy, in press).

For more able individuals, it is often considered that verbal abuse and/or physical violence may arise out of dysfunctional anger (Novaco, 1977), i.e., it may be hostile rather than instrumental (Murphy, in press). The client may then be able to report at least some of the features of situations which make him feel angry (eg, Novaco, 1975) and this can be employed as a starting point for a treatment technique which involves improving the client's ability to control (but not eliminate) his/her anger. The procedures have much in common with stress inoculation training (Meichenbaum, 1985) and stress management techniques. In Betty Benson's model, clients are first taught to identify common anger arousing situations using checklists and anger diaries; they progress to learning to identify their own emotions and to recognising signs of emotions in others; relaxation

213

training (e.g., Lindsay & Baty, 1989) is then taught in order for clients to learn to reduce their levels of arousal in anger-provoking (or anxiety-provoking) situations and this is then practised in role plays of problem situations. Later stages of the training involve teaching coping statements and problem-solving strategies (Benson, 1986, Benson *et al.*, 1986), and a number of similar training techniques have also appeared (Cole *et al.*, 1985; Black 1990; Murphy & Clare, 1991).

It is clear that this approach can result in the reduction of angry outbursts in some client groups (Benson *et al.*, 1986; Black 1990), though it is unclear which part of the treatment package is most useful (Benson *et al.*, 1986, found the relaxation, self-instruction and problem-solving components equally effective to full anger control training). It is possible that some clients will not benefit from such an approach since the procedure is essentially a self-control technique (so it is unlikely to be effective in reducing angry outbursts in someone not motivated to improve his/her control of violent behaviour). Moreover, it is perfectly possible that both instrumental and hostile aggression need to be considered in combination for some individuals, making interventions extremely complex and involving both operant and self-control procedures (e.g., Mr. H. in Murphy & Clare, 1991).

Sexual offences

Some early research suggested that people with intellectual disabilities committed disproportionately more sexual offences than other people (Walker & McCabe, 1973, Gebhard *et al.*, 1965) but more recent studies provide little evidence of this (Craft, 1987). It is generally agreed that people with intellectual disabilities have poorer sexual knowledge (Bender *et al.*, 1983), often as a result of parents and care staff having prohibitive/punitive attitudes to sexual activity (Deisher, 1973; Mitchell *et al.*, 1978) and therefore presumably not providing sex education. Staff attitudes appear to be changing (Rose & Holmes, 1991), however, and a number of sex education packages for use with people with intellectual disabilities are now available (e.g., Craft, 1987).

It is also thought that children and adults with intellectual disabilities are more vulnerable to sexual abuse than others, particularly from within families and friends, as opposed to strangers, partly because of their life-long need for staff assistance and care (Brown & Craft, 1989; Tharinger *et al.*, 1990). Furthermore, people with intellectual disabilities often have difficulty making relationships and may require social skills training (Matson & DiLorenzo, 1986; Bramston & Spence, 1985) as a result of leading a sheltered life and/or not acquiring social skills as readily as others. They may have particular difficulty establishing intimate relationships with others and Marshall (1989) has argued this may be an important precursor to sexual offending. These three factors, poor sex education and knowledge, increased likelihood of sexual abuse and difficulties with social relationships might be expected to increase the vulnerability of people with intellectual disabilities to committing sex offences. There is currently no evidence, however, that the tiny minority who are convicted of sex offences do have significantly poorer sexual knowledge, social skills or higher rates of childhood sexual abuse than other people with intellectual disabilities, so the significance of these factors in the etiology of sexual offending by people with intellectual disabilities is unknown.

The varieties of sexual offences committed have been thought to differ for people with intellectual disabilities and those without. Gebhard *et al.* (1965), for example, considered that assaults against children were particularly likely, whereas Gilby *et al.*, (1989) found 'nuisance' offences, such as exhibitionism, voyeurism, etc, more common. Since it is known that only a small minority of all sex offences are ever reported to the police, however, it is impossible to be certain about the relative proportion of particular sexual crimes that people with intellectual disabilities commit.

Assessment and active treatment following sexual offending is relatively rare in the UK. Perkins quotes the estimate of the Howard League Working Party (1985) that only 2.3% of the 6,614 people convicted of sexual offences go to Special Hospitals, the remainder mainly being sentenced to prison (Perkins, 1988). Few treatment programmes are available in prisons for sex offenders, though Perkins pioneered such a programme in Birmingham in the 1970s (Perkins, 1987). Even in Special Hospital, people with intellectual disabilities may be particularly unlikely to be offered treatment, as the most common form of treatment is that of group therapy, from which people with intellectual disabilities are frequently not thought to benefit. Few reports of group therapy with people with intellectual disabilities appear in the research literature; those which do suggest relatively poor outcome (Swanson & Garwick, 1990). In general, they have followed the 'social work' model and the aims have included learning to be honest about previous sexual abuse/sexual offending, learning to discuss feelings within the group, learning about the difference between violent and sexual behaviour, understanding the victim's view of sexual offending, learning about the harmful effects of offending on victim and perpetrator, setting specific goals for more appropriate sexual activity (see e.g., Salter, 1988; Mezey *et al.*, 1991).

Full psychological assessment of sex offenders normally includes an evaluation of their sexual history (by interview), sexual knowledge (usually by questionnaire), sexual interests (by questionnaire, ratings of slides or taped auditory sequences and sometimes penile plethysmography of responses to photographs, slides or tapes), social skills levels and attitudes to women and/or children (see Salter, 1988). Assessments for people with intellectual disabilities need to be similarly broad and may need to be supplemented, especially for clients with poor language with direct observation of inappropriate sexual behaviour, if the behaviour is frequent enough for this to be possible and not so dangerous that it cannot be permitted to occur.

Individual psychological treatment for people with intellectual disabilities and sexual difficulties used to rely heavily on punishing inappropriate behaviour by

215

electric shock, overcorrection, facial screening, contingent lemon juice or time out, though some reports have appeared of the use of DRO and/or the training of more appropriate sexual behaviours later (Foxx *et al.*, 1986). Foxx and colleagues argued that some treatment strategies appeared to be based on respondent/classical conditioning models (e.g., those aiming to reduce arousal to specific stimuli) while other were more clearly operant (e.g., those aiming to reduce the future probability of sexually inappropriate behaviours) and others appeared to adopt a mixed model. Similarly, Murphy *et al.*, 1983, have proposed a classification of behavioural treatments which included the 'aversion suppression' methods (such as covert sensitisation, odour, taste and electrical aversion, etc.) aiming to reduce arousal to deviant stimuli; methods to generate arousal to non-deviant cues (such as masturbatory conditioning, systematic desensitisation); methods involving skill training (social skills/'courtship' skills/assertive training); sexual dysfunctions treatment and treatments involving training in gender role. The selection of particular techniques from this list will, of course, depend on a particular client's difficulties. The paucity of treatment studies for people with intellectual disabilities makes it impossible as yet to draw firm general conclusions about the efficacy and applicability of the various procedures partly because of the poor methodology in most studies (Foxx *et al.*, 1986). Certainly, current treatment should be aimed at promoting appropriate social and sexual behaviour and should preferably not include aversive elements but should be designed using the principle of the least restrictive alternative. Ideally, if the client has sufficient language, treatment should not just employ a strictly operant or classical conditioning model but should also address the client's cognitions.

Arson
Studies of samples of ordinary children have indicated that for boys, at least, playing with fire is not at all unusual and is not particularly related to psychological or psychiatric disorders (Kafry, 1980). Very few of the total number of fires attended by the British fire service are thought to be 'malicious' in origin and, of those, firesetting for financial gain probably forms an important part (Vreeland & Lewin, 1980). The remaining 'malicious' fires have been considered at length in the research literature concerned with mentally-disordered offenders, mainly with respect to the motivation for the offence.

One example of motivational categories is that of Prins (1986) and he proposes the following list of reasons for malicious arson:

(i)   The 'professional' arsonist.
(ii)   Arson as a cover for another crime.
(iii)   Politically-motivated arson.
(iv)   The politically-motivated self-immolator.
(v)   Arson for mixed or unclear motives.

216

(vi) Arson associated with mental disorder (eg, severe affective disorders; organic disorders; mental impairment; pathological self-immolation).

(vii) The revenge motive.

(viii) Arson motivated by heroics.

(ix) Sexually-motivated arson.

(x) Arson committed by children and young adults.

In general, studies which have examined the motives for arson of convicted offenders have not employed standard measures (Faulk, 1982; Lewis & Yarnell, 1951; Bradford, 1982) and have occasionally categorised people on the basis of case note or similar material (eg, Hill *et al.*, 1982, Prins, Tennant & Trick, 1985). For people with intellectual disabilities, the situation is made even more unsatisfactory by the supposition that simply having such a difficulty in some way 'explains' the arson.

Very few psychological analyses of mentally-disordered offenders have examined the issue of motive. However, Jackson and colleagues demonstrated that mentally-disordered arsonists were in general less assertive than other mentally-disordered offenders (Jackson *et al.*, 1987a) and proposed a model for the functional analysis of such offending (Jackson *et al.*, 1987a). They noted, as had others, that mentally-disordered arsonists tended to have poor social skills and to feel powerless about their future (Jackson *et al.*, 1987b; Harris & Rice, 1984; Hurley & Monahan, 1969) and proposed that an important feature of treatment of such offenders would be social skills training and assertiveness training (see Rice & Chaplin, 1979).

The only systematic study of the setting conditions, antecedents and consequences of firesetting for people with intellectual disabilities convicted of firesetting is that of Murphy (1990). She designed a structured interview to probe people's own view of the setting conditions and antecedents prior to setting the fire(s) and the consequences following the fire(s), within a cognitive-behavioural model. The most common function appeared to be that of gaining attention and the most common feelings reported were anger and 'feeling no-one was listening to them'. After the fire, people sometimes reported consequences consistent with the antecedents and sometimes did not (Murphy, 1990). Murphy argued that the interview could be used to design logical psychological treatments for individual people with intellectual disabilities who set fires and Clare *et al.* (1992) describe a case study employing this approach.

Conclusions

This chapter has tried to place our present day understanding of offending behaviour by people with intellectual disabilities in the context of an historical perspective. The early idea that 'feeble-mindedness' and criminal behaviour were closely linked is no longer sustainable. However, people with intellectual disabilities are vulnerable within the Criminal Justice System and may be particularly open to

217

abuse within prisons. The Legal system allows for assessment and treatment and a legal framework for removing people from prison to hospital or for supporting them within a community setting is available through the Mental Health Act, 1983 and by the use of Probation Orders.

The complexity of factors underlying offending are such that a variety of approaches are required. Individual assessment is essential and there is no place for blanket treatments whether it be medication or the application of behavioural programmes. Intervention needs to be directed by an understanding of the variety of factors (biological, psychological, social and environmental) which may have contributed to that person's offending behaviour.

References

Alberman, E. (1984) Epidemiological aspects of severe mental retardation. In J. Dobbing, A. D. B. Clarke, J. A. Corbett, J. Hogg, and R. O. Robinson (eds) *Scientific Studies in Mental Retardation.* London: Royal Society of Medicine.

Bender, M., Aitman, J. B., Biggs, S. J. and Hang, U. (1983) Initial findings concerning a sexual knowledge questionnaire. *Mental Handicap,*11, 168-169.

Benson, B. A (1986) Anger management training. *Psychiatric Aspects of Mental Retardation Reviews* 5, 51-55.

Benson, B. A., Rice, C. J., and Miranti, S. V. (1986) Effects of anger management training with mentally retarded adults in group treatment. Journal of Consulting and *Clinical Psychology* 54, 728-729.

Black, D. A. (1982) A five-year follow-up of male patients discharged from Broadmoor Hospital. In Guan, J. and Farrington, D. P. (Eds). *Abnormal offenders, delinquency and the criminal justice system.* Chichester: Wiley.

Black, L. (1990) Treatment options for people with a mental handicap who are offenders. In K. Howell, and C. Hollins. (eds) *Clinical Approaches to working with Mentally Disordered and Sexual Offenders.* Issues in Criminological and Legal Psychology, No 16, British Psychological Society.

Bowden, P. (1981) What happens to patients released from special hospitals? *British Journal of Psychiatry* 138, 350-354.

Bramston, P. and Spence, S. H. (1985) Behavioural versus cognitive social skills training with intellectually handicapped adults. *Behaviour Research and Therapy* 23, 239-246.

Bradford, J. (1982) Arson: a clinical study. *Canadian Journal of Psychiatry* 27, 188-192.

Brown, H. and Craft, A. (1989) *Thinking the unthinkable: papers on sexual abuse and people with learning difficulties.* London: F.P.A. Education Unit.

Calnen, T. and Blackman, L. S. (1992) Capital punishment and offenders with mental retardation: response to the Penry brief. *American Journal on Mental Retardation* 96, 557-564.

Carr, E. and Durand, V. (1985) The social communicative basis of severe behaviour problems in children. In S. Reiss, and R. Bootzin, (eds) *Theoretical Issues in Behaviour Therapy.* New York: Academic Press.

Carson, D. (1989) Prosecuting people with mental handicaps. *Criminal Law Review* 87-94.

Clare, I. C. H., Murphy, G. H., Cox, D. and Chaplin, E. H. (1992) Assessment and treatment of fire-setting: a single case investigation using a cognitive-behavioural model. *Criminal Behaviour and Mental Health,* 2, 253–268.

Clare, I. C. H. and Gudjonsson, G. (1991) Recall and understanding of the caution and rights in police detention among persons of average intellectual ability and persons with a mild mental handicap. *Proceedings of the 1st Annual Conference of the Division of Criminological and Legal Psychology,* 1. Leicester: British Psychological Society.

Clare, I. C. H. and Gudjonsson, G. (in press) Interrogative suggestibility, confabulation and acquiescence in people with mild learning difficulties (mental handicap) *British Journal of Clinical Psychology.*

Coid, J. (1984) How many psychiatric patients in prison? *British Journal of Psychiatry* 145, 78-86.

Cole, C. L., Gardner, W. I. and Karan, O. C. (1985) Self-management training of mentally retarded adults presenting severe conduct difficulties. *Applied Research in Mental Retardation* 6, 337-347.

Corbett, J. A. (1979) Psychiatric morbidity and mental retardation. In P. Snaith, and F. E. James (eds) *Psychiatric Illness and Mental Handicap*. Ashford: Headley Brothers.

Corbett, J. A. and Pond, D. A. (1979) Epilepsy and behaviour disorders in the mentally handicapped. In P. Snaith, and F. E. James (eds) *Psychiatric Illness and Mental Handicap*. Ashford: Headley Brothers.

Craft, A. (1987) *Mental Handicap and Sexuality: Issues and Perspectives*. Costello Publications.

Craft, M. (1984) Low intelligence, mental handicap and criminality. In M. Craft, and A. Craft (eds) *Mentally Abnormal Offenders*. London: Balliere-Tindall.

Craft, M. (1985) Low intelligence and delinquency. In M. Craft, J. Bicknell and S. Hollins (eds) *Mental Handicap*. London: Balliere-Tindall

Day, K. (1988) A hospital-based treatment programme for male mentally handicapped offenders. *British Journal of Psychiatry*, 153, 635-644.

Dell, S. and Robertson, G. (1988) *Sentenced to Hospital*. Oxford: Oxford University Press.

Deisher, R. W. (1973) Sexual behaviour of the retarded in institutions. In De La Cruz, F.F. and La Veck, G. D. (eds) *Human Sexuality and the Mental Retarded*. New York: Brummer/Mazel.

Denkowski, G. C., Denkowski, K. M. and Mabll, J. (1983a) A 50-state survey of the current status of residential treatment programmes for mentally retarded offenders. *Mental Retardation* 21, 197-205.

Denkowski, G. C. and Denkowski, K. M. (1983b) Group home designs initiating community based treatment with mentally retarded adolescent offenders, *Journal of Behaviour Therapy and Experimental Psychiatry* 14, 141-145.

Donnellan, A. M., LaVigna, G. W., Negri-Shoultz, N. and Fassbender, L. L. (1988) *Progress without punishments*. New York: Teachers College Press.

Ellis, D. (1986) *Sensory Impairments in Mentally Handicapped People*. London: Croom Helm.

Emerson, E., Cummings, R., Barrett, S., Hughes, H., McCool, C. and Toogood, A. (1988) Challenging behaviour and community services: who are the people who challenge services? *Mental Handicap*, 16, 16-19.

Eyman, R. K. and Call, T. (1977) Maladaptive behaviour and community placement of mentally retarded persons. *American Journal of Mental Deficiency* 82, 137-144.

Faulk, M. (1982) The assessment of dangerousness in arsonists. In J.R., Hamilton and H. Freeman (eds) *Dangerousness: psychiatric assessment and management*. London: Royal College of Psychiatrists, Gaskell Books.

Fenwick, P. (1986) Aggression and Epilepsy. In M. R. Trimble and T.G. Bolwig (eds) *Aspects of Epilpsy and Psychiatry*. London: John Wiley and Sons.

Fidura, J. G., Lindsey, E. R. and Walker, G. R. (1987) A special behaviour unit for treatment of behaviour problems of persons who are mentally retarded. *Mental Retardation* 25, 107-111.

Foxx, R. M., Bittle, R. G., Bechtel, D. R. and Livesay, J. R (1986) Behavioral treatment of the sexually deviant behavior of mentally retarded individuals. In N.R. Ellis and N.W. Bray (eds.) *International Review of Research in Mental Retardation* 14, 291-317.

Foreshaw, D. and Rollins, H. (1990) The history of law and psychiatry in Europe. In R. Bluglass and P. Bowden (eds) *Principles and practice of Forensic Psychiatry*. London: Churchill Livingstone.

Frost, J. B. (1984) Behavioural disturbance in mentally handicapped adults. In Berg, J.M. (Ed). *Perspectives and Progress in Mental Retardation, Vol II, Biomedical Aspects*. Baltimore, MD: University Park Press.

Gathercole, C., Craft, K., McDougall, J., Barnes, H. and Peck, D. (1968) A review of 100 discharges from a Special Hospital. *British Journal of Criminology* 8, 419-424.

Gebhard, P. H., Gagnon, J. H., Pomeroy, W. B. and Christienson, C.V. (1965) *Sex offenders: an analysis of types*. New York: Harper and Row.

Gilby, R., Wolf, L. and Goldberg, B. (1989) Mentally retarded sex offenders: A survey and pilot study. *Canadian Journal of Psychiatry* 34, 542-548.

Gostin, L. O. (1985) The Law relating to mental handicap in England and Wales. In M. Craft, J. Bicknell and S. S. Hollins (eds) *Mental Handicap*. London: Balliere-Tindall.

Grounds, A. I. (1987) Detention of psychopathic disorder patients in Special Hospitals: Critical Issues. *British Journal of Psychiatry* 151, 474-478.

Grubin, D. (1991) Unfit to plead, unfit for discharge: Patients found unfit to plead who are still in hospital. *Criminal Behaviour and Mental Health* 1, 282-294.

219

Gualtieri, C. T., Schroeder, S. R., Hicks, R. E. and Quade, D. (1986). Tardive dyskinesia in young mentally retarded individuals. *Archives of General Psychiatry*, 43, 335–340.
Gudjonsson, G. H. and MacKeith, J. A. C. (1988) Retracted confessions: legal, psychological and psychiatric aspects. *Medicine, Science and the Law* 28, 187-194.
Gunn, J., Maden, A. and Swinton, M. (1991) Treatment needs of prisoners with psychiatric disorders. *British Medical Journal* 303, 338-341.
Gunn, M. J. (1984) The Law and mental handicap. 2. The Mental Health Act, 1983 - Guardianship and Hospitalisation. *Mental Handicap* 12, 8-11.
Gunn, M. J. (1990) The law and learning disability. *International Review of Psychiatry* 2, 13-22.
Harris, G. T. and Rice, M. E. (1984) Mentally disordered fire-setters: psychodynamic vs empiracal approaches. *International Journal of Law and Psychiatry* 7, 19-34.
Harris, P. and Russell, O. (1990) Aggressive behaviour among people with learning difficulties - the nature of the problem. In A. Dosen, A. Van Gennel and G. J. Zwaniken (eds) *Treatment of Mental Illness and Behaviour Disorder in the Mentally Retarded.* Leiden: Logon Publications.
Hill, R. W., Langevin, R., Paitich, D., Handy, L. Russon, A. and Wilkinson, L. (1982) Is arson an aggressive act or a property offence? A controlled study of psychiatric referrals. *Canadian Journal of Psychiatry* 27, 648-654.
Hodgins, S. (1992) Mental disorder, intellectual deficiency and crime: evidence from a birth cohort. *Archives of General Psychiatry* 49, 476-483.
Hogg, J. and Sebba, J. (1986) *Profound Retardation and Multiple Impairment,* Vol I. London: Croom Helm.
Holland, T. and Murphy, G. (1990) Behavioural and psychiatric disorder in adults with mild learning difficulties. *International Review of Psychiatry* 2, 117-136.
Holland, A. J. (1991) Learning disability and behavioural/psychiatric disorders: a genetic perspective. *The New Genetics of Mental Illness.* eds: McGuffin, P. and Murray, R. Butterworth-Heinmann, Oxford.
Hollin, C. (1989) *Psychology and Crime.* London: Routledge.
Home Office Statistical Bulletin (1985) *Statistics of Mentally Disorered Offenders, England and Wales,* 1984. Surbiton, Surrey: Home Office Statistical Department.
Home Office Statistical Bulletin (1988) *Statistics of Mentally Disordered Offenders, England and Wales, 1985 and 1986.* Surbiton, Surrey: Home Office Statistical Department.
Hurley, W. and Monahan, T. M. (1969) Arson: the criminal and the crime. *British Journal of Criminology* 9, 4-21.
Jackson, H. F., Glass, C. and Hope, S. (1987a), A Functional Analysis of Recidivistic Arson, *British Journal of Clinical Psychology* 26, 175-185.
Jackson, H. F., Hope, S. and Glass, C. (1987b), Why are Arsonists not Violent Offenders?, *International Journal of Offender Therapy and Comparative Criminology* 31, 143-152.
Jacobsen, J. W. (1982). Problem behaviour and psychiatric impairment within a developmentally disabled population. I: behaviour frequency. *Applied Research in Mental Retardation,* 3, 121–139.
Kafry, D. (1980) Playing with matches: children and fire. In Canter, D. (Ed). *Fires and human behaviour.* Chichester: Wiley.
Kearns, A. (1988) The mentally handicapped criminal offender: a 10-year study of two hospitals. *British Journal of Psychiatry* 152, 848-851.
Ledbetter, D. H., Riccardi, V. M., Airhart, S. D., Strobel, R. J., Keenan, B. S. and Crawford, J. D. (1981) Deletions of chromosome 15 as a cause of the Prader-Willi Syndrome. *New England Journal of Medicine* 304, 325-329.
Letts, P. (1991) Unfitness to plead: a change in the Law - at last! Mental Handicap 19, 105-108.
Leudar, I. and Fraser, W.I. (1987) Behaviour disturbance and its assessment. In J. Hogg and N. Raynes (eds) *Assessment in Mental Handicap: a guide to assessment practices, tests and checklists.* London: Croom Helm.
Lewis, N. D. C. and Yarnell, H. (1951) *Pathological firesetting (pyromania).* New York: Nervous Disease Monographs, No.42.
Lindsay, W. R. and Baty, F. J. (1989) Group relaxation training with adults who are mentally handicapped. *Behavioural Psychotherapy* 17, 43-51.
Lund, J. (1990) Mentally retarded criminal offenders in Denmark. *British Journal of Psychiatry* 156, 726-731.

Lund, J. (1985) The prevalence of psychiatric morbidity in mentally retarded adults. *Acta Psychiatrica Scandinavica* 72, 563-570.

Marshall, W. L. (1989) Intimacy, loneliness and sexual offenders. *Behaviour Research and Therapy* 27, 491-503.

Matson, J. L. and DiLorenzo, T. M. (1986) Social skills training and mental handicap and organic impairment. In C. R. Hollin and P. Trower (eds) *Handbook of Social Skills Training, Vol 2.* Oxford: Pergamon Press.

MacAchron, A. E. (1979) Mentally retarded offenders: prevalence and characteristics. *American Journal of Mental Deficiency* 84, 165-176.

McAfee, J. K. and Gural, M. (1988) Individuals with mental retardation and the criminal justice system: the view from States' Attorneys General. *Mental Retardation* 26, 5-12.

McGarry, A. (1971) The fate of psychotic offenders returned for trial. *American Journal of Psychiatry* 124, 181-189.

Meichenbaum, D. (1985) *Stress Innoculation Training.* New York: Plenum Press.

Mezey, G., Vizard, E., Hawkes, C. and Austin, R. (1991) A community treatment programme for convicted child sex offenders: a preliminary report. *Journal of Forensic Psychiatry* 2.

Mitchell, L., Doctor, R. M. and Butler, D. C. (1978) Attitudes of caretakers toward the sexual behaviour of mentally retarded persons. *American Journal of Mental Deficiency* 83, 289-296.

Murphy, G. H. (1990) *Analysis of motivation and fire-related interests in people with a mild intellectual disability who set fires.* Paper presented at the International Congress on Treatment of Mental Illness and Behavioural Disorders in Mentally Retarded People, Amsterdam.

Murphy, G. (In press) The treatment of challenging behaviour in people with learning difficulties. In Thompson, C. (Ed). *Science and Psychiatry of Violence.* Butterworth-Heinemann.

Murphy, G. and Oliver, C. (1987) Decreasing undersirable behaviours. In W. Yule and J. Carr (eds) *Behaviour Modification for People with Mental Handicaps.* London: Croom Helm.

Murphy, G., Holland, A., Fowler, P. and Reep, J. (1991) MIETS: a service option for people with mild mental handicaps and challenging behaviour or psychiatric disorder - 1. Philosophy, service and service users. *Mental Handicap Research* 4, 41-66.

Murphy, G. and Clare, I. (1991) MIETS: a service option for people with mild mental handicaps and challenging behaviour or psychiatric problems. 2. Assessment, treatment and outcome for service users and service effectivenss. *Mental Handicap Research* 4, 180-206.

Murphy, W. D., Coleman, E. M. and Abel, G. G. (1983) Human sexuality in the mentally retarded. In J.L. Matson and F. Andrasik (eds) *Treatment Issues and Innovations in Mental Retardation.* New York: Plenum Press.

Nihara, K., Meyers, C. E. and Mink, I. T. (1980) Home environment, family adjustment and the development of mentally retarded children. *Applied Research in Mentally Retardation* 1, 5-24.

Novaco, R. W. (1975) *Anger control: The development and evaluation of an experimental treatment.* Lexington DC Health and Co.

Novaco, R. W. (1977) A stress inoculation approach to anger management in the training of law enforcement officers. *Journal of Community* 5, 327-346.

Oliver, C., Murphy, G. H. and Corbett, J. A. (1987) Self-injurious behaviour in people with mental handicap: a total population study. *Journal of Mental Deficiency Research* 31, 147-162.

Parker, E. and Tennant, G. (1979) The 1959 Mental Health Act and Mentally Abnormal Offenders: a comparative study. *Medicine, Science and Law* 19, 29-38.

Perkins, D. (1987) A psychological treatment programme for sex offenders. In B. J. McGurk D. M. Thornton and M. Williams (eds) *Applying Psychology to Imprisonment: Theory and Practice.* London: HMSO.

Perkins, D. (1988) Sex therapy with male offenders. In M. Cole and W. Dryden (eds) *Sex therapy in Britain.* Milton Keynes: Oxford University Press.

Perske, R. (1991) *Unequal justice?* Nashville: Abingdon Press.

Prins, H., Tennant, G. and Trick, K. (1985) Motives for arson (fire-raising). *Medicine, Science and the Law* 25, 275-278.

Prins, H. (1986) *Dangerous behaviour, the law and mental disorder.* London: Tavistock Publications.

Quen, J. (1990) The history of law and psychaitry in America. In R. Bluglass and P. Bowden (eds) *Principles and practice in Forensic Psychiatry.* London: Churchill Livingstone.

221

Qureshi, H. and Alborz, A. (1992) Epidemiology of challenging behaviour. *Mental Handicap Research* 5, 130-145.

Rasch, W. (1990) Criminal responsibility in Europe. In R. Bluglass and P. Bowden (eds) *Principles and practice in Forensic Psychiatry*. London: Churchill Livingstone.

Reid, A. H. (1972) Psychoses in adult mental defectives, i. Manic Depressive Psychosis. ii. Schizophrenia and paranoid psychosis, *British Journal of Psychiatry* 120, 205-218

Reid, A. H. (1982). *Psychiatry of Mental Handicap*. Blackwells, Oxford.

Reid, A. H., Ballinger, B. R. and Heather, B. B. (1978) Behavioral syndromes identified by cluster analysis in a sample of 100 severely and profoundly retarded adults. *Psychological Medicine* 8, 399-412.

Rice, M. E., and Chaplin, T. C. (1979) Social skills training for hospitalised male arsonists. *Journal of Therapy and Experimental Psychiatry* 10, 105-108.

Richardson, S. A. (1981) Family characteristics associated with mild mental retardation. In M.J. Begab H. C. Haywood, and H. L. Garber (eds) *Psychosocial influences in retarded performance II*. Baltimore: University Park Press.

Richardson, S. A., Koller, H. and Katz, M. (1985a) Relationship of upbringing to later behaviour disturbance of mildly mentally retarded young people, *American Journal of mental Deficiency* 90, 1-8.

Richardson, S. A., Koller, H. and Katz, M. (1985b) Continuities and change in behaviour disturbance: a follow-up study of mildly retarded young people, *American Journal of Orthopsychiatry* 55, 220-229.

Richardson, S. A. and Koller, H. L. (1985) Epidemiology. In A. M. Clarke, A. D. B. Clarke, and J. M. Berg (eds) *Mental Deficiency: the Changing Outlook*. London: Methuen.

Roberts, D. F. (1987) Population genetics of mental handicap. In G. Hosking, G. and G. Murphy (eds) *Prevention of Mental Handicap: a world view*. London: Royal Society of Medicine.

Robertson, G. (1981) The extent and pattern of crime amongst mentally handicapped offenders. *Apex: Journal of British Institute of Mental Handicap* 9, 100-103.

Robertson, G. (1989) The resistricted hospital order. Psychiatric Bulletin 13, 4-11.

Rose, J. and Holmes, S. (1991) Changing staff attitudes to the secuality of people with mental handicaps: an evaluative comparison of one and three day workshops. *Mental Handicap Research* 4, 67-79.

Rutter, M., Graham, P. and Yule, W. (1970) *A neuropsychiatric study in childhood*. London: Spastics International Medical Publication.

Sadoff, R. (1990) Legislation in the United States. In Bluglass, R., and Bowden, P. (eds.) *Principles and practice of forensic psychiatry*. London: Churchill Livingston.

Salter, A. C. (1988) *Treating child sex offenders and victims*. London: Sage Publications Ltd.

Sandford, D. A., Elizingarh, R. H., and Grainger, W. (1987) Evaluation of a residential program for behaviorally disturbed mentally retarded young adults. *American Journal of Mental Deficiency* 91, 431-434.

Shah, A., Holmes, N. and Wing, L. (1982) Prevalence of autism and related conditions in adults in a mental handicap hospital. *Applied Research in Mental Handicap* 3, 303-317.

Slifer, K. J., Ivanic, M. T., Parrish, J. M., Page, T. J. and Burgio, L. D. (1986) Assessment and treatment of multiple behaviour problems exhibited by a profoundly retarded adolescent. *Journal of Behaviour Therapy and Experimental Psychiatry* 17, 202-213.

Steadman, H. and Halfon, A. (1971) The Baxtrom patients: backgrounds and outcomes. In M. Greenblatt and E. Hartmann (eds) *Seminars in Psychiatry* 3, 376-385.

Stein, Z. and Susser, M. (1960) The families of dull children: a classification for predicting careers. *British Journal of Preventative and Social Medicine* 14, 83-88.

Swanson, C. K. and Garwick, G. B. (1990) Treatment for low functioning sex offenders: group therapy and interagency co-ordination. *Mental Retardation* 28, 155-161.

Tharinger, D., Horton, C. B. and Millea, S. (1990) Sexual abuse and exploitation of children and adults with mental retardation and other handicaps. *Child Abuse and Neglect* 14, 301-312.

Tizard, J. (1974) Longitudinal studies: problems and findings. In A. M. Clarke, and A. D. B. Clarke (eds) *Mental Deficiency: the changing outlook*. London: Methuen and Co. Ltd. (3rd Edition).

Tong, J. and MacKay, T. (1958) A statistical follow-up of mental defectives of dangerous or violent propensities. *British Journal of Delinquency* 9, 276-284.

Thomas, T. (1989) The mentally handicapped offender: rights and responsibilities. *British Journal of Mental Subnormality* 35, 108-114.

Vreeland, R. G. and Lewin, B. M. (1980) Psychological aspects of fire-setting. In Carter, D. (Ed). *Fires and Human Behaviour*. Chichester: John Wiley.

Walker, N. and McCabe, S. (1968) Hospital orders. In A. V. S. Reuck, and R. Porder (eds) *The Mentally Abnormal Offender*. London: J. A. Churchill Ltd.

Walker, N. and McCabe, S. (1973) *Crime and insanity in England, Vol 2*. Edinburgh: University Press.

Woodward, M. (1955) The role of low intelligence in delinquency. *British Journal of Delinquency* 5, 281-303.

Wright, E. C. (1982) The presentation of mental illness in mentally retarded adults. *British Journal of Psychiatry* 141, 496-502.

Zarkowska, E. and Clements, J. (1988) *Problem Behaviour and people with severe learning disability: a practical guide to the constructional approach*. London: Croom Helm.

CHAPTER 10

The Functional Analysis of Challenging Behaviours: Some Conceptual and Theoretical Problems

R. Glynn Owens
University College of North Wales, Bangor
and
Shelagh MacKinnon
St Helens and Knowsley Health Authority

Introduction

In a relatively short time, functional analysis has come to be synonymous with the way forward in dealing with challenging behaviour. Increasingly therapists are acknowledging the need for such an analysis as a precursor to successful intervention. The technology available for the conduct of such analyses continues to develop, as do the types of procedure implemented on the basis of the analyses. Thus measures such as the Motivation Assessment Schedule (MAS) of Durand & Crimmins (1988) and the S-R questionnaire of Lauterbach (1990) are available to provide a structure for functional assessments, providing instruments of demonstrable value with at least basic psychometric information regarding reliability and validity. For the more psychometrically sophisticated, the Generalisability Theory of Cronbach *et al.*, (1972) has been implemented in a variety of behavioural contexts providing quantitative information of direct relevance to functional analyses (e.g., Mariotto & Farrell, 1979). Similar development of intervention technology has seen early procedures like punishment and extinction supplemented by more complex procedures like response prevention, DRO, and even occasionally DRL. More recent have been the development of procedures like Functional Communication Training (Durand, 1990) which directly apply the principles of functional analysis in therapeutic activity.

Whilst these developments have done much to alleviate the practical problems of functional analyses it is perhaps suprising then to note that despite all this attention, the basic process of functional analysis is itself still fraught with conceptual and theoretical problems. The aim of the present chapter is not so much to provide solutions to these problems as to highlight their existence and in some cases to suggest the direction which might be taken in seeking clarification or solution.

Functional analysis isn't as easy as ABC

The widespread use of the Antecedents, Behaviour, Consequences (ABC) framework in the conduct of functional analyses has led to the notion that ABC and functional analysis are synonymous. Certainly it is clear that for practical purposes conducting an ABC analysis may provide sufficient information to permit effective intervention. To assume however that functional analysis is nothing more than an ABC may be a serious error.

To take an obvious point first. Exactly what constitute Antecedents, Behaviours and Consequences is itself a question which depends on the reasons for its being asked. That is to say, the categorisation of events into the above sets is a function of the reason for the investigation. It can be argued that any event which has an influence on a subsequent behaviour, and *only such events* can be regarded as an antecedent of that behaviour; indeed, considering the converse, any event which does not influence a behaviour, *no matter how reliably it precedes the behaviour,* is from a functional viewpoint not an antecedent. At its most trivial level, this can be seen when a reliable precursor of a behaviour is incapable of being perceived by the subject. Destruction of the VIIIth cranial nerve produces profound deafness; for such an individual a sound which reliably precedes a behaviour will never, from a functional viewpoint, be an antecedent. At a more general level, only stimuli which exert some degree of control over a behaviour can be regarded as antecedents in a functional analysis.

We are now in a position to see how the classification of events into sets of Antecedents, Behaviours and Consequences is a function of the purpose to which the analysis is to be put. It would be unusual for subjects not to perceive their own behaviour. That they are perceiving their behaviour implies that the behaviour is itself influencing other behaviours - either ones which appear identical but are functionally different (q.v.) or ones which are obviously physically dissimilar (e.g., performing an action and then describing the action which has been performed). What constitutes a Behaviour in one analysis, then, may be an Antecedent in another.

The argument can be extended to all three types of event in the traditional ABC paradigm. From at least one point of view (Premack, 1965) reinforcement can be seen as an issue of behaviour rather than of stimulation; it may not be food that is reinforcing so much as eating, or even seeing the food (Skinner, 1968 has drawn attention to the fact that seeing, hearing etc. are themselves all examples of behaviour). From this point of view, therefore, what are traditionally thought of as consequences in a Functional Analysis can also (in another context) be thought of as behaviours. It is of course uncontentious to recognise that perceiving one's own behaviour can be as much a part of a behavioural system as perceiving any other event; again, therefore, a behaviour may be an antecedent, and arguably an event cannot be an antecedent without the behaviour (seeing, hearing) necessary for it to play a part in the system.

Such a conceptualisation, incidentally, illustrates the lack of sophistication shown by critics of behaviourism who loftily pronounce that 'a person doesn't respond to a stimulus, but to what they perceive a stimulus to be'. Leaving aside the issue of whether such S-R formulations in any case have a role in behavioural formulation, it is apparent that the very act of perceiving a stimulus to be something is itself likely to be the person's first response.

Such observations are not entirely trivial. Firstly they illustrate the need for a certain level of caution in regarding functional analysis as demonstrating any kind of absolute truth; rather functional analysis should be seen as a means of mapping onto an artificial model those aspects of a behavioural system which are most important in achieving some particular purpose. Whilst a functional analysis cannot afford to incorporate elements which are not true, it is important to remember that the 'truth' presented by an analysis is only one of many.

A second point worth noting is that, since (from one point of view) *all* the elements of an ABC analysis are in fact behaviours, such behaviours are themselves subject to change in the light of changing contingencies. Fortunately for most individuals the behaviours with which we are concerned (seeing, hearing etc.) are usually under fairly strict stimulus control. Thus for most people seeing a hedgehog is likely to be primarily determined by whether or not there is a hedgehog in the visual field at that time. Similarly, for most people with intellectual disabilities, seeing a particular individual associated with reinforcement of a particular behaviour is likely to be determined by the presence of that individual. For example, if a particular person has a history of reinforcing some form of challenging behaviour, that person is likely to have become a discriminative stimulus for the behaviour. In a traditional analysis, the presence of that person would probably be regarded as an important antecedent; however an alternative conceptualisation might note that it is the *seeing* of that person by the client with the challenging behaviour which constitutes the important antecedent. In this sense, the antecedent of the challenging behaviour is another behaviour from that same client, the behaviour of seeing the person associated with reinforcement.

Since there will usually be an extremely close correspondence between the client's behaviour of seeing and the presence of the person seen, the distinction will normally be of little more than academic significance. It is important to note however that this close correspondence may not always occur. Common examples include seeing and hearing whilst asleep (i.e., in dreams) and hallucinatory experiences; less extreme examples include 'misperceptions' e.g., the experience of a bereaved relative who hears the voice of a loved one around the house, or who sees the loved one's face amongst the crowds in the street. Such misperceptions could in principle have profound effects on other behavioural systems, setting severe limits on the predictability and controllability of behaviour. Consider for example a client who relates well to another member of a social group. Observing a frightening incident may lead the client to turn to other members of the social group for comfort and support. If however the client in witnessing the incident mistakenly 'saw' a member of this social group involved in the incident, then rather than turn to the group for support, the group (or at least that member mistakenly thought to have been involved) may be more likely to elicit anxiety.

Perhaps most obviously familiar are circumstances in which the client 'fails to see'. Commonly such failure is referred to as a 'lack of attention', but within a behavioural framework such a mentalistic notion sits uncomfortably. More consistent is the replacement of the concept of attention with that of stimulus control, particularly since the factors determining the latter are well known (Terrace, 1966). In principle this provides the therapist dealing with challenging behaviour with the possibility not of removing some particular antecedent but rather of decreasing the degree of stimulus control exerted by that individual over behaviour. Conversely there may of course be circumstances where a therapist is keen to ensure that a client 'attends' to some event; again, the concept of stimulus control provides a framework for therapeutic action.

Changing operants isn't the same as changing responses

Often forgotten in the field of behaviour modification is that the terms operant and response aren't interchangeable. To make matters worse, the distinction implies that our problems are with responses but our interventions are with operants.

The distinction itself is relatively simple. A response is defined in terms of its topography, and can be as precisely specified as needs require. Thus a problem response may be 'striking someone else' or 'hitting someone else with the right hand' or 'hitting with the right hand someone sitting on the left'. What all of these have in common is that they are defined in terms of what the behaviour *looks* like, a characteristic which has an immediate appeal to those with a behavioural background.

What the descriptions *don't* do however is describe operants. Where a response is defined in terms of its topography, an operant is defined in terms of its relationship to other variables. Specifically an operant is a *class* of responses all of which stand in a similar relationship to the variables of which they are a function. Thus to the extent that they provide a means of increasing the amount of attention obtained from others, threats, violence, screaming, headbanging, smiling and laughing may all be members of the same operant. Put another way, the behaviours are *functionally equivalent* - they are interchangeable in terms of their relationship to controlling conditions.

In practice, however, the therapist is not usually concerned with the operant as a whole, but only with certain responses which form a subset of the operant. In the illustration above, for example, it is likely that a therapist will wish to eliminate threats and violence from the individual's repertoire, but may be content to leave smiling and laughing unchanged. Seen in this light, therefore, operant conditioning of problem behaviours can be seen as a modification of the membership of particular operants. Specifically, what the therapist wishes to do is arrange matters such that the problem and non-problem behaviours are no longer functionally equivalent. This may be achieved by various means, including selective punishment of the unwanted responses, selective reinforcement of the desired responses, or a combination of the two. In effect the therapist's aim is to produce a change such that the problem behaviours no longer stand in the same relationship to controlling conditions as the desirable behaviours. Thus the therapist is aiming to change the structure of *operants* as a means of dealing with problems presented by particular *responses.*

It should incidentally be noted here that once again the definitions being used are a function of the purposes of the analysis. Taken to an absolute limit, no behaviours are *entirely* functionally equivalent; even hitting out with right or left hand is likely to involve slightly different relationships to other controlling conditions. The important issue however is whether or not the behaviours are functionally equivalent from the point of view of the therapist, to the extent that it makes sense to change contingencies in a general manner for such a subset.

At this level it might appear that the distinction, whilst possibly interesting from a theoretical perspective, is of little practical significance. There are however practical implications. We have seen how several behaviours which look very different may be functionally similar in the sense of standing in a similar relationship to controlling conditions. The converse also applies; behaviours which look very similar may in fact be members of quite different operants, being physically indistinguishable but functionally dissimilar. Put most simply this means that a person may do the same thing for a number of different reasons - the behaviour can serve several different functions. Thus a client may self-injure as a means of receiving stimulation, a means of attracting attention, a means of communicating a particular need, a means of blocking out some other more distressing stimulation or for other reasons. Any attempt to change the behaviour will need to take account of the variety of different operants of which this single response is a member; indeed, the attempt to produce a functional analysis in the first place may be frustrated if it appears that no variable is consistently or reliably associated with the problem behaviour.

The problem can be particularly acute when the controlling conditions of the behaviour are so different between operants that strategies having a particular effect on one operant have the opposite effect on another. Such a distinction may be seen for example in some forms of aggressive behaviour. It has been noted that at least two distinct processes may give rise to aggression; such behaviour may, like other behaviours, be shaped and maintained by reinforcement, and hence has been termed *operant* aggression. However aggressive behaviour may also occur in the absence of any clearly defined external reinforcement. In an early experiment Ulrich & Azrin (1962) noted that if a pair of rats in an experimental chamber were subjected to electric shock, they would begin to fight; if only one was shocked it would attack the other; a rat shocked when alone showed no such behaviour. Such behaviour, originally termed shock induced fighting can be seen to occur in a variety of contexts; the important issue for the present discussion is that the behaviour may stand in a totally different relationship to controlling conditions.

Consider for example a case in which an individual shows both operant aggression and *reactive* aggression in response to aversive stimuli (analogous to the shock induced fighting). Conceivably some degree of inhibition of the operant aggression will be produced through the natural aversive contingencies (e.g., the fact that the victim may hit back). Aversive stimuli will then be functioning in two quite distinct ways; as a precursor to reactive aggression and as an inhibitor of operant aggression. Note that from the viewpoint of an external observer these two forms of aggression may be indistinguishable. However, if an attempt is made to control such aggression by using drugs like anxiolytics (which reduce the controlling effect of aversive stimuli) complex results may occur. To the extent that the effect of aversive stimuli prompting *reactive* aggression is reduced, a reduction in such aggression might be expected. However, concomitant with this will be a reduction in the effectiveness of the aversive contingencies inhibiting the *operant* aggression, implying that such aggression might be expected to increase. Thus, the use of the anxiolytic could have quite different effects on the probability of aggressive behaviour depending on whether the individual's aggressive behaviour were reactive, operant, or if both, the relative mix of the two. Such a possibility of course reflects exactly what is found when attempts are made experimentally to assess the effects of drugs on 'aggression' without a clarification of the conditions of which such aggression is a function (Owens & Ashcroft, 1985). The implication is that attempts to modify such behaviour in these ways require in the first instance a full behavioural analysis. Going beyond the specific example of aggression we can see that the distinction between operants and responses, and the fact that we are changing the former whilst being concerned with the latter is of both theoretical and practical significance.

As an aside, the example of aggression provides a timely reminder that not all the behaviour with which the therapist is concerned fits neatly into a traditional operant framework (although there is a more complex sense in which reactive

229

aggression *involves* operant processes); other processes, such as habituation and Pavlovian conditioning might also be relevant. It is a reminder also that even when behaviour does not appear to be a direct function of operant contingencies, it may nonetheless be amenable to modification through contingency management.

The 'Skinner box' isn't a good model of real behaviour - even in animals

Most beginning texts on operant conditioning start with a simple description of a rat in a box pressing a lever, with food presentation being used to reinforce the response; if not a rat pressing a lever, we are usually treated to a pigeon pecking at a disc. Much discussion ensues as to the appropriateness of such animal models as a framework for the understanding of human behaviour. Now it is true that there are aspects of human behaviour (e.g., language) which complicate the picture; however it is worth remembering that even in normal animal behaviour the kind of experiment described is inadequate. This is not to say that operant conditioning is not important in animal or even human behaviour; rather it is to say that the *contingencies* in the kind of experiment described do not adequately reflect the complexity of real-life contingencies. Moreover, and this is the greater problem, it is clear that if we *do* attempt to model more closely the complexity of real life contingencies, the picture changes dramatically.

That investigation of a single response leading to a single reinforcement leads to puzzling results has been known since Ferster & Skinner's original (1957) study of different schedules. In one of their experiments, Ferster & Skinner attempted to measure the effect on rate of responding of changing the magnitude of the reinforcer. Intuitively one might expect that as the size of the reinforcement was reduced, so would the rate of responding. One could conversely argue a case that as the size of the reinforcer was reduced the rate of responding would go up (so as to keep the amount of reinforcement at the desired level). What Ferster & Skinner found, much less predictably, was that varying the size of the reinforcer appeared to have little or no systematic effect on responding at all!

As time went on the reasons for this became clear. One of the early developments of the original simple conditioning experiments was the introduction of so-called *concurrent* schedules. In a concurrent schedule the experimental subject has a choice of (usually two) responses, each of which may be reinforced according to its own individual schedule. A moment's reflection reveals that this is much closer to what might be expected in 'real-life' situations. For most of us (and indeed most animals outside a laboratory) there is usually more than one option available to us when choosing what to do. Moreover the consequences associated with each choice are likely to be specific. That is to say, most real-life behaviour is a function of concurrent schedules; the kind of single schedule observed in the original paradigmatic experiments does not usually represent the natural environment. A client in the community will normally have a range of possible activities available. Watching television, going for a walk, visiting friends and other behaviours may all be available and all be associated with particular reinforcers. That is to say, there will normally be a number of comparable concurrent schedules operating.

The study of concurrent schedules led to a number of important findings, not least of which has come to be termed the 'matching law'. In the experimental laboratory, a pigeon working on concurrent variable interval schedules will learn to distribute its effort in such a way that the amount of time spent on each schedule will mirror the amount of reinforcement available on each. Put simply, the subject learns to match the amount of effort to the amount of reward. Interestingly, this also resolves Ferster & Skinner's original problem regarding magnitude of reinforcement; if the schedules on the two responses are identical in density, but one delivers a reinforcer only half the magnitude of the other, then (making certain parametric allowances) the amount of effort expended on the former will be only half that expended on the latter. Moreover, the matching law itself implies that when there is only a single response available, then it is to be *expected* that changing the reinforcement magnitude will have little effect on behaviour. If the individual has two responses available equal time will be spent on them if the reinforcement available is equal. If the reinforcement on one is halved, that will then represent only a third of the total reinforcement. The time spent on this response will then drop from 50% of the total to 33% of the total.

(It should be noted here that there has been considerable debate regarding the extent to which the matching law actually applies to human subjects, a debate which appears to relate to the use of language by human subjects making the relevant contingencies much more a function of stimuli (words) than would normally be the case. It is therefore difficult to establish in the laboratory schedules for humans which are functionally equivalent to those used with other species. Comparison of human and non-human studies is therefore difficult, and probably of little relevance to the present discussion.)

If however the individual has only a single response available, then that response, *irrespective of the size of the reinforcer,* provides 100% of the reinforcement. Thus changing the size of the reinforcer will not produce any change in the amount of time spent on the behaviour until the reduction is to zero. In practice of course there will always be some other behaviours available - the pigeon may preen, walk around the cage etc. However the reinforcers available for these are likely to be relatively trivial compared to those available for pecking at the key. The latter reinforcers can therefore be changed considerably in magnitude before the effect of the other reinforcers is anything but trivial; not surprisingly, this implies that under such circumstances changing the amount of reinforcement will have little effect on behaviour. It should be noted incidentally that in the example given of two concurrent behaviours with equal reinforcers, reducing one by 50% did not reduce the rate of behaviour by a corresponding amount. Although the reinforcement was halved, the time spent in the behaviour drops from 50% of the time not to 25% (half the original value) but to 33% (two-thirds of the original value of 50%). That is to say, reinforcement is halved but rate continues at two-thirds the original level. Thus reducing the rate of reinforcement for a behaviour may not produce anything like the reduction in the behaviour we might expect.

The picture becomes even more complicated when we consider that concurrent schedules may operate on behaviours which are otherwise indistinguishable. That is to say, a single behaviour, as we mentioned above, may be simultaneously a member of several operants. In the experimental laboratory such a situation might be modelled by programming several schedules of (possibly different) reinforcers on a single key press. A schedule like this is known as a *conjoint* schedule - one in which a single behaviour is reinforced according to more than one schedule. Thus a particular challenging behaviour like throwing a tantrum may serve a number of functions, including escape from an unpleasant situation, relief from boredom and achievement of some particular objective. Again, it might be considered that such a schedule more accurately represents the reality of natural contingencies than the single response/schedule model of the classical experiment; it is rare that any single response will have only a single schedule of reinforcement operating, though in many cases there will be a single dominant reinforcer with others having only a minor or trivial effect. To the extent that such schedules actually reflect those reinforcing behaviours of interest they carry serious quantitative implications for therapists. In particular the observations made earlier about the matching law become even more important. If a behaviour is reinforced according to a conjoint schedule (i.e., is a function of several reinforcers) this does not preclude the possibility of other behaviours also being available and reinforced concurrently. Extending the earlier example of two behaviours with identical levels of reinforcement, we can consider what would happen if one of these were on a conjoint schedule itself maintained by two equally powerful reinforcers. An attempt at a functional analysis might run into problems from the start by noting that no single consequence reliably followed the behaviour (since there are two reinforcers operating). Undeterred however the therapist might hypothesise that one of the consequences observed did indeed serve a reinforcing function. Removing this as part of an extinction programme would be equivalent to the earlier example of halving the reinforcement available; as we have seen the behaviour would under these circumstances still continue at around two-thirds of its previous level. At this stage the unwary therapist might be tempted to conclude that this could not after all have been the reinforcer, discontinue the attempt at extinction, and search for other reinforcers (possibly hitting upon the second and repeating the original mistake!). It should be noted in passing that these examples are 'pure' ones; in reality it is likely that various extraneous factors would conspire to muddy the picture and make the programmes seem less clear and the processes less comprehensible.

In terms of modelling natural contingencies, then, it is important that the therapist be aware of the role of concurrent and conjoint schedules and of their parametric effects on rates of behaviour. In passing it might be worth remarking that despite the fact that the single schedule model is such a poor one it has nonetheless had considerable success. To some extent this reflects the application of programmes where the distinction is less important (e.g., in the shaping of new behaviours) but also, soberingly, may reflect the institutional context of much early work; in such settings, it may often have been the case that residents had indeed only a single behaviour open to them and often perhaps only a single source of reinforcement. This contrast between the restrictive environment of an institution and the more open environment of the community may result in changes of behaviour with such changes without any formal programming. For example a client who showed a number of challenging behaviours including verbal and physical aggression was found to exhibit a much lower level of such behaviours when moved to the community where he had access to a much wider range of activities. It appears that in the institution, even a low level of reinforcement for the challenging behaviours was sufficient for them to be maintained; however once returned to the community the reinforcement available for other activities was considerably greater than that previously available. In consequence the overwhelming percentage of his time was now spent on more constructive and positive activities.

Operant conditioning may be the road to chaos
By definition, operant conditioning involves a relationship between behaviour and its consequences. In particular the consequences of a behaviour feed back into the behaviour itself, influencing its future probability. In this sense, operant conditioning represents an *iterative* system, one in which a cycle is passed through over and over again, the output of one loop of the cycle forming (at least part of) the input to the next (c.f. the comments earlier in the chapter about the exchangeability of the terms antecedent, behaviour and consequence). Moreover, as we have seen in the preceding section, several such processes may simultaneously be operating independently.

Recent years have seen, in a number of fields, recognition of the fact that such systems can lead to behaviour which has come to be described as chaotic. A number of simple processes can give rise, under certain conditions, to behaviour which very soon follows no apparent regular pattern. Such processes include models of simple mechanical systems, e.g., of what would happen if instead of two heavenly bodies orbiting, three came to exert a mutual influence (Peitgen & Richter, 1986). They also include simple iterative models of biological and other systems - e.g., what happens in terms of how a population one year is determined by its size the previous year and parameters allowing for rates of breeding and dying (May, 1976). Perhaps the most paradigmatic of chaotic systems is one to which the concept was first applied; the weather. Models of weather forecasting now generally accept that even a simple determinate model does not permit prediction more than a limited time period ahead; any attempt to predict the long term future is impossible, because the dynamic system exhibits what has come to be termed 'sensitive dependence on initial conditions' - that is to say, the slightest difference in the starting point of the system will soon lead to dramatic differences in its behavioural trajectory.

At present it is far from clear to what extent such problems will be apparent in psychology. However the basic ingredients of a chaotic system are certainly present in many of the problems confronting the therapist; a multiplicity of systems interacting concurrently (like the three heavenly bodies) and the existence of non-linear dynamic processes. Thus we have seen that realistic modelling of human activity is likely to involve recognition of the concurrent operation of several schedules; it takes little imagination to recognise that there may often be substantial interactions between these. In a simple case, the occurrence of one behaviour may be affected substantially by changes brought about in another; Willems (1974) has coined the term 'behavioural ecology' to draw attention to such effects. Recognition of the fact that, in addition, the individual behavioural processes may be chaotic (operant conditioning for example is clearly iterative, the results of one cycle feeding back into another) implies that attempts to predict behaviour in the long term may sometimes be as impractical as attempting to make a long-term weather prediction. Rather we may be limited to making short-term predictions, monitoring continually the systems we are trying to predict.

In practice this may be less of a problem than might appear. This is because, like many potentially chaotic processes, it is likely that those in psychology are parametrically sensitive. That is to say, the same process with the parameters at one value may give rise to stable, predictable behaviour, whilst at another value they may give rise to unstable chaotic unpredictability. For many problems confronted in psychology, our task may be to shift the values of such parameters in order to transform behaviour which is currently chaotic to a more stable form. This may mean shifting the parameters of the behavioural systems to an extent that the behaviour of the system determines its future inputs in such a way as to produce stability; in simple terms, it means providing the individual with a behavioural repertoire which is sufficiently successful as to be self-maintaining - a system which will be largely homeostatic. Such a system is exemplified by the difference between teaching someone how to do something and teaching them how to find out how to do something - the difference between teaching the solution to a problem and teaching the problem-solving skill. To the extent that individuals are able to seek out their own environments, the task of the therapist can be seen as developing behaviours which will incorporate their own stabilising mechanisms. Any attempt at generalisable behavioural change needs to take account of the natural reinforcement contingencies in the world at large (Ferster, 1967). A programme which enables a client to obtain access to such reinforcers should also provide the client with a mechanism for maintaining such access in the light of unforeseen difficulties. At the simplest level, this might involve little more than providing the client with social skills to seek out further help when necessary.

The functional analysis that works isn't necessarily the right one

One of the strengths of the whole behavioural approach, and indeed of functional analysis, has been its own sensitivity to feedback. That is to say, by incorporating into the procedures formal mechanisms for evaluation, functional analysis can be seen as testing itself out as it goes along. The formal structure of functional analysis can be described as a feedback process; information is gathered about the problem, on the basis of which a functional analysis is produced. The functional analysis leads to an intervention which then leads back to the gathering of information (about the outcome of the intervention). Either the outcome is successful, in which case the therapist may consider the problem solved, or it is unsuccessful. In the latter case the outcome of the intervention is itself part of the data gathering process which then has to be incorporated into a new functional analysis, on the basis of which a new intervention is devised and so on until the problem is successfully dealt with (Owens & Ashcroft, 1982; Jones & Owens, 1992; Owens & Jones, 1992)

It is worth remembering here that the role of the evaluation of the intervention's effects is asymmetric. If an intervention doesn't produce the expected effect, this shows quite clearly that the functional analysis is inadequate; the converse however does not necessarily apply. That a behaviour changes in the manner predicted by the analysis only shows that the analysis is possible; it does not preclude the possibility that some quite different process is operating according to which the intervention would have the same effect. Put simply, the intervention may work for the wrong reasons. At a simple level it might be argued that this surely doesn't matter if the problem is solved; however, in some circumstances the therapist's confidence in an analysis may form the basis of other inferences about the behaviour, and if the analysis is wrong this could be disastrous. To revert to the earlier example of aggressive behaviour; if a reactive process were mistaken for an operant one, the intervention applied could appear successful yet be based on mistaken assumptions. Imagine an individual who, for some reason, finds the sight of particular individuals extremely aversive and reacts by becoming violent. On admission to an institution that individual may then find that the violence also provides a means to an end. The therapist who treats this violence, by extinction, teaching of acceptable alternatives etc. may well eliminate violence within the institution yet find that the individual reverts to the original level of violent behaviour when returned to the community where the individuals prompting the reactive aggression are again encountered. The implication is that a functional analysis needs to be based not only on careful empirical data collection but also on a firm grasp of the theoretical underpinnings of the processes of importance.

In practice there is probably no point at which any functional analysis can be said to have been proved correct; it can only be proved incorrect. In this sense such analyses accord with the general scientific principle of falsifiability; the aim is not to produce a theory which can be proved correct, but rather to have a theory which is at all times capable of being refuted. From a practical point of view this means that any analysis produced by a therapist should, irrespective of its success, still only be considered provisional. To be capable of refutation is equivalent to saying that it is still capable of making predictions. The only theories incapable of refutation are those according to which anything is possible; such theories are either so ill-specified as to be unhelpful or are simply tautologies. If however an analysis predicts that a particular intervention will have a certain effect on behaviour, the production of that behaviour does not prove the analysis correct (the behaviour may occur for other reasons) but failure to produce the behaviour constitutes a refutation of at least part of the functional analysis. The best that a therapist can hope for is an analysis which is consistent with observation; the possibility that tomorrow a further observation may refute the analysis should be seen as a strength, not a weakness.

Contingency management need not involve modifying a contingency

The typical introduction to behaviour modification outlines the principles of contingency management by illustrating ways in which new behaviours can be shaped by providing reinforcement for increasing approximations to some particular target. Eliminating behaviours will usually indicate the value of removing some reinforcer which is maintaining the behaviour, possibly in conjunction with the introduction of some punishing contingency where the need for change in behaviour is urgent. What these interventions have in common is that they are direct modifications of the individual's physical environment. Reinforcers are added or taken away, punishment is introduced, and in some cases particular controlling stimuli will be introduced, relating either to the existing or the newly introduced schedules of reinforcement and punishment.

It is worth noting however that behaviour may be changed without any modification of the physical antecedents and consequences of that behaviour. Earlier in this chapter it was noted that attempts at behaviour change operate at the level of the operant, not at the level of the response (despite the fact that it is typically the response which is of interest). Examined closely however this implies an alternative strategy to behaviour change. Rather than attempt to produce different physical antecedents or consequences to a behaviour, these can be left as they are and the therapist's effort directed towards modifying the *function* of these events.

In this way the physical relationship between an individual's behaviour and its particular antecedents and consequences can remain unchanged yet the behaviour may be modified dramatically. Put simply, the same physical antecedents and consequences of behaviour occur, but they no longer have the same significance to the individual. Thus an extinction schedule, instead of following a conventional pattern of removing a reinforcing consequence of behaviour, may instead operate by removing the reinforcing *effects* of that consequence.

In one sense, from a purely theoretical viewpoint, any event which functions as an antecedent or a consequence is also one which (potentially) has reinforcing consequences. As far as antecedents are concerned this is fairly obvious; any event which is *functionally* a consequence is, by definition, having an influence on the behaviour. Such an influence can only be to increase or decrease the rate of behaviour (a change in the patterning, apparently a third option, is really nothing more than local increases and decreases), either of which imply that the event is capable of functioning as a reinforcer. Interestingly the same is in a sense true of antecedents; using a traditional notation of S+ and S–, stimuli which precede a behaviour can serve only one of two functions, either to increase or decrease the behaviour. That is to say, if a stimulus serves a function as part of a behavioural system, it is a *discriminative stimulus.* Now while it is arguable whether or not all conditioned reinforcers are discriminative stimuli, it is clear that discriminative stimuli are capable of functioning as conditioned reinforcers. From a theoretical viewpoint, therefore, any stimulus which is part of a behavioural system is one which in principle at least is capable of serving a reinforcing function; from a functional viewpoint, any stimulus is a potential reinforcer.

In practice this is probably of little significance, since the reinforcing properties of particular discriminative stimuli may be weak; moreover the reinforcing effect of an event is itself a function of how it is scheduled. From a practical viewpoint, the functions of many stimuli may be changed with surprisingly little effort. Indeed, most psychologists have considerable experience of doing so, although they may not have conceptualised their actions in this way. Consider for example a psychologist conducting a programme of systematic desensitisation in the treatment of a phobia; leaving aside the debates regarding the effective components of such treatments, it is clear that the objective of such treatments is to change the function of the phobic stimulus so that its relation to the individual's behaviour changes. Before treatment the phobic stimulus functioned to make avoidance more likely; following treatment the phobic stimulus may be considerably less likely to do so (its degree of stimulus control may be weakened) or indeed it may have no effect whatsoever (i.e., it exerts no stimulus control over avoidance behaviour).

The same principle is of considerable significance in the design of treatment programmes to deal with aggression which occurs as described earlier in response to some inescapable aversive stimulus. An individual who has learned to respond aggressively to certain events or individuals can have this function changed using procedures like systematic desensitisation, in which the response to such stimuli is changed from aggression to some neutral response.

Changing the function of consequences is perhaps a little less familiar to most psychologists but does not necessarily involve any greater degree of complexity. To the extent that a behaviour is under the control of a conditioned reinforcer there are several ways in which its reinforcing relationship to the behaviour can be changed. The first of course we have already seen when discussing the relationship between responses and operants; other alternative behaviours can be brought into the same operant and provide an alternative means to access to the same reinforcer; this is for

237

example the principle behind teaching appropriate assertion skills as an alternative to aggressive behaviour. Alternatively (or additionally) the reinforcing properties of a particular stimulus can be changed by changing its relationship to other reinforcers. To the extent that the stimulus is differentially associated with reinforcement, the stimulus will have reinforcing properties. If this association no longer holds, the conditioned reinforcing properties will be lost. This principle has been seen in the operation of token economies, where the stealing of tokens from other people has been eliminated by designing tokens specific to each individual. The stealing still leads to the same consequence of acquiring those particular tokens, but they are no longer associated with any other reinforcer. Many types of challenging behaviour have been shown to be amenable to similar approaches. For example the individual who breaks windows by putting a hand through them will still obtain the same immediate consequences (cleansing of the wounds, bandaging etc.) but the conditioned reinforcing properties of such an event may be reduced or eliminated if there is no association with other reinforcers like social interaction, the opportunity to watch the window being repaired etc.

Summary

The theoretical and conceptual problems outlined in this chapter should not be seen as exhaustive; theoreticians and practitioners are aware of many others (e.g., the relative status of analyses of the aetiology and the maintenance of problems) and there are no doubt more still to be encountered. Nor should these problems be taken to imply that enthusiasm for functional analysis as an approach is misguided; despite its difficulties, functional analysis still represents by far the most promising available approach to the understanding and modification of behaviour.

Nevertheless it is apparent that the apparent simplicity of functional analysis may mask a number of theoretical complexities. The very notions of Antecedents, Behaviours and Consequences appear to be interchangeable, the profound distinction between operants and responses cannot be ignored, and attempts to model contingencies in the laboratory need to consider carefully the way 'real life' schedules of reinforcement actually operate. Disciplines as diverse as astronomy and biology are now beginning to realise that there are limitations on their ability to predict their subject matter, in part from the 'chaotic' nature of the underlying processes. If psychology, too, encounters such chaotic processes (and there is every reason to suppose it might) then similar limitations on prediction may be found, a problem exacerbated by recognition that any analysis devised by the therapist can only be refuted, not proved. That is to say, the therapist may be in the position of knowing that even if an analysis is correct, its predictive ability may be limited; on top of this, the possibility will always remain that the analysis itself may not be correct. Some of these problems have very real practical implications; the applied significance of others remains to be determined. Functional analysis already provides a powerful technology for helping those with intellectual disabilities. Hopefully a recognition of the problems and limitations of functional analysis will permit further development of the approach and thereby enhance the contribution it is able to make.

References

Cronbach, L. J., Gleser, G. C., Nanda, H. and Rajaratnam, N. (1972) *The dependability of behavioral measurements*. New York: Wiley.

Durand, V. M. (1990) *Functional Communication Training; an intervention program for severe behavior problems*. New York: Guilford Press.

Durand, V. M. and Crimmins, D. B. (1988) Identifying the variables maintaining self-injurious behavior. *Journal of Autism and Developmental Disorders* 18, 99-117.

Ferster, C. B. (1967) Arbitrary and Natural Reinforcement. *The Psychological Record* 17, 341-347.

Ferster, C. B., and Skinner, B. F. (1957) *Schedules of Reinforcement*. New York: Appleton Century Crofts.

Jones, R. S. P., and Owens, R. G. (1992) Applying functional analysis. *Behavioural Psychotherapy* 20, 37-40.

Lauterbach, W. (1990) Situation-response (S-R) questions for identifying the function of problem behaviour: The example of thumb sucking. *British Journal of Clinical Psychology* 29, 51-57.

Mariotto, M. J., and Farrell, A. D. (1979) Comparability of the absolute level of ratings on the inpatient multidimensional psychiatric scale within a homegeneous group of raters. *Journal of Consulting and Clinical Psychology* 47, 59-64.

May, R. (1976) Simple mathematical models with very complicated dynamics. *Nature* 261, 459-467.

Owens, R. G, and Ashcroft, J. B. (1982) Functional analysis in applied psychology. *British Journal of Clinical Psychology,* 21, 181-189.

Owens, R. G. and Ashcroft, J. B. (1985) *Violence: a guide for the caring profession*. Croom Helm, Beckenham.

Owens, R. G., and Jones, R. S. P. (1992) Extending the role of functional analysis in challenging behaviour. *Behavioural Psychotherapy* 20, 45-46.

Peitgen, H. O., and Richter, P. H. (1986) *The beauty of fractals; images of complex dynamical systems*. New York: Springer-Verlag.

Premack, D. (1965) Reinforcement theory. In M. R. Jones (ed.), *Nebraska Symposium on Motivation*. University of Nebraska.

Skinner, B. F. (1968) *Contingencies of Reinforcement; a theoretical analysis*. New York: Appleton Century Crofts.

Terrace, H. S. (1966) Stimulus control. In W. K. Honig (ed.), *Operant Behavior; areas of research and application*. New York: Appleton Century Crofts.

Ulrich, R. E., and Azrin, N. H. (1962) Reflexive fighting in response to aversive stimulation. *Journal of the Experimental Analysis of Behavior* 5, 511-520.

Willems, E. P. (1974) Behavioral technology and behavioral ecology. *Journal of Applied Behaviour Analysis* 7, 151-166.

CHAPTER 11

Future Directions

Chris Kiernan
University of Manchester

Introduction

This final chapter will examine three issues which have been raised by several preceding authors in this book. The issues concern the ethics of intervention in relation to challenging behaviour, the development of behavioural theory, and the context of intervention within services. The final section of the chapter will try to evaluate likely developments in the 1990s.

The ethics of intervention

Challenging behaviours are, in essence, socially defined. They are a category of behaviours which people other than the individual with intellectual disability find in some way problematic or unacceptable. In a proportion of these cases individuals themselves may also find the behaviours problematic. There is broad agreement that some challenging behaviours are a function of poor environment or inept management by parents or staff and that a behaviour which one person may find challenging another may find unchallenging. Furthermore, challenging behaviours may significantly affect carers, staff or other people with intellectual disability. For example aggressive or destructive behaviour may lead to injury to others or to significant costs as a result of damage to domestic and other environments. Finally, some people with intellectual disability can clearly understand that certain actions are 'wrong' from a moral viewpoint. Are they to be held responsible if they are aware that their challenging behaviour, for example hurting or harming others, is morally wrong?

This gross analysis raises a number of ethical issues which are particularly troublesome in service provision for people with intellectual disability and challenging behaviour. They may be summarised under the rights and duties of service providers to intervene in the management of challenging behaviour, and the justification of methods of intervention; the right for third parties, carers, staff and other clients, to be considered in intervention; and the responsibility of the person with intellectual disability for their own behaviour.

Concepts in social work and medical ethics relate to these issues. Horne (1987) points out that, within social work values, the idea of 'respect for persons' has been central. Horne quotes Plant (1970) as arguing that the values of individualisation, acceptance and self-direction are implicit in respect for persons and that it is the basic value in casework (Horne, 1987). In medical ethics the principle of autonomy reflects the same notions. Autonomy requires that:

'we regard others as rightfully self-governing (autonomous) in matters of choice and action' (Beauchamp & McCullough, 1984).

Within medical ethics autonomy is balanced against beneficence, the requirement to provide benefits as well as to prevent and remove harmful conditions (Beauchamp & McCullough, 1984). Respect for autonomy will frequently not conflict with beneficence but will conflict under circumstances where the individual is perceived as not being autonomous, for example where the person's competence to make judgments is seriously in doubt. When beneficence and autonomy conflict some element of paternalism, the intentional limitation of the autonomy of the person, will occur if action is taken. Paternalism may be weak, when only substantially nonautonomous behaviour is controlled, or strong when substantially autonomous behaviours are controlled (Beauchamp & McCullough, 1984).

Competence is a difficult concept to apply. It relates to the individual's ability to do a 'task' and turns on the ability or capacity to process information, to understand. Beauchamp & McCullough (1984) point out that judgment of competence is inherently specific to contexts and individual abilities. Furthermore competence will vary across short and across long time periods and may be present in degrees relating to possession of abilities. Although, as Toogood (this volume) points out, Wolfensberger (1980) has recognised the need to assess competence in resolving problems associated with inappropriate choices Kiernan (1991) has argued that the issue of competence to make autonomous decisions is by no means easily resolved. Tests of competence involving the ability to make a choice, to give a rational reason for the choice which is based on an analysis of risks and benefits and an understanding of the issues, are offered by Beauchamp & McCullough (1984) but do not appear to be used systematically (if at all?) in services for people with intellectual disability.

Horne (1987), in discussing social work values, explores the argument relating to respect for persons in terms of short and long term interests. Using the example of preventing a child crossing a road (short-term interest) when a vehicle is coming and thereby preventing him from being run over (long-term interest), Horne suggests that:

241

'. . . "respect for persons" should prescribe that one acts to promote a person's long term interests, even at the expense of violating their autonomy or self-determination in the short term'.

However, as Horne points out, this example is relatively straightforward and uncontroversial. Issues concerned with the removal into residential care against the wishes of the individual because of the inability of the person to care for themselves even with support, are less easily resolved.

People with intellectual disability who show challenging behaviour present significant problems in terms of the issues of autonomy and beneficence, or respect for persons, versus paternalism. In extreme cases intervention to prevent challenging behaviour, thereby over-riding the individual's autonomy, is clearly entirely justified in terms of the principle of beneficence. For the person who is causing significant life-threatening self-injury carers and other staff have the clear moral duty to try to prevent the harm caused. How they do it, for example by use of aversive or non-aversive techniques or by a combination of the two, is a separate question. Their moral duty is to provide positive benefits and to prevent and remove harmful conditions.

Several chapters in this volume point to the confusion caused by inappropriate interpretations of the notion of the right to choice, i.e., respect for autonomy, of people with intellectual disability. Further confusion is added in some service contexts by the insistence that staff should befriend, enable or facilitate in the lives of their clients. These notions can also point staff away from their duty to prevent individuals from harming themselves. For example staff supporting an individual in a small residential setting were expected to accompany him to a local public house where he liked to drink. However, in this public house, he would not infrequently cause incidents through inappropriate approaches to women. Staff found themselves in the position where they knew that his visits to the pub' would lead to him getting into fights but, because of their ascribed roles, could not fail to go with him if he insisted on going.

It could be argued that the staff in question should have been able to devise effective strategies to prevent the harm to the individual. However, for them, there was a conflict between their ascribed roles as enablers and their duties in preventing and removing harmful conditions. The line management did not resolve their dilemma by clearly defining their duties in relation to challenging behaviour.

Further complications flow from the essentially social definition of challenging behaviour. We have suggested that challenging behaviours are defined as such by those who interact with people with intellectual disability. This may be because service provision is inadequate or inappropriate or because individuals interacting with the person with intellectual disability find behaviours unacceptable or difficult to tolerate. In the case of the first category interventions which over-ride the individual's autonomy would clearly be inappropriate in simple terms. Intervention *should* involve improvement in service provision. In the second case interventions over-riding the individual's autonomy may be much more difficult to justify.

In practice this type of argument may involve what in medical ethics is termed an appeal to the needs of third parties. The British Association of Social Workers (1975, quoted by Horne, 1987) draws out as one of the implications of 'respect for persons' that it will involve self-realisation of the individual person 'with due regard for the interest of others'. This approach would apply clearly where an intervention directed at regularising the sleep patterns of an adult with intellectual disability because his parents are under substantial stress through disturbance of their own sleep.

This example is straightforward. Any 'reasonable person' would agree that parents have the right to unbroken sleep at night. However, the reasonable person argument may be more difficult to sustain if staff find a behaviour unacceptable or difficult to tolerate, especially if, as is often the case, different staff rate different behaviours as priorities for intervention.

Although in practice the wishes or rights of their parties are often taken into account in decisions about programmes to manage challenging behaviour, much of this decision making is implicit rather than explicit. Even within well systematised presentations statements about the rights of third parties are lacking. For example the position statement 'The right to effective treatment', drafted by Van Houten and his colleagues (Van Houten, Axelrod, Bailey, Favell, Foxx, Iwata & Lovaas, 1988), does not mention the rights of third parties. Similarly, Wolfensberger's (1980) guidelines concerned with inappropriate expressions of personal autonomy addresses the issue only indirectly. The last suggestion which Wolfensberger makes is that 'if all else fails walk with the person'.

Clearly, there is a distinction to be made between the wishes of third parties and their rights. It seems likely that responsible practitioners would try to follow the rule that the wishes of third parties should be followed only if it can be shown that they are in accord with the best interests of the person with intellectual disability. However it is all too common to hear programmes criticised on the grounds that they were mounted only because 'staff found the behaviour inconvenient'. On the other hand there are, within services for people with challenging behaviour, many examples of heroic programmes which place staff under great stress and run the serious risk of injury or burn-out to staff.

Many of the problems outlined above could be better addressed if more explicit guidelines were developed. These should include explicit recognition of the need to assess competence in decision-making and to make explicit the duty of staff to contain, prevent and, in time, replace behaviours which are causing the individual short or long term harm. Similarly the issue of the wishes and rights of third parties should be made explicit in programme development. It is clear that these are taken into account implicitly. It is also clear that, without being made explicit, there is a serious risk of programmes being distorted either by paying too much regard to the wishes of third parties or by paying too little regard to their rights. Rights which clearly need to be recognised include the right to physical protection and indeed this is already embodied in the UK in the Health and Safety at Work Act (HMSO, 1974), and the right to work in an environment with appropriate management commitment to reduce stress. Here good management support to individuals, including provision of counselling where appropriate, and sensitivity to the possibility of burn-out could be seen as carer and staff rights.

Many of the issues already outlined also apply to the notion of the individual's moral responsibility for his or her behaviour. It can be argued that the ethos of services informed by normalisation is antithetic to judgements about responsibility. Re-casting 'problem behaviour' as challenging behaviour adds to this trend. The argument that such behaviour 'challenges' the people who care for people with intellectual disability carries the implication that if they, and the environments in which they live and work with individuals with intellectual disability, could support the individual more appropriately the 'challenge' would disappear. Therefore the 'responsibility' for challenging behaviour lies not with the individuals with intellectual disability but with the people who interact with them. This position has emerged in a modified way in the United States of America with a ruling that a person with intellectual disability should not be subject to capital punishment (American Journal of Mental Retardation, 1992, 6, pp 557-575).

Carson (1989) has argued that although an individual with intellectual disability may threaten other people or actually assault them, or break or steal the property of others, staff may decide that the behaviour is not really a crime and therefore do nothing except note the behaviour in records. Certainly Department of Health guidelines suggest that police should not be involved unless serious crime could be prevented, detected or prosecuted by doing so (DHSS, 1984). Carson argues that responses resembling punishment do however follow such behaviour. These may include transfers to wards for 'difficult clients', having money removed from their accounts to pay for damage or having medication prescribed to 'control' behaviour. Kiernan, Reeves & Alborz (in preparation) found that difficulty in managing behaviour was a strong predictor of the use of anti-psychotic medication (independent of diagnosis of psychosis) in people with intellectual disability and challenging behaviour.

Carson points out that these service responses may be made without adequate investigation of incidents to establish 'guilt' or 'innocence'. Carson argues that all serious incidents should be investigated by a designated officer and, if allegations are found to have substance, the report should be submitted to a special panel or to the police. Where police feel that they are unable to act the panel would organise a hearing, ensuring that the client has a competent and independent advocate. The role of the panel would be to stress the competence and responsibility of the person with intellectual disability and to emphasise the responsibility of services in creating conditions leading to offending. Carson argues that such a process would emphasise the individual's competence and responsibility, reduce abuses and open up the activities and standards of facilities to scrutiny. In addition such procedures would reduce the tendency for individuals to acquire 'reputations' which are based on exaggerated accounts of incidents for which they were not responsible.

Carson's process may seem to be rather cumbersome. However, he does draw out the necessity for treating people with intellectual disability with a degree of respect in terms of their ability to control their own behaviour and to recognise and learn the differences between right and wrongs acts.

Establishing responsibility is clearly a difficult process. It involves similar problems to establishing competence in terms of working out whether the individual was, at the time when an incident occurred, able to understand what he or she was doing, the consequences of the act, and whether the act was right or wrong. However, even with people with severe intellectual disability instances are not difficult to find where they 'deliberately' harm others. Often responses to such incidents are 'off the cuff' verbal reprimands or punishments, typically varying amongst carers. Arguably programme development should take into account the degree of deliberation involved in challenging behaviour and should have as one of its goals the enhancement of the individual's understanding of moral and legal rules.

Models of Analysis and Intervention
As a 'category' challenging behaviour is, as we have argued, essentially socially defined. As such it represents a totally heterogeneous category. Challenging behaviours vary in terms of intensity, frequency and chronicity. Individuals described as showing challenging behaviours range from people with profound intellectual disability to people with mild to borderline intellectual disability. For example, in terms of language development this represents a range from individuals with no linguistic abilities, either expressive or receptive, individuals with substantial competencies. Challenging behaviours also occur as an aspect of the total behaviour stream of the individual and are under the influence of continuously changing environmental influences, many of which are out of the control of professionals seeking to analyse behaviour and to intervene.

It is against this background that the development of theory has to be considered. What seems to be clear from the outset is that a single all embracing theory is unlikely to be a viable proposition. However it would be dangerous to follow the distressing current trend toward mindless eclecticism on the grounds that 'no one theory is adequate to explain everything'. What needs to happen is that our analytic models should be developed to deal with aspects of different challenging behaviours within an overall internally consistent theoretical approach. Furthermore the theory needs to be usable in the settings in which challenging behaviours occur.

Possibly the most obvious example of the need to develop theory is the dimension of language as it relates to challenging behaviour. Excellent models for the analysis of some challenging behaviours, in particular high frequency behaviours such as self-injury, have been developed within the behavioural tradition (Carr & Durand, 1985). These models have, most commonly, been applied with people with severe or profound intellectual disability and limited communication skills.

The models are clearly only broadly applicable, if at all, to attempted suicide in people with mild intellectual disability. Here the use of language in analysing the 'causes' of attempted suicide is likely to be a far more viable approach in terms of developing a picture of the 'mental state' of the individual. This is partly because of the (hopefully) low frequency of the behaviour, but also because the precipitating factors may well be covert rather than readily identifiable environmental events.

Clearly, interventions based within a broadly behavioural framework, the framework of behaviour therapy, will be substantially applicable to people with mild intellectual disability. In some cases, for example relaxation therapy and systematic de-sensitisation, these procedures may be adapted for people with severe or profound intellectual disability. However their bases do not lie within the framework of the experimental analysis of behaviour.

Social skills training represents another convenient example of the use of broadly cognate models which nonetheless fall outside behaviour analysis. Hollin & Trower (1986) trace the history of development of contemporary social skills training from the development of techniques such as shaping and chaining and the manipulation of environmental contingencies within token economies. However, they argue, interest in human social learning, with an emphasis on 'cognitive processes' such as imitation, modelling and self-reinforcement, (Bandura, 1977) and research on human interpersonal behaviour (Argyle, 1967) were essential elements in the development of contemporary models of social skills training. The Argyle model of social behaviour suggests that acquisition of a social skill involves formulation of a goal, for example making a friend; perception of environmental cues, social cues from a potential friend; translation of perceptions into plans for action, to initiate conversation; and making a motor response, carrying out a piece of behaviour, to begin to talk. The model is completed when the environment changes - in this case when the friend-to-be responds and provides feedback, either positive or negative. None of these processes readily translates into behaviour analytic terminology.

Arguably, much of this literature and the techniques used *could* be re-interpreted within the framework of the experimental analysis of behaviour. The translation would be facilitated by better development in several related areas. The increasing interest in Skinner's (1969) distinction between contingency-governed and rule-governed behaviour has led in this direction. Lowe and his colleagues, (e.g., Lowe, Horne & Higson, 1987) have repeatedly pointed out that available evidence suggests that preverbal human infants perform on traditional FI, FR and DRL schedules in ways indistinguishable from infra-human organisms. However, older children with good verbal skills respond on the basis of rules which they develop for themselves (Bentall, Lowe & Beasty, 1983, 1985; Lowe, 1983; Lowe, Beasty & Bentall, 1983). Other studies have shown that human operant behaviour on single and concurrent VI schedules is determined by covertly formulated rules for responding (e.g., Lowe & Horne, 1985).

Despite this and other evidence suggesting that rule-governed human behaviour may be insensitive to immediate consequences, this line of work has had little impact on the experimental analysis of human behaviour (Jones, 1991). Remington (1991) suggests that, for people with intellectual disability and challenging behaviour who have good verbal skills, the impact of contingencies may be indirect. He argues that their impact may depend on the relations of instructions, or self-instructions, and the consequences provided for behaviour change. Remington also suggests that interventions which succeed in developing functional language skills will produce major changes including a different mode of relating to experience.

Lowe et al., (1987) point out that the exponents of cognitive behaviour therapy have found it necessary to adopt the language of cognitivism apparently out of the belief that the behavioural approach cannot deal with the modification of covert behaviour. Lowe et al., suggest that this is, in part, the responsibility of behaviourists who until recently have ignored Skinner's accounts of the role of verbal behaviour in the development of human consciousness (e.g., Skinner, 1945, 1984). However it has to be noted that, because of the lack of attention to research, only the principle that verbal skills are relevant is established. In addition, theoretical accounts of the role of language are relatively programmatic or relatively inaccessible (e.g., Kantor, 1977; Skinner, 1957).

These observations suggest that it will require considerable development of theory and research before a workable theory will be available. There is, however, a further consideration. Theories are constructions which allow scientists to systematise known phenomena and to test propositions about these phenomena in controlled experiments. Choice between theories with equivalent explanatory power is made on the basis of their parsimony, the degree to which they are economical in terms of the number of processes which they postulate, Einstein's Chopper, and the terms of the number of postulated entities, Occam's Razor (Harre, 1961). We can not predict whether, if it is ever developed, a behaviourist theory of language will prove to be as parsimonious as competing 'cognitive' theories. At present, approaches based on a combination of a broad behaviourist approach and theories derived from pragmatics and conversational or discourse analysis may be the best guides to analysis and intervention (e.g., Calculator & Bedrosian, 1988; Warren & Rogers-Warren, 1983).

A rather different set of considerations apply to other concepts already within the framework of behaviourist theorising. Woods & Blewitt (this volume) well described some of the issues surrounding the concept of 'setting' events. In essence the concept, in its various forms, reflects an attempt to conceptualise the control of behaviour by factors beyond the basic three-term contingency.

Here it seems clear that there is a need for concepts of this type within the framework of behavioural theory. The theory must be able to deal efficiently with the influence of factors such as the physical state of the individual, the influence of environmental factors such as noise or heat, and the influence of proximal and distal events as they may affect behaviour. As Woods & Blewitt point out, since the introduction of the concept by Bijou & Baer (1961), this need has been reflected in the development of a plethora of related concepts.

These concepts vary substantially in terms of their specificity, at least in their initial description. Michael's (1982) use of the term 'establishing operation' and Sidman's (1986) concepts of the four-term contingency (conditional discrimination) and five-term contingency (second-order conditional discrimination) are both fairly tightly specified. Related but less well specified concepts include the notion of the response class (e.g., Spradlin, Karlan & Wetherby, 1976) and of response co-variation (Kazdin, 1982). Others, for example concepts drawn from ecological psychology, are more generally drawn (e.g., Wicker, 1979). However, as has become clear in the use made by psychologists and others of Bronfenbrenner's (1979) ecological perspective on development, these schemas are, at least at the moment, more useful as heuristic or descriptive models than for explanatory and predictive purposes. As with Wahler's interpretation of setting events (Wahler, 1975; 1980; Wahler & Fox, 1981) these approaches can incorporate the individual's history into an account of behaviour. For example Richardson, Koller & Katz (1985) found that unstable family upbringing was related to later behaviour disturbance in young adults with mild intellectual disability. This study is one of a small handful to identify 'risk factors' for behaviour disturbance in populations of people with intellectual disability, although a substantial literature has accumulated on risk factors for conduct disorders in non-handicapped populations (Rutter, 1989). However, as Woods & Blewitt point out in respect of the Wahler studies, exactly *how* these risk factors affect behaviour disturbance is unclear. Clearly studies of risk factors could be of value in informing early intervention, for example suggesting the need to stabilise families or to change coping styles, but are of little explanatory value in the experimental analysis of behaviour unless their precise effects on the three-term contingency can be specified.

Repp & Dietz (1989) present an atheoretical classification of setting events in terms of three dimensions. These are, firstly, the nature of the events, classified as condition, short-term event, response-response interaction and stimulus-response interaction; secondly the temporal proximity of the event, distant, proximate or concurrent and thirdly, the effect, to increase or decrease behaviour. There is an urgent need to go beyond this classification in terms of the analysis of the concepts currently subsumed under the concept of setting events. The object of this exercise should be to synthesise and, if necessary, to prune the existing concepts, and to establish whatever controlling relationships may be operative (Emerson, personal communication). Given the failure of researchers working with Bronfenbrenner's ecological model to operationalise propositions in terms of testable hypotheses, there is a particular need to develop the behavioural model. Within this framework it is likely that some concepts will emerge as redundant, especially in terms of their utility in planning interventions.

Theoretical development is also needed in the conceptualisation of challenging behaviours. As we have pointed out the 'category' is not only diverse and heterogeneous in terms of topographies but is essentially socially defined. Furthermore, classification of behaviours by terms such as 'aggressive', 'self-injurious' or 'destructive' behaviour is superficial in describing the functions which such behaviours may have for the individual. Some progress has been made through analyses examining functions such as demand avoidance, attention-seeking and the like but, although of considerable utility, they represent relatively crude starting points for further analyses.

At a broad level it seems likely that, as in the case of self-injurious behaviour, (Oliver, this volume), progress will be made in conceptualising challenging behaviours through a series of restricted theories consistent with behavioural theory but each containing particular features. This may apply in the case of some of the behaviours under the general classification of aggressive behaviour where reactive and instrumental aspects of the behaviours may be distinguished and may be important in analysis and intervention.

These pleas for theoretical development have to be taken in the context of what can reasonably be expected of analysis and intervention in real-life environments. At the beginning of this section we pointed out that challenging behaviours occur as an aspect of the total stream of behaviour against a background of continuously changing environmental influences, many of which may not be controllable. This imposes an inherent limitation on the degree to which precise analyses are possible. In addition extended detailed analyses of behaviour risk the accusation that behaviour analysts spend too much time analysing and too little time intervening. Theoretical developments must, as in the case of analogue methods, be accompanied by technology which allows their translation into recording procedures which allow rapid, reliable and valid data to be accumulated and interpreted. Clearly, the use of lap-top computers point the direction for development.

The Relation to Intervention and Service Development
Experiences within services shows that there are a limited number of people with intellectual disability with challenging behaviour which is of such a high level of dangerousness, disruptiveness and, in many cases, chronicity, as to challenge even highly skilled behaviour analysts working in ideal environments. Less serious challenging behaviour may also be exacerbated by uninformed management. In the majority of cases, at the moment, it seems clear that the rights of both groups to effective treatment are being violated for a variety of reasons.

Policy developments in the UK are leading toward a position common in other English-speaking countries. The National Health Service and Community Care Act (HMSO, 1990) provides a potentially good framework for the implementation of behaviourally-based intervention programmes for people with intellectual disability and challenging behaviour. What is envisaged is a clear purchaser-provider division. In terms of services for people with challenging behaviour 'experts' in behaviour analysis could be commissioned to establish programmes and to support staff implementing programmes, or to provide special provision with a view to analysing challenging behaviour under controlled conditions, mount programmes and transfer them to other facilities.

There are several problems which make it unlikely that the promise of the new Act will be fully realised. In order to work effectively the model described would need a clear contract between the purchaser, the agency responsible for the individual, most probably a social services setting, and the provider, possibly an individual or team of individuals located in a social services, health or an independent agency. The contract would have to detail what the provider would do in relation to analysing challenging behaviour, an activity which would probably require the purchasing agency to commit its staff to collaborative work. Similarly purchasing agency staff would inevitably need to change their behaviour in order to implement programmes, maintaining both consistency of responding and recording.

It seems very unlikely that management structures in social services and, possibly to a lesser degree, in health settings, could 'deliver' the cooperation of their staff to the level necessary to allow a provider to work effectively. Many commentators have remarked that 'management' within services for people with intellectual disability frequently does not manage. There is a strong tradition of allowing autonomy of decision-making by front-line staff, often bolstered by asinine arguments that they 'know the person best'. In effect, as a 'management' style, failure to direct front-line staff typically conceals a poverty of skills and ideas on the part of managers about what should be done. The other facet of this style of management is an inability and unwillingness to ensure that programmes developed by outside agencies, which under new arrangements would be purchased, are implemented.

Clearly what has been described is an extreme, although all too common, problem. It can be argued that the skills of behavioural experts should include the ability to persuade management and front-line staff to cooperate and to 'own' programmes. However, bringing about widespread change in the organisational culture of an agency is accepted as notoriously difficult. Certainly a great deal of effort would be wasted if such changes had to be brought about every time a programme was mounted.

Not all agencies or parts of agencies operate laissez-faire management. It is to be hoped that more members of senior management, within the new purchaser-provider framework, will learn or realise that money will be substantially wasted if front-line managers do not ensure that programmes are implemented.

A second problem which will affect the realisation of the promise of the new legislation concerns the 'providers' of services, the expert teams. Many agencies have chosen to establish small teams whose role is to work, usually within agencies, in the development of management programmes for people with challenging behaviour. These are variously called 'challenging behaviour teams', 'additional support teams' or the like. They are typically made up of a small number of qualified nurses or social workers, usually with the support of psychologists, and a number of assistants. The impetus for their establishment has been in part the closure of institutions, creating the need for increased support in community settings, and an increased regard to the right to treatment of people with intellectual disability and challenging behaviour.

Although the results of formal evaluations of the effectiveness of these schemes are not yet available it seems reasonable to argue that they will be shown to have had a positive effect on service provision. However, in the context of this book, the effectiveness of the teams in their use of techniques based in behaviour analysis may be seriously questioned. The reason lies in the lack of training designed to prepare 'experts' in the use of behaviour analysis.

In the UK and elsewhere scandals concerning the misuse of behavioural techniques have led to enquiries and working parties recommending standards. In the UK a working party involving representatives of the Royal College of Nursing, the Royal College of Psychiatry, the British Psychological Society and the watchdog organisation MIND, under the general auspices of the then Department of Health and Social Security, concluded that the training of specialist behaviour analysts to work with people with intellectual disability and challenging behaviour was a high priority (HMSO, 1980). Of these organisations only the Royal College of Nursing developed a course, the ENB 705, which could go toward addressing this need. However the initiative for setting up of this type of course rests with centres who decide on their own priorities. In other terms the various validating bodies, including the validating body for social work training, the Central Council for Education and Training in Social Work, do not commission courses or provide significant incentives for their establishment.

The result of this situation has been that only a few centres have mounted the ENB 705 or related courses. These courses are producing only a trickle of trained staff. Setting aside the fact that only a proportion of 'graduates' from these courses could really be considered as top flight behaviour analysts it is clear that, given the widespread establishment of teams, the need for well-trained behaviour analysts is far out-stripping supply. It is also significant that although courses may be open to people qualified in nursing and social work the bulk of graduates are nurses. Within the new purchaser/provider framework specialist teams could be staffed by nurses but, nonetheless, lead responsibility for care of people with intellectual disability will lie with social services. Given this, it is unfortunate that more social service staff are not being seconded for training. One reason for this is the lack of funding for secondment in social services departments but there also appears to be a cultural bias against the use of behavioural techniques in many social services settings which has been exacerbated by misconstrued ideas about social role valorisation.

Other professions have been lax in their approach to training behaviour analysts. Although behaviour analysis has its roots in psychology clinical psychology postgraduate training does not necessarily involve extensive skill building in this area. Add to this the fact that there is a serious overall manpower shortage of clinical psychologists in the UK and that intellectual disability is a minority interest in the profession, it becomes clear that clinical psychology is not a significant source of expert behaviour analysts.

The other professions who might be expected to have significant expertise in behaviour analysis are teachers and educational psychologists. Here again the training of teachers for work with pupils with 'severe learning difficulties' has not normally involved an emphasis on behaviour analysis. As with other professions, teachers who have expertise in behaviour analysis will have acquired it through their own efforts.

I have outlined the position concerning expertise in behaviour analysis in some detail in order to emphasise the massive gap between needs and reality. If we add to this the difficulties which behaviour analysts face in ensuring that programmes are implemented it becomes clear that we can not be too optimistic about rapid change in the immediate future. What is needed is a culture change in many existing services and a coordinated effort within the various regions in the UK to develop the training of qualified professionals to fill the 'expert' roles. Without this dual initiative many services for people with intellectual disability and challenging behaviour are likely to continue to use behaviour analysis in an amateurish and often inept fashion.

Conclusion

Challenging behaviour absorbs substantial service resource. The importance of challenging behaviour for carers and for services for people with intellectual disability has been increasingly recognised with the development of community provision as an alternative to institutional provision. However, although substantial advances have been made in both understanding and in service provision, it is clear from this volume that we still have a long way to go. Theoretical developments and developments of services are all necessary. These developments have, however, to be seen in the context of behaviour analysis being a minority interest in research. It has proved very difficult to persuade funding agencies in the UK to support research on behaviourally-based interventions. A scan of the literature shows that the overwhelming majority of research studies stem from the United States. A good deal of persuasion needs to go on to change this position.

Similarly the last section of this chapter has drawn attention to the absence of adequate preparation of professional behaviour analysts. The same problem can be found in undergraduate courses with the consequence that the majority of researchers in the field are 'self-taught'. A reversal of this position would again be desirable.

Little mention has been made in this chapter of the 'aversives debate'. This debate has, arguably, generated a great deal of heat without furthering the cause of analysis and treatment of challenging behaviour. It is to be hoped that this debate will be resolved rapidly although its depth and quality makes a rapid resolution seem unlikely (Kiernan, 1991).

What then for the future? Substantial advances have been made and the replacement of institutionalisation by community provision informed by positive philosophies should provide a facilitative framework for further development. However, this volume shows that although much has been learned from research and from demonstration services the major development must be the translation of this work into widespread practice. Hopefully the volume will make a contribution to this process.

References

Argyle, M. (1967) *The Psychology of Interpersonal Behaviour*. Harmondsworth: Penguin Books

Bandura, A. (1977) *Principles of Behavior Modification*. New York: Holt, Rinehart & Winston

Beauchamp, T. L. and McCullough, L. B. (1984) *Medical Ethics*. Englewood Cliffs, N.J.: Prentice Hall

Bentall, R. P., Lowe, C. F. and Beasty, A. (1983) Does language produce behavioral rigidity in humans? *Behavior Analysis Letters*, 3, 251

Bentall, R. P, Lowe, C. F. and Beasty, A. (1985) The role of verbal behavior in human learning 11: Developmental differences. *Journal of the Experimental Analysis of Behavior*, 43, 165-181

Bijou, S. and Baer, D. M. (1961) *Child Development 1: A Systematic and Empirical Theory*. New York: Appleton-Century-Crofts

Bronfenbrenner, U. (1979) *The Ecology of Human Development*. Harvard: Harvard University Press

Calculator, S. N. and Bedrosian, J. L. (1988) *Communication Assessment and Intervention for Adults with Mental Retardation*. London: Taylor and Francis

Carson, D. (1989) Prosecuting people with mental handicap. *Criminal Law Review*, February

Carr, E. G. and Durand, V. M. (1985) Reducing behavior problems through functional communication training. *Journal of Applied Behavior Analysis*, 18, 111-126

DHSS (1984) *Code on Confidentiality of Personal Health Data*. DHSS Circular DA(84)25

Harre, R. (1961) *Theories and Things*. London: Sheed and Ward

HMSO (1974) Health and Safety at Work Act. London: HMSO.

HMSO (1980) *Report of a Working Party on Behavioural Modification*. London: HMSO

HMSO (1990) NHS and Community Care Act. London: HMSO.

Hollin, C. R. and Trower, P. (1986) Social skills training: a retrospective analysis and summary of applications. In C. R. Hollin and P. Trower (eds.), *Handbook of Social Skills Training, Volume 1*. Oxford: Pergamon Press.

Horne, M. (1987) *Values in Social Work*. Aldershot: Wildwood House

Jones, R. S. P. (1991) Reducing inappropriate behaviour using non-aversive procedures: evaluating differential reinforcement schedules. In B. Remington (ed) *The Challenge of Severe Mental Handicaps*. Chichester: John Wiley. pp 47-70

Kantor, J. R. (1977) *Psychological Linguistics*. Chicago, Ill: Principia Press

Kazdin, A. E. (1982) Symptom substitution, generalisation and response covariation: implications for psychotherapy outcome. *Psychological Bulletin*, 91, 349-361

Kiernan, C. (1991) Professional ethics: behaviour analysis and normalisation. In B. Remington (ed) *The Challenge of Severe Mental Handicap*. Chichester: John Wiley & Sons. pp 369-392

Kiernan, C. C., Reeves, D. and Alborz, A. (in preparation) The use of anti-psychotic drugs with adults with learning disabilities and challenging behaviour

Lowe, C. F. (1983) Radical behaviourism and human psychology. In G. C. L. Davey (ed.), *Animal Models and Human Behaviour: Conceptual, evolutionary and neurological perspectives*. Chichester: John Wiley.

Lowe, C. F., Beasty, A. and Bentall, R. P. (1983) The role of verbal behavior in human learning: Infant performance on fixed-interval schedules. *Journal of the Experimental Analysis of Behavior*, 39, 157-164

Lowe, C. F. and Horne, P. J. (1985) On the generality of behavioural principles: Human choice and the matching law. In C. F. Lowe, M. Richelle, D. E. Blackman and C. M. Bradshaw (eds) *Behaviour Analysis and Contemporary Psychology*. London: Erlbaum.

Lowe, C. F., Horne, P. J., and Higson, P. J. (1987) Operant conditioning: the hiatus between theory and practice in clinical psychology. In H. J. Eysenck and I. Martin (eds) *Theoretical Foundations of Behavior Therapy*. New York: Plenum Press.

Michael, J. L. (1982) Distinguishing between discriminative and motivational functions of stimuli. *Journal of the Experimental Analysis of Behavior*, 37, 149-155

Plant, R. (1970) *Social and Moral Theory in Casework*. London: Routledge & Kegan Paul

Rutter, M. (1989) Pathways from childhood to adult life. *Journal of Child Psychology and Psychiatry*, 30, 23-51

Remington, B. (1991) Behaviour analysis and severe mental handicap: the dialogue between research and application. In B. Remington (ed) *The Challenge of Severe Mental Handicap*. Chichester: John Wiley.

Repp, A. C. and Dietz, D. E. D. (1989) Using an ecobehavioral analysis to determine a taxonomy for stereotyped responding. In S. R. Schroder (ed.), *Ecobehavioral Analysis and Developmental Disabilities*. New York: Springer-Verlag

Richardson, S. A., Koller, H. and Katz, M. (1985) Relationships of upbringing to later behavior disturbance of mildly mentally retarded young people. *American Journal of Mental Deficiency*, 90, 1-8

Sidman, M. (1986) Functional analysis of emergent verbal classes. In T. Thompson and M. D. Zeiler (ed) *Analysis and Integration of Behavioral Units*. pp 213-245. Hillsdale, NJ: Lawrence Erlbaum

Skinner, B. F. (1945) The operational analysis of psychological terms. *Psychological Review*, 52, 270-277

Skinner, B. F. (1957) *Verbal Behavior*. New York: Appleton-Century-Crofts

Skinner, B. F. (1969) *Contingencies of Reinforcement: A Theoretical Analysis*. Englewood Cliffs: Prentice-Hall

Skinner, B. F. (1984) Coming to terms with private events. In A. C. Catania and S. Harnad (eds.), *The Behavior and Brain Sciences*, 7, 572-581

Spradlin, J. E., Karlan, G. R. and Wetherby, B. (1976) Behavior analysis, behavior modification and developmental disabilities. In L. L. Lloyd (ed.), *Communication, Assessment and Intervention Strategies*. pp 225-263. Baltimore, Md: University Park Press

Van Houten, R., Axelrod, S., Bailey, J. S., Favell, J. E., Foxx, R. M., Iwata, B. and Lovaas, O. I. (1988). The right to effective behavioral treatment. *Journal of Applied Behavior Analysis*, 21, 381–384.

Wahler, R. G. (1975) Some structural aspects of deviant child behavior. *Journal of Applied Behavior Analysis*, 8, 27-42

Wahler, R. G. (1980) The insular mother: her problems in parent-child treatment. *Journal of Applied Behavior Analysis*, 13, 207-219

Wahler, R. G. and Fox, J. J. (1981) Setting events in applied behavior analysis: Toward a conceptual and methodological expansion. *Journal of Applied Behavior Analysis*, 14, 327-338

Warren, S. F. and Rogers-Warren A. K. (1983) Because no one asked. Setting variables affecting the generalisation of trained vocabulary within a residential institution. In K. T. Kernan, M. J. Begab and R. B. Edgerton (eds) *Environments and Behavior*. Baltimore Md: University Park Press

254

Wicker, A. W. (1979) *An Introduction to Ecological Psychology.* Monterey, Ca: Brooks-Cole
Wolfensberger, W. (1980). The Definition of Normalisation: Update, Problems, Disagreements and
Misunderstandings. In J. F. Flynn and K. E. Nitsch (eds.), *Normalisation, Social Integration and
Community Services.* Proed: Austin, Texas.

Author Index

Fryers, T., 5, 11
Fugua, R. W., 58, 61

Gadow, K. D., 123, 144
Gagnon, J. H., 214, 215, 219
Gardner, W. I., 47, 53, 56, 57, 62, 91, 96, 214, 219
Garreri, E., 160, 170
Garvey, K., 140, 143
Garwick, G. B., 215, 222
Gaskell, G., 4, 10
Gathercole, C., 36, 62, 210, 219
Gaylord-Ross, R., 13, 31
Gebhard, P. H., 214, 215, 219
Georigades, N. J., 162, 168, 170
Gertz, B., 160, 170
Geyde, A., 188, 192
Gilbert, P., 160, 170
Gilby, B., 215, 219
Gilman, R., 149, 171
Glass, C., 217, 220
Glenn, L., 71, 84, 86, 98
Gleser, G. C., 224, 239
Glossop, C., 123, 146
Glynn, S. M., 161, 162, 170
Gold, M., 91, 96
Gold, V. J., 13, 15, 21, 32
Goldberg, B., 215, 219
Goldiamond, I., 40, 55, 62, 64
Gonzalez, L., 187, 188, 190, 193
Gorman-Smith, D., 1, 11
Gostin, L. O., 197, 206, 208, 219
Goza, A., 6, 37, 90, 91, 99, 100, 103, 104, 107, 119, 120
Graham, P., 201, 222
Grainger, W., 211, 222
Grant, G. W. B., 135, 136, 144, 145
Graves, M, G., 52, 64
Griffin, H. C., 95, 97
Griffin, J. C., 5, 11, 25, 32, 107, 119, 123, 142, 144
Groden, G., 58, 59, 62
Gross, A. M., 186, 192
Grounds, A. I., 208, 219
Grubin, D., 206, 219
Grusec, J. E., 103, 120
Gualtieri, C. T., 213, 220
Gudjonsson, G. H., 202, 203, 220
Guess, D., 99, 119, 174, 192
Gunn, J., 202, 203, 220

Gunn, M. J., 206, 208, 220
Gunsett, R. P., 188, 192
Gural, M., 203, 221
Gurguis, E. F., 163, 170

Halfon, A., 210, 222
Hall, E. T., 152, 170
Hall, J. C., 95, 97, 148, 171
Hall, S., 20, 29, 31
Haller, R. M., 149, 150, 170
Handy, L., 217, 220
Hang, U., 214, 218
Hanneman, R. A., 2, 11
Hansen, P., 160, 170
Hanson, R. H. 17, 32, 110, 112, 119
Harre, R., 247, 253
Harris, C. J., 129, 143
Harris, G. T., 217, 220
Harris, J. M., 132, 139, 144
Harris, P., 1, 4, 11, 122, 144, 199, 220
Harris, R. T., 94, 95
Hattersley, J., 40, 42, 62
Hartley, J. R., 159, 170
Harvey, E. R., 154, 158, 166, 170
Hawkes, C., 215, 221
Hauber, F. A., 211, 122, 146, 148, 149, 170
Hauck, F., 17, 31
Hauneman, R. A., 148, 168, 171
Hayduk, L. A., 150, 170
Hayes, S. C., 56, 62
Head, D., 8, 12, 29, 129, 130, 145, 184
Heal, L. W., 2, 11, 122, 127, 144, 145, 148, 149, 170
Heather, B. B., 201, 222
Helmstetter, E., 37, 44, 58, 62, 99, 119, 174, 192
Hemming, H., 122, 144
Hemming, J., 122, 135, 144
Heslin, R., 152, 171
Hicks, R. E., 213, 220
Higson, P. J., 42, 65, 246, 247, 254
Hill, B. K., 2, 11, 122, 123, 145, 148, 149, 170
Hill, J., 148, 150, 153, 170
Hill, P., 138, 143
Hill, R. W., 217, 220
Hilliard, J., 139, 146
Hitzing, W., 173, 193
Hobbs, D. C., 91, 96, 174, 175, 179, 180, 181, 186, 191, 193

259

Hodgins, S., 202, 220
Hogg, J., 141, 145, 199, 220
Holland, A. J., 6, 9, 149, 167, 195, 198, 201, 210, 211, 212, 220, 221
Holland, T. (see Holland, A. J.)
Hollin, C., 208, 220, 246, 253
Holmes, N., 212, 222
Holmes, S., 214, 222
Holtz, W. C., 103, 118
Hom, A. C., 123, 146
Hope, S., 217, 220
Horcones, 39, 63
Horne, M., 241, 242, 243, 253
Horne, P. J., 246, 247, 254
Horner, R. D., 58, 63
Horner, R. H., 37, 63
Horton, C. B., 214, 222
Hubert, J., 122, 145
Huff, J., 118, 119
Hughes, H., 198, 219
Humphreys, S., 138, 143
Hurley, W., 217, 220

Infantino, J. A., 160, 170
Intagliata, J., 74, 78, 95, 96
Ivancic, M. T., 16, 25, 32, 213, 222
Iwata, B. A., 13, 14, 16, 17, 18, 19, 21, 23, 25, 31, 46, 51, 63, 104, 115, 119, 243, 254

Jackson, H. F., 217, 220
Jacobsen, J. W., 5, 11, 149, 168, 170, 199, 201, 220
Jacobson, S. G., 91, 96
James, D. H., 2, 11, 148, 149, 170
Jan, J. E., 21, 31
Jansma, P., 58, 63
Jeffree, D., 138, 145
Jenkins, J., 138, 139, 140, 141, 144, 145, 147,
Johnson, F., 139, 146
Johnson, W. L., 16, 31
Johnston, R., 123, 143
Jones, L. J., 175, 187, 192
Jones, M. L., 14, 28, 31, 103, 119, 138, 145
Jones, R. S. P., 1, 2, 6, 7, 8, 11, 91, 108, 109, 129, 152, 173, 175, 179, 181, 182, 184, 187, 188, 189, 190, 191, 192, 193, 235, 239, 247, 253
Jordan, J., 187, 192

Kafry, D., 216, 220
Kalsher, M. J., 13, 14, 16, 17, 19, 23, 25, 31
Kantor, J. R., 35, 49, 50, 51, 53, 61, 63, 247, 253
Karan, O. C., 47, 53, 56, 57, 62, 214, 219
Karlan, G. R., 248, 254
Karsh, K. G., 29, 32
Kassorla, I. C., 13, 15, 21, 32
Katz, M., 200, 222, 248, 254
Kazdin, A. E., 36, 63, 91, 96, 248, 254
Kearns, A., 205, 220
Kedesdy, J. H., 99, 102, 119, 174, 193
Keenan, B. S., 212, 220
Kelley, B., 174, 187, 188, 192
Kelly, B., 174, 192
Kelly, S., 109, 119
Kem, L., 58, 63
Kendall, K. A., 100, 101, 120, 175, 187, 192
Kiernan, C., 9, 10, 14, 31, 78, 90, 96, 138, 145, 240, 241, 244, 253, 254
Kinzek, A. F., 152, 170
Kishi, G., 17, 31
Knoll, J., 174, 194
Knowles, M., 94, 96
Knowlton, S., 99, 119, 174, 192
Koegal, R. L., 37, 58, 63
Koller, H., 198, 200, 222, 248, 254
Krasner, L., 52, 63
Kushlick, A., 122, 123, 144, 145, 146
Kushlick, S., 123, 1444

La Borde, R., 149, 171
La Grow, S. J., 1, 11
Lakin, K. C., 2, 11, 122, 145, 148, 149, 170
Lalli, E. P., 51, 63
Lalli, J. S., 25, 32, 51, 63
Landesman, S., 75, 76, 96, 123, 127, 133, 142, 145
Landesman-Dwyer, S., 79, 94, 96, 127, 142, 143
Langevin, R., 217, 220
Lanzi, F., 109, 110, 112, 120
Larsson, E. V., 112, 115, 116, 119
Lattimore, J., 135, 143
Lauterbach, W., 224, 239
Lavender, T., 123, 135, 144
La Vigna, G. W., 37, 63, 91, 96, 102, 119, 151, 153, 169, 170, 172, 181, 192, 213, 219

261

Miller, C., 123, 143
Millichamp, C. J., 123, 146
Milne, D., 159, 168, 171
Miltenberger, R. G., 1, 11, 150, 170
Mink, I. T., 200, 221
Miranti, S. V., 214, 218
Mirenda, P. L., 17, 31, 45, 62, 130, 143
Mitchell, L., 214, 221
Mittler, P., 94, 96, 141, 145, 148, 171
Monahan, T. M., 217, 220
Mondy, L. W., 136, 147
Moniz, D., 17, 30
Montegar, C. A., 135, 145
Moore, J., 187, 193
Moores, B., 135, 136, 144, 145
Morgan, R. L., 166, 171
Morris, E. K., 52, 63
Morris, P., 123, 145
Moxley, R., 55, 63
Mudford, O. C., 174, 186, 193
Mulick, J. A., 99, 100, 102, 109, 119, 173,
   174, 175, 186, 188, 192, 193
Murphy, G. H., 4, 5, 6, 9, 11, 12, 14, 15,
   16, 17, 18, 19, 22, 25, 32, 46, 64, 92,
   97, 122, 123, 146, 149, 150, 167, 171,
   181, 193, 195, 198, 199, 201, 202, 210,
   211, 212, 213, 214, 217, 218, 220, 221
Murphy, W. D., 216, 221
Musingo, S., 160, 170
Myers, A. M., 118, 119

Nanda, H., 224, 239
Nau, P. A., 152, 172
Negri-Shoultz, N., 213, 219
Nevin, J. A., 39, 64
Newman, D. E., 21, 31
Newman, R. C., 152, 171
Newson, C. D., 13, 30, 104, 119
Ney, P. G., 179, 193
Nihara, K., 200, 221
Nirje, B., 67, 68, 71, 96, 97
Nitsch, K. E., 72, 88, 91, 96
Nord, G., 109, 112, 119
Normand, C., 4, 10
Novaco, R. W., 213, 221
Nowinski, J. M., 56, 62

O'Brien, F., 102, 119
O'Brien, J., 66, 71, 72, 77, 78, 79, 81, 85,
   86, 87, 89, 92, 97, 127, 145

O'Brien, S., 16, 25, 32
Offord, G., 150, 170
Oldenquist, A., 100, 102, 120
Oswin, M., 123, 136, 146
Oliver, C., 4, 5, 8, 11, 12, 13, 14, 16, 17,
   18, 19, 20, 21, 22, 25, 29, 31, 92, 97,
   122, 123, 129, 130, 145, 146, 150, 171,
   181, 184, 193, 199, 213, 221, 249
O'Neill, R. E., 37, 63
Owens, R. G., 9, 48, 184, 188, 224, 229,
   235, 239

Pace, G. M., 13, 14, 16, 17, 19, 23, 25, 31,
   104, 119
Page, T. J., 16, 25, 32, 213, 222
Pagel, S. E., 122, 146
Pahl, J., 95, 97, 122, 146
Paisey, T. J., 107, 119, 187, 193
Paitich, D., 217, 220
Palumbo, L. W., 13, 30
Parker, E., 205, 221
Parrish, J. M., 13, 32, 213, 222
Patterson, G. R., 49, 64
Patterson, M. L., 152, 171
Pavlov, I. P., 38, 64
Peck, D., 210, 219
Peitgen, H. O., 233, 239
Penningroth, P., 156, 171
Perkins, D., 215, 221
Perkins, T. S., 100, 107, 119
Perrin, B., 68, 97
Perske, R., 202, 203, 221
Phillamore, L., 162, 168, 170
Piachaud, J., 149, 172
Pill, R., 123, 135, 144
Plant, R., 241, 254
Poling, A. G., 123, 144
Pollack, D., 152, 171
Pomeroy, W. B., 214, 215, 219
Pond, D. A., 212, 219
Porterfield, J., 58, 64
Powers, T., 153, 155, 171
Praill, T., 162, 168, 171
Pratt, M. W., 136, 145
Premack, D., 225, 239
Presland, J. L., 37, 40, 64
Prins, H., 216, 217, 221

Quade, D., 213, 220
Quen, J., 196, 221

263

Subject Index

reciprocity eliciting (returning value), 180

unconditional valuing, 179

mutual change as a component, 180

techniques, 175-179

Housing, community based, 76, 121-147

Humanistic psychology, 179

Human rights committees, 110

Individual programme plans, 138-139

Institutional treatment, 122-123

Interbehavioural psychology, 35, 50-52

Legal issues, 195-221

historical aspects, 195-197

court procedures, 206-208

Matching law, 231

Microcomputers, 23, 29, 249

Needs (of people with intellectual disabilities), 124

Neural oscillator theory (of challenging behaviour), 130

Neurotransmitters (and SIB), 29

Normalisation, 66-78, 243, 244

definitions, 67, 70-71

five service accomplishments, 66, 71, 78-87

Scandinavian formulations, 66-68

seven core themes, 69

North American formulations, 68-69

PASS/PASSING, 71-72

Ordinary life model, 121

Organic theory (of challenging behaviour), 129-130

Pharmacology, 29, 109, 244

Premack principle, 27, 225

Preventative strategies (for challenging behaviour), 164-166

Psychiatric disorder, 200-202

Psychiatric assessment and treatment, 211-213

Psychodynamic theories (of challenging behaviour), 129

Punishment, 38, 41, 102-103, 244

Quality of life, 127-128

Reinforcement

arbitrary, 39, 40

automatic, 14, 25

definition, 38, 103-104

differential reinforcement, 28

DRO, 36, 102, 224

DRI, 36

DRL, 102, 224

natural, 39

negative, 13, 14, 20

positive, 13, 14, 20

sensory, 47

reinforcer deprivation, 22

Research funding, 252

Restraint, 153-159

Self-injurious behaviour, 12-33, 47, 99, 228, 249

Self stimulation, 14

Sensory stimulation, 47

Sexual offences, 214-216

Social attention, 13

Specialist treatment, 125-126

Staff behaviour, 135-141, 149-153, 159

Staff management, 249-251

Staff motivation, 184-185

Staff training, 159-162

Verbal behaviour, 247

Violence, 149, 213-214